Additional praise for
AMERICAN RADICALS

"Teeming with colorful and long-forgotten characters, Holly Jackson's dazzling new history—at once wide-ranging and fine-grained—recovers anew the restless and improbable spirit of reform that animated America in the nineteenth century. *American Radicals* is a timely and powerful reminder that America has always been a work in progress—and that voices of protest echo with purpose and urgency across the generations. Amid the din of our daunting times, here is a history lined with hope."

—Brian Matthew Jordan, finalist for the
2016 Pulitzer Prize in History for *Marching Home:
Union Veterans and Their Unending Civil War*

"*American Radicals* is a wise and vivid history of the women and men who imagined a nation that would live up to the ideals of untrammeled personal liberty and direct democracy and then dared to build movements and communities dedicated to that purpose. This is a book that will educate and thrill progressives of all ages."

—Michael Kazin, author of *War Against War:
The American Fight for Peace, 1914–1918* and
professor of history at Georgetown University

"Jackson gives readers stories that are inspiring, infuriating, hilarious, frustrating, and meaningful for our complicated present. An outstanding book that any modern radical should read."

—Erik Loomis, associate professor of history
at the University of Rhode Island and author
of *A History of America in Ten Strikes*

AMERICAN
RADICALS

AMERICAN RADICALS

How Nineteenth-Century Protest Shaped the Nation

HOLLY JACKSON

CROWN
NEW YORK

Published in the United States by Crown, an imprint of Random House,
a division of Penguin Random House LLC, New York.
crownpublishing.com

CROWN and the Crown colophon are registered trademarks of
Penguin Random House LLC.

LIBRARY OF CONGRESS CATALOGING-IN-PUBLICATION DATA
Names: Jackson, Holly, author.
Title: American radicals : how nineteenth-century protest
shaped the nation / Holly Jackson.
Description: First edition. | New York : Crown, an imprint
of Random House, [2019]
Identifiers: LCCN 2019016198 | ISBN 9780525573098 (hardcover) |
ISBN 9780525573104 (pbk.) | ISBN 9780525573111 (ebk.)
Subjects: LCSH: Radicals—United States—History—19th century—Biography. |
Social reformers—United States—History—19th century—Biography. |
United States—Social conditions—19th century. | United States—Politics
and government—19th century. | United States—History—1815–1861. |
United States—History—1849–1877.
Classification: LCC HN90.R3 J37 2019 | DDC 303.48/409034—dc23
LC record available at https://lccn.loc.gov/2019016198

ISBN 978-0-525-57309-8
Ebook ISBN 978-0-525-57311-1

Printed in the United States of America

2 4 6 8 9 7 5 3 1

First Edition

For Sari Edelstein

Contents

Introduction: A Second and More Glorious Revolution   *ix*

Part I. Foul Oppression in the Wind of Freedom, 1817–1840

CHAPTER 1	A Tremendous NO	*3*
CHAPTER 2	One Bold Lady-Man	*29*
CHAPTER 3	O America, Your Destruction Is at Hand!	*48*
CHAPTER 4	To Break Every Yoke	*68*

Part II. Infidel Utopian Free Lovers, 1836–1858

CHAPTER 5	Coming Out from the World	*87*
CHAPTER 6	Brook Farm on Fire	*107*
CHAPTER 7	Wheat Bread and Seminal Losses	*123*
CHAPTER 8	Marriage Slavery and All Other Queer Things	*142*

Part III. Abolition War, 1848–1865

CHAPTER 9	The Aliened American	*161*
CHAPTER 10	Treason Will Not Be Treason Much Longer	*182*
CHAPTER 11	The Provisional United States	*209*
CHAPTER 12	Under the Flag	*227*

Part IV. The Radicals' Reconstruction, 1865–1877

CHAPTER 13	To Write Justice in the American Heart	*247*
CHAPTER 14	A Revolution Going Backward	*271*
CHAPTER 15	This Electric Uprising	*297*
CONCLUSION	On Radical Failure	*317*

Acknowledgments   *331*
Notes   *333*
Index   *359*

Introduction

A Second and More Glorious Revolution

On July 4, 1826, Americans woke before dawn. Some squeezed into blue coats that had been folded in trunks for decades and covered what was left of their hair with tricornered hats, long out of fashion. At sunrise, cannons boomed, church bells pealed, and across the nation's scattered villages and modest cities, aged "heroes of '76" fired salutes from flintlock muskets, marching down dirt thoroughfares to drum and fife and the cheers of the crowd. Most parades then proceeded to a grove or a town square for a reading of the Declaration of Independence, followed by high-flown speeches honoring this momentous day: the semicentennial, or "Jubilee," as they called it. Some addresses spun wild visions in which the twenty-four states dotted with family farms and the vast forested territories beyond would one day become a powerful empire. The listeners adjourned to eat barbecue and then headed to the taverns for rounds of toasts—to George Washington, to the flag, to the eagle, to the first half-century of American life.

As orators waxed poetic on "the imperishable names of the founders" who had risked execution as traitors to the Crown in order to bequeath the everlasting legacy of freedom, Thomas Jefferson died in his bed in Virginia. Hours later, sitting in a chair at home in Massachusetts, John Adams followed him. It was exactly fifty years after the Declaration they had drafted together was approved, founding the United States of America. Many regarded this strange historical coincidence as a divine message, God's seal of approval on the American Revolution and a promise of perpetuity for its outcomes. Unmistakably, it was the threshold of a new era, the end of the beginning. The young nation had outlived the men who made it. What was next?

One man in Indiana claimed to know. Robert Owen was a rich industrialist, renowned in this country and in Europe for running philanthropic experiments in a cotton mill he owned in New Lanark, Scotland. As the nation celebrated its Jubilee, he mounted the stage at New Harmony Hall, a former church that he had purchased, along with the twenty thousand acres surrounding it. Intrigued by communal groups like the Shakers and emboldened by his experience applying his social theories to the factory workers he employed, Owen had sailed for the United States to propose a project on a far grander scale. His fame had spread after he addressed the assembled leaders of the federal government the previous year in Washington, D.C., pitching a wholesale reorganization of American life that was surprisingly well received. It was pouring rain on the Wabash River that Fourth of July, but a thousand people packed the building, traveling to this rural outpost from all over the country to hear what this slight Welsh gentleman had to say.

While orators in other cities and towns sang the praises of the American founders, Owen focused instead on the limits of their achievement. They had been forced to settle for mere "political independence," he claimed, hemmed in by the old-world prejudices that still dominated their era. But they could glimpse "a stronger and clearer light at the distance," he explained, and the founders trusted that their descendants would pick up where they left off, completing the transformation they had only begun. Indeed, a second revolution was required, a new battle for freedom "superior in benefit and importance to the first revolution." He asked the crowd, "Are you prepared to imitate the example of your ancestors? Are you willing to run the risks they encountered? Are you ready, like them, to meet the prejudices of past times, and determined to overcome them at all hazards, for the benefit of your country and for the emancipation of the human race?" To launch this revolution, Owen presented his Declaration of Mental Independence to supplant the founding document adopted fifty years before that day. Its object was to slay a "Hydra of Evils" enslaving mankind the world over: specifically, the "threefold horrid monster" of private property, religion, and marriage.

From our vantage point, almost two hundred years later, Owen's social revolution seems destined to fail, his interpretation of the founders as heralds of secular communism laughable at best. Capitalism, evangelical Protestantism, and the nuclear family would ultimately win the day, becoming far more deeply entrenched in American culture during Owen's lifetime. But from where he stood, the future of the United States was wide open, rolling out like a screen on which marvelous utopian visions could be projected. And indeed, Indiana looked a little like Eden in 1826. The woodland areas around New Harmony abounded that summer with persimmons, wild grapes, and flowering vines, punctuated with flashes of tropical green and yellow from wheeling Carolina parakeets, which are now extinct. Fertile land was practically endless, offering the rapidly multiplying population the natural plentitude of timber forests and lakes and rivers teeming with fish.

European visitors like Owen were astounded by the simple, direct dealings of the people carrying out the experiment that was early America: their free and easy manners, the "extreme equality" across classes, and their universal, near-fanatical engagement in politics as a form of social engineering. They seized every local election or civic debate as a new opportunity to invent the country of the future. Railroads and the telegraph would soon join steamships and canals in the network of new technology connecting the expanding country for trade, the exchange of ideas, the development of new towns, new states, new industries. This restless mobility and ambition turned away from the past, pushing further into the vast and magnificent West. The booming agriculture of the South fed the beginning of the Industrial Revolution in the North, where new systems of integrated manufacturing processed these abundant raw materials for global commerce, auguring the great wealth that would one day drive a great nation.

Viewed in another light, of course, this scene was not so utopian.

The workers in these new factories might labor sixteen hours a day, six days a week. Married women were relegated to the status of dependent children, unable to control property, vote, attend college, or sue in a court of law. The land, of course, was far from vacant; it was inhabited by long-established nations battling against extermination at the hands of white settlers. And the economic dynamo driving the young nation to prominence on the world stage was the forced labor of a million and a half people of African descent enslaved in this land of radical freedom, a number that would more than double in the coming decades. The conditions under which they lived were unspeakably brutal, and American law unambiguously doomed their children and their children's children to the same outrages.

Owen was right: a Hydra of Evils threatened the most profound ideals of the American project, and the recently departed founding generation would not be the ones to slay it. As his overflow audience suggests, many were ready to take up the mantle of a social revolution to right the many wrongs created or left unaddressed by the political revolution of their grandfathers. In the next half a century, hundreds of thousands of Americans pledged themselves to a vision of the nation based on collectivity, equality, and freedom. In social movements overlapping and diverging, they built a tradition of radical resistance that would reshape American life. Protest movements influenced westward expansion, southern secession, northern victory, and Reconstruction. They changed American law right up to the Constitution and transformed innumerable aspects of American culture—the breakfast table, the marital bed, and the church pew among them. Carrying the fight from the urban centers of the Eastern Seaboard to Kansas, Ontario, Haiti, Tennessee, Nigeria, and elsewhere, they extended their legacy through centuries and across the globe. This is the story of one constellation of these agitators and the second revolution they effected, though incompletely and imperfectly, in the most turbulent era of our history.[1]

THE FIGURES WHO come to the fore in this story worked across three entwined fields: slavery and race; sex and gender; property and labor. Each of these areas opened into other concerns—prisons, housing, birth control, religious belief, free speech, imperialism, child rearing, and diet among them. Drawn into one flash-point issue, they would soon find that it was inextricable from other oppressive systems. Owen's figure of the Hydra of social evils was apt: one deadly organism with many faces. As Wendell Phillips reflected after thirty years agitating for abolition, universal suffrage, and labor rights, he had been awakened as a young man to the fact that slavery "had poisoned everything it touched." It was not a single institution but the invisible, toxic framework of the entire society. He realized that everyone in power had a stake in preserving it— the press, the merchants, the historians, and the churchmen—so every aspect of the culture was merely another face of the same corruption: "When we tore off the mask the same hideous features were behind it—a sneering and gibbering spectre. This was America."[2]

Inequality was multiple, but so was the resistance that would strike at its root. The abolitionist vigilante John Brown was wild-eyed and armed to the teeth, with a scrawled manifesto and an appetite for martyrdom. Marx Edgeworth Lazarus was a Jewish southerner, writing anti-marriage screeds from a socialist commune but convinced he was slowly dying from nocturnal emissions. James Forten was an affluent black business owner and urban real estate investor. Sarah Bagley was a New England farm girl turned factory worker, editor, and socialist organizer. Some of these radicals were ostentatiously countercultural, wearing bloomers or dashikis, full beards in a clean-shaven era, flowers in their long hair. Some ate only raw vegan foods and whole grains. Some communed with the dead, interpreted skull bumps, douched with prodigious amounts of cold water, abstained from orgasm. Even participants in these movements sometimes found such oppositional affectations to be a distraction from real politics, and for most Americans, they were further evidence that progressive activists were troublemaking misfits. But even the wackiest features of what Henry James called "humanitary bohemia" were protests against mainstream values that helped define the communities of dissent that shaped the era's momentous struggle over the meaning of American democracy.

As we will see, some protests involved battering in a courthouse door and fist-fighting the police. There were strikes, raids, rallies, boycotts, secret councils, hidden weapons, endless rounds of conventions, lectures, resolutions, and petitions. But opposition was also a dance party with a whispered entry password, a group of worshippers walking silently out of a segregated church, a white woman casting an illegal ballot, a couple refusing to recite marriage vows, a woman of color stepping out of her comfortable carriage into a mob of frenzied white men that might have killed her.

Before Owen arrived with his plan to make America more radically free, African American activists across the North were organizing to protest slavery and racial inequality, establishing community institutions to support those whose very lives were a form of resistance. As their struggle mounted in the 1820s for emancipation and citizenship, the first major wave of socialism and workingmen's organizations raised their voices in protest, further revealing American social equality to be a myth. Around 1830, a radical turn in antislavery activism led to the first national social movement to bring together Americans across race, class, and gender, aiming not only to free enslaved people but to rout out tyranny wherever it remained. This intensifying culture of dissent met a violent backlash from the American mainstream. But even as protesters were mobbed, assaulted, and prosecuted, their printing presses smashed, their lecture halls burned to the ground, even as they were murdered, the field of activism expanded.

The country's first philosophical movement called for the end of all external authority and inherited institutions at this time, feeding an increasing embrace of civil disobedience. Many came out of the churches, leading some to "come out from the world" as a new wave of utopian socialism flowered in communes and a growing labor movement. From the beginning, this tradition of protest took aim at private life just as much as traditional politics; marriage was a lightning rod issue for socialists, women's rights activists, and Free Lovers who would liberate women from the bonds of maternity and domestic servitude. But in the midst of debates about the abolition of "wage slavery" and "marriage slavery," westward expansion triggered a national crisis over the fate of millions literally held captive.

As the founding compromise between the North and the South wore thin, antislavery activism took a militant turn around 1850. White activists began calling for the end of the Union. Black activists renewed their deliberations about a walkout on a national scale, abandoning the United States in search of a more promising land. Blood spilled on city streets, across the prairie, and in the halls of Congress. Genteel reformers embraced violence and treason, speeding a civil war waged not against slavery but against abolitionists. After four years of bloody internecine warfare, activists celebrated the victory of emancipation and an unprecedented opportunity to right the wrongs of the country's first revolution. With Reconstruction, ideas that had once seemed fringe were now squarely on the national agenda. But as former fanatics turned to politics, they found their values and their movements tested. By the time the nation rang in its one hundredth anniversary in 1876, patriotic fervor could not mask its tailspin into lawless violence. In the following year, the federal government would permit a white supremacist counterrevolution in the South but crack down brutally on aggrieved workers across the North, watershed reinforcements of inequality that threatened to undo the advances of the preceding half-century.

———

ROBERT OWEN'S CHOICE of the Fourth of July to launch his attack on American society, and his revision of the nation's founding document into a radical manifesto, were common tactics among the agitators of his century. While most Americans saw the Fourth as a day of celebration, activists remembered that it commemorated a protest and kept up that tradition by forcing the nation to reckon with its own ostensible values. Native Americans, industrial workers, women's rights advocates, Free Lovers, insurgent militias, and many others seized the symbolic richness of Independence Day and the language of the Declaration to raise their own calls for freedom and equality. After all, that initial manifesto was a reminder that the United States of America had only recently been no more than an idea for a radical utopian community—a set of principles and practices that a group of men made up together. Perhaps it could be done again, but better.

Thus, even as they aimed to "disorganize" society at its roots, these radicals saw themselves as the true inheritors of the American project who would keep its ideals alive. Indeed, they embraced many elements of the founders' thought that had been jettisoned during the more conservative period of state-making that followed the revolution. Thomas Paine, for instance, an antislavery, working-class immigrant, had rallied the colonies with his pamphlet *Common Sense,* calling not for a simple separation from England but for a new kind of society based on untried social theory: the "United States of America," a phrase he coined. But by the time Paine died in 1809, he was so hated by the American people for his variance from orthodox religious belief that no cemetery would bury him. Clearly, the country had a peculiar relationship to radicalism from the beginning. The Declaration was a monumental articulation of human rights, the Constitution a bulwark of slavery, hanging the union between the states on a morally and politically untenable compromise. These strands remained inextricable in the nation they formed.[3]

Nineteenth-century radicals' battle for social justice, freedom, and equality was defined by their struggle with the nation and its meaning: They refused to vote, demanded to vote, served in the government, and plotted armed coups to overthrow it. They burned the Constitution, hung the flag upside down, and yet returned to the specific form and language of the founding documents again and again to articulate the new versions of America they hoped to bring about. They spearheaded schemes to leave the country en masse, then signed up for military service, ready to die for it. In relation to the founders, they heeded both Owen's injunction to "imitate the example of your ancestors" and the abolitionist William Lloyd Garrison's call to "blush for their self-evident injustice, to shun the evil example they set." They revered Paine but denounced George Washington as a "man stealer." Even those whose solutions involved abandoning the United States altogether, aligning with international networks and denouncing the violent chauvinism of national identity, often declared that they acted in the "spirit of '76." Despite its galling and destructive hypocrisy, the nation never seemed to exhaust itself as a source of radical promise.[4]

Robert Owen believed that his Declaration of Mental Independence would spread around the globe at once and usher in an era of happiness and freedom, inspired by the American founders but reaching heights they had only contemplated in secret. Alas, he did not personally produce this transformation, and his project at New Harmony lasted only two chaotic years. But he indicated a groundswell under way and would remain a touchstone for some, one node in the nineteenth-century activist network that sought at various times to overthrow not only capitalism, Christianity, and the domestic family, as he proclaimed that day, but a range of other systems, most of all slavery, that they believed to be obstructing the nation's radical mission.

And in truth, something along these lines did seem to open up for the next fifty years, a period of upheaval that few of Owen's listeners could have imagined. Indeed, by the nation's centennial, American society would change so rapidly and dramatically that it was common to say that one had lived through a second revolution: even the youngest child alive would never again see the republic into which he was born.

PART I

Foul Oppression in the Wind of Freedom, 1817–1840

CHAPTER 1

A Tremendous NO

On the morning of August 16, 1824, a majestic flotilla appeared on the water in New York harbor: a series of ships decorated like floating palaces, all in the service of escorting one man safely to port. The Marquis de Lafayette stepped ashore to the sound of fifty thousand people cheering wildly, among them the vice president of the United States and two hundred of the city's leading citizens. After a month at sea, the cacophony must have been overwhelming: cannons booming, bells ringing, flags flapping, the West Point band in full swing. Militias stood at attention, wearing Lafayette's portrait over their hearts. Elderly veterans embraced him, openly weeping. Mothers thrust their children into his arms. Men and women fainted. Others approached him so choked with emotion they could not speak. They placed a crown of fresh cypress and laurel boughs on his head and ushered him into a grand carriage drawn by four white horses. The parade proceeded up Broadway to city hall, passing flag-draped buildings and banners stamped with the name of the returning hero, fresh flowers raining down from the windows. The shops were all closed, the business of New York City standing still for the day.[1]

As a mere teenager, the Frenchman had joined the Americans in their War for Independence, not only risking his life in battle, but volunteering his own money to feed, clothe, and pay his battalion. His leading role in the Battle of Yorktown had earned him a place in the pantheon of military heroes whose victory brought into being a new nation. Now that nation was nearing its fiftieth anniversary, and Lafayette was back to help celebrate: the only general from the Revolutionary army alive, and still a robust presence a month before his sixty-seventh birthday. But underneath all the patriotic pride was an undeniable note of anxiety.

The election year of 1824 was the very first in which no founding father appeared on the ticket. From Washington to Monroe, the first five presidents had been active participants in the conception of the new republic, but the country would soon outlive the men who had created it. To survive, it would need to transition from an experimental republic steered and administered directly by its makers to a permanent state, which would require a particular interpretation of its history. Thomas Jefferson had argued that every generation ought to be able to remake American society and all of its laws so that they would not be tyrannically ruled by his generation's dead hand. But by 1824, Americans were looking not for constant reinvention but for stability. Most wanted to believe that the words and deeds of the founders were final and the era of insurrection closed. France loomed as a cautionary tale, having torn up a number of constitutions by this time, its revolution followed by periods of terrible violence, a dictatorship, and finally the restoration of the monarchy in 1814. American society bolstered itself in this troubling changing-of-the-guard moment with a near-religious commemoration of the founding generation—a worshipful attitude that Ralph Waldo Emerson would denounce as the tendency to "build the sepulcres of the fathers," to be "retrospective," or conservative of what had been, rather than following the lead of the founders in daring to imagine what else might be. In short, revolutionary iconoclasm had been replaced with filial piety in American political culture.[2]

Lafayette's return was a landmark event in this culture of commemoration. He and his compatriots were to be remembered no longer as militant radicals, high on Enlightenment theory and ready to die for untried ideals, but as patriarchs of a static lineage that must be revered and preserved. While most of the other founders were dead or nearly so, Lafayette still had the physical wherewithal to reassure the American people at a moment when a certain crucial thread threatened to snap. Congress felt it was so important for him to visit at this time that it offered to send a ship to any port in France to convey him to the United States, to live on America's dime for two years, and receive payments in stock and land for his contributions to the revolution, a show of largesse that made the young nation feel strong and rich as its semicentennial Jubilee approached.

So they rolled out a welcome like no other. Before he left New York, Lafayette was honored by "the fete" at Castle Garden, which one attendee described as "the most brilliant and magnificent scene ever witnessed in the United States." This seems to have been the actual party of the century, a dazzling visual spectacle more lavish than anything anyone present could remember, surpassing even royal coronations. Six thousand partiers with two hundred servants in tow danced the cotillion under an arrangement of chandeliers reflecting the light of a thousand torches. Lafayette went on to tour all twenty-four of the states, paraded around in fine style as the "guest of the nation." Wherever he went, he was greeted with festivals, dances, and speeches. Maidens robed in white and wearing crowns of myrtle marched under newly constructed triumphal arches in choreographed formation with engraved lances aloft. They named streets, towns, counties, and city squares for him; at least one newborn was saddled with the name "Welcome Lafayette." On one occasion, a young army officer sang some verses he had composed, but when he came to the climax of the song, his voice faltered with emotion and he was unable to say the general's name. He fell at Lafayette's feet crying and rushed away.

But on the day of his arrival, Lafayette's mind was occupied with thoughts of one woman, who was at that moment still in the middle of the Atlantic Ocean en route to the United States. From the center of the celebratory hubbub, he wrote to a friend how eagerly he awaited the coming ship that would reunite him with his "beloved." A month behind his hero's welcome in New York, a far less distinguished vessel pulled in to the harbor with no fanfare, with a woman aboard who was too indispensable to Lafayette to be left out of his American tour but already too controversial to have arrived by the same boat or to be mentioned in any of the official accounts of his visit. As the general's intimate friend, she would soon be entertained in the homes of the nation's first families, only to be regarded in the years to come as the most notorious radical in its history.

Lafayette was the revolutionary past, but she was the revolutionary future; the press would call her "the female Tom Paine." No one worshipped the founders more than she did, and for that very reason she refused to regard their accomplishment as mere symbolism, their rhetoric as empty, or their project complete. In 1824, she was the hushed-up younger woman behind the man who was bringing the country they both idolized to its feet. But within five years, her name would be denounced from pulpits and splashed across the front pages of newspapers, shorthand for a festering fusion of interracial sex, Free Love, gender-bending, and atheism that threatened to bring down the Republic: "that she-demon and unprincipled profligate, FANNY WRIGHT."[3]

FRANCES WRIGHT WAS an orphaned Scottish aristocrat who had been raised, along with her younger sister, Camilla, by a string of relatives in England. She spent most of her youth with an aunt who

Frances Wright, 1824 portrait
by Henry Inman.
Luce Center, New-York Historical Society.
Purchase, Abbott-Lenox and Foster-Jarvis funds,
and the James S. Cushman Bequest

lived in a twenty-room mansion in a tiny town called Dawlish, on the southern seacoast of Devonshire. When she was seventeen, Wright happened upon a history of the American Revolution in the library of a family member's estate, later recalling how strange it had been to find a "subject so politically heterodox" in that patrician context. Opening the book had awoken her to "a new existence" in an instant. "From that moment my attention became riveted on this country," she would later write, "as on the theater where man might first awake to the full knowledge and the full exercise of his powers." Restless and bored with the limited round of activities available to a genteel young lady under the watch of a persnickety aunt, she began to dream of the United States as a nearly magical new world "consecrated to liberty," where traditional constraints and distinctions had been abandoned, and vowed to see it in person one day.[4]

Wright went off to live with one of her father's relatives, James Mylne, a professor of moral philosophy at the University of Glasgow, a hotbed of the Scottish Enlightenment; her uncle held the faculty position that had once been occupied by Adam Smith. In this environment, Wright imbibed a devotion to reason and empiricism, a suspicion of received wisdom, traditions, and religious authority that would animate her activist career. Women would not be admitted as students at Glasgow until 1883, so Wright's free access to the university library enabled an education that would remain unavailable to other women for generations. She wrote poetry, a philosophical treatise, later a play.

Realizing her dream at the age of twenty-three, she sailed for the United States with her sister. In 1821, she published a book of her observations, *Views of Society and Manners in America*. It brimmed with praise for the young country, which seemed to live up to her idealized view of its prospects, except for a particularly glaring contradiction of the founding principles she held so dear: "The sight of slavery is revolting every where, but to inhale the impure breath of its pestilence in the free winds of America is odious beyond all that the imagination can conceive." Because she saw "so many seeds of excellence, so bright a dawning of national glory, so fair a promise," she regarded American slavery with "regret, impatience, and anxiety."[5]

Wright's book was widely read and quite popular with what was left of the Enlightenment elite. Corresponding with Jeremy Bentham, who had praised the work, she called the United States "our Utopia." But she was especially exhilarated by an approving note from the Marquis de Lafayette—one of the heroes from the book that had inspired her trip, a Revolutionary legend who would soon change the course of her life. On a visit to France, she set out to meet him on her own and eventually came to live in his house. Perhaps, as Wright claimed, they talked about America until the wee hours of the morning. But rumors soon flew that they were lovers, and it is likely enough that they were: everything about Wright's life indicates that she cared not at all for the rules of sexual propriety, and the French writer Stendhal later described Lafayette at this stage of his life as "solely occupied, in spite of his age, in fumbling at pretty girls' plackets, not occasionally but constantly, and not much caring who saw."[6]

Wright had countless friendships with men as an intellectual equal, not a love interest or a sex object, so it is possible that friendship and philosophical connection truly were the limit of her relationship with Lafayette. But her letters to him were full of romantic pining: "I am only half alive when away from you" or simply "I love you very, very, much." His letters told her she was "beloved" and "cherished" and that he could not wait to hold her in his arms again. Wright proposed that he either marry her or formally adopt her and her sister in order to legitimate their extremely close relationship in the face of the rumors. He did neither. The couple was determined, though, that she would return to the United States as the personal guest of the "nation's guest." Lafayette's family would not hear of them making the voyage together, however, and ultimately Wright agreed to follow a couple of weeks behind. She would rejoin him in New York to begin a tour of her cherished America on the arm of its French hero.[7]

But only a month after she arrived, she wrote, "My heart is sick." Her awareness of "the breadth of distance between American principles and American practice" was finally shaking her faith in the nation's perfection. Her book had already revealed her awareness of the glaring problem of slavery in the land of the free, but now she was no longer willing to countenance this paradox with which all admirers of America must grapple. Her creeping feeling of disappointment began to compromise her enjoyment of all the pomp and celebration for Lafayette. She was both morally and politically offended by the hypocrisy of a nation that was in love with its revolution but had failed to do anything to end slavery half a century later. "The enthusiasm, triumphs and rejoices exhibited here before the countenance of the great and good Lafayette have no longer charms for me," she wrote. "They who so sin against the liberty of their country, against those great principles for which their honored guest poured on their soil his treasure and his blood, are not worthy to rejoice in his presence. My soul sickens in the midst of gaiety, and turns almost with disgust from the fairest faces or the most amiable discourse."[8]

It must have been with some trepidation, then, that she approached one of the tour's highlights: a visit to Monticello, the plantation where Thomas Jefferson, icon of Revolutionary Enlightenment thought, enslaved well over a hundred people. Wright missed Lafayette's emotional reunion with the elderly founder, who walked out bareheaded over his vast lawn overlooking the Blue Ridge Mountains, clenching his friend in a long and tearful embrace. Keeping up the charade of respectability, she and Camilla showed up a day or two later. She didn't make the best impression, at least with the women in Jefferson's household, who plainly disliked her unconventional ways and were unsparing in their evaluation of her as a "bluestocking" who was not interested in conversing with ladies and who proudly displayed "masculine proclivities." They were not charmed by Lafayette's anecdotes of occasions on their travels in which she would "harangue the men in the public room of a hotel and the like." Jane Cary, a Jefferson cousin, offered this caustic account of Wright's appearance: "In person she was masculine, measuring at least 5 feet 11 inches, and wearing her hair a la Niñon in close curls," that is, cut short in the style of a French courtesan. She described Wright's complexion as "thoroughly English," which she seems to have intended as a bitter insult, and charged that "she always seemed to wear the wrong attire."[9]

Wright never cared about clothes or any of the other social niceties that might have made her acceptable to the elite American women among whom she circulated at this time. She was no doubt more concerned with the strange and poignant American outrage on garish display at Monticello. Lafayette's personal secretary, Auguste Levasseur, wrote an account of their tour that offers us the best sense of what Jefferson's home looked like to these European visitors. When one enters Virginia, he reflected, "the soul feels suddenly chilled and the imagination alarmed, in learning that at many points of this vast republic the horrible principle of slavery still reigns with all its sad and monstrous consequences; we demand with astonishment the source of this contradiction between such sublime theories, and a practice so shameful to humanity!" His horror and disbelief plainly shine through his attempt to write cheerfully and respectfully about Jefferson. He observed that the people enslaved at Monticello appeared to be healthy, and he conversed with many who assured him that they were never treated badly and were "nearly certain of not being torn from their homes to be sent elsewhere, during Mr. Jefferson's life."[10] Faint praise indeed.

For Wright as well, seeing firsthand that this titan of the American founding held so many people in bondage was troubling and disillusioning. She talked to Jefferson about slavery while she was his guest, as did Lafayette, who openly opposed the institution, maintaining that he had contributed to the Revolutionary War because he believed it was fought in the name of freedom for all humanity. Jefferson himself had long acknowledged that slavery was immoral and likely to bring down divine retribution. In his *Notes on the State of Virginia,* he wrote, "I tremble for my country when I reflect that God is just; that his justice cannot sleep forever: that considering numbers, nature and natural means only, a revolution of the wheel of fortune, an exchange of situation is among possible events." He hoped that the American Revolution would prepare the way "for a total emancipation" to head off a disastrous race war, so that slaves might be freed "with the consent of the masters, rather than by their extirpation."

But in the same work, he opined that black people were biologically inferior to whites and claimed that this natural inequality made the end of slavery unrealizable, unless the millions of black people currently in bondage could be removed from the population. "Nothing is more certainly written in the book of fate than that these people are to be free," he wrote. "Nor is it less certain that the two races, equally free, cannot live in the same government. Nature, habit, opinion has drawn indelible lines of distinction between them." The solution, for Jefferson and countless others, was to round up all people of African descent for deportation once they were freed. Like all proponents of what came to be called colonization, he believed that it was the only way to avoid much worse outcomes: an uprising that would dwarf the Haitian Revolution, in which slaves had taken up arms and overthrown their enslavers, or (perhaps even more horrifying) the further sexual intermixing of black and white populations.[11]

Indeed, in her time with Jefferson, Wright gathered that the prejudice against interracial sex was the ultimate consideration making it impossible for white Americans to end slavery. From Virginia, she wrote to a friend in London that this taboo "is so deeply rooted in the American mind that emancipation without expatriation . . . seems impossible." One can only imagine how she squared this idea with the conspicuous presence of enslaved people at Monticello with light skin, red hair, and freckles, much resembling Jefferson himself.

Wright was not alarmed by the idea of sex across the color line and noted that the "amalgamation" of the races Americans so feared was already "taking place slowly but surely under the present system . . . in the most degrading and dangerous way possible." But she was hopeful that the panic over interracial sex might motivate white Americans to do something about slavery. "The apprehension of this amalgamation," she wrote, might operate as a "powerful incentive toward active measures." It was an insight that emerged not only from her time with Jefferson but also from a recent brush with the Haitian emigration movement under way in free black communities across the North. On her whirlwind tour of the country in the previous two months, as she became increasingly sickened by the sight of slavery in the land of the free, she learned of a proposal from the Haitian president, Jean-Pierre Boyer, to help black Americans settle in Haiti. She sent word to Jonathas Granville, a Haitian military officer sent to the United States to recruit emigrants, that she wanted to meet with him in Philadelphia when she passed through with Lafayette.[12]

The general met with the aristocratic Haitian in his own quarters and made a point of personally escorting him through the packed front rooms of the boardinghouse, a small protest against American racial prejudice. Wright met Granville at the more private family home where he was staying, but the scandalous news that she had socialized with a man of color spread anyway, leading Martha Washington's granddaughter to freeze her out on the next leg of their visit, blocking her from accompanying Lafayette to the family plantation at Mount Vernon. By the time she left Monticello, Wright had discussed in rapid succession the prospects of elective black emigration with a Haitian gentleman and forced colonization with an American founder, and, in between, had caught a tiny whiff of the panic and disdain that mere conversation between a white woman and a black man could incite. She filed these observations away, but not for long.

———

GRANVILLE HAD BEEN in Philadelphia a number of times that summer before he met Wright, working with the leaders of one of the most robust and politically active free black communities in the country, one that had been debating for many years the question of whether people of African descent should insist on a future in the United States or look elsewhere. Back in January 1817, word reached them that a powerful group of white men, including the incoming president and the Speaker of the House, members of the clergy, and a number of white philanthropists claiming to have their best interests at heart, had met in the nation's capital the previous month to form the American Colonization Society. These men were committed to a large-scale plan that would pluck free people of color out of their hard-won American lives and deport them to West Africa. Alarm spread through Philadelphia's black neighborhoods. They would be dragged from their homes, they whispered, and shipped across the globe to die of disease in a country most had never seen.

Around the time that the first snow of the year fell, more than three thousand free people of color crammed into the sanctuary of Mother Bethel in Philadelphia, the first African Methodist Episcopal church, to learn about the ACS and register their dissent. Founded by Richard Allen, a community leader and organizer, the church was one of the flourishing institutions made by and for the free people of Philadelphia in the previous decades. This particular meeting might have been the first of its kind and scale in history. Despite their considerable worry and agitation, the crowd waited in breathless quiet, sitting stock still through introductory remarks by James Forten, the finely dressed black gentleman who presided. Forten owned his own business—plus a three-story brick town house two blocks away and investment properties around the city—employing both black and white tradesmen in his sail-making loft. Despite his great wealth, he shared with the crowd of poor laborers the vexed position of free black people at this time: they were not enslaved, as hundreds were in Philadelphia in 1817, not to mention the millions beyond, but despite their nominal freedom they were despised, worse than shunned, subject to capricious violence and structural discrimination every day.

Forten, Allen, and other leaders in Philadelphia had been working for a time with Paul Cuffee, another wealthy black gentleman in the seafaring business. Cuffee lived in Massachusetts but hoped to settle African Americans in the new British colony of Sierra Leone in West Africa, where, he believed, they would have brighter prospects than in the United States. Although Forten had no interest in leaving the country himself, he well understood why others might, given the conditions they all faced. He helped promote Cuffee's project, recruiting four black Philadelphians to emigrate at the end of 1815.

Although some free African Americans liked the idea of a home abroad, where they and their children might enjoy the rights and opportunities denied to them in the United States, the idea took on a different valence when white men picked it up and ran with it. Among them was Robert Finley, a minister and educator concerned that "if the people of color remain among us, the effect of their presence will be unfavorable to our industry and morals," who wrote to Cuffee to ask about his experience settling black emigrants in West Africa. Cuffee responded that Sierra Leone was not big enough for the mass exodus that Finley had in mind and instead floated the idea of establishing one colony in West Africa and another all-black colony within the United States. But the prospect of any black population remaining in proximity to white Americans did not appeal to Finley. Although he acknowledged that "to colonize them in Africa would be a much more arduous undertaking" than the far less expensive idea of dedicating a place for them in "our own wild lands," he feared that if free black people controlled a nearby colony, their resentment might make them formidable military enemies. Moreover, their presence would render America's "slaves uneasy in their masters' service" and give them a safe destination for escape. Removing them to a distant shore would create a more sharply bifurcated America: white citizens and black slaves. This was, of course, exactly Finley's aim. In December 1816, he and other prominent white citizens founded the American Colonization Society, an organization backed by both state and federal government funding that would aim "to rid our country of a useless and pernicious, if not dangerous portion of its population," as its first president explained.[13]

The founding of the ACS by pro-slavery whites had the unintended consequence of mobilizing organized resistance from the very community that it sought to eliminate. That January day in 1817, when Forten asked the thousands assembled in Mother Bethel if they were interested in returning to the continent of their ancestors, beginning a new country of their own making, "you might have heard a pin drop, so profound was the silence." Reframing the question, he asked again for the crowd to speak for or against the

Mother Bethel AME Church in Philadelphia, 1829.
The Library Company of Philadelphia

idea of emigration—did they wish to seek a new life, leaving America behind? In response, "one *long, loud,* aye, TREMENDOUS NO, from this vast audience, seemed as if it would bring down the walls of the building. Never did there appear a more unanimous opinion. Every heart seemed to feel that it was a *life and death question.*" In a single voice of dissent, they shouted their determination not to be exiled, to claim their place as Americans, despite overwhelming opposition.[14]

Forten and a colleague wrote up a series of resolutions to represent the community's protest: "WHEREAS our ancestors (not of choice) were the first successful cultivators of America, we . . . feel ourselves entitled to participate in the blessings of her luxuriant soil, which their blood and sweat manured." They viewed "with deep abhorrence the unmerited stigma attempted to be cast upon the reputation of the free People of Colour" by those who wanted them deported. Moreover, they affirmed their unity with enslaved people, refusing to leave millions behind in captivity: "We never will separate ourselves voluntarily from the slave population of this country; they are our brethren by the ties of consanguinity, of suffering, and of wrongs." It was a sweeping statement of black solidarity, free and enslaved, and a categorical rejection of any plan to sever their connection to the United States. Free black communities across the North joined the Philadelphians in denouncing the ACS as a racist scheme and refusing to relinquish their claim to American citizenship. As Allen affirmed, the "land which we have watered with our tears and our blood, is now our mother country."[15]

James Forten had demonstrated by any measure his belonging and allegiance to the young country. Born free to a father who was also born free, his was the fourth generation of his family to live in Philadelphia; his great-grandfather had arrived around the same time as William Penn, the colony's founder. As a nine-year-old boy, Forten squeezed through the crowd gathered outside the Pennsylvania State House as its two-thousand-pound bell—not yet called the Liberty Bell, and not yet cracked—called citizens to hear the first public reading of the Declaration of Independence. A man with powdered hair stood on a platform and read from a sheet of parchment, proclaiming it to be "self-evident" that "all men are created equal, that they are endowed by their Creator with certain unalienable Rights, that among these are Life, Liberty and the pur-

James Forten portrait,
ca. 1818.
Leon Gardiner collection of
American Negro Historical Society
records, Historical Society
of Pennsylvania

suit of Happiness." These high-flown phrases must have revolved in the young Forten's mind with thrilling but uncertain import.

Given his dubious position in the project of this new nation, Forten approached it with an almost unaccountable sense of hope and duty. As the war raged on, he begged his mother to let him volunteer and shipped out in 1781, before he was fifteen years old. His first tour saw a bloody battle with a Royal Navy vessel, resulting in many casualties on both sides. But he survived, returning to port in time to watch George Washington's army parade through Philadelphia, marching south where they would combine with the forces under the Marquis de Lafayette to fight the British at Yorktown. The tall general who would become the country's first president likely commanded the attention of most of the crowd, but Forten's eyes were glued to the "several Companies of Coloured People" from New England who marched into battle with him, rows of black American revolutionaries, "as brave Men as ever fought."[16]

Weeks later, Forten embarked on his second voyage, and just as the troops under Washington and Lafayette were securing the surrender of Cornwallis, his ship was captured by a British warship and he was taken captive—a disastrous occurrence, because black prisoners were usually shipped to the Caribbean and sold into slavery. But the captain had a twelve-year-old son on board and pressed the young Forten into service as a playmate and babysitter. Indeed, as he got to know him, he proposed that Forten accompany his son back to England, offering him a new start as the friend of a rich landowner. But Forten would not cast his lot with the enemy of the United States, replying, "I have been taken prisoner for the liberties of my country, and never will prove a traitor to her interest." Stymied but perhaps a little impressed, the captain wrote a note to the head of the prison ship, recommending that Forten be exchanged for a British POW and returned safely home.[17]

The Philadelphia to which he returned was the new nation's capital and also the capital of free black America, home to organizations for mutual support and elevation founded by and for the nation's largest free black population. Though these projects faced significant government and social opposition (as they did in other northern cities), Philadelphia offered a uniquely favorable context for African American institution building, in part because of its Quaker roots. The city was home to a school for black children, founded by Quakers, as well as the first American abolitionist society, which had been supported by a number of the country's founders, including Thomas Paine, Benjamin Franklin, and Benjamin Rush. The Pennsylvania Assembly passed the earliest American law abolishing slavery in 1780. Grateful for their own deliverance from the "tyranny of Great Britain," the assemblymen declared, "we conceive that it is our duty, and we rejoice that it is in our Power, to extend a Portion of that freedom to others, which hath been extended to us."[18]

But the statute, while groundbreaking, did not actually free anyone. Aiming to phase out the institution very gradually, it provided for children born to enslaved people to be freed when they reached the age of twenty-eight. Some Pennsylvanians remained enslaved until the 1840s. In the meantime, members of the free black community exerted what pressure they could, asking Congress, still meeting in Philadelphia at that time, to end the slave trade. But Congress declined even to consider their petitions, rightly perceiving that affirming black Americans' rights as citizens under the Constitution would be the first step toward a national activist movement and eventually black representation in the government. One member asked his philanthropically inclined colleagues if they wished "to see those people sitting by their sides, deliberating in the councils of the nation." Another declared, "It would teach them the art of assembling together, debating, and the like, and would soon, if encouraged, extend from one end of the Union to the other."[19]

Failing to make inroads at the national level, Philadelphia's free black leadership also approached the state legislature to propose that the city's black residents be taxed to generate the money to free Pennsylvania's remaining slaves. Although this proposal appealed to the house, it was killed in the state senate. It is particularly striking that free African Americans were willing to assume a financial burden to free enslaved people—even against the advice of the city's white abolitionist society—considering that on the whole they were poor, severely disadvantaged by their limited educational and employment opportunities. Forten was an exception, but he knew that even his astonishingly rare position as a wealthy black man did not protect him, or his wife and children, from being kidnapped and sold into slavery on any given day.

Indeed, even as the number of free black Americans grew, their situation was getting worse. After the revolution, other northern states passed gradual abolition statutes, and some scattered white individuals manumitted the people they enslaved, unable to keep up the hypocrisy of holding black men and women as property after waging war in the name of freedom. Moreover, as many as 100,000 enslaved people had self-emancipated during the war period, escaping from large plantations, modest family farms, and urban homes in a time of upheaval. There had been around 1,000 free black people in Philadelphia at the end of the Revolutionary War; in 1810, there were nearly 10,000. White Americans already hated and feared free blacks, and now their numbers seemed to be swelling at an alarming rate, destabilizing the institution of slavery and threatening the ideal of an all-white America.[20]

There were already a number of state and federal laws aimed at managing the perceived threat of racial "mixing" and ensuring the permanent subordination of free people of color, including anti-miscegenation statutes and other formal indications that white citizens intended to keep this population permanently separate and subordinate. The fugitive slave law, which first appeared as a clause in the Constitution but was strengthened in 1793, stipulated that enslaved people who escaped to a free state must be returned to their lawful owners. This made free black people easy prey for kidnappers, who could abduct them under the auspices of this law and then sell them into slavery for a tidy profit, regardless of their previous status. In 1813, Pennsylvania passed a new set of laws cracking down even further. One bill required all free black people, including children, to officially register themselves with the local government. Police could demand to see proof of this registration at any time and, if they were unsatisfied, a free person could end up in jail or on the auction block.

Forten published an outraged response to this bill, opening with a sentiment by then familiar to all Americans but that he had been among the first to hear: "We hold this truth to be self-evident, that God created all men equal." Unlike the founders, he left no ambiguity about how this last phrase should be interpreted: "This idea embraces the Indian and the European, the Savage and the Saint, the Peruvian and the Laplander, the white Man and the African." Because all men have the natural rights described in the Declaration and, he added, many free black men own property on which they pay taxes, they claim their rights as citizens under the Constitution. Underscoring the injustice of their position, he noted that many of them shed blood in the revolution but could not now venture outdoors on the Fourth of July without becoming the target of gang violence from drunken white men.[21]

Four years later, when the founding of the ACS again threatened the status of black Americans, Forten was resolute, despite his earlier support of Cuffee's black-led emigration plan: black people in the United States were indeed Americans and must be given the full rights and equality of citizens. The opposition of free black communities did not, however, encourage the organization to change course. After a delay due to freezing temperatures that locked the ship into the North River, the ACS's maiden voyage launched from New York City in February 1820 with three white agents and eighty-eight black emigrants, a group mainly from New York and Pennsylvania that included farmers, carpenters, a nurse, and dozens of children. The ship was christened the *Elizabeth,* but the organization referred to it as the black *Mayflower* in honor of the two hundredth anniversary of the landing at Plymouth Rock, hoping to position these emigrants as new Pilgrims, the seed of a future black republic. But within three weeks of their arrival, all three whites and twenty-two of the black settlers were dead. Between food scarcity, attacks from the people who already lived there, and a malaria outbreak, conditions were hard. Although the ACS continued to send settlers to the colony of Liberia, founded with the support of the slave-owning president James Monroe, it seemed to many that the plan was turning out to be an exorbitantly expensive failure.[22]

Although most free black communities opposed the ACS and its projects, the possibility of a black nation still appealed to many, and in the 1820s a black-led emigration movement coalesced around a destination much closer to home. The postcolonial republic of Haiti had long been a source of inspiration for black Americans and terror for whites. Its revolution in the 1790s against France proved not only the organizational and military wherewithal of black people but their commitment to the Enlightenment political ideals that had also inspired the American founding. Beginning around 1818, African Americans became interested in moving to Haiti to enjoy freedom and equal rights under a government of black men. The Haitian president, Jean-Pierre Boyer, saw an opportunity: new settlers would bring economic growth, as well as the possibility of diplomatic recognition from the United States, which was eager to off-load its black population. He offered to subsidize the travel of African American emigrants, to meet them personally at the dock, and to provide them with land, provisions, and immediate citizenship rights. He corresponded with Forten and Allen, both of whom embraced the plan and helped promote it. The editor and activist Benjamin Lundy, the most prominent white abolitionist of the time, also backed the Haitian emigration movement, printing a series of supportive articles in his newspaper, the *Genius of Universal Emancipation,* and traveling to Haiti at least twice himself with emigrating free people, sending firsthand accounts of life there back to Philadelphia.[23]

In 1824, Boyer mounted a major publicity push with the help of his American colleagues. That summer, he sent Granville to the United States to drum up interest among potential emigrants. Finding the racism of the United States deeply offensive as he traveled from city to city, Granville earnestly appealed to free African Americans across the North with stories of the better life that awaited them in Haiti. He met repeatedly with Forten and Allen in Philadelphia, holding one particularly large meeting at Mother

Bethel in July, during which fifty members of the congregation signed up to emigrate. But he was soon summoned back to the city, not by James Forten, but by another Revolutionary veteran, the one with superstar status touring the country as the nation's honored guest: the aged Marquis de Lafayette, accompanied by his strange young mistress, on their way to Monticello.

———

THE WRIGHT SISTERS stayed on in Virginia after Lafayette departed, taking in some local sights with their host, including Harpers Ferry, where the Shenandoah River meets the Potomac amid forested rolling foothills. Jefferson likely pointed out the national armory that had been built there during his presidency, one of two sites in the young nation where the government manufactured and stockpiled weapons. Decades later, it would play a pivotal role in American history and the fight against slavery that neither Jefferson nor Wright could have imagined nor would live to see.

Rejoining Lafayette in Washington, D.C., the sisters accompanied him that winter through rounds of celebration by the capital city's elite as the previous year's controversial and still unresolved presidential election continued to unfold. Andrew Jackson had received more popular votes and more electoral votes than his rival, John Quincy Adams, but neither had the number of electoral votes required to declare a victory, so the decision went to the House of Representatives. Wright went to the Capitol to witness the vote on February 9. Henry Clay, the Speaker of the House, handed the presidency to Adams, who had been the loser by any measure, and was promptly appointed his secretary of state. This deal would go down in history as a "corrupt bargain," and historians date the end of "the Era of Good Feelings" in American politics to this day. From the visitors' gallery, Wright had a front-row seat at this circus, which she felt turned the presidency, "that office, the noblest that exists upon the globe," into a trifling and crooked game. America's grand institutions were quickly losing their utopian sheen.[24]

Fatefully, another event in the very same room later that month sparked Wright's imagination with renewed hope for the republic she had once loved. Kept in D.C. by a bad cold, she happened to be in town when Robert Owen delivered his lectures in the Hall of Representatives. Although he would soon be known as the leader of the first national socialist movement in the United States, he was welcomed by American leaders as a successful capitalist who had improved workers' lives in his cotton mill in addition to extracting their labor, providing them with education, childcare, and high-quality affordable goods in the company store, all while turning a tidy profit for himself. To the sitting president, the president-elect, and members of Congress and the cabinet, Owen proposed to help Americans realize "a much more perfect system of equality and liberty" than the War for Independence had achieved. "By a hard struggle you have attained political liberty," he explained, and yet Americans remain in a state of "mental bondage." Like Wright, he deplored the inequality still to be found in the country, declaring that capitalism gives "surplus of wealth and power to the few" and inflicts "poverty and subjection on the many."

His plan to end inequality through communal living rested on a theory of social determinism he had previously outlined in his book *A New View of Society,* published in 1813. In it, he wrote that man is the passive product of his environment, "formed to be irresistibly controlled by external circumstances." Inequality was the result of faults in society, not natural and unavoidable in human nature. Thus, to create true equality, every citizen would need to be shaped by the same environment, receiving an identical, communal education and upbringing. Owen believed that if the influences all around them were properly calibrated, children could be "formed" to have "any human character." In designing a new system to supplant the private family, he believed he could design a new people.

In the United States, Owen's philosophy morphed into a vision for the country and the world that struck an unmistakably utopian chord: "Old things shall pass away, and all shall become new, and beautiful, and delightful." Over the course of two lectures, he described to this assembled government body a socialist commune situated on "1,000 or 2,000 acres of land," a magnificent square palace enclosing schools for students from infancy through the university level, facilities for cooking and eating, a brewery, laundry, laboratories, and chapels, as well as rooms for lectures, committee meetings, concerts, and dancing. As a parting gift, he left a scale model of this gorgeous American community of the future, and it was displayed for a time in John Quincy Adams's White House.[25]

Wright was deeply stirred by Owen's radical call for a second revolution that would address inequality and invent a new society, just as Lafayette and his brothers-in-arms had done fifty years earlier. Owen's plan offered a solution to one manifestation of the contradiction and corruption that had troubled her for the past six months. She shared his Enlightenment belief in the perfectibility of all people, in education rather than inborn traits and inherited status. Moreover, she must have longed for a plan that would uproot private as well as public life, freeing women from their circumscribed sphere. As for Owen's "science of circumstances," she already believed that gender, race, and other aspects of identity were the product of culture, not nature. She had written to Lafayette three years earlier, "Trust me . . . the mind has no sex but what habit and education give it, and I who was thrown in infancy upon the world like a wreck upon the waters have learned, as well to struggle with the elements as any male child of Adam."[26]

She determined to visit the property Owen had recently purchased in Indiana and intended as the site of his utopian community, breaking off from Lafayette's grand tour. At the side of a founding hero, she had seen how short the United States had fallen of its full potential, hampered even by the very people who had put it into motion. Now she turned from the nation's mythic past toward an unprecedented future, a new horizon for the unfinished American Revolution.

When Owen and his followers arrived in Indiana in 1825, they walked into a ready-made utopia on the banks of the Wabash River set up by the Rappites, German peasants who had fled persecution in their homeland for following a Christian splinter sect with a charismatic leader. Their lives were simple and celibate, united in their devotion to Jesus Christ and George Rapp. The beautiful and prosperous town they called Harmony was nestled in the midst of

over two thousand acres of fertile land they had fenced and cultivated with orchards, vineyards, and vast vegetable gardens. They
built manufacturing facilities for everything they needed to live in-
dependently on the rural frontier, to brew beer and distill whiskey,
to spin fabric and dye it, to make soap, candles and glue, boots and
shoes. They had massive granaries to store wheat and a gristmill to
grind it into flour. There were rows of neat log cabins and several
two-story homes, as well as five or six large community buildings
housing sixty to eighty people each and two magnificent churches.
In this prosperous, well-ordered town, they lived much more com-
fortably and abundantly than other settlers in the surrounding area.
Owen bought them out for $135,000, and the Rappites moved on
to build a new commune in Pennsylvania.

Wright arrived just before the Rappites' departure and was
amazed at the wealth they had generated through hard work carried
out in cheerful, organized equality, with all their worldly goods
held in common. In fact, it gave her an idea. Owen specifically excluded people of color from his community, unless they were
brought along as servants by white people joining him "to promote
the happiness of the world." But Wright conceived of another project that would combine Owenite socialism with the Rappite system
of united labor to prepare enslaved people for freedom and resettle
them outside the United States. Like Forten and other free black
activists, Wright opposed the ACS because it did not take direct aim
at the institution of slavery. But having seen how deeply prejudice
was ingrained even in the North, she doubted there was anywhere
in the United States where black people could enjoy their full rights
as Americans. Remembering what Jefferson had told her about
white Americans' horror of interracial sex and their refusal to live
alongside free black people, she adopted the idea widely held by
white Americans that it was best to eliminate them from the body
politic: "Emancipation should be connected with colonization."[27]

Specifically, she decided "to purchase two sections of government land, within the good south western cotton-producing areas,
either in Tennessee, Alabama, or Mississippi," and "to place on this
land from fifty to one hundred negroes, and introduce a system of

cooperative labor, promising them liberty after five years of service, along with liberty and education for their children." From there, the communes would spread: "It is hoped that, after one successful experiment, a similar establishment will be placed in each state." She believed this would allow for the gradual abolition of slavery, "without danger or loss to the citizens of the south." Enslaved people would live and work communally like the Rappites, generating the money for their own purchase and deportation, meanwhile receiving an education that would prepare them for whatever life awaited them in freedom, somewhere far from the only home they had ever known.[28]

She sent this proposal to Benjamin Lundy, who issued it as a pamphlet and published notes on her activities in his newspaper. But she had laid out her ideas first in a long letter to a friend, advising her to read it only in private. She posted this letter from Philadelphia, where perhaps the most powerful of the country's many free black communities prospered despite formidable opposition and without, of course, having been prepared to do so by any organized scheme. Although many of them supported the black-led Haitian emigration movement, they had denounced in their historic inaugural protest the attempts of white people to control their destinies or "resettle" them away from their native land, the United States. From her meeting with Granville and her familiarity with Lundy's paper, she knew that hundreds of free people of color were choosing to relocate to Haiti. Instead of backing this black-led project directly, as Lundy was doing, or hammering out her ideas for racial uplift with Forten, Allen, or any other of the community leaders who had been working on these issues for decades, she devoted her considerable energy, connections, and financial resources to spearheading her own experiment.

As she prepared to execute her plan, she called on her powerful friends for support. Lafayette was on board. Jefferson responded supportively but demurred from becoming personally involved, saying that he was too close to death to start new ventures but commending her for taking on this great subject, "which has been thro' life that of my greatest anxieties." He wrote encouragingly, "The abolition of the evil is not impossible; it ought never therefore to be despaired of. Every plan should be adopted, every experiment tried, which may do something towards the ultimate object. That which you propose is well worthy of trial. It has succeeded with certain portions of our white brethren, under the care of a Rapp and an Owen; and why may it not succeed with the man of colour?"[29]

In the early fall of 1825, Wright rode hundreds of miles to scout land for her project, heading to Tennessee with the English-born farmer George Flower, who had brokered the deal between Rapp and Owen for New Harmony. He had much-needed experience with frontier life in Illinois as well as with shepherding freed people out of the country; before he met Wright, he had worked with President Boyer to move approximately thirty African Americans to Haiti from property he owned in Illinois. Flower was married with children, twice over in fact: he had abandoned his family in England and now had a technically illegal American wife and children. Wright had no regard for marriage or conventional morality, and people who knew them openly remarked that they were lovers during these months of sightseeing and scheming out in nature on horseback, far from society and its rules.[30]

They went to meet with Andrew Jackson at his cotton plantation in Nashville, which Lafayette had visited earlier that year. A hero of the War of 1812 against the British, as well as the Creek War and First Seminole War against Native American peoples, and a founding member of the ACS, Jackson was stewing at home, having recently been robbed of his electoral and popular victory in the presidential election. Historians have attached his name to the fifteen-year stretch of history opening around this time that saw rapid development in transportation, communications, and industry. As a rugged westerner, Jackson emblematized a shift in American political culture away from the aristocratic leaders of the founding generation to a more populist orientation, as property requirements for the vote gave way to "universal" white male suffrage.[31]

Jackson, who enslaved around a hundred people at this time, supported Wright's plan for a cooperative community where black workers would pay for their own colonization. He suggested some land about three hundred miles away near a muddy trading post called Memphis, on the bluffs where the Chickasaw people had lived for hundreds of years. Wright and Flower rode out to see the site, and Wright bought the first area of an estate that would eventually total around eighteen hundred acres. Adopting the Chickasaw name for the Wolf River, she called her commune Nashoba.

Jackson ran for president again in 1828 and won in a landslide. One of his signature accomplishments in the White House was the Indian Removal Act of 1830. When the government forced the Chickasaw out of the Nashoba area, tribal leaders managed to negotiate a financial settlement for the land, planning to purchase an area of their choice in Indian Territory, but both the money and the dream of a new homeland would prove elusive in the coming years. On July 4, 1837, they gathered in Memphis with whatever belongings they could carry to begin the grim westward march that has come to be called the Trail of Tears.[32]

CHAPTER 2

One Bold Lady-Man

Between Memphis and Nashoba was swampland. Getting to the commune required navigating a provisional bridge made of felled tree trunks. If it had rained, one stream would be too deep for a carriage to ford, so the only way to cross was on the back of a horse submerged belly-deep. There were stumps three feet high in the middle of the road and the woods were full of wolves and cougars. Wright's companions observed that she navigated this route like a seasoned backwoods trapper. When Nashoba was "finished," it consisted of about a hundred mostly cleared acres with inferior soil where residents would plant apple trees, potatoes, corn, and cotton. Wright hired workmen to throw up a few buildings made of roughly hewn wood; her bedroom had no ceiling and only loosely laid planks for a floor, thus providing little respite from the region's swarming mosquitoes. There was only rainwater to drink.

An English friend who visited the property at Wright's urging recalled that "one glance sufficed to convince me that every idea I had formed of the place was as far as possible from the truth." Wright had lured her there with descriptions of a beautiful new way of life illuminating a path to human freedom. But at the real Nashoba, "desolation was the only feeling—the only word that presented itself." Although Wright, too, was accustomed to the comfort and refinement of the European upper class, "her whole heart and soul" were occupied with a near "religious fanaticism" for the project's aims, and the material conditions there, even the lack of basic necessities, seemed to be beneath her notice.[1]

By this time, Wright had purchased a number of slaves. Whether it was a surreal and awful experience to pay for human chattel at auction in the process of pursuing universal freedom, or whether this too was something she took in stride, convinced of her project's eventual impact on the entire economy of slavery, her letters do not reflect. The initial group consisted of five men and three women: Willis, Jacob, Grandison, Redrick, Henry, Nelly, Peggy, and Kitty, plus three children. They were joined by a family from South Carolina consisting of a pregnant woman named Lukey and her six daughters, who ranged in age from three to twenty: Maria, Harriet, Elvira, Isabel, Viole, and Delilah. They had recently been inherited by a man who did not wish to keep them, and when he read Wright's "Proposal," he set off to sell them to her. She publicly promised to "feed them plentifully; treat them humanely; employ them industriously," and emancipate and colonize them in fifteen years, or sooner if they had paid back by their labor what Wright had spent

Sketch of Nashoba in 1827.
Houghton Library, Harvard University GEN (WKR 20.1.15)

on them plus the cost of their resettlement abroad. Flower thought it could be done in five.

Nashoba officially commenced in early March 1826. Wright and Flower sent regular progress reports to be published in Lundy's paper, assuring readers that "the slaves in this establishment" are not forced to work by fear of the lash or the presence of an overseer. "They are directed in the usual way that free laborers would be," Wright wrote in one of her dispatches, noting that the slaves were also given clothing, three good meals a day, and "advice" on their behavior or "bad habits." In June, they reported that they had "so far only resorted to 'coercion' once," in "a bad case of theft, malice, and obduracy, in one of the Nashville girls. After persuasion and gentle means without effect, we had recourse to solitary confinement and diet of bread and water. In 24 hours her obduracy gave way and we were enabled to release her. As this was the first punishment inflicted, it made a considerable impression."[2]

Wright and the other white leaders of Nashoba did not intend to profit from the labor of the enslaved people under their control, and they were risking their own lives in a pestilent swamp in their attempt to educate and free them. And yet they slept and ate in quarters separate from the slaves, and they always called them "the slaves." The slaves were not allowed to receive money, clothes, food, or anything else from visitors. They were not allowed to eat anywhere or at any time other than at the public meals they were provided. This was not an "interracial community," as it has sometimes been called. It was a southern plantation on which black people were held by white enslavers who forced them to work, monitored their behavior, and punished insubordination, all while Wright developed a philosophy of human freedom, not unlike Thomas Jefferson before her.[3]

At the end of 1826, Wright fell deathly ill for several months. She eventually decided to leave Nashoba for a time to recover her health and went on hiatus to Europe, leaving her sister, Camilla, and James Richardson, a bookkeeper she had hired in Memphis, in charge. Things got bad fast. Word reached Wright in France that Richardson had assumed her communications with Lundy's *Genius of Universal Emancipation,* publishing excerpts from the log he kept of Nashoba's activities. The content of the article disturbed her so much that her friends began to worry about her sanity. Her hair rapidly turned white, and she would at times tremble uncontrollably.[4]

Richardson wrote, "If any of the slaves neglect their duty, and thus retard the object of the plan, we will exclude such slaves from the benefit of the plan, and will treat them, according to the slave system, until it shall appear that their habits are changed for the better." Enslaved children were put into what was passing for school at Nashoba, with all communications with their parents prohibited except by permission. The most disturbing entries dealt with the sexual climate of the plantation: Isabel complained that Redrick had come to her bedroom uninvited, "endeavoring without her consent to take liberties with her person." Camilla and Richardson refused the woman's request for a lock on the bedroom door, insisting that she—and everyone living at Nashoba—would be perfectly safe once they had adopted the views on sex on which they had been lectured repeatedly, namely that it must be governed "by the Unrestrained choice of both parties." Finally, Richardson had informed the residents that "Mamselle Josephine [a free woman of color] and he began to live together, and he took this occasion of repeating to them our views on color, and on the sexual relation." It seemed that Nashoba's white leaders intended not only to practice their avant-garde sexual ideas but also to require them of women under their control.

Lundy's readers were shocked by this clear and unapologetic report that sex outside marriage and across the color line was not only endorsed but practiced at Nashoba. The commune was henceforth regarded as "one great brothel," in which "the wild and wicked system of Owen (the elder)" had "been realized, or partially surpassed." A letter from one reader declared that just as abolitionists detest the libidinous practices of slaveholders, "any thing that contains a semblance of the same character must be as pointedly condemned if tolerated by those who are laboring to destroy the system of African oppression." This reader incisively points out that these shocking excesses are the inevitable "consequences of slavery." To wit, these enslaved people, like all others, were completely subject to the whims and demands of their enslavers: "Here are a number of purchased slaves, drawn from their former residences, subject to the will of their new masters and mistresses, who impose on them, as a fundamental principle, that the ties of marriage are to be disregarded, that promiscuous intercourse between the sexes is to be substituted, that violence only is to be avoided. The slaves, whose moral and religious instruction is in the hands of their licentious owners, are thus taught, we may say compelled, to become accomplices in guilt."[5]

Richardson wrote back affirming his behavior and dismissing the religious tenor of his critics: "I am an Atheist, and on the diffusion of Atheism rests my only hope of the progress of Universal Emancipation." An even more shocking entry from the surviving log did not make it into the paper: "Two women slaves tied up and flogged by James Richardson in presence of Camilla and all the slaves. Two dozen and one dozen on the bare back with a cowskin." Nashoba reproduced the worst aspects of the slave system they were purportedly trying to eradicate: sexual assault, the separation of parents from children, even the lash.[6]

Upon receiving this dreadful news, Wright sailed for America. On the way, she wrote an explanatory account of Nashoba and its goals. One would think that she intended this essay to salvage her reputation and allay some of the public outrage over the sexual ideas that Richardson had revealed to be at the heart of the project. Far from backpedaling, though, she blazed on even further and made things much worse. Although the primary goal of Nashoba was evidently the ultimate abolition of slavery, her account emphasizes sexual liberation to an equal degree. In detailing the community's membership rules, she declares, "The marriage law existing without the pale of the institution, is of no force within that pale. No woman can forfeit her individual rights or independent existence, and no man assert over her any rights or power whatsoever." She goes further to denounce "the tyranny usurped by the matrimonial law" and "the unjust" public opinion of "unlegalized" attachments.

Piquing curiosity about her own experience with "unlegalized" relations, Wright's "Explanatory Notes" launches into a celebration of sex, charging that "false opinions and vicious institutions" like marriage "have perverted the best source of human happiness—the intercourse of the sexes, into the deepest human misery." She argues that children should be taught about sex rather than having mystery and condemnation thrown over their bodies, desires, and affections: "Let us correct our views of right and wrong . . . let us not teach that virtue consists in crucifying the affections and appetites." This affirmation of the goodness and power of sex would have been shocking coming from any author; that it came from an unmarried lady was a genuine scandal.

Why this sex-education tirade serves as the bulk of Wright's notes on Nashoba is unclear until she lays out her belief that whites and blacks should "gradually blend into one their blood and their hue." Although she planned to bow to American prejudices by taking the first of Nashoba's slaves out of the country, her long-term vision was not just a racially integrated society but a racially mixed population. Although she had learned from Jefferson and others that interracial sex, though common enough in practice, was a defining phobia of American society, Wright insisted that proper schooling would eradicate this prejudice by giving people of color equal standing with whites and putting the populations together from childhood. As a final nail in the coffin of her reputation, she joined Richardson in a candid avowal of atheism, affirming that "religion occupies no place in the institution." Wright wrote this at sea on December 4, 1827, sitting on a coil of rope and reading passages to a sailor who was mending his pants. History is silent on his reaction, but when the "Explanatory Notes" was published in the United States, Wright received death threats, and some started to say she had gone crazy. The essay's heady mix of radical ideas against marriage and religion, in favor of abolition, socialism, and interracial sex, combined with the author's anomalous personal status as an empowered and independent public woman, was more than people could take. Ultimately, it was not her antislavery position but her atheism and ideas about sex that put her permanently at odds with mainstream society, which had previously extended a kind of hesitant respect for her "patriotic philanthropy" because of her class position and powerful connections. Many of her fellow activists disavowed her as well. Lundy had always supported Wright but now declared that "her present plan for proceeding" was "too wide a departure from the rules sanctioned by wisdom and experience, and calculated to break up the foundation of social order, instead of improving the edifice at present erected."[7]

Soon after Wright's return to the property in January 1828, she abandoned the Nashoba project. She could not force enslaved people to prove her theories by turning a ramshackle backwater into paradise, so she hired an overseer to manage the estate and departed. Nashoba was hell at the end of a road paved with good intentions. Wright sincerely found slavery reprehensible, and she was the first white woman in the United States to try actively and publicly on this scale to end it. She did not understand the American obsession with "race" as a marker of inborn inequality, as it was beginning to be imagined. But her behavior makes it clear that she also did not recognize the full humanity of enslaved people. Her plan for emancipation was at once too accommodationist and too convoluted, succeeding only in providing Wright herself with the adventure of a grand crusade. In her first revolutionary battle, Wright emulated the national founders only too truly, replicating the same forms of hypocrisy that had marred their accomplishment from the beginning.

———

WRIGHT PUT NASHOBA behind her. She returned to New Harmony but found that it, too, was in a state of disintegration. Owen's addresses in Washington had brought national attention to his plans, and when he put out an invitation to join the New Harmony community, people poured in from nearly every state in the Union, and many from abroad: refined urban ladies, tradesmen and laborers, pioneers and hillbillies, eminent scientists, European educators, and families with children as well as unmarried men and women. Owen's son Robert Dale Owen, who managed much of the commune's daily operations in his mid-twenties, later described the group as a "heterogeneous collection of radicals, enthusiastic devotees to principle, honest latitudinarians and lazy theorists, with a sprinkling of unprincipled sharpers thrown in." There were a thousand people on the property, more than one hundred of them children, and they soon overwhelmed the community's resources.[8]

New Harmony's most successful venture was its schools; the community housed the country's first preschool and kindergarten, as well as a trade school and an upper school that may have been the best in the country at the time. All were coed, focused on practical knowledge, and taught by leading innovators in a range of scientific and educational fields. Of course, some might find the students' lives at these boarding facilities rather spartan. They slept in bunks suspended by cords from the ceiling, making a game of swinging themselves into midair collisions. They milked the cows in the morning, and the milk was boiled with mush in big kettles for their breakfast. For lunch they had soup, then milk and mush again for dinner. As one student recalled, "I thought if I ever got out, I would kill myself eating sugar and cake." She reported seeing her parents only twice in their two years at New Harmony.[9]

Among the adult members, splinter groups had broken off almost immediately and formed other Owenite communities on the same land. One thing these communities seemed to share was a love of music. They were all "passionately fond of dancing" and had a concert every week as well as a ball, featuring their own musicians under a bandleader named Josiah Warren. At the cotillions, dancers drew numbers for their partners to prevent class-based "partialities."

But these partialities persisted nevertheless. Although many community members adopted the distinctive shared attire of New Harmony, a plain and androgynous costume of pantaloons with jackets that made them all look like children, some upper-class residents still dressed up in finery for the evening entertainments and only associated with one another. The entrenched class differences posed problems for those on both sides of the social spectrum. One aristocratic visitor found that "the much vaunted equality" of the community resulted in strange juxtapositions, such as when the eminent Owen or another high theorist was delivering a formal lecture with some raggedy hayseed stretched out on the stage beside him. Those truly committed to economic equality were disappointed that Owen never fully dispensed with private property as he promised. Unless they surrendered all their assets to the community, one such member reasoned, the wealthy members were withholding vital resources and risking nothing by joining what was supposed to be a socialist venture. He said there was no intimacy between these supposed brothers and sisters, no community feeling, that they were all strangers.

Those who pushed Owen to declare full community of property were ultimately asked to leave New Harmony, but they were invited to form another community on Owen's land and under his rules. Many demurred, declaring that they would not be treated like "man-machines" by the paternalistic Owen. That approach might have worked in the Scottish mill where he had tightly monitored his workers' behavior in an attempt to mold their characters, but it was proving ineffective on the American scene. Declaring a new start, community leaders flushed out their most vocal opponents and also shot all the dogs that constantly rambled in from the country, because they were not even producing enough food to sustain the human residents.

But the "perfect community" they desired never materialized. It seemed that everyone complained of everyone else's laziness. Meanwhile, members invested untold hours in theorizing different ways to organize the society and divvy up the labor even as the grounds lay fallow. All the bricks they had fired to construct the palatial quadrangle of Owen's model remained piled in a field. The fences broke and were not repaired, so the livestock wandered about and feasted on the beautiful gardens laid out by the Rappites. Despite their official opposition to the tyranny of marriage, the domestic drudgery was all foisted on the women, who were expected to be "community wives" in the sense that they did all the cleaning and sewing not just for their own husbands but for hundreds of others. The Owenites planned to build new houses to reflect their particular system, with no rooms for children and no kitchens, because all the rearing and cooking would be done communally. But when one visitor went to see the progress they had made at the construction site, there was only one worker there and he was fast asleep. Nearly everyone was gone by the spring of 1828.[10]

To the stragglers who remained, Wright delivered a Fourth of July speech two years after Owen's Declaration of Mental Independence and from the same stage. Though a few women had braved controversy to preach in public before this time, including Puritan dissenter Ann Hutchinson, Shaker leader Mother Anne Lee, and Jarena Lee of Philadelphia's AME Bethel Church, this was likely the first public political address by a woman in American history. She warned her audience against a narrow patriotism that would worship the founders instead of their principles, that would inculcate love of the country above love of justice for all humanity. Her speech focused in particular on one aspect of American government that made it superior, in her view, to any other system ever devised: "the principle of *change*." In the amendment system, she argued, the Constitution enshrined a built-in expectation that the nation must advance and improve, so that as the public mind became more enlightened, so too would the government. The revolution and the nation's founding were meant to be an ongoing process, shaped by each successive generation, an idea that Jefferson had endorsed before her.[11]

To catalyze that process, Wright embraced a new career as a lecturer. Her speeches characteristically returned to the idea that the founding fathers had initiated a new era in human history but that Americans must continuously ask themselves what they had done to make good on their "daring experiment." For a year and a half, she traveled all over the country and spoke everywhere: Boston, St. Louis, New Orleans, Cincinnati, Syracuse, and so on. She spoke in grand theaters packed with thousands and sordid, smoky little rooms to a few loiterers. In some cities, she was booed and hissed; windows were broken, gas lines cut, fires started. In others, she was cheered and applauded, carried off the stage triumphantly on the shoulders of adoring fans. Government, business, and church officials tried to close venues, gag the press, and do anything they could think of to stop her from appearing in their city and spreading her insidious influence.

It is difficult for us to imagine how shocking it was in the 1820s to see someone in a dress up on a stage, speaking to a crowd of both men and women. It simply had never been done before. And this woman was not some genteel Christian matron but a notorious spinster who believed in the equality of the sexes, denounced religion, and championed the amalgamation of the races and the end of marriage. Fanny Wright became a household name during this period in part because she was an irresistible spectacle and provocation for the press. They reported, "She comes among us in the character of a bold blasphemer, and a voluptuous preacher of licentiousness." If her "pestilent doctrines" were adopted, "she would break down all the barriers to virtue, and reduce the world to one grand theatre of vice and sensuality in its most loathsome form." They referred to her as "a super-infamous advocate of promiscuous intercourse" and "one bold lady-man."[12]

Throughout Wright's career, a central subject of attack for her critics was her obvious gender-bending: she was taller than the average American man, wore her hair short, and spent all of her time doing things that literally only men did. One reporter called her "a great awkward *bungle* of womanhood, somewhere about six feet in longitude, with a face like a Fury, and her hair cropped like a convict." Catharine Beecher, daughter of the eminent minister Lyman Beecher and foremost representative of the cult of true womanhood, looked on Wright with "disgust and abhorrence." "There she stands," Beecher imagined, "with brazen front and brawny arms . . . with her great masculine person, her loud voice, her untasteful attire, going about unprotected, and feeling no need of protection, mingling with men in stormy debate." She declared, "I cannot conceive anything in the shape of a woman, more intolerably offensive and disgusting." Wright's appearance and behavior sinned against the expectations for femininity, but even more frightening was the gender revolution she seemed to embody, as well as advocate, on the lecture platform.[13]

In 1829, Wright moved to New York City with a group of fellow travelers, including her friend Robert Dale Owen. She rented a historic mansion with generous grounds on the East River at Seventy-fifth Street, envisioning it as a home where like-minded men and women could live and work communally, a new harmony away from New Harmony. For $7,000, Wright also purchased the building that had been the Ebenezer Baptist Church on Broome Street and rechristened it the Hall of Science. When she gave the hall's opening address in April 1829, it was clear that her advocacy of "scientific subjects" was another way of talking about atheism. One newspaper called it the "Beelzebub Institute" and warned that the "debauchery" expounded there by "this atrocious woman" threatens New Yorkers with divine retribution. Wright had sharply criticized religion her entire career, but it became a primary focus in this period as she hosted and delivered lectures for workingmen on rational thought and socialism. At the Hall of Science, Wright and Robert Dale Owen displayed the portraits of infidels like Thomas Paine and sold the newspaper they edited, *The Free Enquirer,* a leading organ for free thought, Free Love, women's rights, birth control, workers' rights, and socialism, an early landmark in the history of radical magazines.[14]

The Hall of Science and office of *The Free Enquirer* on Broome Street, New York.
From The Free Enquirer, *October 31, 1829*

From Wright's perspective, religious belief was just as irrational as racial prejudice and would need to be rooted out if Americans were ever going to realize the radical potential of their own founding ideals. Having sidelined slavery as a target of her critique, she believed that what the whole country needed was education aimed at destroying these "superstitions." Her solution was a system of "national, rational, republican" public schools that would inculcate both social equality and scientific thought from earliest childhood.

After the revolution, Jefferson had recognized the necessity of a national education system but did not manage to bring it about. In Wright's time, schooling was wildly uneven between the states. In Massachusetts, the Boston Latin School had been operating since 1635, and Boston English, the nation's first public high school, opened in 1821. But Mississippi did not create a school system until 1868, and the education of children was not legally mandated there until 1918. In proposing a system of free and universal schooling, Wright was a decade ahead of Horace Mann, who would become the hero of American public education; such a system, they believed, was the only way to produce republican citizens and minimize class stratification.

Of course, the schools Wright had in mind were quite different from the ones Mann would ultimately help create. While education was crucial to Wright's goal of a rational citizenry, the schools she advocated for would perform an equally important social function by removing children completely from the system of private families by which socioeconomic classes were created and reproduced. Under Wright's plan, parents "could visit the children at suitable hours, but, in no case, interfere with or interrupt the rules of the institution." She and Owen felt that even a free and equal education would do nothing to eliminate social distinctions if, at the end of the school day, some students returned home to luxurious wealth and some to poverty. They specified that all children should receive the same simple food and wear the same simple clothing and be taught the same fields of study so that "nothing savoring of inequality, nothing reminding them of the pride of riches, or the contempt of poverty, should be suffered to enter these republican safeguards of a young nation of equals."[15]

An associate of Wright and Owen from this time later explained how this plan to root out class inequality would also, they hoped, make marriage obsolete. By his account, Wright and Owen wanted public schools to mold rational children but, just as important, to "liberate the parents." With children no longer dependent on them for support and stability, men and women "would be free to co-habit together, according to their mutual likings, and for as long a time as they found it mutually agreeable, and no longer." Just as educating black and white children together and equally would re-move the stigma from interracial sex, she believed, a proper school system would produce a more secular America, one in which class distinctions would soon be eroded—and, as a bonus, couples would not be obliged to stay together for the sake of their children.[16]

Wright and Owen began to pursue this agenda through the labor movement emerging in the urban Northeast at this time. As indus-trial capitalism expanded with little regulation, the American work-ers who generated enormous wealth for factory owners toiled eighty hours each week in dangerous conditions, often living in substandard housing on the edge of poverty. In the 1820s, strikes became increasingly common and labor associations, newspapers, and parties appeared in Philadelphia, New York, and New England to protest "an unequal and very excessive accumulation of wealth and power into the hands of a few," as the Mechanics' Union of Trade Associations put it. Many of these groups aimed first and foremost to secure or protect a ten-hour workday, but they had a broad agenda of ways to improve the lives of the working class. In 1829, the New York Workingmen's Party appeared to be a promis-ing up-and-coming force in politics, and Owen in particular was eager to get involved, eventually becoming the group's secretary.[17]

Among the items on the workingmen's agenda was a free school system for their children, paid for by taxes, so the plan that Owen championed at their meetings likely appealed to them, even if it went much further than what they had imagined. While Owen ad-vocated state guardianship and education for all American children

Robert Dale Owen, ca. 1847.
*National Portrait Gallery, Smithsonian
Institution; gift of Andrew Oliver*

as the central plank of the party's platform, the group's other emergent leader, Thomas Skidmore, demanded the equal distribution of all property and the abolition of inheritance. Factionalism and infighting bitterly divided the group, and in the end the organization rejected both Skidmore and Owen as too radical. Rightly perceiving that the unstated goal of Owen's education plan was to undermine the family unit, they resolved to "leave to the father and the affectionate mother the enjoyment of the society of their offspring." Dispensing with the private family, and monogamy in the bargain, continued to be a bridge too far for most Americans.[18]

Although Wright was not involved with the "Workies" to the extent that Owen was, she was so infamous that any whiff of her influence was enough to bring on attacks from the press. In the run-up to the fall of 1830, members of the Workingmen's Party were accused of being "in strict accordance with the rule of *Wright,*" and the scandal of Nashoba was rehashed. The papers suggested that Wright was driven by unnatural passions, "a sorceress" who attempted to overturn society as revenge for the sexual inattention of men, and her name was regularly invoked to discredit the party, an early instance of the pattern that would characterize the press's treatment of activists for the rest of the century. The election dealt a clear defeat to the Workingmen's Party, but Wright was not there to see it.[19]

DURING ALL OF her adventures in 1828 and 1829—touring American cities and scandalizing audiences, writing lectures on intellectual and social freedom, fighting against officials who challenged her right to speak, founding the Hall of Science and addressing crowds of workingmen and freethinkers there—Wright still enslaved around thirty people who remained in bondage at her Nashoba estate. She finally decided to do something about it, planning a lecture route that would bring her to New Orleans, where she would sail with them to Haiti and free them at long last. As many as thirteen thousand African Americans had moved there in 1824 and 1825 during the height of Granville and Boyer's publicity push for the Haitian emigration movement, bolstered by supporters like James Forten. By this time, however, many had returned to the United States, and African American backing for Haitian emigration had waned as settlers' hopes for full citizenship rights and economic opportunity were disappointed. But the people enslaved at Nashoba did not have the opportunity to weigh their options. Wright chose for them.[20]

She brought along an associate from New Harmony, William S. Phiquepal d'Arusmont, to accompany her and help with business matters. Phiquepal had experience in the Caribbean, but he was neither well liked nor respected. Acquaintances regarded him at best as undistinguished and at worst as a fraud or a "madman." They described him as stupid and vain, harsh and irritable. Robert Dale Owen later reflected that Phiquepal was "gifted with a certain enthusiasm which had its attraction" but proved to be "from the first, an unwise, hasty, fanciful counselor" to Wright. "His influence was of injurious effect, alike on her character and on her happiness." In January 1830, Wright had her slaves transported from Nashoba down the Mississippi to New Orleans and chartered a brig. They departed on a monthlong sea voyage for what she thought would be a quick trip.[21]

Wright and her party were welcomed profusely by Boyer, his government, and the Haitian people. He defrayed her expenses and settled Wright's former slaves on his own land, promising that he would soon set them up on their own farms. Wright and Phiquepal ended up staying longer than she had expected, enjoying dinners and garden parties with the mixed-race Haitian aristocracy, exploring Port-au-Prince, and no doubt savoring this respite in a lush tropical setting after years of hard living at a breakneck pace, riding horseback over mountain ranges to frontier outposts, and battling the press and angry crowds in dirty city streets.

At the end of March, Wright sailed for Philadelphia. She felt nauseated and constantly fatigued during the long voyage, but she was not seasick. She was pregnant. It turns out that she and Phiquepal had been more than just colleagues. She had thought of her trip to Haiti as a momentary pause to settle some unfinished business, from which she would quickly return to her lecture career, her plan for American public schools, fomenting a movement at the Hall of Science—and now we can only speculate what she might have tackled next. Instead, the trip effectively ruined her life. For years, she had openly embraced sexual freedom—and likely practiced it herself with George Flower, the Marquis de Lafayette, maybe others—and managed to dodge the consequences. But finally this historically unique woman would be destroyed by the same kinds of private struggles that loomed over all women of her time.

Returning to New York that spring, Wright hid her pregnancy and continued to lecture to packed houses and fend off attacks from the press, whose venom was renewed by her connection to the Workingmen's Party. One might think she could have confided in Robert Dale Owen, who was well aware of the social and political ramifications of unwanted pregnancies. Indeed, apparently by coincidence, later that year he published the first work in the United States to advocate and explain birth control methods, writing, "If we cannot prevent every misery which man's selfishness and the world's cruelty entail on a sex which it ought to be our pride and honour to cherish and defend, let us prevent as many as we can."[22]

But Wright kept her secret, announcing obliquely that she planned to leave the United States for a time to attend to some "private interests." Her parting address in June at the Bowery Theatre had three thousand people in the audience, half of them reportedly "respectable females." Instead of notes, she unrolled a copy of the Declaration of Independence on the table in front of her, as she had done many times on her lecture tour, and said, "This is my text book—this is my Bible—my holy Bible—the holy Bible of American Independence, and must soon be the holy Bible of the whole earth." On July 1, 1830, she sailed for France, not only disappearing mysteriously from her public work, but cutting contact even with close friends.[23]

From this point on, information on Wright's life becomes sparse, by her design. The American press would have gleefully written Wright into the cautionary narrative of the fallen woman that the country's first novels had primed their audience to love. It would have been delicious, scandalous proof that they had been correct in accusing her of sexual misconduct, of departing from the most cherished norms of social life all these years. It would have been her fitting comeuppance and a reason for them to dismiss everything she ever said. She did not give them this satisfaction. She gave birth to a daughter she named Silva at the end of the year, or possibly in the first days of 1831. She told no one. She soon made an appearance at a party her old companion Lafayette hosted in Paris but was apparently shunned. People remarked on the strange and sudden alteration in her looks and personality, which they were at a loss to explain. The difficulty of her secret pregnancy and motherhood was quickly followed by another hard blow: her sister, Camilla, her only true witness and companion since their lonely childhood, died in early February. All this tragedy wiped her out. In the next five years, Wright became increasingly remote and alienated all of her remaining friends.

She married Phiquepal in July 1831, something she said she would never do. At nearly thirty-six, she was so long past the age when it was appropriate for a woman to remain unmarried that she and everyone else must have regarded the question as settled. She had lamented the legal oppression of "the unhappy female who swears away, at one and the same moment, her person and her property, and, as it but too often is, her peace, her honor, and her life."

One of two quotations from her work later engraved on her tombstone was her declaration that she had "wedded" the cause of human freedom. Having developed a detailed feminist critique of the institution of marriage, she knew well how immolated her identity must now be, her legal personhood effectively subsumed under her husband.

Wright tried her best to disappear completely. She did not answer letters and told no one where she lived or how. One old friend who managed to track her down later regretted it. She found Wright in her nightgown, cooped up in a meager room in Paris with a bed and a few chairs in it, with a naked, unclean one-year-old child, the scene overpowered by the smell of food cooking on a stove in the same room. She told friends that she wished that Fanny had drowned herself rather than ending up this way. Wright's patrician upbringing had not prepared her to perform domestic chores or care for children. She went nowhere and saw no one, completely sequestered in this oppressive private world—exactly the kind of existence she wanted to eradicate for all women and the furthest thing imaginable from the rigorous public life and travels that she had expected to continue for the rest of her life. She would return to the United States five years later, appearing to everyone who knew her to be inexplicably changed, and much for the worse.[24]

CHAPTER 3

O America, Your Destruction
Is at Hand!

In 1829, as Fanny Wright unwittingly hurtled toward personal disaster, she reached the pinnacle of her national notoriety, touring the country from her base in New York City to expound on a range of radical issues. But strangely, her capacious list of activist commitments omitted abolition and black civil rights, the causes that had so recently shaken her to the core. She claimed that four years of observation, reflection, and experience "have convinced me that American negro slavery is but one form of the same evils which pervade the whole frame of American society," and thus could not be combated in isolation. In her lectures, she did not address the topic at all, but focused instead on the neglect of women's minds and their subsequent dependence on men, the quackery and undue influence of religion, and the ineptness and corruption of the press. She also took aim at this last item directly as a co-owner of and chief contributor to *The Free Enquirer*. But the newspaper did not publish articles on slavery or agitate for the rights of free people of color; moreover, it took no apparent notice of *Freedom's Journal,* the nation's first black-owned and black-operated newspaper, though its office was mere blocks away.[1]

Freedom's Journal had launched in 1827 in New York City to counter the racist treatment of African Americans in mainstream papers, to rail against the ACS, and to provide a venue for communication within and between black communities. Its chief editor, Samuel Cornish, had secured funding and support from James

Forten, his brother's employer, and teamed up with John Russ-wurm, the first black graduate of Bowdoin College, as junior editor. Having so recently spent a fortune and destroyed her reputation advocating abolition and interracial sex, Wright apparently had no relationship whatsoever with the black press and activist community flowering in the same city.

But they seemed to keep an eye on her. Back when Nashoba was still operating, *Freedom's Journal* reprinted an article from a mainstream paper about her "strange project of philanthropy," noting, "This delicate female proposes intermarriages between the whites and blacks, and argues that such an amalgamation will in a little while be all efficient in removing the distinction between the colors." *Freedom's Journal* attached an editorial comment to this reprint, insisting that there was nothing particularly absurd or offensive about her plan "to purchase slaves and to them render freedom possible by their own industry." Only time would tell, Cornish wrote, if the undertakings of "this singular lady" will ultimately be for good or evil, but her plan should be lauded if it makes one person free. He also criticized the article's "personal reflections" on Wright's private life, defending any "unmarried lady [who] has the boldness to exchange a life of blushing and smiling behind her fan for one which contemplates solid good, the giving of Liberty to her fellow creatures."[2]

Despite this admirable defense of unorthodox women, *Freedom's Journal* soon soured on Wright because of her atheism. At the end of 1828, the paper noted that at the nearby Hall of Science she was selling Paine's notorious free-thought opus *"Age of Reason,* and another book equally vile. This woman ought to get into pantaloons immediately, she is a disgrace to the fairer part of creation." The following month, it reprinted another article, this time with no comment, that declared, "Miss Wright pretends to be a philanthropist. Now let that woman answer how she dares assume the name, while endeavoring to undermine the happiness of society" by "tearing up root and branches the dearest tendrils of the heart," a reference to her opposition to legal marriage or her belief that all children should be taken into state custody as toddlers, or both.[3]

These scant mentions aside, *Freedom's Journal* was pledged to spreading the message of black activist communities, rather than worrying about white well-wishers. As its opening editorial proclaimed, "We wish to plead our own cause. Too long have others spoken for us." To this end, the editors published articles by and of interest to free African Americans, from national news and social commentary to opinion pieces on manners and frequent coverage of the American Colonization Society. Black leaders like Forten and Allen in Philadelphia, Nathaniel Paul in Albany, John Vashon in Pittsburgh, and David Walker, the paper's agent in Boston, contributed content.[4]

The paper's core political commitments were the abolition of slavery and opposition to black colonization. Condemning the ACS, Cornish insisted that free people of color were "as truly Americans, as the President of the United States and as much entitled to the protection, rights, and privileges of the country as he." Affirming his devotion to the nation of his birth, "with all her imperfections," he trusted that a time of true equality, however distant, would come. Russwurm, who soon took over as the paper's editor, heartily agreed. That is, until some point in early 1829, when he decided to emigrate himself. In March of that year, he announced in a bombshell editorial that he had come to believe "it far preferable, for the man of color, aspiring after wealth and respectability, to emigrate to Liberia, where every incentive to virtuous action, is before him continually, than to remain here, where the mere name of colour, blocks up every avenue." He had previously mocked the ACS for luring emigrants with descriptions of Liberia as a land flowing with milk and honey. But now he cast the colony as a black Eden, where at long last a man of color could "walk forth in all the majesty of his creation—a new born creature—a Free Man!" *Freedom's Journal* folded; Cornish founded a new paper, *The Rights of All,* again with financial backing from James Forten, but it lasted less than a year.[5]

As we'll see, colonization remained a flash-point issue for black activists for decades, even after emancipation. They continued to debate whether it was worth fighting the overwhelming racism of

Freedom's Journal, March 16, 1827.

the United States in the hope of transforming it into an integrated society, or whether black Americans should invest their allegiance and energy in autonomous projects—black social movements, institutions, and even new nations—rather than in the improbable dream of a free and equal America.

BY THE END of that year, a voice arose from this increasingly networked free black community in the North that put the entire nation on notice. In September 1829, David Walker, member of the Massachusetts General Colored Association and the Boston agent of *Freedom's Journal,* began distributing a pamphlet affirming a bold proposition: "America is more our country, than it is the whites." Denouncing colonization as a racist trick, Walker's *Appeal to the Colored Citizens of the World* asked, "Will they drive us from our property and homes, which we have earned with our *blood*?" A used-clothing dealer with a shop near the Boston wharves, Walker smuggled his *Appeal* on board ships with help from both black and white sailors, sometimes sewing it into their clothes. He also sent copies through the mail and otherwise disseminated it by any means possible.

By December, the pamphlet had reached Savannah, Georgia, and within weeks copies could be found in Virginia and across the Carolinas. As Fanny Wright hustled her slaves aboard a New Orleans steamer in January 1830, it had already traveled a thousand miles to reach even that faraway port. The State of Louisiana soon made the distribution of the pamphlet a capital crime. Southerners put a price on the author's head, aiming to have him killed or, even better, brought to a slave state alive. Walker's message was read aloud at black churches and passed through free communities to the enslaved, inspiring legislation, outraged backlash, and, most important, hope.[6]

Walker had previously called for a national movement that would "unite the colored population"; *Freedom's Journal* published an address to the Massachusetts General Colored Association in which he urged listeners to "protect, aid, and assist each other to the utmost of our power," rather than "stand[ing] as neutral spectators" and trusting white allies to improve their condition. The *Appeal* contained a similar call for black pride and unity, and also offered a key departure from earlier antislavery arguments with its insistence on immediate emancipation by any means necessary, up to and including deadly force. Walker clearly aimed to incite and empower the enslaved to be the agents of that necessary violence, noting that a single armed black man could dispatch a crowd of whites and encouraging his readers to shoot to kill: "If you commence, make sure work—do not trifle, for they will not trifle with you." Even the certainty that bloody retribution would follow such an attack should not deter enslaved people from taking up arms.

"Had you not rather be killed," he asked, "than to be a slave to a tyrant, who takes the life of your mother, wife, and dear little children?"

Walker minced no words in describing white people as the enemy, "an unjust, jealous, unmerciful, avaricious and blood-thirsty set of beings, always seeking after power and authority." The pamphlet brims with threats of the vengeance that would be visited upon them by both divine justice and the armed revolt of the people they kept in chains. Walker forecast not a utopian future of integration but rather the end of America in violent, apocalyptic retribution, "the final ruin of this happy republic, or land of *liberty*!!!!" Ominously, he declared, "Your DESTRUCTION *is at hand*." Like so many American radicals, Walker looked to Thomas Jefferson and the founding generation as a major source of ammunition for his takedown of the country they created. Long quotations from the Declaration of Independence at the end of the pamphlet indict the hypocrisy of a slaveholding republic, asking whites, "Do you hear your own language?" He referred to the War for Independence as the "first revolution in this country," plainly suggesting throughout the text that there would soon be another, placing his pamphlet in the tradition of social protest that saw itself as the sequel to an inadequate national founding.

Walker died of a respiratory illness in the summer of 1830, but his pamphlet had lit a torch. In Boston, throughout the North, and beyond, an emerging network of black and white activists stood ready to carry it forward.

———

INDEED, WALKER'S HEIR APPARENT had made his debut in Boston on July 4, 1829. The town buzzed that summer with the news of Fanny Wright's impending visit on her lecture tour. A group of business owners tried to bar her from all speaking venues and circulated a petition requesting a coverage blackout from the city's newspapers, asking that they not publicize or report on her lecture or even mention her name. Ministers denounced her from the pulpit, convinced that she was converting even "respectable females" to her subversive agenda. Nevertheless, she lectured to a packed house at the end of the month, still at the height of her powers, "the subject of conversation in almost every circle, in almost every house in the city of Boston."[7]

While Wright's impact on oppressive American institutions remains difficult to figure, a nervous young speaker mounted a nearby stage that month and launched one of the most consequential activist careers in American history. This newcomer received no fanfare and little notice; the media did not need to be asked to ignore him. William Lloyd Garrison was a carefully dressed but ordinary-looking young man, baby-faced but already balding, even in his twenties, wearing spectacles with little round frames. He had grown up poor in a coastal town north of Boston, the son of a ship's captain who abandoned his family, and had worked as a printer's apprentice from the age of thirteen. With his mild and humble demeanor, he was unlikely to be picked from a lineup as the revolutionary and "pestiferous fanatic" that everyone would soon know him to be, the despised extremist with a price on his head who transformed the nation's political landscape and was credited by Abraham Lincoln himself with the ultimate emancipation of American slaves.[8]

Garrison's initial appearance in the pulpit at Park Street Church did not bode well for a brilliant career as a leader or public speaker. "My very knees knock together at the thought of speaking before so large a concourse," he wrote to a friend in the days before the address. The church was one of Boston's most prominent, located at the head of the Boston Common, adjacent to the Granary Burying Ground, where Revolutionary heroes lie, including Paul Revere, three signers of the Declaration of Independence, and Crispus Attucks, a black man killed in the Boston Massacre and the first American casualty of the War for Independence. It would have been an intimidating venue even for a seasoned speaker, and indeed, when Garrison started delivering the words he had painstakingly prepared, his faltering voice could hardly be heard. But as he continued, his voice gained strength, fired by his conviction in the words he spoke.[9]

William Lloyd Garrison
portrait by Robert Douglass Jr.
*Portrait collection of the Historical
Society of Pennsylvania*

Unlike Fanny Wright's Fourth of July jeremiads, which called audiences back to the principles of the revolution, Garrison warned his generation to reject the example of the founders, finding much of their legacy objectionable and their grievances against England "trifling." Rather than rallying the audience around the American flag and the memories of the dead Revolutionary heroes surrounding them, Garrison declared, "I am ashamed of my country." With menacing prescience, he warned that the country was in imminent danger from "an earthquake rumbling under our feet—a mine accumulating materials for a national catastrophe." Following the example of African American activists in Albany and elsewhere, he held that the Independence Day holiday that occasioned his talk should be one of "fasting and prayer, not of boisterous merriment and idle pageantry—a day of great lamentation, not of congratulatory joy."[10]

Despite this anti-Americanism, he energetically defended the citizenship rights of one group that had no legal claim to that status: the more than two million people then held in slavery. "This is their country by birth, not by adoption," he said. "Their children possess the same inherent and unalienable rights as ours." Yet he warned that white America would not acknowledge the rights and the humanity of enslaved African Americans without a vicious fight: "If any man believes that slavery can be abolished without a struggle with the worst passions of human nature, quietly, harmoniously, he cherishes a delusion. It can never be done, unless the age of miracles return. No; we must expect a collision, full of sharp asperities and bitterness." That collision soon came.[11]

Garrison became an able enough speaker, but his strength was not as a charismatic iconoclast like Fanny Wright but rather as a writer and an untiring organizer who harnessed the energies of those excluded from official politics. Distressed and outraged by the fact that millions of people suffered in captivity, he centered his life on the biblical directive to "remember those in bondage as bound with them." Bringing together African American activists who demanded the immediate emancipation of enslaved people and refused all plans to expatriate them from the United States along with a new wave of white allies, a radical abolitionist movement coalesced around Garrison. It would become the first social movement in the country's history to mobilize Americans across divisions of race, class, and gender to oppose slavery and tackle an expanding range of social issues along the way. While Fanny Wright had, in her own unorthodox way, made certain concessions to make white people more comfortable with her abolition plan (its gradualism, compensation for enslavers, and ultimate goal of colonization), the new wave of antislavery agitation would make no such accommodation. When the abolition of slavery seemed a dangerous and utopian dream to the vast majority of Americans, the Garrisonians did not attempt to make it safer or more practical but stretched instead toward its most disruptive and far-reaching implications.

THIS MOVEMENT, OF course, did not materialize on the spot. In the summer of 1830, while the black community in Philadelphia organized the first National Convention of Free Persons of Colour and the secretly pregnant Fanny Wright left the United States, William Lloyd Garrison sat in a Baltimore jail cell. After his address at the Park Street Church in Boston, Garrison had moved to Baltimore to work for Benjamin Lundy's *Genius of Universal Emancipation*. As co-editor of Lundy's newspaper, he had written an article accusing a Massachusetts shipper of involvement in the (fully legal) domestic slave trade. He was sued for libel and also brought up on criminal charges by the State of Maryland. Found guilty, he refused to pay the fine and was sentenced to six months' imprisonment. He was bailed out after seven weeks by a fellow abolitionist.

By that time, Garrison had traveled even further down the path to radicalization. As Lundy mentored Garrison as a writer, two black activists with whom they lived, William Watkins and Jacob Greener, schooled him on black civil rights, leading him to firmly reject all plans to expatriate African Americans and to demand the immediate, not gradual, end of slavery. His stint in jail gave him a personal taste of the injustices perpetrated in the name of the law, strengthening his resolve to help those captives who would be confined for a lifetime. He wrote from his cell, "It is my shame that I have done so little for the people of color; yea, before God, I feel humbled that my feelings are so cold, and my language so weak. A few white victims must be sacrificed to open the eyes of this nation, and to show the tyranny of the laws."[12]

Garrison returned to Boston in the fall of 1830 ready to be "persecuted, imprisoned and bound" for advocating black rights and willing to die as one of the white martyrs he believed would be necessary to awake mainstream America to the cause of black suffering. When he set out to deliver an address on the subject, the only venue he could find was in a building used by a group of "infidels" led by the freethinker Abner Kneeland, an associate of Fanny Wright's. Garrison was not a religious skeptic like Kneeland and argued against slavery on scriptural grounds. But by the end of the decade, his evolving vision of Christian anarchism wholly aligned him in the public mind with the Owenite atheists who appeared on the same stage that year. He would soon be called an "infidel" too often to track.

Garrison opened his speech with a scorching denunciation of the ACS and apologized for having ignorantly supported it in the past. His fiery new commitment was palpable in this talk. One

Brahmin minister in the audience was moved as he had never been by any other speech. Laying eyes on Garrison for the first time, he felt convinced, as he later recorded, that "he is a prophet; he will shake our nation to its center." Moved to help Garrison reach a larger audience, he and other admirers secured a spot for him at the Boston Athenaeum, where he repeated the address. To the handful of African Americans in the audience, all of whom had known the recently deceased David Walker, his message would have sounded familiar and yet utterly new coming from a white man.[13]

Walker's colleagues in the black Bostonian community—most notably a committee headed by two women, Elizabeth Riley and Bathsheba Fowler—started raising money for the newspaper Garrison wanted to start. Like Walker, Garrison understood print to be the most powerful weapon he could wield for liberation. Having no personal wealth himself, Garrison could not even cover the ream of paper he needed to print the first issue until a check arrived from James Forten: an advance on twenty-seven subscriptions he had secured in Philadelphia. John Vashon of Pittsburgh was also an important financial backer in these early years and became the paper's agent in that city. Nathaniel Paul of Albany would soon join with many other African Americans who helped pay Garrison's passage to England, securing connections with abolitionists there to advance an international movement.[14]

Thus, especially in its beginnings, Garrisonian abolitionism was powered by its black constituency, and the editor made his paper a megaphone for communicating their concerns and publicizing their work. He covered, for example, their protest of racial segregation in the Park Street Church, where he got his start, and the work of Maria Stewart, a member of Boston's black activist community and the first American-born woman to deliver public lectures. Forten wrote frequently for *The Liberator,* as did his children after him, along with numerous other black contributors. Of the 500 subscribers receiving *The Liberator* in its first year, 450 were African Americans. Three years later, the paper had 2,300 subscribers, and about a quarter were white. Unlike Fanny Wright, Garrison valued his personal and professional relationships with African Americans across the country, and this was the core of his movement's strength. Black activists had been calling for immediate abolition and denouncing the ACS as racist for years. Garrison gained their trust and respect by collaborating in the projects already under way in their movement, using his trade as a printer to publicize their message to both white and black audiences.[15]

The first issue of *The Liberator* appeared on January 1, 1831. In it, Garrison publicly recanted his previous belief that slavery would have to be ended gradually, establishing a firm commitment to an immediatist movement that would no longer tolerate calls for patience or compromise: "I do not wish to think, or to speak, or write, with moderation. No! no! Tell a man whose house is on fire to give a moderate alarm; tell him to moderately rescue his wife from the hands of the ravisher; tell the mother to gradually extricate her babe from the fire into which it has fallen;—but urge me not to use moderation in a cause like the present. I am in earnest— I will not equivocate—I will not excuse—I will not retreat a single inch—AND I WILL BE HEARD." Garrison was twenty-five years old. He would publish *The Liberator* every week without fail for thirty-five years, until slavery was abolished by constitutional amendment in 1865.

From the beginning, the paper furiously attacked not only the institution of slavery but also the oppression of the working class and Native Americans, indicating that Garrison's commitment was always to "human rights" broadly defined. He was willing, too, to address subjects other activists shied away from. The topic of interracial marriage, always the third rail of American civil rights discourse, appeared with regularity in *The Liberator*'s first year. Reprinting David Walker's remark "I would not give a pinch of snuff to be married to any white person I ever saw in all the days of my life," Garrison agreed with his view that laws prohibiting marriages between whites and blacks were meant to maintain for blacks the legal status of nonhuman animals. In May, Garrison penned two columns demanding that Massachusetts lift its ban on marriage across the color line: "Intermarriage is neither unnatural nor repugnant to nature, but obviously proper and salutary." Indeed, it will tend to "break down" the meaningless distinctions in appearance that irrationally lead to "oppression, war, and division among mankind."[16]

The future America envisaged by *The Liberator* is not one in which slaves are legally manumitted while the rest of American society remains intact. It calls not for a reform but for total social transformation, a world without prisons or poverty, where slavery and all forms of racial prejudice are long forgotten. The entire front page of the April 2 issue is devoted to a utopian short story in which the narrator wakes up, Rip van Winkle–style, to a future America where blacks and whites mix freely after a violent "revolution" has emancipated the slaves. Society has been transformed through racial "amalgamation and reconciliation," and African Americans have "married into respectable white families." Furthermore, the narrator learns that the racist belief in African American intellectual inferiority has been ended once and for all by the first black president of the United States, "a man of such distinguished talents, that none chose to risk their own reputation for discernment by not acknowledging it." Sadly, the end of the story reveals that this transformation has all been a dream. The narrator awakes to the sound of slaves being driven past his window in chains, back in the real United States of 1831, where, as we now know, interracial marriage was outlawed in places until 1967 and the election of the first black president was 177 years away.[17]

————

ALONG WITH THE DISSEMINATION of Walker's *Appeal* and the commencement of Garrison's *Liberator,* the beginning of abolitionism's radical turn can be dated to a third event, this one originating inside the slave system, where the fight for immediate emancipation had been raging for centuries. In late August 1831, an enslaved man in Virginia named Nat Turner led a group of around seventy black men, both enslaved and free, who went from house to house in the dark of night, freeing slaves and murdering every white person they found, including Turner's legal owner, who was a nine-year-old boy, along with two dozen other children and infants asleep in their beds, using weapons like fence posts and axes. Turner was literate and intensely religious, regarded by his family as a prophet for his preternatural intelligence and the spiritual visions he had experienced from a young age. He believed that he was an agent of God's divine retribution for the outrage of slavery, and he also wanted to position his insurrection as a new chapter of the American Revolution, having initially chosen the Fourth of July as the date but delaying it due to illness.

When whites discovered what had transpired during the night, their counterrevolution was swift. Many of the insurgents were captured and executed, and scores of black people as far away as North Carolina who had nothing whatsoever to do with the revolt were killed by the state or by mobs in retribution. Turner and his band had killed 60 whites; historians estimate that 120 African Americans were murdered in response. Turner himself managed to hide from authorities for two months but was eventually found, tried, and executed that November. After hanging, his body was beheaded, dissected, and skinned as a message to other would-be insurrectionists. White people stole parts of the corpse as souvenirs; some of his skin was made into a change purse, and his severed head was passed around for decades. His skull was finally recovered in 2016 from the possession of the former mayor of Gary, Indiana, and returned to Turner's descendants after DNA testing.[18]

Newspapers and government leaders placed the blame for this rebellion squarely on the Boston abolitionists, with the governor of Virginia calling out the "incendiary publications" of Walker and Garrison by name. *The Liberator* was termed "diabolical" and its editor an "instigator of human butchery." Boston's mayor was flooded with demands to silence Garrison and shut down his paper, some suggesting that he deserved the death penalty for inciting slaves to kill innocent whites. Garrison published some of the death threats he received in *The Liberator,* along with the response that he was ready to die for the cause: "Such a sacrifice may be necessary to hasten the day of deliverance." He was clear-eyed about the fact that those blaming him merely sought to divert attention away from the sadistic institution of slavery that had produced this bloody counterattack. His initial coverage of Turner's attempted coup presented it as the beginning of a full-blown slave revolution, the initial drops of blood to be spilled in the violent apocalypse that the first issue of *The Liberator* and Walker's *Appeal* had forecast.[19]

Despite its leader's grisly execution, Turner's uprising almost succeeded in ending slavery in Virginia: a vote in the state legislature came surprisingly close to decreeing that it was simply too dangerous for whites to maintain the institution any longer. But it also led to a violent nationwide crackdown on African Americans both free and enslaved, along with an assault on the First Amendment rights of anyone with antislavery views. Across the South, legislators tightened restrictions on black education, assembly, and access to firearms. These states also began to limit abolitionist speech and publications, petitions and peaceable assemblies. In some southern towns, it became illegal to receive *The Liberator* through the post office. In North Carolina, Garrison was indicted for distributing incendiary matter. In South Carolina, there was a $1,500 reward posted for the capture of any white person circulating *The Liberator* or other "seditious" materials. The Georgia legislature offered $5,000 for anyone who apprehended Garrison and brought him in to stand trial. This response wasn't limited to the South. To name only one example, in upstate New York, a grand jury resolved that those organizing "abolitionist societies in the Northern states," and those who circulate "inflammatory publications" to southern blacks, "are guilty of sedition, and of right ought to be punished; and that it is the duty of all our citizens who are friendly to the Constitution of the United States, and the future quiet and happiness of this people, *to destroy all such publications whenever and wherever they may be found.*"[20]

These attacks on free speech were one indication of rapidly escalating anti-abolitionist sentiment in the 1830s. Earlier opponents of slavery who advocated gradual emancipation and colonization had been respected as "philanthropists," and southern states had been home to a number of societies espousing these views. As Jefferson had explained to Fanny Wright only a few years before, many southerners regarded slavery as an immoral and unfortunate inheritance that they could not justify, even as they perpetuated it. But by the end of the decade, they had shed this ambivalence. In Congress, John C. Calhoun famously gave voice to the emerging position that slavery was actually "a positive good," repudiating the new crop of fanatics who attacked the system. In both the North and the South, abolitionists were now regarded as an odious and dangerous fringe, destroyers of peace and stability who threatened the constitutional union holding the country together.

———

GARRISON WAS EAGER to take the views articulated in *The Liberator* from the page into the world and set out to form an organization dedicated to achieving them. Yet even among the antislavery crowd, he could not find many white men who agreed that immediate abolition was "right and safe" and who were not concerned that this extremist position would unduly alarm the public and drive people away from the cause. He eventually found eleven to join him— which he considered enough for a movement, citing the twelve apostles' success in establishing Christianity—and wrote a constitution for an organization under which "the friends of the people of color" would work alongside *the people of color themselves.*" In January 1832, with a nor'easter dumping frozen slush on the city, they founded the New England Anti-Slavery Society in a basement schoolroom of the African Baptist Church on Belknap Street in Boston. Their founding document holds that everyone has a right to freedom from bondage, that no one can be the property of another, that anyone who enslaves a human being is guilty of a grievous wrong: "We hold that a mere difference of complexion is no reason why any man should be deprived of any of his natural rights, or subjected to any political disability."

In addition to beginning their program of "popular agitation" and petitions to Congress for the abolition of slavery at the national level, they aimed to act locally, pledging to help young men of color into trades, to improve the schools for black children while they worked on integrating the public schools, and to look into the cases of any New England residents kidnapped as fugitive slaves and pay for their freedom with the society's funds. When the final version of their constitution was later approved, seventy-two men signed it, around a quarter of them African Americans. A year later, the General Colored Association was formally enfolded into the NEASS, marking the end of what was likely the first black organization for abolition and racial uplift alongside the birth of the first integrated one. Less than two years later, the society had almost two thousand members.[21]

As the representative of the NEASS, Garrison traveled to Philadelphia to attend the 1832 National Convention of the Free People of Colour, staying with James Forten's daughter Harriet and her husband, Robert Purvis. This was to be the third meeting of an association formed to organize free black communities across state lines. It had come into being after the Ohio legislature passed restrictive laws aimed at limiting new black residents from coming to Cincinnati and expelling as much of the existing population as possible. Then, in August 1829, a mob of whites, hundreds strong, descended on the black community there, violently attacking them and burning their homes and businesses. Some stayed to rebuild, but about half of Cincinnati's black population left, some crossing the border into Ontario, then called Canada West, to seek new lives far from the reach of white America.

The increasingly connected free black leaders of the North sought to discuss and respond to the situation in Cincinnati and other issues of concern, and Richard Allen had offered up Mother Bethel AME Church as a meeting space—the site of the massive 1817 protest against the ACS and a flagship black institution that had expanded to include outposts in many states. Allen was seventy years old at this point and would die the following year, but he took the lead in organizing the American Society of Free Persons of Colour, scheduling their first convention for September 20, 1830.[22]

After the inaugural meeting, Allen and the convention delegates issued a strong statement of support for emigration to Canada, promoting it as a destination for refugees forced from their homes, as well as for others seeking economic or educational opportunity, an alternative to white-led colonization to Liberia. Addressing all free people of color in the United States, Allen and his colleagues proposed to help the Cincinnati emigrants in their plan to purchase land in Ontario and found black colonies there, but interestingly, they introduced the idea by quoting the American founding documents. Having been "taught by that inestimable and invaluable instrument, namely, the Declaration of Independence, that all men are born free and equal, and consequently endowed with unalienable rights, among which are the enjoyments of life, liberty, and the pursuit of happiness," they declared that the best hope for improving "our forlorn and deplorable situation" was to come together to "plant and support" a black settlement in Canada.

At the following year's conference, they proudly announced that with their support two thousand black settlers in Canada had built two hundred log cabins on eight hundred acres of land and laid the foundation for a settlement to provide asylum for refugees from American racism. Determined to establish their own economically sustainable society where they and their children would be not only physically safe but could become educated landowners in control of their political destiny, the settlers founded a village they called Wilberforce. It was named after a leading English abolitionist—fitting for a group that had found refuge from the United States in the British Empire.[23]

The following year—Garrison's first in attendance—saw a pivotal change in the convention's attitude toward the emigration project that it had been founded to support. Wavering from their previous enthusiasm for securing additional land in Canada where people of color from the United States could settle en masse, by 1832 some members were concerned that emigration projects sent a message that black people wished to relinquish their claim to American citizenship. Furthermore, although Canadian law was measurably more equitable than American law, some white residents of Ontario had petitioned Parliament to prohibit a further influx of black migrants. Even though the previous year, which had included the Nat Turner rebellion and the grisly white backlash, had "swelled the tide of prejudice until it has almost revolutionized public sentiment" against their communities, convention members were hesitant to abandon their homes, a warmer climate, and democratic institutions for a situation "almost similarly precarious, for an abiding place among strangers!"[24]

Although Garrison spoke eloquently against the ACS at this meeting, he stayed out of the long and heated debates on Canadian emigration and did not serve on the subcommittee appointed to write the convention's statement on the project. But soon after the meeting, he published a pamphlet that summed up the black response to white-led colonization schemes and capped, for a time, most discussion of emigration projects within the movement. His *Thoughts on African Colonization* is almost entirely devoted to collecting and reprinting the "Sentiments of the People of Color" against the ACS. He recounted the 1817 protest in Philadelphia led by Forten, Richard Allen, and others and included similar statements from communities in New York, Baltimore, Washington, D.C., and elsewhere. To white readers, he declared, "*This is their country.*" The idea of colonization, he worried, had hoodwinked moderates into believing that the problem of slavery would be solved by and by, lulling the conscience of the American public into a fatal slumber.[25]

Forten bought and distributed this pamphlet in huge numbers, so although Garrison was in England during the following year's meeting of the Free People of Colour, his belief that black people should commit their full energy to a fight within and for the United States was spreading. The tide began to turn against all emigration projects, including those with black leaders. The convention's committee on the Canada project declared, "There is not now, and probably never will be actual necessity for a large emigration of the present race of free coloured people." They urged constituents "to devote their thoughts and energies to the improvement of their condition . . . in this their native land, rejecting all plans of colonization anywhere."[26]

Later that year, when Garrison returned from abroad, many of the leaders of the Convention of the Free People of Colour met again in Philadelphia, along with white activists from New York, New England, and elsewhere, embodying the goal of racial integration in a new organization, the likes of which the country had never seen before. Garrison took the lead in articulating the group's aims, drafting a statement of purpose at the home of James McCrummell, a black dentist who hosted him during his stay. This Declaration of Sentiments positions the American Anti-Slavery Society in relation to the American Revolution but takes the opportunity to criticize the founding fathers rather than holding them up as a virtuous precedent. Again describing their grievances against England as "trifling" when compared with the situation of the enslaved, it posits that their project remains unfinished while slavery endures: "We have met together for the achievement of an enterprise, without which that of our fathers is incomplete; and which, for its magnitude, solemnity, and probable results upon the destiny of the world, as far transcends theirs as moral truth does physical force." Six black men were named to leadership positions, including Purvis; the editor Samuel Cornish; Abraham Shadd, an active participant in the Philadelphia Conventions of the Free People of Colour; and James Barbadoes, a Boston stalwart. In total, sixty-three people affixed their names to the founding document of the AASS in 1833—more signatures, as Garrison pointed out, than appear on the American Declaration of Independence.[27]

CHAPTER 4

To Break Every Yoke

Before the Declaration of Sentiments for the AASS was signed, Garrison took his draft to the members for review and revision. Lucretia Mott assumed a prominent role in wordsmithing the document. Mott was a Quaker, to all appearances a sedate and motherly figure, but she was also an admirer of both Fanny Wright and Mary Wollstonecraft and was regarded as a religious "heretic," shunned even by some within the abolitionist circle. When she suggested that they switch the order of references to the Bible and the Declaration of Independence in one passage, one young delegate whipped around in his seat to get a look at the woman who was bold enough to speak in a mixed public forum and who knew the word "transpose," to boot. Just as Garrisonian abolitionism hinged on the integration of black and white activists, it was also the first American social movement powered by the ideas and energy of women, who were otherwise excluded from politics and public life. As Garrison's son later wrote, these women were the "great army of silent workers, unknown to fame, and yet without whom the generals were powerless." Women's participation in abolitionist activism was held by many to be as radical as the tenets of immediatism and proved to be a defining bone of contention within the movement itself.[1]

A Philadelphia colleague and friend of the Fortens and Purvises, Mott was a staunch participant in the active Free Produce movement, a transatlantic consumer boycott with roots in eighteenth-century Quaker communities. Free Produce activists committed not to buy or use the products of slave labor, like sugar, cotton, rice, and tobacco. Hundreds of Philadelphians pledged themselves to this program of abstention in the late twenties. Women and African Americans were the backbone of the movement, leveraging their authority over their own households to protest slavery when public interventions in official politics were largely denied to them. Although James Forten continued to trade in cotton for his sails, his family was actively involved in the movement. The early Conventions of the Free People of Colour advocated Free Produce, and in 1834, African American activist William Whipper established a Free Labor store next door to Bethel Church.[2]

Boycotting implicated goods was a rigorous undertaking because the American economy relied so extensively on slave labor. Mott banned the products of the institution from her house, doing all of her shopping at a Free Produce store a block away from Independence Hall in Philadelphia, owned by her colleague Lydia White. Mott's husband, James, a textile merchant, switched from dealing in cotton to wool. Her family was not always thrilled to suffer the privations required of Mott's convictions, as her granddaughter recalled: "Free calicoes could seldom be called handsome, even by the most enthusiastic; free umbrellas were hideous to look upon, and free candies, an abomination."

Immediately after the founding AASS convention, Mott helped establish the Philadelphia Female Anti-Slavery Society with a number of black colleagues, including Forten's wife, Charlotte, and their daughters Margaretta, Sarah, and Harriet. In 1836, the organization issued an address "to the women of Pennsylvania," urging them to their "duty" of making themselves heard in the "halls of Congress" by petitioning against slavery, one of their only avenues for intervening in politics when women's suffrage was nearly a century away. "Yes, although we are *women,* we still are citizens," they declared, "and it is to *us, as women,* that the captive wives and mothers, sisters and daughters of the South have a particular right to look for help."[3]

Garrisonian women staked their claim for legitimacy as abolitionist activists on gender, asserting that enslaved women suffered

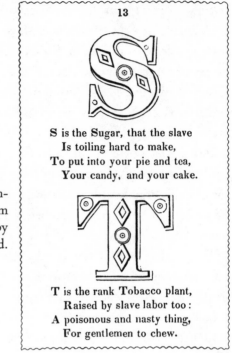

13

S is the Sugar, that the slave
Is toiling hard to make,
To put into your pie and tea,
Your candy, and your cake.

T is the rank Tobacco plant,
Raised by slave labor too :
A poisonous and nasty thing,
For gentlemen to chew.

A lesson in the Free Produce consumer boycott for children from *The Antislavery Alphabet* (1846) by Hannah Townsend.

specific and extreme forms of oppression that free women had a duty to address, especially sexual violence and the particular anguish of motherhood under the slave regime. As a group in Ohio declared, "We consider that we are *not moving out of our proper sphere* as females when we assume a *public* stand in favor of our *oppressed sisters*." The founding of the Anti-Slavery Convention of American Women in 1837 took these arguments to a national stage; Mott considered it the beginning of the women's rights movement. The group published a pamphlet outlining their ideas, to which Sarah Forten contributed a poem that ends with the couplet "Our skins may differ, but from thee we claim / A sister's privilege and a sister's name." The "sisterhood is powerful" argument may be mostly associated today with the "second wave" of American feminism, but when it originated in the 1830s, it was an explicit claim of feminist solidarity across the color line and a core reason to imagine women's political activity into being.[4]

Women's central role in the antislavery movement was a defining aspect of its counterculturalism in relation to the rigorously sexist and pro-slavery American mainstream. This movement did not just lay the groundwork for the postbellum suffrage movement; a feminist movement was already under way in radical antislavery in the 1830s, and by the end of the decade it would be the cause of a major shake-up.

———

THE AASS DECLARATION OF SENTIMENTS concludes with the signers' pledge to do everything in their power to overthrow slavery and secure black rights, "whether we live to witness the triumph of Liberty, Justice and Humanity, or perish untimely as martyrs in this great, benevolent, and holy cause." The mention of martyrdom may seem like a dramatic flourish, but it was far from purely rhetorical: in carrying out their work, abolitionists constantly exposed themselves to verbal abuse and physical violence. Over the course of the decade, white Americans increasingly believed that slavery must be violently defended by anyone who loved the Constitution— and its critics, free or enslaved, black or white, silenced at any cost. Especially after Nat Turner's raid, reactionaries drawn from a broad swath of the white population claimed that they were acting in self-defense against the fanatical antislavery forces endangering public safety along with the Union. Abolitionists were attacked with a variety of weapons, beaten, clubbed, stoned, pelted with rotten eggs and other garbage, lashed, and even murdered. Anti-abolitionist violence was not only ignored but actively sanctioned by the police and other state forces. To name only one example, in 1844 a federal judge in Florida ordered the hand of the abolitionist Jonathan Walker to be branded with the letters *S S* for "slave stealer" when he was found guilty of helping enslaved people escape to the British West Indies. Of course, violence against African Americans was even more endemic throughout this period; Philadelphia's politically active black community was one of many attacked by white mobs in the 1830s.

Within a couple of months in 1835 alone, Garrison was mobbed in the streets of Boston, gallows were built in front of his house as a death threat, and he was burned in effigy. In October of that year, another mob gathered outside his office, where a meeting of the Boston Female Anti-Slavery Society, a pathbreaking group founded by the radical author Lydia Maria Child, devoted fundraiser Maria Weston Chapman, and others, was under way. They had intended to capture, then tar and feather, the British abolitionist George Thompson, whom the women had invited as a guest speaker. Failing to find him, they were happy to have an opportunity to attack Garrison instead. The women carried on the business of their meeting despite the intensifying noise from the street, even as boards were being pried off the door. They refused to leave and affirmed aloud their commitment to work for the slave's cause even if they were killed. The city's mayor finally persuaded them to adjourn to another location, and they walked out through the mob two by two, white women and black women arm in arm. Garrison jumped out of a second-story window onto the roof of an adjacent shed, then ducked into a carpenter's shop. He was accompanied by his colleague Charles Burleigh, whose outlandish appearance (long, tubular red ringlets with a chest-length red beard to match, gangly ankles and wrists protruding from too-short pants and jacket) was no doubt aggravating to a crowd seeking to rid the community of reform weirdos.

The vigilantes found Garrison in the carpenter's loft and dragged him out, covered with sawdust and wood shavings. They tore off his pants and broke his glasses, tying a rope around his body and leading him down to the street like an animal on a leash. The mayor put Garrison in jail, ostensibly to keep the crowd from seriously hurting him, though he also formally charged him and at least thirty abolitionist women with provoking disorder. The Boston papers called Garrison "a public agitator" and said that the mob, described in their pages as "gentlemen of wealth and standing," had been trying to *prevent* a riot that might damage their property, incited by a group of unnatural women carrying on as reformers.[5]

In this and other instances, the activities of antislavery women seemed to particularly gall the violent mainstream opposition. When a female abolitionist society was founded in New York City in 1834, mobs vandalized the homes and churches of both African Americans and white activists, throwing furniture through windows and setting fires, rioting all over the city. As Fanny Wright and her haters knew, antislavery activism unsettled not only racial hierarchies but gender norms as well, compelling American women onto lecture platforms and other public political venues for the first time. (Strangely enough, Wright returned to the United States around this time and actually contributed to the escalating climate of anti-abolitionist violence. Supporting the party of Martin Van Buren and Andrew Jackson in their suppression of dissent, she "became a partizan on the other side, and for a season was politically insane." Dismissing immediate emancipation as "impossible," she said the label "abolitionist" now belonged to violent agitators who opposed the rule of law and used slavery as "a pretext for the fomenting of disorder and the breeding of disunion.")[6]

One dramatic example of the attacks on abolitionists came in 1838, when a grand lecture hall in Philadelphia was burned to the ground a mere three days after it opened. Abolitionists including the Forten and Mott families had raised funds to build Pennsylvania Hall as a site for reform meetings. It was an imposing neoclassical building on a corner lot, one of the largest and most beautiful in the city. In the days leading up to a convention of antislavery women to be held there, handbills posted around the neighborhood invited all "citizens who entertain a proper respect for the right of property and the preservation of the Constitution to interfere, *forcibly if they must* and demand the immediate dispersion of said convention."

The women took the podium anyway, attempting to make their addresses heard over the din of swearing and shouting. Rocks and brickbats smashed into the windows. Angelina Grimké, one of the earliest women well known as an antislavery and women's rights lecturer, urged her colleagues to continue, reminding them that even if the mob intended to break in and "commit violence on our persons," this would be nothing "compared to what the slaves endure." The women left the hall that night through a dense pack of men screaming threats. When an even rowdier crowd assembled around the building the following day, the association of reformers

Executive Committee of the Pennsylvania Anti-Slavery Society, 1851.
Lucretia Mott and Robert Purvis are seated second and third from the right.
Garrison Family Papers, Sophia Smith Collection, Smith College (Northampton, Massachusetts)

that had just dedicated the hall three days earlier asked that the black women stay away for the remainder of the convention in an attempt to quell the mob. Both the white and the black delegates refused this request. Reviving a tactic from the Boston riot in 1835, white and black women linked arms as they left the hall that night, a show of solidarity in case the women of color were singled out for especially violent attacks.[7]

Once the women were gone, the crowd burst into the hall with axes. They piled furniture, books, and papers around the stage, then opened the gas jets and set torches to the new building and everything in it. The Liberty Bell, which still crowned the Pennsylvania State House at that time, rang an alarm that pealed through the city streets. But when the firemen arrived, they sprayed down the neighboring buildings instead, watching alongside a mob of as many as thirty thousand people as the roof and the floors of the massive hall collapsed in flames.

As for the antislavery women, they carried on with the last day of their convention the next morning at a schoolhouse across town. In the public's mind, they were fully to blame for the situation that had endangered their lives. According to the newspapers, the convention had been "an open violation of *common decency*—the association of *black and white*—male and female." Claiming to have seen an interracial couple stepping out of a fine carriage (likely Harriet Forten and her lighter-complexioned husband, Robert Purvis), reporters described the cause of the riot as "the ridiculous and ostentatious amalgamation of colors in Chestnut Street. . . . Whites and blacks, arm-in-arm, were thronging the streets by scores, whereat the populace became greatly excited. Such a course, on their part, was exactly calculated to create a popular commotion." Again the papers sided with the violent anti-abolitionist mob. *The Philadelphia Gazette* described the rioters as a group of "respectable and well-dressed" men who effected their purpose "with a quiet resolve." Readers were assured that "the whole affair took place without

Pennsylvania Hall on fire in 1838.
The Library Company of Philadelphia

unnecessary violence or noise." The article celebrates the firemen for sharing the feelings of the crowd and not allowing one drop of water to fall on the burning building.[8]

––––––

IN THESE HARROWING YEARS, Garrison became increasingly convinced that violence and physical domination were the corrupt core of American society. He knew that he risked assault and death every day he continued as the acknowledged leader of the hated abolitionist movement, especially because the attacks often targeted editors like himself. In Cincinnati, a throng of prominent citizens had broken in to the printer James Birney's office in 1836 and thrown his press into the river. In St. Louis, mobs had smashed Elijah Lovejoy's printing press three times. Lovejoy moved to Illinois, a free state, and resumed publishing his antislavery paper, but armed men attacked again, this time shooting him dead.

Almost anyone else might have tried to make his message more palatable to stanch the violence and save his own life. Garrison instead turned a corner that took him even further to the fringes and made him unpopular with many of his associates, ultimately leading to a formal schism in the abolitionist movement. But for those who stuck with him, he became an even more visionary leader, one whose far-reaching radical program would inspire civil rights movements across the globe.

In his search to articulate a more radical vision of abolition that would abrogate the violence endemic to American culture, Garrison was aided by his close colleague Henry C. Wright. A traveling agent of the Anti-Slavery Society, Wright was disliked by moderates in the organization because he was suspected of being an atheist. He rejected the authority of all human governments and balked at every form of domination or hierarchy, including traditional child-rearing practices, against which he had published a book. He was a nonviolent anarchist, in other words, and also a venomous critic of organized religion. Like many others in the movement, he felt that the unresponsiveness of Christian churches to the atrocity of slavery revealed them to be hollow and false. Wright's perspective, which many viewed as fringe ultraism that could prove troublesome for the movement, turned out to be exactly the new direction that Garrison sought.

As the movement took its anarchist and anticlerical turn, Henry Wright's influence dovetailed with that of a surprising, controversial figure, undeniably an extremist but far from alone in this period in his millenarianism. One day in 1837, a young man named John Humphrey Noyes, with a high forehead and a chin-strap beard, appeared in Garrison's office bearing ideas that would have a profound effect on both the antislavery movement and the tradition of American radicalism more broadly. At the time, he was leading the Putney Bible School in Vermont. A decade later, after being arrested for adultery, he would leave for New York and establish his community of Perfectionists in Oneida. For over thirty years, this group would live out the sexual dimensions of Noyes's philosophy, including "male continence," meaning intercourse without ejaculation; complex marriage, meaning that all members of the community were "married" to all others and therefore to no one. But his earlier contribution to the history of American radicalism through the abolitionist movement is lesser known.

In a letter that Garrison subsequently published in *The Liberator,* Noyes explained that he had "subscribed my name to an instrument, similar to the Declaration of '76, renouncing all allegiance to the government of the United States and asserting the title of Jesus Christ to the throne of the world." This antigovernment declaration, in which Noyes revealed that he was free from sin and therefore not obliged to obey the usual rules of society, had resulted in his expulsion from Yale Theological Seminary in 1834 and the revocation of his ministerial license. But the version he presented to Garrison emphasized a total withdrawal from all of the evil promulgated by the United States: "I have renounced active cooperation with the oppressor, on whose territories I live; now I would find a way to put an end to his oppression." He looks forward to a millennium that will commence "AT THE OVERTHROW OF THIS NATION."

Noyes impressed on Garrison the urgency of starting at once to live "without being a hypocrite, or a partaker in the sins of the nation." After all, the Bible directs believers unambiguously to "cease to do evil" and even to be "perfect, as your Father in Heaven is perfect." Noyes insisted that there was no excuse for even the subtlest forms of complicity and that every person who participates in any way as a citizen of the United States—by voting, for example—is "a subject, and a ruler in a slaveholding government." Reminding Garrison of his position at "the forefront of the hottest battle of righteousness," Noyes urged him to aim for "*perfect* holiness," but accurately prophesied that if Garrison followed him on this path, "you will be deserted by many of your present friends."[9]

The month before Garrison received this letter, Noyes had written to a friend expressing the view that the scriptures advocate sexual freedom rather than monogamous marriage. Those Free Love beliefs were public knowledge when Garrison published Noyes's letter in *The Liberator*. Keeping this kind of company, if only intellectually, brought accusations that "Garrison, as a Perfectionist, believed in spiritual wives." Indeed, after this point, his detractors within the movement increasingly wondered if he was a charismatic leader organizing his followers into a radical cult. Garrison did not claim to be sinless, nor did he attempt to organize a commune as such, but he and others were increasingly convinced that ideological purity as antislavery activists required nothing short of publicly disavowing the U.S. government.[10]

———

THESE IDEAS PROVED CONTROVERSIAL among Garrison's colleagues, but many embraced them wholeheartedly. The Quaker schoolteacher Abby Kelley had been present at the riot at Pennsylvania Hall, initiating a speaking career there that established her as a leader in the movement. She wrote to Garrison to express her support of Noyes's ideas soon after his publication of the letter: "The time is now *fully* come when thou will take a decided stand for *all truths,* under the conviction that the whole are necessary to the permanent establishment of any *single one.* I believe the *Liberator* will not be rejected by many of its present subscribers should it *lay the axe at the root of the tree.*" In his translation of Noyes, Garrison was indeed turning to an attack on American society aimed at its very roots, and Kelley took up a central role in embracing this radical agenda that would soon splinter the official national abolitionist movement as it then stood. Only a year later, she would be called "the bombshell that blew up the society."[11]

The first decisive step in a chain of events leading to this division in the movement was the Peace Convention held in September 1838 in Boston. Garrison's radical intentions were evident from the very beginning when he asked that everyone present, around 160 people, write "his or *her* name" on a piece of paper so that it could be entered correctly into the membership roll. Understanding that the new society to be formed that day would be fully inclusive of women, a number of men walked out. Indeed, not only were women allowed to speak at this convention, but a number, including Abby Kelley, were appointed to leadership positions. Taking advantage of this newfound equality, Kelley called to order a minister who she felt was speaking out of turn and who then stormed out of the meeting. But the convention continued, and two days later, the participants founded the New England Non-Resistance Society, announcing the new organization with a declaration written by Garrison, Kelley, Wright, Alcott, Maria Weston Chapman, and others articulating a brand of radicalism that became synonymous with their movement and that many other abolitionists simply could not tolerate.

In this document, the society's members "profess to belong to a kingdom not of this world, which is without local, geographical, or national boundaries," open to "any person, without distinction of sex or color," devoted to revolutionary peace. They would not serve in the military or take legal action against anyone. They refused allegiance to all governments and vowed not to vote or participate in traditional politics in any way. They did not condone violence of any kind, by individuals or by states: they declared that no one had the right to take a life, not as the punishment for a crime and not even in self-defense.

They regarded the violence they encountered firsthand as one manifestation of a thoroughly violent society, founded and maintained by war and fueled by slavery. They hated the nationalist valorization of that violence and refused to play any role in a system that countenanced slavery. Rather than fighting back with the same tactics used by the corrupt system, they would use abstention and critique as their weapons. The Non-Resistants imagined a society without slavery, but also without sexism, prisons, the military, the death penalty, imperialism, or guns, a rejoinder to the long-standing charges that they were "cut-throats" and "men of one idea." They aimed to "break *every* yoke," to oppose all oppression, and to live in such a way that would withdraw their allegiance from a culture of violent domination. Garrison wrote to his wife after the declaration was adopted, "Never was a more 'fanatical' or 'disorganizing' instrument penned by man. It swept the whole surface of society, and upturned almost every existing institution on earth."[12]

The no-government, anti-American turn became a calling-card Garrisonian doctrine, the culmination of the first decade of the movement. In *The Liberator,* Garrison declared, "Mankind shall hail the TWENTIETH OF SEPTEMBER with more exaltation and gratitude, than Americans now do the FOURTH OF JULY." The public had long accused Garrison of disrespecting American institutions, of wanting to destroy the Union and the Constitution. Now he was embracing these goals explicitly. But as anti-abolitionist violence spiked, his adoption of radical pacifism robbed the pro-slavery mainstream of its ability to align itself with social peace and order. He staked his movement on morality and religious conscience, while the pro-slavery side resorted to violence and murder.

The Non-Resistants disapproved of all monuments "commemorative of violent victories, all trophies won in battle, all celebrations in honor of military or naval exploits," such as the project of finishing the Bunker Hill Monument in the Charlestown neighborhood of Boston. Indeed, the following year, the society published a book by its member Charles Whipple called *Evils of the Revolutionary War,* which argued that the founding fathers were not justified in turning to violence to effect their separation from England. Beyond the violence subtending all state governments, the Non-Resistants rejected the logic of nationalism, the magical significance attached to the idea of "America" both in mainstream culture and among many reformers. Embracing Thomas Paine's motto "Our country is the world, our countrymen are all mankind," they declared, "We love the land of our nativity, only as we love all other lands. The interests, rights, liberties of American citizens are no more dear to us, than are those of the whole human race." Abolitionism was a transatlantic movement, just as slavery was a transatlantic phenomenon, but for Garrison the main enemy, the primary stumbling block, was the U.S. government. There had never been an America that was not founded on racist oppression. Because there was no way to call on this society to live up to its lost ideals, they imagined a string of new "societies" while they worked to disorganize the existing one.[13]

———

NON-RESISTANCE SIGNALED the ratcheting up of Garrison's radicalism not only in its open no-government stance but also in its full inclusion of women, both of which a significant number of abolitionist leaders found extremist and distasteful. This intensifying anarchism and feminism led to dissension in the ranks of the national movement and, before long, a formal parting of ways. Members of the clergy, as well as a contingent of the AASS based in New York City, tended to hold conventional views as to women's roles and also believed that abolition must be pursued through electoral politics. They increasingly believed that "Mr. Garrison was a Fanny Wright man—an infidel—a Sabbath-breaker—a bad and dangerous man," and that he had gone so ultra that he was now disgracing the cause. Henry B. Stanton, a New York–based leader of the American Anti-Slavery Society, declared that anyone who subscribed to the doctrine of Non-Resistance was not a true abolitionist because it was "a moral and religious duty for every abolitionist entitled to vote to go to the polls." Any man who "refused, on any ground whatever," must be regarded as "a recreant to the cause of the slave."[14]

Stanton and his allies argued heartily against Non-Resistance, insisting that if abolitionists gave up the power of the ballot box, they would have no voice in American politics and their cause would be lost. This faction objected, too, to the admission of women "because it was repugnant to the wishes, the wisdom, or the moral sense of many of the members" and would "bring unnecessary reproach and embarrassment to the cause of the enslaved." They also noted that granting women a position of equality in the society would be "at variance with the general usage and sentiments of this and all other nations"—which, for the Garrisonians, was part of the point.[15]

This faction wanted a new journal, feeling that *The Liberator* had gone off the radical deep end and granted too much space to causes beyond the emancipation of slaves. Stanton wrote to a colleague that he was mobilizing a group of abolitionists who shared his belief that "the non-government doctrine, stripped of its disguises, is worse than Fanny Wrightism, and, under a Gospel garb, it is Fanny Wrightism with a white frock on. It goes to the utter overthrow of all order, yea, and of all purity. When carried out it goes not only for a community of goods but a community of wives."[16]

These issues soon brought the American Anti-Slavery Society, which had grown by this time to encompass over a thousand local chapters and 200,000 members, to its breaking point. At the 1840 national convention, after Abby Kelley was nominated to serve on the organization's business committee, the New York faction withdrew from the proceedings and formed a separate association, the American and Foreign Anti-Slavery Society. In the split, the women leaders stuck with Garrison, and Boston's black community also came to his defense. For one, William Powell, who operated boardinghouses for black sailors and also housed fugitives from slavery in nearby Bedford, affirmed that he was not alarmed by Garrison's *"ultra notions,"* namely that "women were to all intents and purposes—*persons*" and that "divine government is preferable to human governments." One of the crowded meetings they held to discuss the growing conflict within the movement published resolutions affirming that "so far from our confidence being shaken" in Garrison and the projects under his leadership, "daily proofs of their real merits increase our attachment, and bind us stronger to them." The new anti-Garrisonian splinter organization nominally held together for a decade but did not accomplish a great deal between annual meetings, always struggling to attract and energize members.[17]

RIGHT AFTER THE New York meeting that saw the schism of the AASS, the Garrisonians sailed for England to attend the World Anti-Slavery Convention in June 1840. Having just weathered the splintering of the movement in part over the question of women in leadership positions, Mott and other female delegates were greeted in London with the news that they would not be seated at the convention, because it departed too profoundly from established ideas about the roles of the sexes. They were instead offered positions behind a bar from which to silently observe the proceedings.

Arriving a few days later, Garrison joined the women behind the bar in protest, as did a few other male colleagues, including Charles Lenox Remond, the convention's only African American delegate. Garrison was regarded as the leader of the most important

Charles Lenox Remond,
ca. 1850s.
Boston Public Library

antislavery movement in the world, so his abstention from the convention was embarrassing to its hosts and hamstrung the conversation. Whenever his name was mentioned in the course of the proceedings, the entire room would turn and applaud toward the balcony where he, Remond, and Mott were sequestered, trying to encourage him to rise and address them. But he sat in silence.

Mott and Garrison were staying at the same boardinghouse as Henry B. Stanton, who had just led the charge against them in New York. Indeed, this trip doubled as Stanton's honeymoon. Mott walked with his vivacious young bride through the streets of London arm in arm, talking about her exclusion from the convention, women's role in the antislavery movement, and the injustice of all the wrongs against them. Elizabeth Cady Stanton was floored. She had never met a woman before who believed in the equality of the sexes, openly espousing a view that broke with orthodox religion. Mott "opened to me a new world of thought," Stanton later recalled. Siding with Mott and the Garrisonians, she managed to persuade her husband to vote with them in favor of the inclusion of female delegates. "Mrs. Stanton is a fearless woman, and goes for woman's rights with all her soul," Garrison wrote to his wife. For her part, Stanton admired Garrison's commitment to women's equality and his refusal to abandon his principles on that score even to advance the antislavery cause: "After coming three thousand miles to speak on the subject nearest his heart, he nobly shared the enforced silence of the rejected delegates. It was a great act of self-sacrifice that should never be forgotten by women."[18]

PART II

Infidel Utopian
Free Lovers,
1836–1858

CHAPTER 5

Coming Out from the World

In the fall of 1840, readers opened *The Liberator* to find an announcement for a convention to be held at the Chardon Street Chapel in downtown Boston, "to examine the validity" of the Sabbath "and to inquire into the origin, nature, and authority of the institutions of the Ministry and the Church, as now existing," including the "corruptions, abuses, and spiritual tyranny" that have always attended these institutions. Outraged, many promptly canceled their subscriptions.[1]

Garrison had just returned stateside after sitting in silent protest alongside Charles Lenox Remond and others in London at the World Anti-Slavery Convention. He did not write the announcement, nor did his name appear at the bottom alongside the names of the convention's organizers, all of whom were his close friends and colleagues. But he promoted their project by publishing the call in his paper, which was more than enough to further convince the names on the other side of the schism that he and his radical cohort would bring down the movement by associating abolitionism in the public mind with the most outrageous and offensive ideas: first women's rights and anarchism, now atheism. Garrison, they complained, "will not content himself with the one heresy of immediate emancipation, but must ever and anon be broaching others."[2]

The mainstream papers were even more incredulous. "WHAT NEXT?" they asked, branding the announcement the worst affront to date from the "male and *female* brethren" of the "woman-voting, no-government clique at Boston." One warned that the "ultras, transcendentalists, and zealots" of the Garrisonian set had launched "a fresh assault upon the holiest bulwarks of human happiness, and a fanatical *crusade* waged against the church of Christ." One reporter remarked, "We verily believe that Garrison would clap his hands for joy, if he could place his foot on the neck of the church, and press it into the dust." Another penned a spoof, announcing a convention to examine "the institution of the marriage relation, the right of parents to recognize, discipline and educate their children, and the right of men to claim exclusive privilege of the use of pantaloons." It is signed by "men of both sexes."[3]

This reactionary conflation of gender-bending, abolition, and religious free thought harked back, of course, to Fanny Wright, one of the country's most widely known freethinkers at a time when evangelical Protestantism was climbing to unprecedented prominence in American life. The early nineteenth century saw the rapid de-secularization of America from the Enlightenment-era, Deist founding fathers that Wright idolized. Between 1800 and 1840, the number of Baptists tripled, the number of Presbyterians quadrupled, and the Methodists multiplied by seven. The Second Great Awakening burned through the country as charismatic preachers drew thousands to daylong events punctuated by groaning and fainting and speaking in tongues. The converted were given to wild bodily contortions or "exercises" such as falling, jerking, barking on all fours, singing, and shrill laughter. Wright recalled witnessing one emotionally overheated camp meeting—"a *revival,* as such scenes of distraction are wont to be styled." She pinpointed a disturbing gender imbalance in these scenes: "The victims of this odious experiment on human credulity and nervous weakness, are invariably women." Wright was horrified by the sight of women contorting themselves on the ground in reaction to what she regarded as superstitious humbug.[4]

Historians generally point to the Second Great Awakening as the primary catalyst of the reformist zeal of the antebellum period, but it is important to note the avowed secularism of most of the activists that figure in this story. As mainstream America flocked into the Christian churches, radicals were coming out. Wright and the Owenites belong to a tradition that later came to include Martin Robison Delany, Elizabeth Cady Stanton, and Ezra Heywood, all of whom pointed to Christianity as a conservatizing force in American life, a source of oppression against African Americans and women and of indifference to the poor. Even social radicals who were devout Christians, like Richard Allen and John Brown, practiced a variant liberation theology that put social justice in the center of their religious mission. Certainly, something of the millenarianism of the period's religious movements, the belief that a glorious epoch of heaven on earth was approaching, translated into political and social schemes, but even those who were not acknowledged freethinkers openly criticized religious practices that the mainstream regarded as sacrosanct. Some, like Wright, saw faith itself as a negative force in the world, while others, like Garrison, grounded their activism in Christian belief but rejected institutional orthodoxy.

For religious precursors to the protest movements described here, we might look instead to the Quakers, for whom social justice had long been a spiritual priority. Back in the 1730s, the Quaker activist Benjamin Lay had committed to a lifestyle of abstention, eating a strict vegetarian diet and refusing to wear or consume anything produced from the exploitation of animals or slave labor. He published pamphlets against slavery, prisons, and capital punishment, and staged dramatic protests at church gatherings, like splattering an audience with fake blood and sitting outside the entrance in freezing temperatures with his bare foot plunged deep into the snow as a reminder to all who passed that the suffering of enslaved people was a bodily reality.[5]

While Quakerism was a vital source of inspiration for some, many others traced their social values to the Enlightenment secularism of the founders. They defiantly identified themselves as the descendants of the working-class immigrant abolitionist Thomas Paine when the mainstream rejected him as an atheist: *The Liberator*'s masthead motto was a quotation from the radical founder; Free Lovers and freethinkers in multiple cities celebrated his birthday every year with large parties; Elizabeth Cady Stanton kept a volume of his works on her desk. Like him, they believed that "we have it in our power to begin the world over again," not by way of a supernatural Second Coming, but by writing, protesting, organizing, and, if necessary, in violent revolution.[6]

Which is why, despite the diversity of this network of activists, most of them were denounced as infidels by the anti-reform mainstream at some point in their careers. "Infidelity" was the charge leveled against religious skeptics, to be sure, but also against anyone advocating ideas that undermined social institutions considered to have a theological basis, including slavery and the subordination of women. As one women's suffragist noted, reflecting back on Fanny Wright's role as a pioneer of their movement, "infidel" was the core of the attacks against her, "though the true meaning of it all was, that plain, simple-minded men were scared out of their wits, lest their wives should learn from her example something that would induce them to question masculine supremacy." The constant use of this epithet might suggest that her atheism bothered Americans more than her advocacy of interracial sex, but the term is better understood as convenient shorthand for damning all forms of social progress as immoral.[7]

Predictably, the papers denounced the Chardon Street meeting to examine the Sabbath as *"an infidel Convention"* and called out the anti-slavery movement's "constant advance toward infidelity" under Garrison's influence, even declaring that "his pretended interest for the welfare of the colored people seems to be only a cloak to cover his real designs." Although Garrison was actually a devout Christian—indeed his antislavery strategy rested on framing the peculiar institution as uniquely offensive to God—there was nevertheless plenty of truth in the accusation that many in his movement sought to undermine the church. By 1840, they had turned their fanatical interrogation of the institutions at the heart of American life on the mainstream religious practices that propped up the slave system. They believed that the teachings of Jesus commanded them to bear witness against slavery, especially because pro-slavery apologists in the South called on the Bible as a key source in defense of the institution, but mainstream churches in the North clearly intended to stay out of the fight.

Activists had become disillusioned with the lack of moral leadership from the pulpit, and they refused to be quiet about it. Henry C. Wright, the Non-Resistant, published an open letter to his church, declaring, "While you thus continue by your silence or otherwise to sustain this system of wrong and outrage . . . I DO HEREBY RENOUNCE YOU AS A CHRISTIAN CHURCH."[8]

The abolitionist belief that coming out or "seceding" from a negligent church was the duty of all Christians was inspired by a verse from Second Corinthians that commands, "Come out from among them, and be ye separate, saith the Lord. Touch not the unclean thing, and I will receive you." In a similar verse in Revelation, God commands his people to come out of Babylon, "that ye be not partakers of her sins, and that ye receive not of her plagues." Inspired by this idea of a righteous separation from corruption, a radical sect on Cape Cod called themselves the Come-Outers, claiming that they could better commune with the Almighty by spending Sunday mornings fishing or otherwise outside the church walls. The term eventually came to apply more broadly to abolitionist renunciations of politically "neutral" religious institutions.[9]

Many Come-Outers were not satisfied merely to let their memberships lapse and sleep in on Sundays. Instead, they confronted church leaders and members face-to-face, disrupting worship services and refusing to leave until they were arrested or physically ejected by the congregation. Abby Kelley's husband and fellow Non-Resistant, Stephen S. Foster, was particularly infamous for his Sunday morning protests. He would enter a church along with the congregation, sit quietly through the opening prayer, and then before the minister could begin his sermon, Foster would rise and deliver as much of an antislavery lecture as he could until he was physically seized. He would then go limp, forcing his detractors to carry the awkward bulk of his long frame down the aisle while he continued to hold forth. He would be thrown out the door, or occasionally a window, and then usually roughed up as he lay on the ground where he landed. The New Hampshire legislature passed a law in response to his activities, making it a crime to interrupt a church service. But he continued his protests anyway, spending time in jail in that state and others. Abolitionist women also took part in these direct-action church protests, arguing with pastors, defying segregated seating, and the like. One Come-Outer woman, clicking her knitting needles to interrupt a sermon, made such a racket that church officials carried her out and had her arrested. Although she was convicted of "contempt of worship," the jailer refused to lock her up.[10]

In addition to interrupting church services, Foster made his anticlerical views known on the antislavery convention circuit, where he was a regular speaker. He opened his speeches by declaring that it would be better for the moral character of a town to have dozens of bars, gambling houses, and brothels than one church. In 1842, he incited a riot on Nantucket Island when he delivered an address calling ministers the "pimps of Satan" and a "brotherhood of thieves." On another occasion, he said that every member of the Methodist Church was guiltier in the sight of God than a prostitute or an assassin. At a meeting in Boston, he mounted the platform wearing a coat that had been torn in half when he was forcibly removed and severely beaten by the deacons of a church in Portland,

Stephen S. Foster.
Massachusetts Historical Society

Maine. But more striking than his one-tailed coat was the iron collar he wore around his neck: a heavy instrument with four long spikes projecting toward his face, used for torturing and dehumanizing enslaved people. In each of his hands were manacles and chains that had been worn by a fugitive from New Orleans. Holding these aloft for the crowd, he shouted, "Behold the emblems of the American church and clergy!"[11]

These Come-Outer demonstrations recalled a landmark protest that had taken place in Philadelphia's free black community decades earlier. After a renovation of the city's Methodist church in the 1790s, white church leaders had decided that black congregants were no longer welcome to sit in their usual pews and must relocate to a segregated balcony. One Sunday morning, they enforced this new seating arrangement even as the congregation knelt in prayer, pulling Absalom Jones, co-founder of the city's Free African Society, up off his knees and dragging him down the aisle. Seeing this, all of Jones's fellow black worshippers rose and "went out of the church in a body."[12]

Under the leadership of Richard Allen, a portion of this group went on to found the African Methodist Episcopal Church and built the meetinghouse that came to be known as Mother Bethel, site of the inaugural anti-colonization protest in 1817, the Conventions of the Free People of Colour beginning in 1830, and other key events in black community organizing and the history of radical activism. James Forten had regarded black nationalism as a walkout of this kind, but on a massive scale, writing to Paul Cuffee that black Americans "will never become a people until they come out from amongst the white people," extending the biblical injunction to describe a more thoroughgoing disentanglement from an oppressive mainstream.[13]

This tradition of righteous separation was the spirit that animated the 1840 Chardon Street Convention and brought together the textured and diffuse counterculture on display there. One attendee called it "the most singular collection of strange specimens of humanity that was ever assembled," which was saying a lot in the heyday of reform conventions. There were "men of every shade of opinion, from the straitest orthodoxy to the wildest heresy, and many persons whose church was a church of one member only. A great variety of dialect and of costume was noticed; a great deal of confusion, eccentricity, and freak appeared, as well as of zeal and enthusiasm. If the assembly was disorderly, it was picturesque." A mainstream reporter covering the event noted, "If there is any body that has a queer conceit of religious or social matters, if anyone has a moral maggot in his brain, if any one is disposed to run a tilt against all the forms, customs, and received ideas of society . . . let him be assured that he had his representative in this congregation of world-improvers."[14]

The convention had initially been called to consider matters of religious observance, and indeed there were plenty of controversial statements on that topic. Substantiating the claims of his detractors to some degree, Garrison firmly stated that Sabbath observation was unnecessary. To those who came to combat these notions by quoting scripture, N. H. Whiting responded, "If others are disposed to dig up the musty records of former times, they can do so; I shall not. I go against the Sabbath as false in philosophy, as false in physiology, and false in morals and religion." But the discussions at Chardon Street strayed wildly from theological questions as this diverse assortment of dissenters competed to ride their various hobbyhorses to the center of attention.

One vegetarian warned meat eaters that their diet was slowly causing their very bodies to convert into the flesh of cows, pigs, and geese. Another objected to this line of argument on the grounds that his body was not becoming a squash or a stinkweed. Calling the Sabbath into question had opened the floodgates to both the profound work and the silly excesses of the drive toward total social transformation. Diet, clothing, sex, kinship, government, work, money, violence, animal rights, medicine—all were up for discussion. Abolitionism aimed to snap white Americans out of their apathy about oppressive practices that they had accepted as facts of the sociopolitical landscape, as had generations before them. The interrogation of matters as settled and sacred as the Sabbath meant that any number of social institutions and practices might now be unsettled and reconsidered.

———

IN THE MIDST of the oddball assembly at the Chardon Street Chapel, among the "Madmen, madwomen, men with beards, Dunkers, Muggletonians, Come-outers, Groaners, Agrarians, Seventh-day-Baptists, Quakers, Abolitionists, Calvinists, Unitarians, and Philosophers," was a gentleman with a beak of a nose, piercing eyes, and an expression both bemused and detached. Though he much preferred his quiet book-lined study to mixing with the reformer rabble, Ralph Waldo Emerson's religious ideas made him an ideal attendee of the Sabbath convention: he had resigned from the ministry a few years earlier because he did not care to perform the Communion ritual anymore, regarding it as a rote gesture that stifled true spirituality.

Emerson was well known in the Boston area for his controversial lectures, which some found abstruse and atheistic but others hailed as "our intellectual Declaration of Independence." He challenged listeners to recognize themselves as God's greatest and most revealing works, far outweighing the scriptures and churches. Disparaging conformity to religious convention, he claimed that firsthand experience, especially in nature, would bring about the kind of metaphysical revelation on which belief should be based. These addresses, along with his poetic treatise "Nature," came to be regarded as core texts of Transcendentalism, an American brand of romanticist philosophy developed in opposition to the bulwark of New England Unitarianism in which Emerson and his coterie had been trained. For the past four years, he had been meeting in the genteel homes of a number of like-minded men and women around Boston and its suburbs for earnest discussion of these ideas, with a few inevitable dashes of erudite posturing and inane jargon thrown in.

"The Club," as some called it, included a rotating selection of participants and guests, not only elite theologians, but others drawn from a broader progressive intelligentsia, including the working-class radical minister Theodore Parker; the pioneering feminist philosopher Margaret Fuller; and Bronson Alcott, a longtime Garrisonian and an educational reformer. Their projects and publications are now regarded as the first American philosophical movement, widely read and taught as key intellectual accomplishments of the century, although at the time their innovations often met with ridicule and censure. Transcendentalism contributed to the erosion of traditional religious authority that made the Chardon Street Convention possible in 1840, one of many points of overlap between radical reform and the eminent New Englanders whose work is now synonymous with antebellum American high culture.

It was Emerson's bookish and bespectacled cousin George Ripley who had the initial idea of the Transcendental Club and hosted its first meeting in 1836. Ripley had been embroiled in controversy that year after publishing an article suggesting that Christians need not believe that the miracles performed by Jesus were historical facts. The Unitarian establishment in which he lived and worked was instantly up in arms because Ripley seemed to be calling into question Jesus's divinity and the biblical account of his life, a shocking and heretical theory. The conservative Andrews Norton, who had taught Ripley at Harvard, denounced him and all of Transcendentalism as the "latest form of infidelity," the bugbear term thrown at Owen, Garrison, and all other social activists of the period. It was particularly resonant in that time and place because Fanny Wright's Boston colleague Abner Kneeland had just been convicted of blasphemy and served sixty days, the last American jailed for the crime.[15]

And in truth, the Transcendentalists deserved their association in the public mind with the Garrisonians, ultra Non-Resistants, and infidel socialists. A decade after Owen and Wright called for free inquiry into the religious conventions they believed were hoodwinking Americans, these Harvard-trained professional ministers serving some of Greater Boston's most prominent congregations took up a surprisingly similar line of thought. Emerson had followed Owen's activities with interest in the late 1820s, but by the time he met the socialist at Alcott's house in late 1845, he had

George Ripley.
Library of Congress

worked out an entire philosophy glorifying the individual, specifically hammered out in part against critics like Owen who focused on the power of social systems. Emerson charged that Owenite socialism "skips the faculty of life, which spawns and scorns system and system-makers" and overturns a thousand "New Harmonies with each pulsation."[16]

Emerson's responses to the socialists and their reformer descendants almost always used them as a straw man or a laugh line against which to argue for the all-powerful individual in opposition to any form of collectivism. And yet his most significant works bear unmistakable resonances of those radical theories he rejected. By the time of the Chardon Street Convention, Emerson was infamous for warning the graduating class of Harvard Divinity School that "the evils of the church that now is are manifest" and inciting newly minted ministers against "the falsehood of our theology." This speech got him banned from his alma mater for decades but was cheered by a growing cohort of New Englanders disillusioned with orthodox religion.

Like Owen before him, Emerson called for "new views." Like

Wright, he chastised his generation for resting on the achievements of the American founders, a tendency to "grope among the dry bones of the past," rather than making living contributions to their own time. His aim was to catalyze readers to "cleanse their vision" with direct experience in nature in order to read the text of the world anew. Indeed, although the resonance was certainly unintentional, some of Emerson's most celebrated ideas surprisingly echo Wright's earlier addresses. At the opening of the Hall of Science, for example, Wright complained that we "receive our knowledge" from books, "instead of seeking it for ourselves in the bosom of nature and the occurrences passing around us," thus "closing our eyes upon this beautiful world." She asked individuals to look to their own perceptions as the most important authority, just as Emerson would in the following decade. We turn to the priest and the schoolmaster, she admonished, "willing to see with his eyes, to hear with his ears, and to think with his thoughts, so that we may but escape the labor of exercising our own." Thinking our own thoughts and seeing with our own eyes, refusing the clergy or the philosopher for the authority of ourselves, seeking knowledge in the bosom of nature and not from the musty authority of books— this is the very heart of the philosophy that made Emerson famous less than a decade later.[17]

He was no doubt aware of Wright and the ideas she spread across the country on her lecture tours. When her visit to Boston blew up the local papers in the summer of 1829, Emerson was living in the city and working as an associate minister at Second Church, and she was an active topic of discussion among his colleagues in the clergy. Even assuming that Emerson found Wright appalling, as essentially everyone did, perhaps it is still possible that her iconoclasm, her extreme rejection of social conventions, made an impression on the young Emerson, modeled for him the fearless fidelity to one's unruly self that he would soon come to champion.

Thus, mistaking Transcendentalism for merely a mannered reworking of New England Unitarianism would be to underestimate its risky alignment with both the infidel socialism that preceded it and the mystical millenarianism that surrounded it. Take, for instance, Jones Very, a poor boy from Salem whose parents were never married because his mother was a staunch supporter of Fanny Wright, believing in neither God nor legal matrimony. He read "Nature" as a Harvard undergraduate and was taken under the wing of the Transcendentalists, impressing them with his contributions to one of the Club meetings. He was in the audience when Emerson delivered the Divinity School address that appalled the entire religious community. It seems to have nudged him over the edge on which he had long teetered. Very took the Transcendentalist belief in the divinity in all humanity literally, declaring himself the Second Coming. He went to Club member Elizabeth Peabody's house, placed his hand on her head, and rebaptized her. He then tried the same process with some clergymen and was committed to the McLean asylum. After his release, Emerson helped him publish his book of poems, which some consider among the finest sonnets in all of nineteenth-century American poetry, lit with divine madness.[18]

Although Transcendentalism was not one of the offbeat religious sects of the Come-Outer era, when a wave of new denominations seeking heaven on earth—Mormons, Perfectionists, Millerites, Adventists, and the like—promoted unorthodox ideas about the Second Coming, Very was not the only Transcendentalist who thought he had identified Christ's successor. Their fevered longing for the end of the world and the dawn of some unprecedented new one vibrated through a wave of socialist agitation that they helped propel, when coming out of the churches led to coming out of the world.

Moreover, whether or not her 1829 lecture tour impressed the young Emerson, Fanny Wright managed through another channel to infuse the teachings of radical socialism into the minds that would produce Transcendentalism. Delivering a lecture in a filthy, broken-down building previously used by a circus in Utica, New York, the usual public venue having been closed to her by local religious authorities, Wright met a tall, bearded young man named Orestes Brownson. An avid reader of the utopian socialists, Brownson became fast friends with Wright. Soon after their initial meeting, she persuaded him to leave the Universalist ministry, become the corresponding editor of *The Free Enquirer,* and join her and Robert Dale Owen's quest to rout out class inequality by turning the care of all American children over to the state. Looking back on his time with Wright and Owen, Brownson claims that he was an agent in a secret society working to get these national schools adopted and make marriage and religion obsolete in the process. Although he soon parted ways with the Free Love socialists and became a minister for a Unitarian congregation outside Boston, some tinge of this radical past followed Brownson into his new context, in which he mentored the Harvard undergraduate Henry David Thoreau, tutoring him in German, taking long nature walks with him, and helping him get a job.[19]

The same year Emerson published the Transcendentalist cri de coeur "Nature," Brownson brought out *New Views of Christianity, Society, and the Church,* seemingly a nod to Owen's earlier work with a very similar title but countering its secularism with a utopian vision of religion as it could be. Brownson called for a "church of the future" that would reclaim Christianity's roots as a radical social movement, claiming, "No man can be a Christian who does not refrain from all practices by which the rich grow richer, and the poor grow poorer, and who does not do all in his power to elevate the laboring classes." Like Emerson, he wanted to abandon religious ceremonies that had become dry husks, but instead of replacing them with inward revelation, he called for "substantial acts of piety and love which do really tend to the melioration of the condition of all men, especially of the poorest and most numerous class."[20]

Emerson popularized the idea that each individual was miraculous and divine; for Brownson, this meant that the degradation of any person was intolerable and allowing so many to live in poverty was an outrage on religious grounds. Brownson attended the inaugural Transcendental Club meeting and later hosted the group himself, but he soon wore out his welcome. Eventually, other members found him "unbearable" because he loved to argue, chew tobacco, and pound the table. But his contributions indicate that Transcen-

dentalism had from the beginning a strand defined by social conscience, in tension with the better-known element of Emersonian
individualism, a division that became even starker when the U.S.
economy fell off a cliff, bringing questions of structural inequality
to the fore.[21]

————

IN MAY 1837, as this historic American philosophical movement
was coalescing in parlors around Boston, a bank panic kicked off a
long and disastrous period of deflation and unemployment, the
country's first major depression. Starvation was widespread, as was
suicide. Rather than bringing about limitless expansion and opportunity as the Jacksonian "market revolution" seemed to promise,
capitalist excesses had cast Americans into ruinous poverty. Emerson wrote in his journal that "the world has failed" and "young men
have no hope." But one upside to the failure of the world is that
other worlds become imaginable. Starting in 1840, proposals for a
postcapitalist America gave thousands of people an astonishing kind
of hope.[22]

The Panic of 1837 led Brownson to issue a radical warning about
the growing inequality of American society that some have seen as
an American precursor to Karl Marx's *Communist Manifesto*. In "The
Laboring Classes," Brownson declared that the distinctions of
wealth and poverty must be destroyed and that doing so will require a bloody revolution. "No one can observe the signs of the
times with much care, without perceiving that a crisis as to the relation of wealth and labor is approaching," he wrote. Sometimes
shouting in all caps, he called for the destruction of banks and mo-
nopolies, and more generally "of all PRIVILEGE," and forecast an
apocalyptic class war in all corners of the globe.

By Brownson's own account, the essay was "received by my
countrymen with one universal scream of horror." As disaffected by
capitalism as many Americans might have been, they did not want to
hear his dire prediction of its overthrow in a violent revolution. As
had become commonplace, when faced with socialist critique, the

conservative press accused Brownson of everything outrageous they could think of, including Free Love, atheism, and anarchism. Brownson was an active Democrat, so the Whigs circulated the article widely, brandishing it as evidence that the rival party wanted to forcibly bring about a socialist redistribution of property. The resulting public debacle contributed to President Martin Van Buren's defeat in his bid for reelection. It was also a significant personal blow, reorienting Brownson politically. He said that this election "disgusted me with democracy, destroyed what little confidence I had in popular elections, and made me distrust both the intelligence and the instincts of 'the masses.'" He soon underwent yet another conversion, this time to Catholicism, and abandoned radical politics. Looking back on this time in his memoir, he recalled, "In 1840 I had not wholly ceased to believe it possible to introduce such changes into our social and economical arrangements as would give to the political equality asserted by the American Democracy a practical significance. I have got bravely over that since."[23]

The financial panic did not propel Emerson into radical action. Like the Garrisonians, he acknowledged that injustice and exploitation were so endemic to American society that every product was tainted, every individual implicated. Striking a note that echoed the Free Produce movement that exposed how completely American consumerism relied on slave labor, he admitted, "We eat and drink and wear perjury and fraud in a hundred commodities." Yet despite his general agreement with the many activists of his acquaintance, he claimed that attempting to extricate oneself from these evils, as the Come-Outers did, and live entirely according to one's conscience was a kind of zealotry that would bring all progress to a halt: "If we suddenly plant our foot, and say,—I will neither eat nor drink nor wear nor touch any food or fabric which I do not know to be innocent . . . we shall stand still." Refuting Garrison's uncompromising demand for ideological purity, Emerson held that perfectionism was at odds with actual progress.

Moreover, Emerson was not a joiner. By his own admission, he was constitutionally averse to taking action to address the social problems that he plainly saw around him: "I was born a seeing eye, and not a helping hand." The growing popularity of socialism in his time and place drove him to articulate his signature philosophy of individualism, becoming a key cheerleader for economic liberalism. Confronted with collectivist plans from every direction, he increasingly idealized market capitalism and denied that anyone was personally responsible for improving the conditions of others. "Are they *my* poor?" he asked in his 1841 essay "Self-Reliance."[24]

Part of the reason he demurred from political extremism was simply that it necessarily separates one from the mainstream: "I do not wish to be absurd and pedantic in reform. I do not wish to push my criticism on the state of things around me to that extravagant mark, that shall compel me to suicide, or to an absolute isolation from the advantages of civil society." Once a person started down this road traveled by the Come-Outers, where could he stop? The rare individual who refuses to benefit from a society propped up by the misery of others must abandon it completely: "Nothing is left him but to begin the world anew."[25]

For Emerson, this was an impossibility, and he believed that individuals should look inward to renovate themselves instead. But beginning the world anew is exactly what a number of his closest friends attempted in the 1840s. Bronson Alcott, for example, was not deterred by the fear that his social critiques would be called extravagant. Instead, he "planted his foot" and demanded a full separation from the goods and practices that offended him. Even other radicals snickered about how his house was pitch-black after sundown because he refused to burn whale oil, which required the slaughter of an animal. In an attempt to live out this perfectionist disentanglement, Alcott and his family endured a bone-chilling New England winter at his Fruitlands commune on a strict vegan diet. And, true to Emerson's prediction, he indeed came very close to suicide when this project failed. He was one of thousands of Americans willing to risk appearing absurd in order to come out of a society they regarded as immoral and contaminating.[26]

Alcott had been a follower of Garrison's since 1830, an activist educator and philosopher for whom abolitionism was one motor of a restless utopian yearning. He left one meeting of the Non-Resistance Society feeling certain that "a few years will bring changes in the opinions and institutions of our time of which few now dream. All things are coming to judgment, and there is nothing deemed true and sacred now that shall pass this time unharmed." Alcott was not alone in imagining that the toppling of settled ideas and customs would bring about total transformation. Beginning in 1840, the process of societal deconstruction kicked off by antislavery agitation flowered into a golden age of American utopianism. Come-Outer separatism inspired many to believe that they could and should distance themselves from institutions beyond the church, separating from the whole of a corrupt society.[27]

Within just a handful of years, attendees of the 1840 Come-Outer conventions, including one in Groton, Massachusetts, in addition to Chardon Street, had founded six separatist living experiments. To avoid the "unclean thing," they came out of capitalism and out of American life, aiming not just to extricate themselves from an exploitative system but to begin the world anew. Among the motley crowd was Alcott, the founder of Fruitlands; Adin Ballou of the Hopedale community, a fellow Non-Resistant; David Mack and four other future leaders of the Northampton Association of Education and Industry, an abolitionist commune centered on a silk mill in western Massachusetts. John Collins, one of the Chardon organizers and general agent of the Anti-Slavery Society who worked closely with both Frederick Douglass and Abby Kelley, founded a vegetarian community of around one hundred members who wanted to abolish government and private property in Skaneateles, New York. His neighbors simply called it "No God" because the communitarians were also atheists. And then there was Henry David Thoreau, who came out of the world on July 4, 1845, for a solo utopian experiment on the bank of Walden Pond.[28]

Indeed, Thoreau came to translate so much from Garrisonian political theory that most people assume he came up with it. Thoreau was not a member of the Non-Resistance Society, but he was close friends with Alcott and had publicly debated Non-Resistance principles with him at the Concord Lyceum (it was Alcott who first refused to pay the poll tax and went to jail in protest, another form of oppositionality that Thoreau copied). Indeed, he disagreed with some of the Garrisonians' core principles and specifically differentiated himself from "those who call themselves no-government men."[29]

But his famous theorization of civil disobedience asks, "How does it become a man to behave toward this American government today? I answer, that he cannot without disgrace be associated with it. I cannot for an instant recognize that political organization as my government which is the slave's government also." Disgusted by slavery and imperialist westward expansion, he wrote, "I think that it is not too soon for honest men to rebel and revolutionize." As the Non-Resistants had done years earlier, Thoreau declared, "Those who call themselves Abolitionists should at once effectually withdraw their support, both in person and property, from the government of Massachusetts."[30]

Like Garrison and John Humphrey Noyes, Thoreau found voting distasteful and held that no reformer could remain loyal to the U.S. government without becoming part of the problem: "Those who, while they disapprove of the character and measures of a government, yield to it their allegiance and support are undoubtedly its most conscientious supporters, and so frequently the most serious obstacles to reform." He articulated most powerfully how an individual's refusal to hypocritically follow rules that outrage his conscience can ultimately disorganize the workings of society: "Let your life be a counter-friction to stop the machine. What I have to do is to see, at any rate, that I do not lend myself to the wrong which I condemn."

Finally, in the Come-Outer tradition, Thoreau's removal from a corrupt society allowed him to imagine a new one. "Is a democracy, such as we know it," Thoreau wondered, "the last improvement possible in government?" He concluded with a projection that echoed not only Robert Owen but many of his own friends who, in the intervening decade, acted on the belief that the American civilization they knew was merely a passing stage in an approaching utopian future. Like them, Thoreau dreamed of a society that "would prepare the way for a still more perfect and glorious State, which also I have imagined, but not yet anywhere seen."

CHAPTER 6

Brook Farm on Fire

A few months after the Chardon Street Convention, George Ripley came out of the church, not as an interloper in the pews like Foster, but from the pulpit. In the wake of the Panic of 1837, Ripley found his famous cousin's philosophy flawed in its "profound indifference" to social injustice. He was deeply disturbed by the poverty everywhere apparent in the streets of Boston and equally appalled by the callousness of those who called themselves Christians—especially the congregants practically stepping over the starving and homeless to enter the Purchase Street Church, where he served as the minister.

On October 1, 1840, around the time Alcott and the other organizers had penned their call for the anti-Sabbath convention, Ripley wrote a letter to church leaders expressing dissatisfaction with the constraints he felt in his position. He needed to do more, he explained, than deliver polite speeches that did not broach the issues he cared about most deeply: "Blame me for it if you will, but I cannot behold the degradation, the ignorance, the poverty, the vice, the ruin of the soul, which is every where displayed in the very bosom of Christian society in our own city, while men look idly on, without a shudder." Attending closely to the anticlerical screeds of the Come-Outers and the anticapitalist arguments of his close colleague and friend Orestes Brownson, Ripley decided he would quit his job, separating from an institution he increasingly regarded as contaminated.[1]

His farewell sermon in March 1841 served as a kind of confession, a "coming-out" in the contemporary sense in which he proudly owned beliefs that some of his parishioners regarded as "infidelity." He addressed his congregation in order "to give a full disclosure of all my heresies; to confess that I was a peace man, a temperance man, an abolitionist, a transcendentalist, a friend of radical reform in our social institutions." In one of the most moving calls for social justice to emerge from Transcendentalism, Ripley affirms that "human equality" is "a deep, solemn, vital truth, written by the Almighty in the laws of our being." He explained to his parishioners that he could no longer muzzle the radical demand for social justice he felt Christianity required, and he argued that what they needed was a revolution, not a Sunday morning get-together to recite words that had become dead to them. He believed that all preaching should aim to overthrow slavery, labor oppression, and poverty and to end war. Ripley's embrace of the most radical theoretical implications of Christianity had made him hate its pantomimed practice, along with capitalism and the society it structured. The congregation wished him well. He and his wife, Sophia, packed their things and left Boston for good.[2]

Ripley had decided that if the church would not redeem the world, he would have to do it himself. He would establish a cooperative, equal society apart from the ugly competition of the capitalist mainstream and hope that the rest of mankind would eventually join him. He floated the idea to the Transcendental Club, and *The Dial,* their magazine, ran two articles promoting the Ripleys' scheme, likely written by Elizabeth Palmer Peabody. In the first, she describes a group of men and women who felt it necessary to "come out from the world" to claim a truer life, no longer benefiting like hypocrites from the system they critiqued. If people started to live truly as Christ directed, they would be enacting the kingdom of God on earth: they would be the Second Coming. She enjoins readers to move beyond merely hearing the words of Jesus, to manifest them instead: "Now let us see him, *let us be him,* and see what will come of that." At the Chardon Street Convention, Alcott had recently articulated the same shocking idea that all people should embrace their equality with Christ: "For a man to be a Christian, is to be in degree and kind what Jesus was. It is to believe that he is inspired as Jesus was, and holy as Jesus was, and divine as Jesus was." The Transcendentalists openly declared that right-living men and women could *be* Christ, the very idea that landed Jones Very in the madhouse.[3]

Ripley and his wife, along with ten others, including the author Nathaniel Hawthorne, came out from the world and went back to the land. They bought a two-hundred-acre former dairy farm in West Roxbury with rolling hills, grassy meadows, a pine forest, and a brook running through it. Brook Farm. They would perform all the domestic and agricultural work of the place themselves rather than relying on the labor of others. They would institute gender equality as well, compensating male and female members at the same rate. The group moved in to the farmhouse already standing on the property and called it the Hive. The dining room and library there would continue to serve as central community spaces even when they had constructed a number of other buildings, including greenhouses, shops, and those they called the Nest, where classes were held and overnight guests stayed, and the Eyrie, the Ripleys' house. They invited Emerson to become part of the venture, invest some money, and live with them communally; he thought about it for five weeks, then wrote to Ripley, "I have decided not to join it, yet very slowly, and I may almost say with penitence."[4]

Ripley was thirty-nine years old. He grew out his beard and curly brown hair, put on some muscle, and got a suntan. He traded his ministerial robe for a bohemian farmer style that caught on with the rest of them. The women wore short skirts over trousers, their long hair streaming down loose, often adorned with flowers and vines. The men wore brightly colored peasant tunics, sack trousers, heavy work boots, and straw hats, a getup that got them pelted with rocks by laughing Bostonians on their visits back to the city.[5]

For some, the vision of elite gentlemen getting a kick out of washing dishes and shoveling manure—or Hawthorne's proud report in a letter to his fiancée: "I have milked a cow!"—will occasion eye rolling. They were dabbling for the first time with performing their own domestic and agricultural work, while most Americans labored all day on a farm or in a factory with no breaks for discussions of Spinoza and Shakespeare. But Brook Farm was more than just a pastoral summer camp for the gifted and talented. Their excitement about crossing social boundaries was driven not by mere escapism or experimentation but by a desire to prefigure a classless society, an attempt to blaze a path out of industrial capitalism that others might follow. Disillusioned with American society, the Brook Farmers and other communitarians of the 1840s channeled the religious fervor of the age into social theory: the promise of conversion, the dream of redemption for all mankind, global regeneration. Their experiences testify to the crucial but ambivalent role of activist hope, the utopianism that is essential to social justice work but that can also discredit and overshadow it.[6]

But even more important than their visions for the future was the simple joy these artsy farmer-intellectuals began to find in daily life. Their memoirs describe an air of merriment and effervescence that they never knew off the commune. They were constantly outdoors in all kinds of weather, chopping firewood, planting and harvesting, rambling through the woods. There were rounds of picnics, boating or ice-skating on the nearby Charles River, putting on plays. They ran a school, their most successful venture, which Harvard endorsed for its incoming students' preparatory work; it was attended by the younger relatives of the Transcendentalist set, but it also had a reputation beyond New England, drawing students from the southern states and even abroad. The communal food at Brook Farm was simple, and they went through periods of retrenchment when it was quite sparse. But sitting together on rough pine benches in a whitewashed room, like-minded men and women laughing and quipping over a meal they made together, they felt that they had truly created the world they wanted, far from the stuffy lives they left behind.

Thousands of visitors came to get a taste of it. Margaret Fuller and Emerson came occasionally to read works in progress. Many evenings, residents would quickly wash the dinner dishes and clear the dining hall for a dance. Special "fancy parties" were held out in the grove. A group would occasionally walk all the way to Boston for a concert on a warm night, looking at the stars and chatting on the long walk back, going to bed only shortly before they had to get up to start their farm chores. One evening, the Hutchinson Family Singers from New Hampshire came to stay overnight. They were celebrities in the United States and Europe, lending their voices to abolitionism and other causes with activist folk songs in tight four-part harmony. One of their best-known songs was called "There's a Good Time Coming," and they likely sang it for the Brook Farmers. Perhaps everyone sat outside that evening after dinner, or on the floor and stairs of the Eyrie, listening to the three brothers and their sister harmonize and likely joining in for the refrain. The lyrics describe a future world with no war or poverty, and universal literacy for children whose limbs and minds grow strong from the outdoor play that replaces industrial toil. There's a good time coming, each verse promises. We may not live to see the day. Wait a little longer.[7]

———

COMMUNITY MEMBERS WOULD long remember those early years on the farm as an arcadian idyll. But financially, the picture was not as pretty. It turned out that Brook Farm did not have excellent soil, and even in the best scenarios farms require a huge initial investment and generally do not become profitable right away. Ripley implemented austerity measures where he could, but he needed a bigger change to make the place run more efficiently and attract new investors. To these practical concerns, he applied a startling solution.

Like thousands of others, the Brook Farmers subscribed to the *New-York Tribune,* a leading daily newspaper edited by Horace Greeley, champion of a range of progressive causes. Since 1842, the paper had run a column by a man named Albert Brisbane on the front page. From this large platform, Brisbane spread a doctrine that he called Association. The Brook Farmers would have found a lot to like in Brisbane's columns, nodding their heads in agreement with his claim that "isolated man without social interests and sympathies is, like a single note in music, valueless. We must combine and associate large masses to develop the harmonies of human nature." They likely approved of Brisbane's insistence that life could be more pleasurable and fulfilling, that mainstream American life was not only repressive but also ugly.[8]

Ripley was already aware of Brisbane and his ideas by the time they began appearing in the paper, having read his book-length presentation of Association when it first appeared in 1840 and reviewed it for the Transcendentalist *Dial*. Brisbane's *Social Destiny of Man* was at once more minutely practical and more wildly idealistic than Brownson's "Laboring Classes," the other major anticapitalist work to appear that year. Brisbane's vision offered an escape from the dysfunction of mainstream America without the apocalyptic class warfare predicted by Brownson. Indeed, although Brisbane's proposal for the reorganization of industry and society was unsparingly critical of the status quo, its tone was imbued with the dazzling, possibly deranged utopianism of Brisbane's guru, the late French philosopher Charles Fourier.

Brisbane was a rich young New Yorker who had gone to Europe to study philosophy with Hegel and other luminaries, eventually coming upon the works of Fourier. Instantly converted, he set out to meet the master, settling in Paris among a group of young French intellectuals who were equally enraptured. Fourier was by then an old man. He never smiled, nor did he care to defend or further explain the perplexing ideas set out in his books. He was waiting for a millionaire to drop by his apartment and offer to fund the construction of a glorious palace on a massive tract of land, as his work had described. In the meantime, he took the young American's money in exchange for a series of lectures on the material. Brisbane became Fourier's key disciple, bringing his ideas to the most sympathetic and proactive audience they would ever find, precisely at the moment when Americans were casting around for alternatives to the capitalist economy that seemed a volatile and dangerous failure.

Fourier held that human society and the planet Earth itself were evolving through a series of stages. The current state, "Civilization," was "monstrously defective," but it would eventually yield to a future utopian state of "Harmony," in which nature itself would be re-formed: seas would brim with lemon soda, helpfully revised animals like the "anti-lion" would roam the earth, and people would be seven feet tall and amphibious, sporting a long tail with a hand at the end. At the core of his theory of social life were "the passions," or desires and drives, which he believed should be allowed freest rein, propelling people to make fulfilling contributions to their communities. Civilized life, with its insistence on "morality," was miserable and oppressive, he believed, demanding that we deny our desires like hypocrites rather than understanding them as the forces meant to steer our decisions and behavior. In the coming state of Harmony, people would live in groups of 1,620 in communal palaces called phalanxes. Their days would be structured to gratify a catalog of desires, with special attention to sensual enjoyment, fulfilling work, and near-constant socializing, including sex of every imaginable variety, interrupted only by four and a half hours of sleep. Fourier had minute plans for every aspect of life in the phalanx, dictating what varieties of fruits would be grown, how children would be cared for and educated, how living spaces would be ventilated. He specified the menus for glorious feasts, as well as myriad configurations for sexual intercourse that would take place once monogamy was obsolete (although that last part of his plans remained an open secret among his American followers, at least initially).[9]

Brisbane returned to the United States and in 1840 published *Social Destiny of Man*, a translation of Fourier's ideas about industry, the economy, and communal life. The book introduced American readers to an idiosyncratic vocabulary of passions, aromas, and adhesiveness, which would be aped by the most affected radicals for the next twenty years. In it, Brisbane called for the wholesale reorganization of society, starting from the premise that labor could and must be made attractive and pleasurable. On the phalanx, he explained, workers would cycle through a variety of useful labors in a single day, moving quickly from shepherding to gardening to fishing, contributing to the work that attracted them most, a reaction against industrial labor that had also been articulated by Emerson and the Transcendentalists. The hope for a beautiful, harmonious society was an irresistible lure for many in this dark time, and Americans flocked to Brisbane's proposal for a utopian socialist future of pleasure and satisfaction in work and at leisure.

Brisbane left the sexual stuff out of that first translation—though, of course, plenty of Americans could read French and sought out the original texts. He retained, however, Fourier's focus on women's rights and his attack on marriage. For Brisbane, the cherished institution of the family and the domestic home were the rotten core of American oppression: "The cabin, the cottage, or the dwelling house of civilization, with its monotony, with the daily repetition of its petty and harassing cares, with its antisocial spirit . . . debilitates the energies of the soul and produces apathy and intellectual death."[10] The Transcendentalists, a group that included brilliant women like Elizabeth Palmer Peabody, Sophia Ripley, and Margaret Fuller, were already primed for these ideas as well. The Brook Farmers were actively seeking an alternative to the isolated household, and Fuller's trailblazing writings and conversations made inquiry into gender and marriage a core strand of their intellectual project.

The impact of Fourier's thought on American culture has been underestimated, probably because it is difficult to believe that thousands of Americans, including highly educated members of the elite, earnestly embraced these ideas. But they did. Fourier's proposals (as presented by Brisbane) gained immediate traction, and phalanxes quickly sprang up in New Jersey, Massachusetts, Wisconsin, Ohio, Michigan, Pennsylvania, and beyond. There were twenty-nine phalanxes in the United States, with a total of some 3,800 members occupying thirty thousand acres of land. And these full-time residents represented only a small percentage of Associationists, as American Fourierists were called. Tens of thousands more read Fourierist pamphlets and newspapers, or attended lectures, or joined a Fourier Club in places like Pittsburgh, Rochester, Cincinnati, and rural Maine. The leading contemporary historian of this movement estimates that it had 100,000 members at its peak.[11]

Without a doubt, Fourier's socialism was "utopian," as Marx and Engels later labeled it, but we should resist the temptation to dismiss it on that score. American national rhetoric has always been utopian and futurist in character. Indeed, many ideas that once seemed quixotic have since taken on the appearance of common sense, becoming major motors of national history and identity. "Manifest destiny," for example, was coined in 1845 to express the view that Americans were a special people fated to overtake the continent and all the people who already inhabited it: "The far-reaching, the boundless future will be the era of American greatness. In its magnificent domain of space and time, the nation of many nations is destined to manifest to mankind the excellence of divine principles." This rhetoric literally shaped the nation as we know it, fueling the imperialist push to the Pacific. Evangelical Christianity was another key utopian discourse of the time, drawing Americans by the thousands to the revival tent with the dream of being converted into something new, born again, redeemed by selfless love, living on forever in paradise after death.[12]

Thus, in examining the utopian tendency of nineteenth-century American radicalism, we might consider what competing forms of utopianism it countered. Rather than musing at the imaginative excesses of the communitarians, we should consider the larger battle of speculative visions for what America might mean and become. Fourier is a flamboyant exemplar of the relationship between social critique and utopian imagining, both of which dare to insist that another and better world is possible.

———

THE NEW YORK–BASED Associationists, with Greeley and Brisbane at the lead, had already helped to establish a model phalanx in New Jersey, and they were looking for others. Their growing movement could tap into funding for anyone who would give it a serious try. Brisbane started visiting Brook Farm in May 1843, hoping to convince Ripley that Association would save his project. At the end of that year, Fourierism hit Boston with a major convention that drew the area's many reformers and ultras; William Lloyd Garrison and Frederick Douglass were among the attendees. As we have seen, abolitionists were hearty supporters of many causes not directly focused on the emancipation of the enslaved. But they had reason to feel wary of the way the Associationist movement regarded itself as the "total reform" that would contain all others. The Fourierists charged that movements for the abolition of slavery or for women's rights were trying to repair a rotten plank when the whole framework of society needed to be replaced. Ripley, for example, believed wholeheartedly that chattel slavery should be abolished, but he charged that the abolitionists would merely deliver the freed slaves into the hands of greedy capitalists, while Association would liberate all of humanity, including the industrial "wage slaves" of the North. Ripley had come to see in Fourier's theories the sweeping, millennial regeneration he sought. By the time of this convention, he was a true believer and decided to convert his commune into a Fourierist phalanx.[13]

This involved a few changes. First, the Brook Farmers reorganized their labor into series and groups, as Fourier had described. They created the Agricultural Series (which contained the Farming Group, Orchard Group, and Garden Group), the Domestic Series (for the Kitchen Group, Laundry Group, and Waiters' Group), the Manufacturing Series, and the Festal Series (for overseeing entertainment and celebrations). They began construction on a large "unitary edifice," or phalanstery, to house them and their activities in the grand communal style Fourier had indicated. Putting their unparalleled intellectual firepower to work for the movement and creating a new source of income, they became the publishers of the leading Associationist periodical, *The Harbinger,* in June 1845. Thus Brook Farm became the nucleus of Fourierist propaganda in the United States.[14]

Ripley and his colleagues regarded their movement not as a utopian experiment but as a practical agenda for the fight against capitalism. Instead of hanging all their hopes for Association on Brook Farm and the other model phalanxes, they also worked with the labor movement to bring Fourierism to the working class. Industrial workers in New England were beginning to organize on a mass scale, and Association was poised to become their method. In the 1830s, women factory workers led some of the first organized labor actions in American history, marching through Lowell en masse, making public speeches for "the rights of women" against "monied aristocracy," and staging a number of successful strikes and work stoppages to protest wage cuts. After 1840, many workers were attracted by Fourier's plan for a cooperative society that would abolish poverty and provide recreation and fulfillment for all. Both male and female laborers in factory towns were active in Fourier Clubs, cooperative stores, and Unions of Associationists. A leading labor newspaper, *Voice of Industry,* had three Fourierist editors in a row. Sarah Bagley and Huldah Stone, millworkers who had founded the Lowell Female Labor Reform Association, became involved with the national Associationist movement as well, speaking alongside Brisbane on convention platforms.[15]

In 1844, the Fall River Mechanics' and Laborers' Association called for a New England labor convention to bring together workers across the region to agitate for shorter hours and higher wages. The convention met in October in Boston's Faneuil Hall, well known to the attendees as the site of American Revolutionary speeches. In attendance were large delegations from Massachusetts mill towns like Lynn, Lowell, and Fall River, as well as from the Brook Farm Phalanx. The convention issued a general call for the end of capitalism and considered methods for achieving the more immediate goal of a ten-hour workday. They formed the New England Workingmen's Association and elected the Brook Farmer Lewis Ryckman as president. Ryckman was a cordwainer (a shoemaker) who had moved to the commune from New York City. His leadership in the group suggests that there was not a hard line dividing the "real" workers in the labor movement from reformer-intellectuals versed in socialist theory, although tensions between these groups shaped labor movements throughout the century.[16]

Ryckman appointed Ripley to the organization's executive committee, and he and Brisbane drafted a resolution presenting the basic tenets of Association, which was popular with most of the delegates. They endorsed "attractive industry" and the organization of workers into groups and series. At their meeting the following spring, Brisbane gave a rousing Associationist speech, and then Ryckman introduced a resolution calling for an immediate revolution in industry and for "the formation of an Industrial Congress analogous to that which fostered the liberties of the American Republic." He also proposed that they organize "a permanent Industrial Revolutionary Government," on the model of the confederation of states under the U.S. Constitution—in other words, a splinter socialist America to fight the capitalist one.[17]

The fact that this proposed workers' revolution to install French socialism would keep the structure of the government intact indicates how central American exceptionalism was to Associationist propaganda. Although communitarians like Ripley had come out of American society, founding separatist colonies explicitly in opposition to mainstream values, they did not share the virulent anti-Americanism of the Garrisonians. Indeed, they argued that "the peculiar history of this nation convinces us that it has been prepared by Providence for the working out of glorious issues. Its position, its people, its free institutions, all prepare it for the manifestation of a true Social Order." Despite the undeniably foreign origin of their philosophy, the Associationists presented their plan as the culmination of the American Revolution. In Ripley's mind, Association would be the realization of the founders' vision for America, not its end. The national motto *E pluribus unum,* he noted, "is but another expression of Universal Unity." The Associationists described Fourier as a new Columbus, the model phalanxes as "cities set on a hill." In other words, Fourier was the discoverer of a newer, truer America, and the Associationists were living closer to the founding fathers' intentions, beginning with colonies inside the territorial United States that would soon cover the continent and then the world.[18]

More astonishingly, Ripley believed Fourier to be the fulfillment not just of American national destiny but also of Christian teleology. He had spilled a lot of ink criticizing the church as an institution, but rather than abandoning Christianity, he seemed to want to update the Holy Trinity with a new member. The birthday party the Brook Farmers threw for the late philosopher in 1845 indicates the extent to which he was venerated as much more than an intellectual influence. They assembled in the evening in the dining hall, where the ceiling had been hung with evergreen garlands. The corners of the room were decorated with fragrant roses, jasmines, and calla lilies from the greenhouse. In the center, tables bearing food and more flowering plants were arranged in the shape of a cross. One wall was emblazoned with a biblical verse promising that God will send a teacher, paired with a quotation from Fourier suggesting that he was in fact that teacher, the Holy Spirit. Others displayed brightly striped banners with Associationist key words. At one end of the room, a plaster bust of Fourier, recently arrived from Paris, was crowned with myrtle. Huge boughs had been arranged nearby to spell out his name and the year of his birth, 1772. Flanking this were a number of important symbols—a beehive representing industry and an anchor representing hope—and a large white lyre, entwined with flowers, with strings painted in rainbow colors, an emblem of the seven spiritual passions he theorized. Ripley read from the Bible, choosing verses that prophesied a coming time of "sublime harmonies." The Frenchman's sacred status at Brook Farm was made even more explicit when someone proposed a toast to "Fourier, the second coming of Christ!"[19]

But not all of the Brook Farmers worshipped Fourier. Amelia Russell recalled that the culture changed after the conversion to a phalanx in a way that destroyed its Transcendental charms: "there was much loud talking" in the new Fourierist phase, "and a bustling air given to the place which destroyed its pleasant quietness." Although the new system was ostensibly based on individual passions, she felt that "a compulsory feeling which gave you the sensation of not belonging to yourself" had replaced "the voluntary labor we had before enjoyed." She didn't like Brisbane, who had come to live with them for a time and lectured them in the evenings so that the rank-and-file members could understand the philosophy behind the changes. Russell recalled that she "annoyed my associates by showing my amusement at some of the wild theories advanced." She had been astounded by the notion that their activities could physically affect the earth to the point that there would be two suns and a lemonade sea, but many of her friends believed it. For some, it was exciting to rush through the day's revolving variety of attractive labors on the new model in their work groups and series. But it also caused inconveniences—like when an escaped pig was discovered eating up the cornfield and a member of the Miscellaneous Group could not be found to go catch him.[20]

———

FOURIERISM SEEMED TO BE paying off for Brook Farm. In 1845, its second year as a phalanx, Ripley balanced the books for the first time and ended up with a cash surplus. The community also welcomed an influx of new residents, most of whom were tradesmen and artisans who could help it become financially sustainable. The prospects of the phalanx and the Associationist movement it headquartered looked promising right up until March 3, 1846—when someone dashed into one of their dance parties shouting, "Fire!"

It was the phalanstery, the linchpin of Brook Farm's full operation as a model Fourierist community. Residents had been working on this massive structure for almost two years, and construction had just resumed that day after a winter break. A stray spark left over from the carpenters' fire caught the woodwork as the community members gathered to celebrate the project's pending completion. When they looked toward the construction site, they saw flames shooting out of the upper windows and blowing out doors, rapidly engulfing the unfinished rooms. The blaze spread quickly; a nearby building was smoking and too hot to touch, apparently saved only by the heroic work of a neighbor on the roof. Fire engines pushed through snowbound roads from the neighboring towns of Newton, Brookline, and Jamaica Plain, but there was little they could do. Within an hour and a half, the phalanstery burned completely to the ground.[21]

Some onlookers "wept, and some stood in mute despair." Sophia Ripley hid her face, unable to bear the sight of the destruction.

But other community members had a very different reaction. Marianne Dwight remarked, "It was glorious beyond description." The next morning, in an enraptured letter to a friend, she recounted the pleasure and beauty she found in the destruction of her community's grandest undertaking:

> An immense, clear blue flame mingled for a while with the others and rose high in the air,—like liquid turquoise and topaz. It came from the melting glass. Rockets, too, rose in the sky, and fell in glittering gems of every rainbow hue—much like our 4th of July fire-works.

Her admiration of the exquisite flames consuming the project in which her community had invested so much time and money was not a uniquely perverse response from one young witness swept up in the spectacle. Another resident, John Codman, also recalled the fire as "a grand and magnificent sight!" He ran to the greenhouse for buckets of water to throw on the blaze but stopped in his tracks and "uttered an exclamation of surprise at the lovely display." The flowers were "lighted up with a heavenly glow of color, and so startlingly beautiful that in spite of my haste I lingered a moment to look on them."[22]

The fire reflecting off the deep, bright snow was visible nine miles away in Boston and lit up every inch of the Brook Farm Phalanx at a time before electric lights, when no one saw much of anything at night beyond what a whale-oil candle could reveal. One man set out from the city toward the glow to offer his help, always thinking the fire must be just over the crest of the next field, eventually finding that he had walked for miles and still not arrived. One neighbor brought all the food he could spare from his house and ran to other nearby farms for milk to help feed the firemen and some two hundred bystanders. The Brook Farmers brewed coffee and sliced up the bread that was supposed to have fed the community the following day. Somehow, they pieced together a late-night picnic that fed a "hungry multitude," virtually reenacting the Gospel miracles that their leader had controversially disavowed a decade

Brook Farm, oil on panel by Josiah Wolcott, ca. 1846.
Massachusetts Historical Society

earlier. Ripley climbed up on a table to address the crowd, even managing a pun about greeting them with a *warm* reception. But under his forced smile, he was pale and stricken, fully aware that they had all just witnessed the funeral pyre of his experiment at Brook Farm. No one knows how the Fourierist zeitgeist might have played out if this grand new headquarters had been put to use.

This fast, beautiful fire is an irresistible if ambiguous metaphor. The awed communitarians seem like wild-eyed romantics high on a hit of the sublime, finding beauty and splendor everywhere but without enough sense to fear physical danger and financial loss. The fire was the harsh intrusion of reality, unstoppably eating up utopian dreams. But its glow was a beckoning horizon always almost reached, calling you to walk into the night to lend what help you could. It was an alternative Independence Day celebration, as Marianne Dwight described it. It was Brook Farm itself and all the utopian projects of its time: it lit the dark with a dazzling shock, mobilizing a community around an urgent common cause, their faces radiant with a weird illumination.

CHAPTER 7

Wheat Bread and
Seminal Losses

The Brook Farmers started to disperse in the months after the fire, some living communally in Boston; by the following year, the commune was closed, and *The Harbinger*, with Ripley still at the helm, moved its operations to New York City. Most of the other Fourierist phalanxes founded in the early 1840s also folded by the end of the decade. All had been plagued by financial troubles, but some radical commentators argued that there was another reason they failed: the members had held on to traditional marriage, even though they knew it was incompatible with Fourier's vision of community. In his initial 1840 translation, Brisbane had used the model of passional attraction to propose a new system of labor, but Fourier's central tenet that society must fulfill human desires clearly applied to sex as well as to work.[1]

By the end of the decade, other Associationists put monogamy squarely on the table for dissection. A handful of works on Fourier appeared hinting that there was more to his philosophy than the reorganization of industry, crowned in 1848 by Henry James Sr.'s anonymous translation of *Love in the Phalanstery*, a work on sexual and domestic arrangements in Harmony. After that explosive publication, Fourierist lingo—"passional attraction," "harmonial attachments," "amative affinities," and the like—was the chosen mode of expression for a generation of sex radicals. Brisbane issued a volume on the "human passions" in 1856, followed the next year by a new edition of *Social Destiny of Man* containing a chapter titled

"The Marriage Question." Published with Henry Clapp Jr.—the "King of Bohemia" and a key figure in the poet Walt Whitman's life and career—this new material stated frankly that in the phalanxes of the future there would be innovative erotic arrangements to address all "amatory varieties."[2]

In his writings on sex, Fourier had worked out minute theories and plans for countless erotic circumstances, including group sex, lesbianism, and the copulation of planets, a whole "new amorous world." Fourier believed there was a broad diversity of sexual preferences and also that people's desires often changed. He argued that society must provide a "sexual minimum" to ensure that all people—including the ugly, the elderly, and those with unusual predilections—were gratified. He described the love of self-obsessed monogamous couples as "indecent" and regarded the marital bed and the family dinner table with particular horror, believing that they turn life's greatest pleasures into monotonous duties to be endured.[3]

Thus, even as the relevance of Fourierism as a socialist plan for reorganizing industry faded, its critique of marriage and the home inspired multiple strands of American feminism, including cooperative housekeeping movements and, perhaps most surprisingly, the women's suffrage movement. But the clearest product of this shift was the robust second act that Fourierism enjoyed in the 1850s as the basis of Free Love. Among the sexual dissidents who espoused this goal, some called unequivocally for the abolition of marriage, denouncing it in the strongest terms possible as "the prolific mother of disease and crime" and "a system of rape." Others hoped that simply making divorce easily accessible would purify and strengthen the institution by rendering it truly voluntary. There were "exclusivists," who practiced serial monogamy, and "varietists," who saw no reason that sex and love should be limited to two people. Some even ventured beyond heterosexuality, affirming that "adhesiveness between the same sex can be, sometimes, stronger than death." What those who claimed the Free Love label shared was the conviction that marriage was the root of women's oppression and that sex should only be regulated by the individual, not by the church, the state, or popular notions of respectability.[4]

Although "Free Love" conjures a vision of anything-goes hedonism—and that was certainly what contemporary critics imagined—the movement's ideas about sex were surprisingly ascetic from the beginning. Many antebellum anti-marriage radicals believed that people should have less sex, and specifically that men should almost never ejaculate. While this perspective was not universally adopted—others claimed that tens of thousands of Americans of both sexes were dying annually from "sexual starvation"—infrequent sexual intercourse and the conservation of semen were accepted tenets of the Free Love creed, pillars of their feminist argument against marital rape. Many recommended that men only expend semen a few times in a lifetime when trying to conceive a child and otherwise enjoy conserving it in their bodies, where it would impart the glow of healthful energy. Too much sexual stimulation, they warned, would lead to diseases of the lungs and digestive organs, memory loss, insanity, violent convulsions, mysterious death, and the conception of "deformed" children. Strangely, these ideas all started with white bread.

———

ALTHOUGH THE BOOMING modernization of American life that began in the Jacksonian period thrilled many, others lamented the traditional ways being wiped out by industrialization. Goods were no longer made at home, and even bread, that symbolically laden foodstuff, was increasingly produced by commercial bakers with flour derived from the cheapest wheat on the market. Consumers developed a taste for the soft, thin-crusted white bread they supplied, tossing aside the unrefined farmhouse loaves that had once been a daily staple. This offense against the traditional American diet cut Sylvester Graham to the quick. Graham was a rather sickly and nervous temperance preacher who had come to blame Americans' increasingly processed diet for a range of ills. He advocated old-fashioned, hand-milled whole wheat bread, made at home by a wife and mother. And his recommendations reached far beyond bread to condemn a range of "stimulating" substances. Tea and coffee, vinegar, mustard, sugar, meat—any rich or highly seasoned food, Graham warned, caused the body to be "debased, degraded, diseased, and destroyed!" His uncompromising rhetoric led him to be attacked by mobs three times in the 1830s, one of which was made up of butchers and bakers furious at his assault on their trades.[5]

Graham's dietary proscriptions gained traction with progressives and reformers for the remainder of the century, including Abby Kelley, William Lloyd Garrison, Henry David Thoreau, and Victoria Woodhull. His vegan teetotalism appealed to them as a form of radical abstention from what they perceived to be the excesses of mainstream culture. There was a Grahamite table at Brook Farm, and the diet was followed so strictly at Oberlin College that one professor was fired for using black pepper.

Graham's nutritional theories went hand in glove with a program of sexual abstinence. His goal in insisting on bland, wholesome fare was to cool down bodies erotically overheated by modern life. Believing that the loss of semen debilitates a man more than the loss of twenty times as much blood, he declared that it was not necessary for a man to ejaculate a single time between puberty and death, even if he lived a hundred years. To avoid dangerous seminal emissions, he prescribed methods to cool the body inside (through a bland vegan diet) and out (with cold baths in the middle of the night and special pajamas and beds designed to avoid genital contact).

Reading Graham and his disciples in the medical literature of the 1830s, you could become convinced that young Americans were dropping like flies from mysterious illnesses brought on by rampant masturbation. Although Graham considered any ejaculation a potentially harmful drain on a man's "mental faculties," masturbation was the most dangerous because it requires the violent concentration of the whole body toward an artificial and pointless end. Sex outside marriage was more damaging, because more exciting, than sex between a husband and a wife. In single men, "the genital organs are kept under an habitual excitement, which is reflected or diffused over the whole nervous system; and disturbs, and disorders all the functions of the body, and impairs all the tissues." But with a husband and wife, "all these causes either entirely lose, or are exceedingly diminished in their effect. They become accustomed to each other's body, and their parts no longer excite an impure imagination." Best of all, at least for Graham, is that the married couple's "sexual intercourse . . . is very seldom."[6]

Still, even as Graham vaunted marriage as "an institution founded in the constitutional nature of things, and inseparably connected with the highest welfare of man," he warned that it offered no safe haven from the danger of sexual overindulgence: "Beyond all question, an immeasurable amount of evil results to the human family from sexual excess within the precincts of wedlock." For many of Graham's most significant intellectual descendants, the numerous radical followers he never could have foreseen or desired, this was his most important insight. The possibility that sex within marriage could be denounced as unnatural or unhealthy opened a world of possibility for the Free Lovers. Although Graham might have intended his sex theories as conservative backlash against anti-marriage agitators like Owen and Wright, he ultimately introduced a legitimate way to talk and write publicly on the topic. His ideas about sex were adopted and adapted into the critiques of marriage by the next generation of Free Love socialists, who framed their discussions of erotic life in terms of health.[7]

Because of their roots in this program of bodily self-denial, nineteenth-century American countercultures sometimes conjured visions of a perverse and laughable asceticism, the flip side of the lush scenes of hedonistic indulgence dreamed up by the sensational media. Herman Melville's novel *Pierre,* for example, finds the protagonist cohabiting with three women in a communal settlement with the Apostles, a group of "strange nondescript adventurers and artists, and indigent philosophers of all sorts." These "Teleological Theorists, and Social Reformers, and political propagandists" scrub their scrawny bodies with a stiff brush with the windows open on frigid winter mornings. At their parties, the only refreshments are "a bushel-basket of Graham crackers" and "a huge jug of Adam's Ale," which is to say, cold water.[8]

IN THE WAKE of Graham's death in 1851, Free Lovers blended his austere hypochondria with the hallucinogenic eroticism of Fourier. The marriage of these strange bedfellows is apparent in the major works of the 1850s that presented bold cases for abolishing marriage. Chief among them was Marx Edgeworth Lazarus's 1852 *Love vs. Marriage,* a lengthy takedown of "civilized marriage—that perpetual offense against spontaneity, against decency, and against humanitary devotion." Lazarus was the son of a prosperous, southern Jewish family. He had long hair and a long beard, sparkly dark eyes, and a Fourierist vocabulary that made his conversational style quirky at best. Five years earlier, he had lived part-time at Brook Farm to work on *The Harbinger* alongside George Ripley, promoting Association with the Transcendentalists.

Lazarus describes marriage as "a compound selfishness, an *egoism a deux,*" in which "the parties contracting it have virtually asserted their independence of society, and embezzled each other in perpetual

Marx Edgeworth Lazarus.
Joseph A. Labadie Collection, University of Michigan Library

monopoly from the passional public." The work's utopian mysticism mimics the style and substance of Fourier, referencing, for example, the aromas of the stars and the future harmonization of the earth's climates. The author's time among the Transcendentalists clearly shows in his citations of Emerson's poetry and essays. Aligning himself with a tradition of radicalism going back to Robert Owen, Lazarus proclaims that just as political liberty had been "the subject of a life-struggle for the American people" some years ago,

> now comes the question of Passional and Social Liberty, and there is another declaration of independence to be made, and another revolution to be achieved for the conquest of that happiness, the right to whose pursuit constitutes one of the prominent articles in our last declaration. That was the shadow, the sham fight, the parade, the external contest with foreign powers, but now comes the substance, the real fight, the battle of souls, the struggle without quarter between the forces of heaven and hell in our midst, and the hottest of the fight must be fought upon this central position of the love relation between the sexes.

A new declaration of independence, the next frontier in the fight for liberty: this rhetoric was de rigueur in radical texts throughout the century, as we've seen. But to most readers today, some of Lazarus's ideas about sexual physiology would seem far from revolutionary.

After singing the praises of variety in love for three hundred pages, Lazarus concludes his tome with an appendix offering a scientific analysis of the dangers of losing semen. However, he gave this Grahamite warning an important Free Love revision, arguing that in the current state of civilization many men live in "forced privation of natural coition, either by want of opportunities, or by moral and religious prejudices," and consequently "fall victims to the abominable practice of self-pollution, which is suicide of the most degrading and horrible kind, destroying soul and body by inches." If sexual relations were free, sperm would not become dangerously bottled up and then be expelled involuntarily or in masturbation, which everyone knew could kill you. Lazarus offers a list of treatments for those suffering from involuntary seminal losses, including sweeping nitrate of silver over the urethra to cauterize it, two cold waist-down baths a day, refraining from stimulants such as eggs, cheese, oysters and other shellfish, animal and fish skins, mushrooms, asparagus, and celery. He also recommends wrapping the pelvis in a wet towel overnight to keep the area cool.

Finally, a single sentence in this long postscript makes it clear that this issue had deep personal significance for the author: "It is no longer ink that stains this paper, it is the blood-tear of agony wrung from the collapsed heart of the victim of seminal losses!" Despite his lively career as a writer and activist, Lazarus was tortured by a secret illness. When he was living at the Brook Farm Phalanx, he called on George Ripley to witness his last will and testament. Perhaps believing himself close to death, Lazarus wanted to bequeath his inheritance to advance "the cause of Human Redemption" through the founding of another Fourierist phalanx. He was sick with "spermatorrhea," meaning in this case nocturnal emissions (and, presumably, the symptoms caused by his anxiety about them). As a devout Grahamite, he believed that he had to fear for his sanity, even his life, if he continued to lose semen. Afraid to sleep at night and becoming unhinged, he went to Providence, Rhode Island, for electric shock treatments. Other prescriptions for his problem at this time included encasing the penis in a miniature iron maiden, applying anal leeches, using suppositories of toxic substances, even castration. Not long after the publication of his pioneering anti-marriage book, Lazarus married, the most recommended treatment for his ailment, and disappeared from the movement. Returning to his native section, he served briefly in the Civil War, a doctor in the Confederate army.[9]

———

When Lazarus's book was published, his former colleague George Ripley had just become the literary editor at the *New-York Tribune* and sent it out for review by none other than Henry James Sr., whose contribution to the sexual literature of Association years earlier had inadvertently paved the way for the movement. Both James and the paper's editor, Horace Greeley, were eager to distance themselves from the new crop of Fourierists like Lazarus who were frankly embracing the sexual elements of the philosophy. James used Lazarus's book as an occasion to articulate a far tamer call for more accessible divorce so that people who had come to hate each other could separate rather than drag down the institution by remaining married. This led to a printed exchange between James and Greeley, who defended indissoluble marriage and rejected any loosening of the divorce laws. Of course, Greeley was also a Fourierist leader, second in importance only to Brisbane in the spread of these ideas nationwide, and a president of the American Union of Associationists in the 1840s. He was still a socialist in the 1850s, but he had no truck with Free Love and regarded sexual questions as a distraction from the real issue of labor and capital. When a third interlocutor shoved his way into the debate, it took a turn into precisely the territory that both of them would likely have preferred to avoid.[10]

Stephen Pearl Andrews was a self-proclaimed "Individual Sovereign," a racy version of Emersonian individualism that drove his advocacy of reforms in everything from sex to the alphabet. With his fellow anarchist Josiah Warren, who had developed ideas about how to run a socialist commune from his time at Owen's New Harmony, Andrews founded Modern Times on Long Island in 1851. The community ran on an alternative, labor-based currency and exchange system, and residents purportedly tied or untied a red string around their fingers to signify their availability for passional attachments.[11]

Andrews took aim at the obvious hypocrisy of James and Greeley, old-guard Fourierists espousing such prim views about marriage. He claimed that "the same evils which exist under the Institutions of Despotism and Slavery exist likewise under the Institution of Marriage and the Family" and that the fight for justice against one of these oppressive institutions will not leave the others unscathed. Although Greeley was initially willing to entertain and

Modern Times labor currency.
American Antiquarian Society

print Andrews's anti-marriage arguments, Andrews soon crossed a line in the sand. In a rare move, he had cited a woman expert at length. Specifically, he repeated her graphic account of the medical consequences of the sexual perversion rampant in traditional marriage:

> In the Medical College at Albany there is an exposition of indissoluble marriage, which should be studied by all those who begin to see that a legalized union may be a most impure, unholy, and, consequently, unhealthy thing. In glass vases, ranged in a large cabinet in this medical museum, are uterine tumors, weighing from half a pound to twenty-four pounds. A viscus that in its ordinary state weighs a few ounces is brought, by the disease caused by amative excess,—in other words, licentiousness and impurity,—to weigh more than twenty pounds. Be it remembered, these monstrosities were produced in lawful and indissoluble wedlock.

This was too much for Greeley. He responded in a private letter to Andrews that this medical illustration was "offensive to the public sense of decency" and "unfit for publication." Andrews defended his "lady correspondent" as "a noble and pure-minded American woman, one to whom the world owes more than to any other man or woman, living or dead, for thorough investigation and appreciation of the causes of disease and the laws of health, especially to all that concerns the sexual relations and the reproduction of the race." And Andrews was not the only one to hold Mary Gove Nichols in such high esteem as a medical expert; prominent surgical journals had lauded her lectures on women's sexual health. This mainstream goodwill wore out, however, when the focus of her activism evolved from the Grahamite demand for less sex, specifically between husband and wife, to a Free Love attack on the institution of marriage.[12]

———

WHEN SHE WAS newly married, the young Mary Gove had been shocked by her husband Hiram's sexual appetites. She suffered multiple miscarriages and stillbirths in addition to one harrowing live birth that almost killed her. She believed this misery was caused by her husband's abusive sexual demands, especially during her periods of illness and recovery. Graham's warnings about the dire health consequences of sexual excess, even in marriage, struck her with the force of a revelation. They offered a scientific reason to reject sexual victimization, affirming her right to protect herself from practices that experts declared dangerous to her health. Gove quickly absorbed these new teachings and took up the genre for herself, gaining recognition as an expert sanctioned to address other women frankly about sexual health and physiology. Lucretia Mott attended one of Gove's lectures, and Elizabeth Cady Stanton likely did as well, because she and Gove were correspondents at the time.[13]

In 1839, Gove published *Solitary Vice,* an application of Graham's masturbation theories for girls and women. She also became a water-cure practitioner, learning the methods by which patients were treated for a variety of complaints with immense amounts of cold water delivered by all possible means: drinking it, bathing in it, washing isolated body parts with it, having it dropped from buckets eighteen feet overhead, and being wrapped in wet sheets for hours. Supporting herself on her earnings as a health reformer, she left her

Mary Gove Nichols.
The Library Company of Philadelphia

husband. He fought her for custody of their daughter and refused to divorce her.

Gove toured a number of communes looking for a place to live with her child among like-minded folks. She tried to join Brook Farm, offering her services as a lecturer there in exchange for her daughter's tuition, but the air of scandal already followed in her wake and Ripley denied her application. She managed to spoil the original plan for Bronson Alcott's Fruitlands, entangling one of the Englishmen who had come to found the new society in an immersive love affair that diverted him from ever setting foot on the property. Luckily, she met Marx Lazarus, and he rented a brownstone for her on East Tenth Street in Manhattan that they turned into a Grahamite commune, water-cure facility, and general hangout for unconventional reformer types. Eight or ten unmarried men and women, mostly artists of various kinds and all vegetarians, lived there as housemates. Gove administered water-cure treatments and taught classes on natural health to well-to-do ladies who sat on the floor of the unfurnished parlor.

This bohemian boardinghouse hosted regular Saturday night parties, where around forty guests—including, at various times, Greeley, Brisbane, Herman Melville, and Edgar Allan Poe—would gather for dancing and conversation. At one of these parties, Gove met a mustachioed dandy named Thomas Nichols, and once Hiram granted her a legal divorce at long last, she married him in 1848. For the next decade, the Nicholses worked as Free Love collaborators, publishing the magazine *Nichols' Monthly* and co-authoring their screed *Marriage: Its History, Character, and Results* (1854).[14]

Their work indicts marriage for turning love into disgust, making people bad citizens, wasting resources, and most of all enslaving women and making them vulnerable to rape, forced maternity, illness, and death. "Abolish all marriage this day—leave all men and women free to have or to refuse the sexual embrace, and there would ensue ten times the moral purity, and consequent health and energy, that now exists," it beseeches. "It is marriage, and the license which it gives, which debauches, enervates, degrades, and pollutes society!" At the prompting of Stephen Pearl Andrews, the couple moved to Modern Times and broke ground for an institution they planned to call Desarrollo, one of several grand projects that never got off the ground.[15]

The following year, the Nicholses attempted to deliver the Free Love message to a wide audience in a novel, as Harriet Beecher Stowe had recently done for the antislavery cause with *Uncle Tom's Cabin*. Mary Nichols's lightly fictionalized autobiography, *Mary Lyndon; or, Revelations of a Life* (1855), caused a cry of alarm from the mainstream media, but it also succeeded in generating public interest in the growing Free Love movement. *The New York Times* panned the novel at length, and the review touched off a series of alarmist, almost hysterical articles on the mounting menace of sex radicalism. It describes the author as "a coarse, sensual and shamelessly immoral person" and "a zealous propagandist of vice and immorality" eager to extol the benefits of "fine art and fornication." It suggests that previous Free Love tracts, dense with opaque Fourierist lingo, had given way to more easily digestible and therefore more dangerous works of fiction aimed at abolishing marriage. The reviewer states that the novel's goal is to "instill into the public mind that the legal institution of *Marriage, with its restraints and its duties, is at war with personal enjoyment,*—meaning thereby the indulgence of personal passions and appetites,—and *ought to be destroyed, or suppressed by the free intercourse of the sexes, without any other restraint than that of personal inclination.*" Despite the sensational italics, the *Times*'s account of Nichols's message is entirely accurate.[16]

Three weeks later, the paper ran a massive article detailing the history of the "disgusting and detestable" anti-marriage movement, revealing its philosophies, print outlets, and leading practitioners. Harking back to the recent review of *Mary Lyndon,* the article warns readers that the novel was the product not of one wayward individual but of a fully operational social movement: "It belongs to a series of efforts, skillfully devised and carried forward with systematic ingenuity and perseverance, of which the ultimate aim is to subvert the present organization of society,—destroy the institution of Marriage, as recognized by the religion and laws of Christendom, and substitute for it a Free Love System." Mentioning dozens of groups and individuals affiliated in some way with Free Love, from Margaret Fuller to the Oneida Perfectionists, this article piqued public interest by referencing a secret society in Manhattan, which had the unintended effect of ushering hundreds of curious new visitors to the gatherings hosted by Andrews in the place that some considered the headquarters of Free Love.[17]

The New York papers were obsessed with this place, where, as they reported, "every section of queerdom" was to be found, mingling promiscuously and plotting the overthrow of decent society. In an undercover exposé, a reporter who claimed to have taken the oath of membership and secrecy revealed the address at 555 Broadway and the magic words to utter to the doorman for admittance: "Passional Attraction." Walking up three dingy staircases and through a system of passageways, the reporter ultimately finds nothing more scandalous than 150 people having a rather ordinary party, with dancing and discussion, even if the average male attendee was "exceedingly hirsute," carelessly dressed, and a "rabid socialist."

The police busted the club on October 18, 1855, citing immoral speech and disorderly conduct, and arrested Albert Brisbane. (Andrews was at home with a bad cold.) In the days that followed, the leaders issued an official statement explaining that the club was not the sex den that the media made it out to be. But they stuck to their Free Love guns and took the opportunity to restate to the readers of the *Times* their radical commitments: "Stephen Pearl Andrews, the Chief of the League, is a Free-Lover, and wishes in no way to shrink from any stigma or responsibility which may be attached to that name. He is openly opposed to marriage as a compulsory bond, and rejects the idea of legal interference in love affairs. . . . He would abolish not only the conjugal idea but the private household itself." Albert Brisbane acknowledged his position as the "head of the Fourierist Party in this country, and, as such, is opposed not only to marriage, to the family, to the isolated household, to fragmentary labor, but to civilization, itself, and all its institutions."[18]

CONSIDERING THE OUTRAGE that *Mary Lyndon* inspired as a salvo from the anti-marriage movement, it is all the more surprising, perhaps even disappointing, to note that the novel ends with a wedding, the most conventional of conclusions and a seeming affirmation of the very practice the book sets out to critique. After detailing not only the injustices but the horrors of marriage and finally securing a divorce with much difficulty, Mary weds again, rejecting "false marriages" or "merely legal" marriages but championing "true marriages" based on love, equality, and, importantly, the right to terminate the relationship at will. The novel culminates with the chapter "A Divorce and a Wedding," in which Mary is released from the marital yoke only to take it up again almost immediately, as the author had done in real life.[19]

Mary Lyndon's odd recourse to the traditional marriage plot reflects the fact that most American Free Lovers were legally married, even as they were fomenting a movement against the institution. These radicals were not afraid to live their politics in other ways; they were willing to go to jail, be lambasted in the press, and endure the miserable conditions of communes. Why did they call publicly for the abolition of marriage while privately contracting legal marriages themselves?

Within the movement, opinion was mixed as to the ethics of Free Lovers who married. Francis Barry, leader of the Berlin Heights community in Ohio, criticized colleagues like the Garrisonian turned sex radical Ezra Heywood, the Nicholses, and their friend Marx Lazarus for presenting themselves as marriage abolitionists and yet being married. "Your *example* is inconsistent with your precepts," giving people "the idea that marriage is a decent rather than a disgraceful thing." Barry himself had met his partner, Cordelia Benschoter, through a "matrimonial ad" she placed in *The Water-Cure Journal*. When he moved to Ohio and they founded the commune together, her father registered a marriage in their names at the county courthouse, though the couple denied that any legal ceremony had taken place. Community members at Berlin Heights were expected to dissolve their families and reorganize into groups based on affinity.[20]

In response to Barry's criticism, Heywood claimed that he and Angela Heywood did not use the terms "husband" and "wife" and, moreover, that they did not regard their relationship as permanent or indissoluble: "My relation to my partner in love and labor, is one of attraction and agreement, and, (whatever statute laws decree to the contrary), will be cancelled if ever experience shows that mutual choice ceases to sanction it. Until that period arrives, I know of no article of the free love faith that requires its dissolution." He argues that lovers are forced into marriage by the state and that marriage represents one of many ways he is required to breach his own values: "Taxation is tyranny; yet I pay taxes because I cannot, now, carry on my business from the inside of a jail." The choice was pragmatic, Heywood claimed: he could be more useful to the movement by marrying to avoid incarceration. Yet he would later be jailed twice for violating obscenity laws, indicating that he willingly faced these consequences to advance Free Love in his writings while personally marrying for the sake of expediency.[21]

Of course, many Free Lovers did flout traditional marriage norms in their personal lives as well as in their public activism. Brisbane had a track record both inside and outside the marriage institution that the mainstream considered scandalous, and all of those dance parties at the Free Love communes and clubs resulted in the reshuffling of plenty of passional attractions. For those who braved the risks and partnered without the state's blessing, a number of criminal cases resulting in significant jail time illustrated that the dangers of defying legal matrimony were very real. One such case in 1886 was the "Lucifer match." Edwin Walker and Lillian Harman, the daughter of the anarchist feminist Moses Harman, editor of the Kansas Free Love periodical *Lucifer, the Light-Bearer,* declared themselves married without the state's imprimatur. After sharing a bedroom for one night, they were arrested on the charge that they had "unlawfully, feloniously lived together as man and wife without being or having been married." The case ultimately went to the state supreme court; they were found guilty and spent six months in jail.[22]

But these cases were exceptions. As Heywood and Nichols lamented in their apologias, it's hard to live one's radical values within the practical limits of the real world. Still, this equivocation seems inexcusably gutless in the context of the 1850s, when even many moderate northerners came to see civil disobedience as a moral imperative in relation to slavery. Garrisonian Perfectionists had been coming out of the corruption of the world for decades, practicing radical forms of separation to avoid lending themselves to the evils they rejected and risking everything from injury and destitution to imprisonment and death.

By comparison, the solution adopted by most Free Lovers feels like a half measure. "Free marriages," or marriages "under protest," had been performed regularly for decades, going back to New Harmony. The Owenite community had passed a resolution that "previous to the performance of the marriage ceremony" there, the couple would enter "a protest against the usual form of marriage" by standing up, taking each other by the hand, stating that they take the other as their husband or wife, and then declaring, "I submit to any other ceremony upon this occasion only in conformity with the laws of the state."[23]

Although his father's commune had long since gone bust, Robert Dale Owen composed a document to establish his marriage to

Mary Robinson in 1832 that clearly echoes this tradition. There was no ceremony, just a mutually agreed-upon compact drawn up in the presence of a small group of witnesses. Their statement outlines the reasons for their opposition to marriage and for utilizing the institution in spite of these principles: "we contract a legal marriage, not because we deem the ceremony necessary to us, or useful . . . to society," but because if they were to live together as unmarried partners, they would have to either lie about it constantly or else navigate an array of "annoyances originating in a public opinion which is powerful, though unenlightened, and whose power, though we do not fear or respect it, we do not perceive the utility of unnecessarily braving." They did not want the trouble of keeping their relationship secret but were aware that they would open themselves to a variety of hazards if they did not. Perhaps Owen and Robinson did not regard their marriage as a sacrifice of their principles because their agreement departed so widely from the established mores of marriage. Their statement declares that their relationship is not necessarily permanent or unbreakable, and in keeping with his feminist values, Owen denounces the power over his wife that the marriage relation grants him.[24]

This practice spread to reformers beyond the Free Love set as well. Lucy Stone and Henry Blackwell, genteel abolitionists and members of the women's movement, staged a similar marriage protest in 1855. Their friend and fellow activist Thomas Wentworth Higginson officiated, reflecting, "I never perform the marriage ceremony without a renewed sense of the iniquity of our present system of laws, in respect to marriage." The couple read aloud a statement objecting to coverture and all the other economic, legal, and personal disadvantages for women under marriage: "We deem it a duty to declare that this act on our part implies no sanction of, nor promise of voluntary obedience to such of the present laws of marriage, as refuse to recognize the wife as an independent, rational being, while they confer upon the husband an injurious and unnatural superiority." They signed the document and then sent it to the newspapers, in the hope "that others may be induced to do likewise."[25]

These protest weddings or "free marriages" resemble Fourier's anti-lion in their oddly limited intervention; the dangerous thing is conveniently revised to be more useful and less harmful but remains disappointingly familiar in the context of an otherwise capacious utopian vision. Still, these couples' refusal to assume the roles of "husband" and "wife" to which they objected, especially their pointed rejections of lifelong commitment and sexual exclusivity, represented a challenge to the meaning and function of marriage. At the very least, Free Lovers who married crafted a negotiated engagement with an institution they felt they could not escape without unlivable sacrifices, and they analyzed this inescapability as part of the tyranny they worked to abolish.

Or, perhaps "free marriage" is just one more brick of proof that the Free Love movement was always compromised by unshakable elements of conservatism, like its early reliance on sex-negative philosophies like Grahamism and its eventual incorporation into the eugenics movement at the turn of the twentieth century. To bolster their demands for "voluntary motherhood" and birth control, many adopted racist arguments about who was fit to reproduce, as Noyes did at Oneida. And Lazarus was not the only notable Free Lover to fly to conservatism and never look back. After they had spearheaded a community called Memnonia in Ohio that advocated total celibacy, the spirit of Saint Ignatius of Loyola appeared to Mary and Thomas Nichols, urging them to convert to Catholicism. In 1857, they abandoned the United States along with their sex radicalism, residing in England for the rest of their lives, rubbing elbows with Charles Dickens and other respectable company, and even issuing new editions of some of their earlier works, with the scandalous content expunged.[26]

CHAPTER 8

Marriage Slavery and All Other Queer Things

Back in 1840, after the World Anti-Slavery Convention in London and her honeymoon European tour, Elizabeth Cady Stanton had relocated to Boston, home to the most dynamic set of progressive intellectuals in the country. She took full advantage of the city's humming reform culture, attending constant rounds of lectures, conventions, "conversations," fundraisers, and the like. For Sunday morning services, she sat with two thousand others in Boston Music Hall to hear the radical message of Theodore Parker's Free Church. She stayed overnight at Brook Farm in its heyday, visiting with the "charming family of intelligent men and women" there as they went about their gardening, housework, and games, getting to know the Ripleys and also Horace Greeley, who visited the commune frequently as it transitioned into a phalanx. She knew Bronson Alcott and Charles Lane of Fruitlands, as well as Orestes Brownson. Any one of these acquaintances might have been the one who pressed a copy of Albert Brisbane's *Social Destiny of Man* into her hand.

Around the time Brook Farm disbanded, Stanton moved to upstate New York with her husband and young children. Their new home was a rambling old farmhouse with clapboard siding located on the outskirts of a small town called Seneca Falls. After the exhilarating urban social scene Stanton was used to, fired by literary genius and righteous political indignation, her new rural digs were a dreary contrast. "My life was comparatively solitary," she recalled, and "somewhat depressing." Her existence seemed to shrink around her domestic duties: "to keep a house and grounds in good order, purchase every article for daily use, keep the wardrobes of half a dozen human beings in proper trim, take the children to dentists, shoemakers, and different schools." Stanton had always enjoyed financial privilege, and in Boston she had hired help to watch her young brood while she engaged in public life. But the nanny had not accompanied the Stantons to New York and had not yet been replaced. As she faced the drudgery of housekeeping alone, without the sparkling conversation of her many friends to provide intellectual stimulation, the restrictions that most women struggled against began to dawn on her. She was powerfully reminded of Brisbane's description of the doleful condition of women under the present social system, "obliged to pass their entire time in the dirty and repugnant occupations attendant upon the care of young children, and in the menial occupations of the kitchen." His call to Association snapped into place. "Fourier's phalansterie community life and co-operative households had a new significance for me," Stanton recalled.

Transcendentalist Margaret Fuller and abolitionist Angelina Grimké had dismantled the workings of gender inequality in their writings and advocated for women's participation in public life—as, of course, had Fanny Wright before them. But Brisbane's translation of Fourier outstretched these writings with its virulent critique of the burdens placed on women by marriage and the private home. Presenting domesticity as poisonous to society and deadly to women's individual fulfillment, he lambasted "the trifling occupations of the isolated household" and vowed that "in Association, the foolish error will not be committed of excluding women from the profession of medicine and the higher branches of teaching, and of reducing them, as in civilization, to the insignificant occupations of cooking and sewing." For Stanton, viewing her own discontent in light of Fourier's analysis "impressed me with a strong feeling that some active measures should be taken to remedy the wrongs of society in general, and of women in particular." She understood

Elizabeth Cady Stanton
with two of her children
in 1848.
Library of Congress

that her isolation and boredom were systemic, not personal, and were intimately related to the larger exclusion of women from public life, politics, and full citizenship rights.[1]

Just as this new perspective congealed, she was invited to spend the day with Lucretia Mott, whose exclusion from the London convention on the basis of sex had so impressed her eight years before. Stanton recalled, "I poured out, that day, the torrent of my long-accumulating discontent, with such vehemence and indignation that I stirred myself, as well as the rest of the party, to do and dare anything." Together, they resolved to take action, bringing women together to identify and protest the injustices they suffered as a group. They rushed an announcement into the local paper for a convention to be held only five days later, on July 19 and 20, 1848, at a church in Seneca Falls.[2]

In the days before the meeting, Stanton wrote up a declaration of sentiments modeled on the Declaration of Independence, launching a women's revolutionary war against what would come to be called the patriarchy. Following but revising the original founding docu-

ment, she affirmed as "self-evident" that all men and *women* are created equal and that any laws interfering with their lives, their
property, or their pursuit of happiness are invalid. The declaration
insists that women's subordination is the dictate not of nature and
religion but of a long, unjust tradition, not unlike the political system that had to be overthrown for American democracy to take
root: "The history of mankind is a history of repeated injuries and
usurpations on the part of man toward woman, having in direct object the establishment of an absolute tyranny." At the convention,
Stanton read these lines aloud to an audience of around three hundred men and women. The idea of women speaking in public was
still so novel and taboo that other participants in this convention,
and those in the years to come, often quaked visibly as they stood to
read the minutes. Some had difficulty raising their voices above a
nervous whisper. But Stanton herself was not afflicted by shyness.[3]

When word of the event spread, most men were stymied by this
sudden revelation of women's dissatisfaction. The relative positions
of the sexes, unequal in sociopolitical power certainly but comple-
mentary and equally important to the functioning of American life,
had been the bedrock of human society and religion from time im-
memorial. These distinctions were written by God in the human
body, not man-made, they argued. The press treated the convention and its declaration with a mix of condescension, ridicule, and
genuine alarm. Stanton clipped a number of these articles for her
scrapbook, presumably both thrilled and amused that men were unsure whether to dismiss her and her collaborators or fear them, as
they warned readers that women "are on the eve of inciting a Pet-
ticoat Revolution." One writer opined that the meeting "must have
been composed almost entirely of aged spinsters, who have been
crossed in love." They "have become the butt of ridicule among the
sensible and discreet of both sexes," he claimed. "We don't believe
they will hold another convention in a hurry." But the women held
a follow-up conference two weeks later in nearby Rochester. Indeed, their conventions continued unceasingly for twelve years,
when they were interrupted by the Civil War.[4]

The Seneca Falls Convention is widely regarded as the beginning of the movement that would, after seventy years of relentless agitation, win for American women the right to vote. But the objectives of the women gathered there, many of them dedicated Associationists, were far more capacious. Stanton, for example, was at least as interested in reforming marriage as in gaining the vote, as were many others in the room that day. Indeed, the attendees at Seneca Falls almost decided not to make the vote a priority for the movement. Suffrage was mentioned in the ninth of eleven resolutions, preceded by many other concerns: women's status as civilly dead in marriage and the inaccessibility of divorce that held them there; their unequal access to property, wages, and work opportunities, as well as education and religious leadership positions; the psychological warfare carried out by men "to destroy her confidence in her own powers, to lessen her self-respect, and to make her willing to lead a dependent and abject life." Of all the resolutions, only the one about women's suffrage was controversial with the attendees, and it was nearly abandoned after a debate in the assembly.

First of all, it raised a conflict for Non-Resistants, who did not endorse voting or any other political approach to the deep injustices of American life. Mott herself, who was both a Quaker and an old-school Garrisonian, objected to making women's suffrage a goal of the movement on these grounds. Avowed Come-Outers like Abby Kelley would not have dreamed of casting a vote under the pro-slavery U.S. Constitution at this time. Even those who did not frown upon the franchise itself worried that the idea of women exercising it seemed so outrageous that it would discredit the other goals they regarded as "more rational" and "make the whole movement ridiculous." But Frederick Douglass, the formerly enslaved abolitionist orator, author, and leader in the National Conventions of the Free People of Colour, stepped up in this debate to defend the women's suffrage resolution as indispensable to the platform, arguing that it "was the right by which all others could be secured." After his speech, the resolution passed, but only by a small margin.[5]

At their follow-up meeting in Rochester, the assembly took the daring step of electing a woman to preside over the convention, a move to which both Mott and Stanton were opposed, describing it as "a most hazardous experiment." Stanton later regretted her timidity in those early days as "foolish." But their wariness of going too far, of discrediting their movement by disturbing the mainstream too much, persisted for the rest of the century. Stanton was relieved, for example, that Mary Gove Nichols steered clear of the annual conventions they held throughout the 1850s as alarm about Free Love—the other American feminist movement, more clearly spawned by Fourier—screamed from the headlines. Though they had once been friends, Stanton had stopped speaking to her by 1852, by which time, as one historian has put it, Nichols had morphed from respectable physiology expert to socially "radioactive" Free Lover. But Stanton did not disagree with her. She wrote to her colleague Susan B. Anthony that year that "the right idea of marriage is at the foundation of all reforms," and she aligned herself with Free Love in a number of ways in the coming decades, much to the chagrin of her more cautious colleagues.[6]

In contrast to radical strains of abolitionism that boldly prodded a range of hot-button social issues not directly related to emancipating the enslaved, the women's rights movement was frequently hemmed in by internal debate about which issues were up for discussion, how their priorities should be ranked, how conservatives would react, and what role adjacent groups and causes should play. Free Love, antislavery, and labor movements invested in the conditions of working women significantly overlapped with—some would have said intruded upon—the now widely known organization Stanton and Mott founded. These intersections were crucial to the emergence of women's rights and gave rise, at times, to formidable coalitions. But at other times they were stifled, exploited, or contested by the women's rights women as they defined their agenda.

———

DOUGLASS'S CRITICAL INTERVENTION at Seneca Falls is perhaps the most striking example of how activists known primarily as abolitionists shaped the women's movement. A number of antislavery men and women were regular speakers at the National Women's Rights Conventions that met annually beginning in 1850, including William Lloyd Garrison, Sojourner Truth, Stephen S. Foster, Sarah and Charles Lenox Remond, and Margaretta and Harriet Forten Purvis. Indeed, Susan B. Anthony became involved in the women's movement after attending an antislavery meeting in Seneca Falls; Garrison was staying at Stanton's house, and as she walked home with him after the meeting adjourned, the two women were introduced on the street. The participants in these movements overlapped to such a degree that by the end of the decade, the women's conventions were scheduled in conjunction with the AASS for convenience. Yet despite this overlap, the question of slavery's relevance to women's rights was a controversial one.

At the 1850 meeting, Wendell Phillips, a leading abolitionist, feminist, and labor activist, stood to urge the group of predominantly white women never to forget "the million and a half of slave women at the South, the most grossly wronged and foully outraged of all women," calling for a platform that would honor "the tram-

Wendell Phillips, ca. 1850s.
Library of Congress

pled womanhood of the plantation, and omit no effort to raise it to a share in the rights we claim for ourselves." This was a provocative resolution, raising the question of the role of race in a movement for the equality of the sexes. Some insisted that "in a Woman's Rights Convention, the question of color has no right to a hearing," that the new movement must be respected as a separate endeavor and not expected to accomplish "everything at once."[7]

In their eagerness to affirm that the wrongs against white women deserved sustained attention at a time when millions of people of color were enslaved, many women argued that their situation was in fact more similar to slavery than men like Phillips realized. One speaker from the Hopedale commune declared, "No matter if the yoke we wear is soft and cushioned, it is nevertheless a yoke. No matter if the chain is fastened by those we love, it is nevertheless a chain." They were regarded as naturally inferior, subject to economic limitations, and barred from the rights of citizenship. And in marriage, they stressed, women were exposed to all kinds of horrors under the complete power of despotic, sometimes drunken men. Even in its best form, the institution took away their property and their very selves, because the legal system of coverture subsumed a woman's civic identity under her husband.[8]

Talking down marriage this way was daring, because one whiff of sexual heterodoxy was enough to permanently discredit any person or set of ideas to which it became attached. Social conservatives and the mainstream press were eager to lump women's rights and antislavery together alongside Free Love under the red flag of Fanny Wrightism, warning the public that "Fanny organized a war which has been vigorously carried on by her strong-minded successors." In these anti-reform screeds, all the movements of the day were represented as covers for the same devious plot: "Whether they be Oneida Communists, Individual Sovereigns, Berlin Heights Freelovers, Spiritualists, Advocates of Woman Suffrage, or Friends of Free Divorce, we find them all united for the accomplishment of one object—the total destruction of the marriage relation." One critic claimed to have interviewed a well-known abolitionist who said, "Let us free the blacks first; then we will break the bonds of woman." But he clarified that he did not mean a mere reform of the voting laws. "Woman suffrage is a very small affair—a very inconsiderable part of this great question. It is the stepping-stone only to the abolition of marriage, which must follow woman suffrage." In short, "monogamic marriage is doomed."[9]

Most of Stanton's compatriots blanched at the Free Love label. Yet as the antislavery movement gathered irresistible force, making freedom the essential watchword of reform culture, both the sex radicals and the women's movement strove to brand themselves as next-wave abolitionists. As attention turned to the myriad subtle means by which Americans were held captive, many hoped the next abolition movement would break the bonds of marriage.

Although the most avowed Free Lovers were not active in the fight to emancipate enslaved people, they leaned heavily on rhetoric developed by the antislavery movement. Many adapted the "higher law" argument—which held that individual Americans should follow the antislavery mandate of their own conscience, even if it meant breaking the law—to attack marriage and mainstream sexual mores. Others made the metaphor explicit: any woman trapped in a sexually exploitative marriage, wrote one Free Lover, "is a slave, not less degraded than any ever bought or sold upon the auction-block; and she entertains to her master the feelings which such a relation must produce. Marriage, to her, becomes the name for all that is debasing and disgusting." Joseph Treat, a member of the Berlin Heights commune, claimed that every married person is both slaveholder and chattel: "You have enslaved somebody else, too; you are a tyrant, as well as a slave." The Nicholses were particularly fluent in this analogy: "The great wrong of slavery consists in the power which it gives to one human being over another. A husband has almost precisely the same power over the wife that the master has over the slave." Indeed, they went so far as to suggest that there is more cruelty, evil, and violence in legal marriage than in chattel slavery, that there may be "more freedom and enjoyment, in the domestic relations of our negro slaves, than among the same number of our free white population."[10]

The future Confederate army recruit Marx Lazarus had the most alarming relationship to slavery of the major Free Lovers. He finished his work *Love vs. Marriage* in a family home in Alabama, among the people his family enslaved, who he claimed "have never known aught but comfort, security, the mild yoke of well-assorted labors, and that elevating influence which the Caucasian race, superior in intellect and culture, invariably extends over the negro." During his time working with George Ripley on *The Harbinger,* he wrote an article proposing that southern plantations institute Fourierist attractive labors to make slaves more productive. Ripley disclaimed responsibility for Lazarus's views, finding his attitude toward slavery most unfortunate. But he printed it anyway.[11]

Stanton, a northerner, came from a slave-owning family as well, and though she supported the abolition cause in which her husband was a leader, she was not above using slavery as a metaphor for the status of white women. Addressing the New York state legislature, she drew parallels between "the slave of the Carolinas" and the condition of "the mothers, wives and daughters of the Empire State." Noting their similarities in rhetoric and aims, the Free Lovers recognized the women's movement as sisters-in-arms, if only they would admit it. Surely if Stanton and her allies acknowledged that the marriage institution was a form of slavery, they hoped to abolish it, as the Free Lovers did. At the 1858 National Woman's Rights Convention in New York, Stephen Pearl Andrews turned up to register his support for their movement and perhaps spark a collaboration on this front.[12]

The Modern Times project he and Josiah Warren had established on Long Island was still operating, and that very month he helped found the Unitary Household with Ned Underhill, a working-class socialist and one of the signers of the original Declaration of Sentiments at the 1848 Seneca Falls Convention. He had been brought along by an aunt when he was eighteen. Their commune on Stuyvesant Street in Manhattan was a Fourierist boardinghouse with around twenty residents that hosted regular social events for the city's bohemian clique. Taking the platform, which any attendee was allowed to do, Andrews noted that he had often sat in the audience of their conventions but never spoke because he was aware that association with his name would cast them and their leaders into further controversy. His speech alluded to the principle of "voluntary motherhood," meaning that women must have the unfettered right to choose when and with whom they conceived children, a loaded term that hinted at not only marital rape but also birth control and non-monogamy.[13]

It was an uncomfortable reminder that as long as the women's movement critiqued the oppressions of private life, they were toeing the line of Free Love, and it did not escape the notice of the press. The *New York Times* reporter covering the convention relayed that Andrews "seemed to claim for women the right to be unchaste" and that "the convention does not appear to have expressed any disapprobation of his views." On the contrary, many of the women disapproved deeply. Some, like Stanton and Ernestine Rose, had long been branded Free Lovers and were not particularly concerned about it. But most supporters of women's rights denied that their movement was related to "theories which claim unlimited indulgence for appetite and passion." Julia Branch, a member of the Unitary Household, had accompanied Andrews to the convention that day. A petite woman in her twenties, with long brunette curls, Branch was also a committed Free Lover. She managed to buttonhole Lucy Stone, a celebrated antislavery and women's rights speaker famous for her "marriage under protest," and extract from her the declaration, "The marriage question will and must someday be discussed." Branch countered, "Why are you not willing that it should be discussed now and here?" But Stone "did not think it a proper place."[14]

How could activists ever form meaningful coalitions if there was no "proper place" to address shared concerns? Branch was no doubt frustrated. But as the women's movement tried to push controversial issues aside, organizers in Rutland, Vermont, were preparing for a three-day meeting with no limitations on what might be discussed. Their "Free Convention" offered a time and place for dissenters of every stripe to air their views and mingle after hours, with a free platform where spiritualism, pacifism, individualism, and all the other isms of the day could be addressed. They called "every section of the great army of reform" together "to challenge the institutions that claim control over humanity." Although Branch and others headed to the Free Convention to strengthen ties between divergent social movements, the event ultimately revealed a profound disagreement about the value and limits of a multi-issue approach to injustice. For some, the social transformation they sought would require equal attention to a spectrum of issues at once, with marriage front and center. But for others, issues like Free Love were dangerous distractions at the very moment when radicals were called to duty as never before.[15]

———

IN THE LAST WEEK of June 1858, they stepped off the trains into dazzling sunshine in the small but bustling town: short-haired women and long-haired men, sporting bloomers and Byron collars, conspicuous hats and checkered suits. As the smirking *New York Times* reporter would write in his evening dispatch, they were "a medley of people, of all sorts of shades; of heterodox notions; white, black, partially black, badly sun-burned and fair in face," who had convened in this Green Mountain hamlet "to discuss abolitionism, spiritualism, free-love, free-trade, and all other queer things." Finding the vacant lot on the east side of Grove Street, they bought root beer and gingerbread from the locals who had set up booths around the perimeter and then gathered under a tent some one hundred feet across, decorated with bunting that sagged heavily in the airless heat. They talked all day and late into the evening, barely breaking for meals and musical interludes from the Harmonial Glee Club. Colorful countercultural types came out of the woodwork. The *Times* reporter claims to have walked into one gathering in a hotel parlor just as a woman freestyling improvised poetry and accompanying herself on an antique accordion was interrupted by an adolescent in a trance who began flailing around the room and mumbling messages from a departed spirit.

The convention's resolutions affirmed their belief in spirit communications; rejected war, the death penalty, and Sabbath observances; and stated that "the American Union was a crime in its formation" and "has proved a curse ever since." The influence of the radical Garrisonians was evident in these declarations, and indeed among the first to speak was Henry C. Wright, a founding Non-Resistant. He traveled widely to lecture on these doctrines, and his letters were published in *The Liberator* as a regular column. But his most impassioned remarks at the Rutland convention pertained to "sham" marriages, abortion, and the gender politics of sexual consent.

It turns out that Wright chose to be a traveling agent of the antislavery cause because he could not stand to be at home. When he was twenty-five, he had married a forty-three-year-old widow with four children. Even as the newlyweds embarked on a Niagara Falls honeymoon, he knew he had made a mistake: "Within 24 hours after the ceremony my eyes were open to see the gulf into which I had blindly leaped. I saw that my heart never had been & never could be given to that woman. She could not receive it—nor understand it. From that hour I commenced a course of *concealment*." He later confided to his journal, "No marriage love is between us. She was past child-bearing when I first knew her—we have not had intercourse as husband and wife for 15 years—it is many years since we have slept in the same bed." Staying in other people's homes as he traveled, he was tortured by the sight of happy couples embracing, newborns nursing, and other blissful domestic scenes that he was denied. He felt he was trapped in his marriage as in "a living death."[16]

But his travels presented other opportunities as well. Passionate affairs with at least one woman and likely multiple women in Europe led Wright to question the traditional standards that deemed his sexless marriage the only legitimate form of intimacy. By the time of the Rutland convention, and while still actively at work for the antislavery movement, he had published *Marriage and Parentage; or, The Reproductive Element in Man* (1854). In it, he explains that sex must be taken up as an object for reform alongside movements like abolition and temperance. Extending no-government principles to private life, Wright declares that "no human law, or license or authority, or social custom" can make a true marriage. People living together as husband and wife, even if they have a state-issued marriage license, are committing adultery if "there is no longer true marriage in the heart," and sex between them is "legalized prostitution." Thus, because neither the church nor the state has the power to sanction a marriage, if either of the parties wishes to separate, they need not worry about procuring a legal divorce from these institutions. Wright's call at Rutland for "the immediate abolition of all external authority" was a wide net cast to encompass not only the slave power, the government, and the churches but the institution of marriage as well.

All participants in the Free Convention had their own causes to add to this list of external authorities to be abolished, and they were practically climbing over one another for the floor—Spiritualists butting in after proposals for free trade, freethinkers one-upping abolitionists. An impassioned advocate for Native Americans tried valiantly to call attention a number of times to a recent massacre and the condition of "the aborigines of this country" more generally but could gain no traction with the crowd as it jumped from one topic to the next.

Julia Branch was a star of the convention. For the *New York Times* reporter, "It produced an odd sensation to see a good-looking woman rise to avow herself a Free-Lover." The marriage-slavery analogy was on full display in her speech. "Women are bought and paid for as the negro slave is," she declared. Feminist talk of "marriage slavery" was matched by others decrying "mental slavery," "spiritual slavery," and man's "enslavement" by religious conventions. They seemed to compete over which of these could be proved worse than the "slavery of the body" practiced in the South.

Stephen S. Foster, the cantankerous Come-Outer, was there as well, listening intently to two days of such speeches on marriage and communications between the living and the spirits of the dead.

Responding to Branch's declaration "that the slavery and degradation of woman proceed from the institution of marriage," he countered that marriage was the only institution he had ever found to be
untarnished, indicating that his relationship with his wife and antislavery colleague, Abby Kelley, was for him "the glory of this fallen
world." Still, he had engaged in the Free Love discussions with an
open mind, insisting that the real problem was gender inequality
but granting that if a truly egalitarian marriage did not work for
others the way it had worked for him, then he would support them
in trying an experiment of a different kind.

But by Saturday afternoon, Foster was tired of listening to all of
this talk. Not just tired, furious. He rose and addressed the convention in the same Come-Outer spirit with which he harangued un-
suspecting churchgoers at the Sunday services he crashed. He would
not allow these self-styled reformers to feel comfortable while in
the South the lash continued to fall. Frankly disgusted by so much
talk, Foster demanded action. "My heart has been pained and sunk
within me as I have listened to the discussions which have been
going on before this audience," he said. "I call upon you, in the
name of four millions of slaves, to go to work." He charged that
when his listeners sit and chat about communications from beyond
the grave, they fall deaf to the cries of millions of living people
bound in chains. How can they speak abstractly of women's rights,
he wonders, in the very moment that enslaved women are being
raped, or the politics of maternity while newborn babies are torn
away from mothers sold at auction with cattle and swine? The Free
Convention threatened, in Foster's view, to splinter activist energy
into offshoots that seemed distressingly apolitical, doing nothing to
save lives and end unjust suffering. In response, he made his commitment clear: "Let me say here and now, that I never intend to lay
aside the question of slavery, come what may. I never intend to turn
my eye from the slave until the last shackle falls." Ending with a
sanguinary note, which was becoming inescapable in the late 1850s
even in the rhetoric of devoted Non-Resistants, he warned, "I leave
the responsibility with you; and God is my witness, if you go down

to the grave with this crime upon your souls, my soul is clean of your blood."[17]

Foster's foreboding remarks, lobbed into what had been a boisterous reformer shindig, suggest something of the precipice on which they and the entire country teetered. In a few short years, all Americans would be living in the shadow of mass death, and the long crime of slavery would meet its end in apocalyptic bloodshed. There would soon be little time to debate who should be emancipated next, when the national crisis the abolitionists had long desired finally arrived.

PART III

Abolition War, 1848–1865

CHAPTER 9

The Aliened American

A decade before Stephen Pearl Andrews was a New York City sex radical and "Individual Sovereign," before he founded Modern Times with Josiah Warren, the Free Love Club with Albert Brisbane, and the Unitary Household with Julia Branch, before he defended Marx Lazarus and Mary Gove Nichols in the *Tribune* or crashed the Woman's Rights Convention, he became a Texan. As a young man, Andrews had left his native Massachusetts for Louisiana, practicing law in New Orleans. After the Texas Revolution, he moved to Houston, watching the fledgling city rise from muddy prairie and pine forest. He hoped to make some money (he had lost most of his in the Panic of 1837) and to shape the slavery debate as the laws and lands of this new country, the Republic of Texas, were settled.

Mexico had abolished slavery in 1829, but the new Texian government enshrined the right to own slaves in their 1836 constitution. The new republic's leaders also hoped to draw American settlers from the neighboring states and territories of the Southwest, who would expect to bring enslaved people with them as property and laborers. By the early 1840s, Texas seemed to be on a path toward annexation by the United States as a slave state—or even as five separate slave states—which would mean a huge expansion of the institution and a new crop of pro-slavery representatives in the federal government.

But Andrews dreamed up another foreign policy option that

would claim this massive territory for free labor: he would persuade England to recognize Texas as an independent nation and a lucrative investment. England, he thought, could offer Texas loans and favorable trade conditions in exchange for abolition. Enslaved people from Arkansas and Louisiana could then seek sanctuary in the state, weakening the institution throughout the South.

Andrews tried to keep his antislavery views somewhat under wraps, but he blew his cover during a talk at the Houston courthouse in which he painted a picture of a future Texas without the institution. After that, a mob rode out to his house for a heated discussion that involved threatening him with a rope. He fled with his wife and infant son in the dark of night, but he did not give up on his plan.[1]

In June 1843, he went to London to broker a deal personally with the British foreign secretary that would abolish slavery in Texas. The plan was discussed favorably by the House of Lords. But then the official Texas ambassador to England caught up with him, letting the peers know that Andrews was an unauthorized meddler and warning those back home about his efforts at international diplomacy. Even though the Texas government was not interested in pursuing the deal Andrews had formulated, the threat of it pushed the United States into action. The new secretary of state, proslavery firebrand John C. Calhoun, moved swiftly toward annexation, claiming it was "impossible for the United States to witness with indifference the efforts of Great Britain to abolish slavery there." Thus, acting in "self-defense," the United States brought Texas into the Union as a slave state in 1845, then went to war with Mexico almost immediately in a dispute over its boundaries, with the expansionist president James K. Polk eyeing the regions that now constitute New Mexico and California as well. Bitter debate bloomed over this conflict and what might result if the United States took control not only of Texas but of a landmass extending all the way to the Pacific. Whigs in Congress regarded it as "an aggressive, unholy, and unjust war" and refused to play a part in "the murder of Mexicans upon their own soil, or in robbing them of their country." But Democrats waxed poetic on this landgrab as the

country's "manifest destiny." The United States was divinely ordained to conquer the continent and expand from ocean to ocean,
they claimed. The South, meanwhile, salivated not only at the expansion of the institution of slavery but at the pro-slavery representatives these new states would send to Congress, giving them
control of the federal government indefinitely.[2]

Winning the Mexican-American War in 1848, the United States
seized not only the whole of present-day Texas but also the immense territory now carved up into California, Nevada, and Utah,
plus chunks of New Mexico, Arizona, Colorado, Kansas, and on up
to Wyoming—all of it inhabited at the time by tens of thousands of
Mexicans and many nations of indigenous people. This acquisition
catalyzed an all-out crisis in Congress as parties splintered into new
factions, largely along regional lines. David Wilmot, a representative from Pennsylvania, introduced a proposal that would exclude
slavery from all of the territory acquired in the war with Mexico.
Calhoun warned this would result in "political revolution, anarchy,
civil war." Another possible solution was to extend the boundary
line drawn by the Missouri Compromise of 1820, which had stayed
civil war decades before by maintaining political equilibrium between slave and free states. Or they could let the settlers of these
territories decide for themselves. In the heated atmosphere at the
Capitol, fistfights broke out between northern and southern congressmen. During one debate, a Mississippi senator pulled a loaded
revolver.

As the Garrisonians lamented, the Constitution had been carefully drafted to create a union premised on compromise between
free and slave states. The threat of upsetting this balance was at the
center of the controversy—meaning so was the Constitution itself.
There was debate over the extent to which the document protected
slavery and allowed its expansion but, more critically, over the
value of continued fealty to the union between the sections that the
Constitution had brokered. Southern "fire-eaters" made clear that
their principal loyalty was to the slave system. A representative from
Georgia said that if the federal government sought to keep southerners from bringing their human property to California, *"I am for*

disunion." Those on the other end of the political spectrum were ready to let the Constitution go as well. The antislavery New York senator William Seward affirmed that the founding document allowed Congress to limit the spread of slavery, but even if it didn't, he declared, "there is a higher law than the Constitution."[3]

A version of these debates was also under way within the antislavery movement. Of course, radical activists opposed the imperialist Mexican-American War and the expansion of slavery it augured. Frederick Douglass said, "I would not care if, to-morrow, I should hear of the death of every man who engaged in that bloody war in Mexico, and that every man had met the fate he went there to perpetrate upon unoffending Mexicans." Thoreau famously refused to pay his taxes in protest and spent a night in jail. Garrison had publicly wished the United States a devastating defeat in the conflict, calling it criminal and unconstitutional, "cruel, unprovoked, and diabolical." But he was not biting his nails over the threat this debate posed to the Constitution or the survival of the Union. In fact, he hoped it would bring about the destruction of both.[4]

Garrisonians had called for the national union to dissolve years before Texas forced the question, denouncing the compromise between the North and the South that had created an intrinsically pro-slavery nation. At a Faneuil Hall rally in 1842, speaking before a crowd of Brook Farmers and other Boston-area agitators, Wendell Phillips exclaimed, "My CURSE be on the Constitution of these United States!" He published a long pamphlet presenting the Constitution as "A Pro-slavery Compact" and declaring it "the duty of each individual to trample it under his feet." They believed that the nation itself must be overturned for slavery to be abolished. But not all in the activist community agreed.[5]

After the 1840 schism that split the AASS—in part over whether abolitionists had a duty to vote or on the contrary to shun any involvement with the U.S. government—sharp divisions over the role of official politics in the fight against slavery had continued. The "political abolitionists" had heartily endorsed electoral approaches and founded the Liberty Party to pursue them. Elizabeth Cady Stanton's husband, Henry Stanton, and more prominently her cousin,

Gerrit Smith, tangled with the Garrisonians, insisting that the Constitution was actually an antislavery document that empowered the federal government to abolish the institution.[6]

A number of African American leaders, including Frederick Douglass, supported the Liberty Party, and for many, allegiance to other key Garrisonian tenets waned as well. While black activist communities took part in the nationwide conversations at this time about the Constitution, territorial expansion, and the varieties of disunion, even treason, that seemed increasingly desirable, their internal deliberations also concerned their relationship as a group to white Americans, including their allies. Was violence a justified response to slavery in the South and racism in the North, although most white abolitionists had condemned it? Should the American political system be engaged strategically or abandoned altogether? Was the destiny of black people bound up with that of the United States or profoundly separate? New leaders emerged to revisit these persistent questions and define a revolutionary era in antislavery and black radical agitation as a national crisis unfolded.

———

LEGALLY SPEAKING, Martin Robison Delany was born free and black in 1812 in Charles Town, Virginia, but he would spend his life searching the country, the continent, the globe, for a place where it was truly possible to be both. One of his earliest childhood memories was of the day a neighbor ran to tell his free mother, Pati Peace, that his enslaved father, Samuel Delany, was in jail. After refusing to let a white man whip him, he had faced off with the police who came to arrest him. The sheriff wanted to shoot him, but his enslaver objected because Samuel's body was such valuable property. So they knocked him unconscious with a rock. Every day after that, Martin saw the scar on his father's face as the mark of "all the humiliations and bestial associations to which their hapless race was subjected." Although he was not a slave, Delany was nevertheless tightly constrained by Virginia's harsh laws for free people of color. He, his mother, and his siblings had to register themselves with the county and carry proof of that registration at all times. They were not allowed to move between towns, and free blacks from other states were forbidden to enter Virginia. Anyone manumitted in the state was required to leave within a year. Pati found herself in court twice about her children before Martin was ten years old. The first time, a local white man had attempted to sell him and his sister into slavery. Then another white man discovered that he could read, which was against the law. They wanted to jail his mother and put the children in state custody. To avoid this fate, Pati moved the family across the border for a new start in Pennsylvania; Samuel soon bought his freedom and joined them.[7]

When he was nineteen, Delany moved to Pittsburgh and quickly became part of its vital black intellectual and activist scene. He met John Vashon, a community leader who introduced him to all kinds of radical antislavery materials, including David Walker's *Appeal*, Samuel Cornish's newspapers, and *The Liberator*, of which Vashon was a financial backer and subscription agent. Delany was one of the first pupils at the community school Vashon had founded with Lewis Woodson, a teacher, AME minister, and advocate of black nationalism.

Although most black leaders at this time supported racial integration, Woodson remained a powerful proponent of separatism, urging free people to differentiate black-led plans from the enforced exile of colonization. In the pages of *The Colored American,* Cornish's newspaper that succeeded *Freedom's Journal* and *The Rights of All,* Woodson argued that black people were a distinct class within American society, sharing a history and experience only with one another and not with even the most sympathetic and activist whites. They must cultivate this "national feeling" in all-black churches, schools, and settlements, he wrote. Against Cornish's objections, he called for the establishment of black colonies within the United States, citing the Declaration of Independence as precedent for such a separatist venture. Years earlier, Woodson had explored the idea of founding a black town called Africania in Ohio, specifying the need for at least three thousand acres to ensure that residents would be free from white laws and surveillance. He was less interested in small-scale experiments than in exodus, calling for the entire black population to come out from white America as a group. Many disagreed with him. But the idea of an all-black state of the kind Woodson proposed appealed to Delany profoundly.[8]

His first thought was Texas. It was 1839, when the fate of the independent republic was still unclear, and Delany wondered if thousands of black men might come together to lay claim to one area of the vast territory. He set off to explore it, risking enslavement and murder for a trip through Mississippi, Arkansas, and Louisiana. When he arrived in Texas, however, he realized that it was not a promising site for a black state; he could perceive immediately the violent racism and entrenched pro-slavery outlook that Stephen Pearl Andrews was blithely trying to circumvent at that time. He headed north into Native American territories, where Choctaw leaders welcomed him gladly, telling him of their hopes for forming an Indian state with representation in Congress.[9]

This first plan for colonization tabled, Delany returned to Pittsburgh and resumed his medical practice in cupping and leeching, as well as his activism. He supported the Liberty Party, worked to amend the Pennsylvania Constitution to allow free black men to vote, and also started a weekly newspaper for black readers, *The Mystery*. He married and started a family that would eventually include six sons, all bearing the names of black heroes, and a daughter, Ethiopia.

He met Frederick Douglass in the summer of 1847 when the celebrated author and orator passed through Pennsylvania on a speaking tour with William Lloyd Garrison, spreading the doctrines of religious Come-Outerism and its political counterpart, disunion. Douglass had packed the house with an admiring crowd at Mother Bethel in Philadelphia, but he and Garrison were greeted with hurled stones and rotten eggs in other venues around the state. Traveling alone on some legs of the trip, Douglass encountered even worse. Railway staff refused to serve him, and he had gone without a meal for forty-eight hours when he staggered off the train to a hero's welcome from the black community in Pittsburgh, led by Vashon and Delany.

Douglass's time with Delany on this trip proved to be an

important turning point in his career. Although Garrison, his mentor, had tried to dissuade him from the idea of running his own newspaper, he raised the subject with Delany, who was slightly older and had experience as an editor. Finding inspiration and encouragement in these conversations, Douglass firmly resolved to found a publication that would focus on slavery in the South, prejudice in the North, and the successes and challenges of African American communities across the nation. He believed that a staff of black men could accomplish what "would be wholly impossible for our white friends to do for us."[10]

Enlisted as co-editor, Delany joined Douglass and William C. Nell in Rochester, New York, to lay out the first issue of *The North Star*. All three were also staunch supporters of women's rights, as the paper's masthead motto indicates: "Right is of no Sex—Truth is of no Color." They ran the original call for the Seneca Falls Convention, where Douglass played a pivotal role in defining the nascent movement's agenda; Nell, a second-generation Boston abolitionist who would soon publish pioneering works of African American history, joined them at the follow-up convention in Rochester weeks later.

Delany spent much of his brief tenure as an editor of *The North Star* on the road. Traveling across the Midwest to Detroit, he drummed up subscriptions, although not as many as Douglass had hoped, and wrote dispatches for the paper on the state of black America. This lecture tour nearly proved deadly at a stop in Marseilles, Ohio, when a gang of white men followed him through the street and back to his hotel. Delany went inside, but the men continued to congregate. They broke open a barrel of tar and set it on fire; their initial plan was to tar and feather him, but then they decided to burn him alive. They also considered burning down the hotel, dragging out Delany and his associate, Charles Langston, and selling them south as slaves. Delany blocked the stairwell with furniture and appeared at an upstairs window with a hatchet and a butcher knife. He would not be taken quietly. The mob rioted around the hotel and kept the fire going, howling, swearing, beating drums and tambourines until one in the morning. Delany and

Langston got away the next day, the crowd showering their buggy with stones as they pulled out of town. Defiant in the face of this near lynching, Delany reported, "We left this place unharmed, and even unfrightened."[11]

Delany fully embraced the use of violence in the antislavery fight, as had a number of other black activists. Perhaps the most profound statement of black militance in this period came from Henry Highland Garnet, a formerly enslaved man from Maryland who became one of the foremost black orators of the century, in an incendiary address at the 1843 National Convention of Colored Citizens. "However much you and all of us may desire it," he said, "there is not much hope of redemption without the shedding of blood." Although he delivered this speech to an assembly of free men, he directly addressed the vast population of enslaved people, expressing solidarity and hoping to incite them to revolution. It was "sinful," he claimed, for them to remain in bondage. In a crystal clear rejection of Garrisonian pacifism, Garnet declared, "Let your motto be resistance! resistance! resistance! No oppressed people have ever secured their liberty without resistance."

Douglass spoke against the convention's adoption of the ideas in this address. It was "war-like," he said, and so radical that if convention delegates endorsed it, they would have to fear for their lives. The assembly voted it down twice, omitting it from the convention proceedings. Garnet and Douglass remained in a bitter dispute for years, exacerbated by Garnet's advocacy of black emigration.[12]

Delany was with Garnet ideologically, as his own controversial contributions to the national convention five years later confirm. He offered up a number of resolutions the 1848 assembly found too extreme. Delany was not supported in his proposal that black people "use every means in their power" to learn military tactics so that they can successfully engage assailants and invaders. He and Douglass were also overruled in committee on a resolution affirming the equality of the sexes and support for women's full participation in the conventions thereafter as delegates. But Delany brought back the motion before the full assembly, and Douglass called on a white Quaker woman to speak on its behalf. She wished the assembled black men swift and sweeping success in their fight for citizenship rights and affirmed that women wanted the same for themselves, in part, she hinted, because so many felt called to duty for racial justice but were politically powerless. The delegates endorsed the resolution resoundingly, responding with "Three cheers for woman's rights!" The Seneca Falls Convention had met only two months before, with Douglass playing a key role there as well. Thus, the movement represented by the National Conventions of the Free People of Colour worked apace with the emergent white-majority women's rights movement in declaring gender equality a natural fact and a social goal.[13]

Delany's most controversial resolution at the 1848 convention proposed that no black person should work in a menial job like domestic service. The crowd, which comprised many barbers, porters, and bootblacks, found this position offensive. Douglass, the convention's president, intervened once again to smooth over the tension, insisting that useful labor was not degrading, a theory that the Brook Farmers and other white socialists also championed that decade. Delany's professional position as a lecturer, editor, and doctor was a privileged one when considered in relation to many of his colleagues in the movement, not to mention the four million people held captive or on the run.

Although Delany was never enslaved as his father had been, he was plagued nonetheless by the low ceiling of possibility that hemmed in all African Americans, even those like himself who were nominally free. He was deeply frustrated about his prospects. For one thing, he could not gain admission to a medical school despite all his years of study and experience. In 1850, he took a bold step to address this problem, seeking out the dean of Harvard Medical School, Oliver Wendell Holmes, for an interview. Holmes was a fellow traveler of the Transcendentalists and a cousin of the antislavery radical Wendell Phillips. He admitted Delany along with another black student who was training for a career as a doctor in Liberia and would soon emigrate. But their white classmates called foul, threatening to withdraw from Harvard if they were forced to share a classroom with people they would not welcome in their homes or even acknowledge on the street. The admission of these two African Americans was detrimental to Harvard's reputation, they argued, and the university would soon have all black students and very few whites if they did not adopt a firm policy to stop the turning tide. Bowing to this pressure, the administration asked the black students to leave. Delany wrote to Garrison, hoping the editor would use his platform to shine a light on the racist discrimination taking place in his own city. But Garrison's attention was turned, along with the rest of the nation's, to a watershed in the slavery debate, the Rubicon of a coming revolution.[14]

In 1850, after four years of rancorous debate over the territories seized from Mexico, Congress crafted a compromise to keep the number of free and slave states balanced. In the bargain, they passed a tougher law that made residents of free states responsible for the return of fugitive slaves. It became a crime to assist someone escaping enslavement, and the new law offered financial incentives for judicial rulings in favor of slaveholders when fugitive cases went to court. There was no longer anywhere in the United States that enslaved people might consider a sanctuary, and indeed the law tended to encourage the kidnapping of free African Americans as well. Many northern whites finally realized that there was no staying out of the issue. The law had appointed them slave catchers, and if the situation arose, they would have to serve as agents of the slave system or else break the law and face the consequences. To be a law-abiding American citizen, it was finally clear, was to be personally responsible for enforcing the country's slave regime. While Washington, D.C., celebrated the end of a four-year crisis in Congress that had threatened to dissolve the Union, abolitionist communities erupted with infuriated disbelief, and a new phase of the movement began.

———

AFTER THE COMPROMISE OF 1850, more and more abolitionists came to believe, as Garnet and Delany did, that violence in the service of ending slavery was both justified and necessary. Soon after the new law was passed, clashes broke out in Syracuse, New York, and Christiana, Pennsylvania, where fugitives were defended by force. In August, two thousand people convened in an apple orchard in Cazenovia, New York, including Douglass and dozens of other formerly enslaved people, along with Gerrit Smith and a number of old-guard Garrisonians. They issued an address that exposed the rising tension between Non-Resistants and those who supported the use of physical violence. "Some of us have become non-resistants," and have rejected the use of physical force and weapons, they explained to the enslaved people they hoped to reach. "But in point of fact," they clarified, "it is only a handful" of free men of color who hold these views. "When the insurrection of the Southern slaves shall take place," they assured them, the great majority of the North's black men "will be found by your side, with deep-stored and long-accumulated revenge in their hearts, and with death-dealing weapons in their hands." Even the Non-Resistants believed that "if the American revolutionists had excuse for shedding but one drop of blood, then have the American slaves excuse for making blood flow 'even unto the horse-bridles.' "[15]

But as calls mounted for a new revolution that would overthrow slavery, Delany took a different tack. As many of his colleagues in the movement expressed the desire to bring about a free and equal United States at the point of the bayonet, Delany published a book titled *The Condition, Elevation, Emigration, and Destiny of the Colored People of the United States.* In it, he entreated black readers to realize that they shared an identity only with one another, not with white Americans, and that mass exodus from the country was their only viable future. "We are a nation within a nation," he declared. He began by calling out white abolitionists, proclaiming that "the colored people are not yet known, even to their most professed friends among the white Americans," who, he claimed, have "presumed to *think* for, dictate to, and *know* better what suited colored people, than they knew for themselves." He said in essence that white allies, motivated by racial guilt, had worked too slowly, never delivering what they had promised. Even within the antislavery movement, he argued, blacks occupy "a mere secondary, underling position." His goal was black power, not integration.

Gerrit Smith, Frederick Douglass, and others at the Fugitive Slave Law Convention in Cazenovia, New York, 1850.
J. Paul Getty Museum

Working up to his proposal, Delany affirmed black claims to citizenship. Given their centuries of economic contributions and military service, "this is our country," he declared, to which African Americans have natural rights that can be obstructed but never annulled. And yet, he insisted, "we are politically, not of them, but aliens to the laws and political privileges of the country." Black Americans deserved "a new country, a new beginning." Rejecting Liberia as a racist scheme of the ACS to rid the United States of free blacks—not an independent republic, but a "miserable mockery" of one—he proposed instead Central and South America as "the ultimate destination and future home of the colored race on this continent." He specifically pointed to Nicaragua and New Grenada, which he described as fertile and resource rich, gorgeous, accessible, a preordained paradise for black Americans.

Despite Delany's enthusiasm for the Western Hemisphere as a God-given refuge for the oppressed, his book also proposed a second plan, fully articulated but buried in an appendix. He called for a "confidential council" of the intellectual leaders of the race to plan an expedition to the eastern coast of Africa to establish a settlement there. For funding, they should approach European allies as "a distinct nation of people," although "enveloped by the United States." In brief, he projected that this settlement would serve as the center of commercial trade within Africa and with East Asia and the Americas. To accomplish this, he proposed the construction of "a great rail road" through the mountains, across the continent to the Atlantic coast: "All the world would pass through Africa upon this rail road, which would yield a revenue infinitely greater than any other investment in the world." Indeed, he believed the project would pay for itself with the natural resources they would mine from the land it would occupy, the gold and other precious metals and minerals under the earth, "ten-fold greater than all the rich productions of California." This theory of black manifest destiny was conspicuously similar to the white American model, including westward expansion, a transcontinental railroad, a gold rush, and settler colonialism. It unfortunately also borrowed from white American imperialism a total disregard for the peoples already inhabiting the vast swaths of land in question. "The land is ours," Delany declared, "there it lies with inexhaustible resources; let us go and possess it."[16]

It likely came as no surprise when reviewers in the antislavery press blasted Delany's book because emigration schemes remained anathema for many activists. *The Liberator* gave it a polite notice but frowned on its black nationalist message, restating Garrison's hope for an integrated United States in which citizenship would no longer be racially defined: "We are desirous of seeing neither white nor black republics, as such." Delany answered with a letter pointedly assuring Garrison that he would have no particular objection to living among white people, except for the slight complication that it doomed him and everyone like him to permanent inferiority. As for Garrison's criticism of the book's "tone of despondency," Delany reiterated, "I have no hopes in this country—no confidence in the American people." Douglass's response to Delany's treatise was even worse: the editor of the country's leading black newspaper

(*Frederick Douglass' Paper,* which succeeded *The North Star*), and Delany's longtime colleague in the struggle, completely ignored the book. Months later, he printed an angry letter from the author, calling him out for this disregard: "You heaped upon it a cold and deathly silence. This is not the course you pursue towards any issue, good or bad, sent you by white persons."[17]

Delany had a specific white person in mind. His *Condition, Elevation, Emigration, and Destiny* had been overshadowed by a literary juggernaut published the same year. *Uncle Tom's Cabin* by Harriet Beecher Stowe was the best-selling novel that the United States had ever seen. More than a book, it was a culture-wide sensation with numerous stage adaptations and merchandise tie-ins. The publisher could not print fast enough to meet the demand—300,000 copies in the United States in the first year and even more in England. It was read feverishly on both sides of the Mason-Dixon Line, across Europe, in Moscow, and beyond. Fanny Wright, on her deathbed in Cincinnati that year, begged a copy from her lawyer, writing, "I am in great anguish and require something to draw me out of my suffering."[18]

Uncle Tom's Cabin intertwines two plots that begin on a Kentucky plantation. In one, the docile, pious title character is sold south away from his wife and children, ultimately suffering a martyr's death at the hands of a sadistic enslaver. In the other, Eliza Harris flees north with her child, leaping and teetering desperately on moving ice floes to cross the Ohio River. She is joined by her husband, the brilliant George Harris, whose revolutionary speeches place him in the tradition of the American founding fathers. And indeed, like them he declares, "I want a country, a nation, of my own." Although the Harrises are safe and prospering in Canada at the novel's conclusion, we learn that their ultimate happy ending will be in Liberia: "The whole splendid continent of Africa opens before us and our children."[19]

Douglass raved that Stowe "has evinced great keenness of insight into the workings of slavery and a depth of knowledge of all its various parts, such as few writers have equaled, and none, we are sure, have exceeded." How, Delany wondered, could he approvingly overlook Stowe's emphasis on old-school colonization but reject Delany's proposal for black-led emigration? Delany hated Stowe's insistence on submissive Christianity, which he had long considered one of the main obstacles to black freedom, and he was astonished that Douglass would look favorably on any suggestion that African Americans belong in Liberia. Learning that Douglass had met with Stowe and hoped to work with her to establish a black college, Delany wrote to warn him about relying on white patrons in his plans for the elevation of the free black community. She *"knows nothing about us,"* he exclaimed, and "neither does any other white person—and, consequently, can contrive no successful scheme for our elevation; it must be done for ourselves." Still on the rampage weeks later, Delany wrote to Douglass's paper again to suggest that Stowe give a portion of her profits to all of the black people whose stories she had appropriated into her novel, especially the authors of fugitive slave narratives, from which she borrowed heavily.[20]

Delany was not the only radical calling foul. Robert Purvis, the prominent antislavery organizer in Philadelphia, longtime colleague of Lucretia Mott's, and son-in-law of James Forten, declared that "the terrible blow which the closing chapter of this otherwise great book inflicted . . . should cause its condemnation as pernicious to the well-being of the colored people of this country." Even Garrison, still a stalwart Non-Resistant at this time, was troubled by the pious pacifism of the novel's title character. Pointing to the novel's celebratory attitude toward the founding fathers, who shed blood to overthrow tyrants, he asked, "How is this to be explained or reconciled? Is there one law of submission and non-resistance for the black man, and another law of rebellion and conflict for the white man?" Moreover, his review concluded, "the work, towards its conclusion, contains some objectionable sentiments respecting African colonization, which we regret to see." Even the author herself had misgivings about the novel's ending almost immediately after publication, possibly swayed by the offended responses of free black readers and the radical antislavery community; Stowe admitted "that if she were to write 'Uncle Tom' again, she would not send George Harris to Liberia."[21]

But after the passage of the fugitive slave law, even the black leaders most devoted to the idea that African Americans must stand their ground as citizens were increasingly pessimistic about the possibility of American integration. In 1853, Douglass conceded that free and enslaved blacks together constituted "a nation, in the midst of a nation which disowns them." He hosted a convention in Rochester that year to denounce emigration and to propose instead the permanent "National Council of the Colored People," a black governing body within and under the United States. Quoting extensively from the American founding documents, the convention's resolutions affirm, "We address you not as aliens or as exiles" but as "American citizens asserting their rights on their own native soil." The National Council of the Colored People would manage all the needs and concerns of the black population, including recording its history in an official library and museum. The convention proceedings devote many pages to denouncing colonization yet also contain a special resolution of thanks and approval to Stowe and her novel. Delany snubbed the assembly and countered it with a radical response.[22]

While the men at Douglass's convention ultimately clung to middle-class American values, calling on black people to renew their commitment to marriage, domesticity, and religious morality, Delany's National Emigration Convention in August 1854, in which women served as delegates and on leadership committees, advocated militant black nationalism. Activists from all over the country, including southern states, as well as Ontario, gathered to pledge racial solidarity and pursue mass exodus. There were resolutions calling for equal education for black girls and others affirming racial identity and pride—departing from the long-standing position of the antislavery community, both black and white, who insisted that people were fundamentally the same across lines of so-called racial difference.

This meeting also differed from Douglass's convention in its antipathy not only toward slavery but toward the United States generally. One resolution notes that the fugitive slave law and its aftermath had "measurably alienated our feelings toward this country;

dispelled the lingering patriotism from our bosoms, which compels us to regard as our common enemy every white, who proves not himself to the contrary." The assembly was rapt listening to a young delegate from New Orleans offer to take up arms against the United States. "I can hate this Government without being disloyal," he claimed. "I can join a foreign enemy and fight against it, without being a traitor, because it treats me as an ALIEN and a STRANGER." Warning his listeners not to fall for the "sickly sentimentality" of American patriotism, he said, "I am willing to forget the endearing name of home and country, and as an unwilling exile seek on other shores the freedom which has been denied me in the land of my birth." The audience reacted with a "ferment of emotion" to this affirmation that violence was justified not only to combat enslavers but also to confront the U.S. government as a military enemy.

Delany took the floor and delivered his most powerful speech to date. He posited black racial specificity, even superiority, as the basis of their bond with one another, their distinction from the majority of Americans, and the basis of a future state: "Our friends in this and other countries, anxious for our elevation, have for years been erroneously urging us to lose our identity as a distinct race, declaring that we were the same as other people." But "the truth is," he argued, "we are not identical with the Anglo-Saxon or any other race." He continued: "We have then inherent traits, attributes— so to speak—and native characteristics, peculiar to our race," and when these can be cultivated and developed "in their purity," they will be desirable and emulated by the rest of the world. Indeed, "we barely acknowledge the whites as equals—perhaps not in every particular." Finding it pernicious and degrading for black children to see every respectable and prominent position filled by a white man, he insisted, "A people, to be free, must necessarily be *their own rulers*" and control their "political destiny." To this end, the convention affirmed its support for black emigration from the United States to some other site in the Western Hemisphere, proposing to consider plans for Canada, the Caribbean, and Central and South America.[23]

The emigration convention was a hot topic for debate in the

black press, many of the responses attacking Delany and his movement. When Douglass reprinted one of these critiques, Delany sent an insinuating response: "We have no quarrel with those who love to live among the whites better than the blacks, and leave them to the enjoyment of their predilections." And leave he did.[24]

———

THE BLACK REFUGEES who fled Ohio for Canada in 1829 to found the Wilberforce colony with the initial support of the National Conventions of the Free People of Colour had been joined in the intervening years by other emigrants. By the 1840s, Ontario was dotted with settlements like the intentional communities of Dawn and Elgin, as well as regular towns with concentrations of expatriate black families. These communities north of the border became even more attractive in the following decade as the fugitive slave law continued to endanger every free person of color in the North, but especially the many who had once been enslaved. Then came the 1857 Supreme Court decision in the *Dred Scott* case, which declared that no person of African descent could ever be an American citizen, indeed that black Americans had no rights at all that white men were bound to respect. Thousands of African Americans crossed the border, streaming into Canada West from every city in the North.[25]

One particularly popular destination was Chatham, Ontario, which sits across Lake Erie from Cleveland, a quick ride from Detroit by train or steamboat. Around a third of the residents of Chatham were black exiles from the United States, and the town soon became large enough to support a newspaper, two churches, a school, and a firefighting company. Black settlers could also claim the same legal rights and protections as white Canadians, including the vote. This city was called "a mecca" and "the colored man's Paris" of the mid-nineteenth century for the robust black community that sprang up there. Ontario was not utopia, of course, and the settlers still encountered racial prejudice despite their improved legal status. Some white Canadians took legislative action in an attempt to limit any further influx of black immigrants. But many

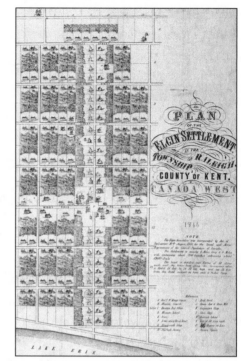

Plan for the
Elgin settlement.
Archives of Ontario

African Americans found this kind of racism far preferable to the situation in the United States, fleeing a supposedly free democracy for the protections of a monarchy.[26]

Chatham's black newspaper was run by Mary Ann Shadd, the daughter of a prominent leader in the early antislavery and Free People of Colour conventions, who had emigrated late in 1851. Mere months after her family's arrival, she published a pro-emigration piece describing Canada in utopian terms and urging African Americans to make a permanent home there. Her pioneering work as an editor and black emigrationist in Canada laid the groundwork for her long activist career. Many others joined in her enthusiasm for post-American black life across the border. In 1856, the African American poet and activist Frances Harper wrote, "I have just returned from Canada. I have gazed for the first time upon a free land," adding, "Tears sprang to my eyes and I wept." Even Frederick Douglass, in his 1852 story, *The Heroic Slave,* rhapsodized on the refuge of Canada. When his protagonist finally crosses the border, he declares, "I nestle in the mane of the British lion, protected by the mighty paw from the talons and the beak of the American eagle. I AM FREE."[27]

Delany made good on his disavowal of the United States and in 1856 moved his family to Chatham, where he and his wife, Catherine, bought a house and a quarter acre of land. But he saw Canada as a stopgap measure only and continued to pursue the sweeping solution he had floated to a select few colleagues in "secret sessions" of his emigration convention. For the next three years, Delany raised money and made final preparations for the trip he felt he was born to take.

CHAPTER 10

Treason Will Not Be Treason Much Longer

Anthony Burns worked for a used-clothing dealer near the Boston wharves, just a couple of doors down from the shop from which David Walker's pamphlet advocating violent resistance had found its way to the enslaved people of the South back in 1829. At the corner was Brattle Street Church, where John Hancock and Samuel Adams had worshipped years before. The building still had a cannonball fired during the Siege of Boston embedded in one wall, preserved there as a memorial to the revolution. As Burns walked down the street after work on May 24, 1854, a man approached and laid a rough hand on his shoulder, telling him he had been accused of robbing a jewelry store. In fact, his only crime had been to escape from the plantation where he had been enslaved. The law said that he owed his labor, indeed his whole person, to a man in Virginia. Six or more men jumped out of hiding and secured his limbs, carrying him horizontally to the courthouse. If he had resisted, the slave catcher intended to shoot him dead in the street.[1]

This was the third highly publicized case of a man escaped from slavery being held captive under the Fugitive Slave Act in Boston, an epicenter of abolitionist organizing. The first had involved the arrest of Shadrach Minkins in February 1851. Having escaped from Virginia the previous year, Minkins was seized in the coffeehouse where he worked as a waiter. During his trial, a group of black Bostonian activists entered the courtroom and physically carried him out, ferrying him through a number of Massachusetts safe houses and on to Canada. Secretary of State Daniel Webster, the former Massachusetts senator who had been an architect of the Compromise of 1850, called the Minkins rescue "treason, and nothing less," charging those involved with "levying war against the United States." Thomas Sims, a skinny teenager escaped from Georgia, was arrested just months later. Determined not to lose the prisoner this time, over one hundred armed policemen and militia guarded the courthouse and actually wrapped chains around the building, under which the judges had to stoop to enter—symbolism that was lost on no one.[2]

After the Compromise of 1850, the work of "Vigilance Committees," associations of antislavery men willing to take physical action to protect and aid fugitives despite the law, intensified. Robert Purvis had founded a group of this kind in Philadelphia—the Vigilant Association—back in 1837 to facilitate freedom missions, and there were similar associations across northern cities. The Boston Vigilance Committee held a meeting in the *Liberator* office in April 1851 to hatch a plan for Sims's escape. Among the attendees was the minister Thomas Wentworth Higginson, who recalled that despite the unfaltering commitment of this group, "it is impossible to conceive of a set of men, personally admirable, yet less fitted on the whole than this committee to undertake any positive action in the direction of forcible resistance to authorities." Half of them were Non-Resistants, pledged to absolute pacificism. The other half were "political abolitionists" who believed in working within the system, "personally full of indignation" and yet "extremely anxious not to be placed for one moment outside the pale of good citizenship." Higginson helped hatch a plan in which Sims would jump from a third-story window onto a pile of mattresses to be spirited away in a waiting carriage. But that same day, his captors reinforced the windows with iron bars. The second plan was to overtake the vessel returning him south, board it pirate-style, and take him away in another boat. This plan, too, was abandoned as impractical. In the end, Sims was marched through the city at four in the morning to a ship waiting to take him to Savannah, Georgia, where he was publicly whipped upon arrival.

Thoroughly ashamed of this inadequate response, Higginson came away from the Sims case lamenting his "great want of preparation" for bold acts of defiance against the government. After a lifetime of good behavior, he reflected, "it takes the whole experience of one such case to educate the mind to the attitude of revolution." Like many other white abolitionists, Higginson—a Boston Brahmin whose illustrious family went back to the first Puritan settlers and signers of the Constitution—had always considered himself a law-abiding patriot. "It is so strange to find one's self outside of established institutions; to be obliged to lower one's voice and conceal one's purposes; to see law and order, police and military, on the wrong side, and find good citizenship a sin and bad citizenship a duty, that it takes time to prepare one to act coolly and wisely, as well as courageously, in such an emergency," he wrote. When Anthony Burns was captured three years later, Higginson and his colleagues were more prepared. They swore that this man would not be returned to slavery while they stood quietly by.[3]

When word got out that another fugitive was locked in the city courthouse, a rally was swiftly arranged for Faneuil Hall. Higginson and the Vigilance Committee made a plan to harness the energy of this protest into a rescue mission. They appointed someone to

Thomas Wentworth Higginson.
Massachusetts Historical Society

interrupt the speakers once they had stirred the crowd to a fever pitch and to announce that a group of black men had launched a direct attack on the courthouse, as they had in the Shadrach Minkins rescue; from the stage, the speakers would urge the crowd to run to their aid. At the sound of the throng approaching, Higginson and the committee members would begin an assault on the building where Burns was held, to be backed by the reinforcement of the crowd flowing in behind them.

At the Faneuil Hall rally, Theodore Parker, the Transcendentalist minister who preached to thousands of progressives in the city every Sunday, took the stage. He had already taken a public stance against the fugitive slave law and had also hidden Ellen Craft, a member of his congregation, in his home when slave catchers came to Boston to find her and her husband. He wrote his sermon that week with a loaded revolver in his desk and was prepared to use it. At the protest to free Anthony Burns, he asked the people of Massachusetts how they liked being subjects of Virginia, watching slave catchers reach into the land of the Pilgrims to kidnap men over the very graves of the founders. There is no North, he boomed: "The South goes clear up to the Canada line." He called for a change in the antislavery movement from argument to action: "I ask you, are we to have *deeds* as well as words?" Departing from Garrisonian orthodoxy, Parker indicated that the time for violence had arrived. "I am a clergyman and a man of peace; I love peace," he averred. "But there is a means and there is an end; liberty is the end, and sometimes peace is not the means toward it."[4]

Although Parker's encouragement of direct action, and violent resistance if necessary, aligned perfectly with Higginson's plan to transform the assembly into an insurrection, neither Parker nor the other leading speaker, Wendell Phillips, had received the message about the role they were supposed to play in the rescue plan. The announcement was made that an attack on the courthouse had begun, and hundreds poured out of Faneuil Hall, but with no clear aim. Reaching the courthouse steps, working-class immigrants and black abolitionists jostled against white men who had never protested anything before. From the street, they threw stones and bricks through the windows of the imposing government building. Someone climbed a lamppost and extinguished the streetlight. They hacked at the massive doors with axes and then, finding a wooden joist around ten or fifteen feet long in an alley, took hold of it for a battering ram.

At the front stood Higginson and Lewis Hayden, one of the city's leading black abolitionists and businessmen. As an enslaved fourteen-year-old in Kentucky, Hayden had turned out to see the Marquis de Lafayette parade through Lexington during his 1825 visit, perching on a fence away from the white admirers who had come to see the Revolutionary hero's carriage pass by. Catching his eye, Lafayette bowed in Hayden's direction. He "was the most famous man I had ever heard of," Hayden recalled, "and you can imagine how I felt, a slave-boy to be favored with his recognition. The act burnt his image upon my heart. . . . After that I allowed no moving thing on the face of the earth to stand between me and my freedom." As a young man, Hayden was married to a woman enslaved by Henry Clay, the founding president of the American Colonization Society who became secretary of state in the "corrupt bargain" that Fanny Wright had witnessed after the 1824 election. Hayden and his wife had a child together—a boy. But Clay soon sold both mother and son. Hayden never saw them again. With his second wife, Harriet, he escaped Kentucky in 1844, and after a brief stay at the Dawn settlement in Ontario, they settled in Boston. Hayden helped hundreds of others to freedom, spearheading the Minkins rescue in 1851 and leading an organization of black Bostonians active in the fight against the Fugitive Slave Act. He and Harriet kept their Beacon Hill home stocked with kegs of gunpowder, ready to blow it up rather than turn over the hunted people they harbored.[5]

The men slammed the beam into the door again and again. Higginson later recounted that these strokes echoed through the streets "like the first drum beat of the Revolution." With one final swing, a hinge broke and the door opened wide enough for one person to pass through. Anyone bold enough to enter would pass directly into a group of policemen on the other side, with the impossible mission of reaching the stairwell to the third floor, overpowering more armed guards, and bringing the prisoner down safely. Higginson recalled, "I glanced instinctively at my black ally. He did not even look at me, but sprang in first." Following him in, Higginson was slammed against a wall. He and Hayden fought back with their fists against the crowd of armed police. Higginson was slashed in the face with a cutlass. Caught up in the fight, he was not even aware he had been injured, but he would have a scar for the rest of his life, a reminder of the first time he put his body on the line for the cause.[6]

A gunshot rang out, and one of the guards, a deputy marshal named James Batchelder, cried out. Seeing Higginson penned in a corner and being hammered with clubs, Hayden had drawn a concealed pistol and fired. The deputy fell to the floor of the courthouse entrance and died. Despite the identifying wound on his face, Higginson managed to slip out of the courthouse and make it home to Worcester, although a number of others were arrested. Hayden got away as well and skipped town later that week. No one ever figured out that he had killed Batchelder; the coroner's inquest

Lewis Hayden.
Houghton Library, Harvard University,
MS Am 2420(14)

declared that the wound was long and deep, made by a knife, not a round pistol ball. But Hayden had loaded the gun with a slug that tore through the guard's femoral artery lengthwise.[7]

After decades in which antislavery activists had been the targets of mob violence numerous times, the tables had turned. One of the defining principles of the Garrisonians was Non-Resistance, but a different approach was coming to the fore. The Burns riot launched a sequence of violent clashes between antislavery dissidents and the state-supported pro-slavery regime in the 1850s that would lead from the Boston courthouse through Kansas, Washington, D.C., and Harpers Ferry, Virginia, directly into the war that, after four blood-soaked years, would ultimately settle the question.

———

Local media coverage framed the Anthony Burns protest as a battle not between liberty and slavery but between law and anarchy, with the abolitionists on the wrong side. They blamed Parker and Phillips for Batchelder's death, alleging that they had incited the crowd to homicide. Newspapers in Boston and New York called for them to be charged with murder, treason, and "war against the union," suggesting the gallows as the appropriate punishment or simply recommending that they be "shot down like dogs." Indeed, Parker and Phillips were both indicted in the coming days, although the charges were eventually dropped.[8]

As for those who did more than give speeches, the papers described the assault on the courthouse as an act of treason carried out by "bold, bad men." They cautioned all good citizens, no matter their views on slavery, to stay at home, warning them that "Burns is in the hands of the law. Those who engage in the work of attempting to take him away from the officers will commit treason against their country, and must suffer its penalties." Yet in the same breath, they framed the protesters' failure to free Burns in this revolt as evidence that abolitionists "are mighty with the tongue—great in holding conventions and passing resolutions"—but will never successfully *do* anything for their cause.[9]

For the next six days, downtown Boston was under martial law.

After the attempted rescue, President Franklin Pierce—a northerner and close friend of the former Brook Farmer Nathaniel Hawthorne—deployed federal troops to join the local militia in putting down any further resistance to Burns's rendition. Armed soldiers trained weapons of war on civilians; a cannon was pulled up the street by two horses and positioned in front of one of the courthouse entrances, facing into the crowd. Protests continued every day, men and women, white and black, demanding that the authorities of their free state release its prisoner. For some in the crowd, this was a turning point in their relationship to the law and its enforcers. The American military was there to defend against them as traitors and lawbreakers in the name of one enslaver's property claim. They were ready to fire upon the crowd if a rescue was attempted again. The protesters' refusal to aid personally the smooth functioning of the slave system constituted a mass act of civil disobedience.[10]

On June 2, Burns was brought out of the building. He was twenty years old and six feet tall, his hands tied in front of him, and wearing a top hat, by all accounts looking broken in both body and spirit. On his cheek was a large scar that seemed to be the result of branding or some other torture. One of his hands was deformed by a projecting bone, a break never treated or healed. A regiment of soldiers armed with muskets formed a hollow square around him. They were reinforced by militiamen with loaded revolvers in one hand and drawn swords in the other. Marines rode a line of horses pulling the cannon. The U.S. artillery did a drill of rapidly loading and firing their guns as a show of force. This bellicose display was intended as a warning not to the prisoner but to the throng of fifty thousand people packing every balcony and roof, hanging from every window, booing the soldiers, hissing, "Shame!" Heavy folds of black crape festooned the streets in mourning. A huge American flag hung upside down and draped with black was suspended on a rope across State Street. One group of protesters displayed a coffin they had labeled "Liberty," later lowering it out the window of a building, high above the crowd. The soldiers marched Burns a third of a mile to the harbor, past the statehouse and the site of the

Boston Massacre. They loaded him onto the waiting ship, headed for Virginia.

In the age of the Black Lives Matter movement, some speak of being or staying "woke," meaning aware of systemic racism, vigilant for its manifestations and opportunities for resistance. In the nineteenth century, Americans described a similar experience of being "waked up." Early in his career, Garrison had received a letter from a reader announcing, "I have waked up—I have *thought* myself awake for years, but I begin to be convinced that I have only been *dreaming*—I mean I have waked up on the subject of slavery." The kidnapping, trial, and rendition of Anthony Burns were the events most credited at the time with having "waked up" the antislavery spirit and general indignation of the North at the aggression and overreach of the slave power. A correspondent from Boston re-

As many as fifty thousand people assembled in Boston
to protest the re-enslavement of Anthony Burns in 1854.
E. Benjamin Andrews, History of the United States from the Earliest
Discovery of America to the Present Day, Volume III *(New York:
Charles Scribner's Sons, 1898), 214*

ported that it had revolutionized public sentiment, making people of color in that city more certain of their white allies and the eventual success of their movement: "Thus, while poor Burns has been sacrificed, his trial and rendition, with the horrible circumstances attending them, have waked up more minds, and set in motion more anti-slavery forces in this state, than could have been done by ten years of ordinary effort." The most famous usage of the phrase came from Amos Adams Lawrence, scion of a Boston mercantile family worth millions. He wrote to his uncle to describe the effect of the Burns case on Bostonians like himself who had always stayed out of the fray: "We went to bed one night old fashioned, conservative, Compromise Union Whigs & waked up stark mad Abolitionists."[11]

Like Lawrence and many other white northerners, Higginson had been waked up by the Anthony Burns case, even though he had been steeped in reform culture for years. He had entered Harvard University when he was thirteen, in the Transcendentalist heyday when Emerson was disavowed by his alma mater for his infidel notions. Jones Very, the young poet committed to McLean for proclaiming himself the Second Coming of Christ, was Higginson's tutor and friend. Through the Fourierist minister William Henry Channing, Higginson imbibed the ideas of Brook Farm, although when he visited, he was turned off by the "variety of dirty men, boys and girls" who lived at the community. By 1854, he was already active in the women's movement, having organized a temperance convention the previous year with Elizabeth Cady Stanton, Lucy Stone, Lucretia Mott, and others and published in the new feminist periodical *The Una*. But he had initially joined the Boston Vigilance Committee as much for adventure as for politics, regretting that he had missed the excitement of the Minkins rescue. Although Higginson had been a committed abolitionist since he was a teenager, any action he had taken up to that point might have been driven in part by his self-regarding desire to be manly, heroic, and talked about. But his role at the head of a battering ram in Boston emboldened him to a new level of engagement.[12]

After his leading role in the insurrection at the courthouse,

Higginson returned to his congregation in Worcester and preached a sermon with his face still bandaged. Like Parker, he felt that a change in the movement was long overdue: "We have been surfeited with words for twenty years. I am thankful that this time there was action also." Importantly, the events led him to articulate his profound hostility not just to slaveholding but to the United States: "I am glad of the discovery—(no hasty thing, but gradually dawning upon me for ten years)—that I live under a despotism. I have lost the dream that ours is a land of peace and order. I have looked thoroughly through your 'Fourth of July,' and seen its hollowness; I can only make life worth living for, by becoming a revolutionist."

Others in the abolitionist movement felt called to revolution at this time as well. The Independence Day demonstration held by the Garrisonians that year made clear that further fealty to the United States had become morally impossible and that the movement's long commitment to pacifism was wearing thin. Trains and carriages brought a huge crowd out to Harmony Grove in Framingham that hot day. Carrying picnic lunches, the visitors arrayed themselves around a stage crowned with an American flag hung upside down and draped in black. Among the other flags adorned with mourning crape, one implored, "Redeem Massachusetts."

Higginson was not present; he had a bad cold, but as he explained to William Lloyd Garrison in a letter, he also had a quarrel with how *The Liberator* had covered the courthouse raid, having described it as ill-advised and hasty. "Of course, I do not expect you, as a Non-Resistant, to sympathize with such an attack," Higginson wrote, but he was annoyed at the lack of respect from the abolitionist paper of record. After all, the crowd at the courthouse had finally *done* something to act on an entire community's outrage. He insisted that *nothing* would have been done otherwise to try to save Anthony Burns, insinuating that Garrison's whole program of moral suasion, speeches, meetings, articles, and the like was worthless.[13]

When Garrison took the stage in Framingham, he delivered the most famous speech of his long career. He began by praising the

Declaration of Independence as "the most radical political instrument in the world," noting the hypocrisy of "conservatives today making ostentatious venerations of the Declaration of 1776 filled with distress and horror at the thought of radicalism." The Declaration severs all chains, he averred, and if it were ever truly carried out, the world would be redeemed. "What is an abolitionist," he asked, "but a sincere believer in the Declaration of '76?" But this profound dedication to American ideals demanded a direct attack on the perverted system that had forgotten them. He wanted to burn the country down, and he would start that day.

He held high a printed copy of the fugitive slave law and set it on fire. He burned the decision in the Burns case and the charge of treasonable assault against the courthouse protesters, cheers roaring from the crowd as the flames consumed the documents. Finally, he pulled out a copy of the U.S. Constitution, which he called "the source and parent of all the other atrocities, a covenant with death, and an agreement with hell," and burned it up, shouting, "So perish all compromises with tyranny!" This symbolic violence became the most notorious of Garrison's calls for the death of the Union. He had found a way to represent the vehemence of his words with a destructive physical act, indicating that speech alone no longer felt sufficient, even to the most committed pacifist, a newspaperman whose life's work was a war on slavery with words.[14]

He was followed on the platform by several other multi-issue abolitionists, including the formerly enslaved communitarian Sojourner Truth, the Come-Outer Stephen S. Foster, the feminist Lucy Stone, and the Transcendental anarchist Henry David Thoreau. Like Higginson, Thoreau's dominant feeling on that Fourth of July was that America was over. "I have lived for the last month," he explained, "with the sense of having suffered a vast and indefinite loss. I did not know at first what ailed me. At last it occurred to me that what I had lost was a country." He said that he tried to forget the horrifying state of politics and go outside, but "the remembrance of my country spoils my walk. My thoughts are murder to the State, and involuntarily go plotting against her." With disgust, he talked about his Concord neighbors celebrating the Fourth of

July, congratulating themselves on the role of their town in the American Revolution decades in the past, when a travesty of those values just happened under their noses. He observed that Massachusetts "praises till she is hoarse the easy exploit of the Boston tea party," but predicted that in the future "she will be comparatively silent about the braver and more disinterestedly heroic attack on the Boston Court-House, simply because it was unsuccessful!"[15]

Thoreau was right about the comparative silence. The Boston Tea Party museum is elaborate even by the standards of a city in which Revolutionary history is a prime tourist attraction. The tax protest is commemorated with a museum perched on the water, fully restored sailing vessels from the eighteenth century, historical reenactors, fife music piped over speakers, eighteenth-century cocktails, and a multimedia documentary. But the site of the courthouse in Boston, where Anthony Burns, Shadrach Minkins, and Thomas Sims were held as slaves by the free Commonwealth of Massachusetts, receives no such fanfare. The nearby "Freedom Trail" lionizes the valiant insurrectionists of a previous generation, and the Black Heritage Trail and Museum of African American History in Beacon Hill work tirelessly to preserve the memory of the black Bostonians like Lewis and Harriet Hayden. But as Thoreau suspected, 26 Court Street stands without so much as a historical marker to acknowledge Anthony Burns and the interracial group of protesters who risked their lives to try to free him.

He might have been wrong, however, to call the protest unsuccessful. While the protesters failed to rescue Burns, their efforts prefigured, and arguably helped to inspire, the soldiers who marched south when the federal government ended its armed defense of slavery at long last. Treason would soon switch sides.

———

As ANTISLAVERY SENTIMENT HEIGHTENED in the North, the South's defense of the institution took on revolutionary new dimensions as well. Inverting Garrison's two-step with the founding documents, southerners clung fiercely to the Constitution while rejecting the Declaration of Independence. The Constitution's "three-fifths clause" granted extra representation to slave states, bolstering their control of the government and, arguably, sanctioning and protecting the institution by acknowledging it as part of the country's political organization from the beginning. In the 1850s, pro-slavery pundits like George Fitzhugh went so far as to deride the Declaration as a sham theoretical exercise that no one took seriously until the antislavery crowd started making a fuss about it. Moreover, he insisted that free society was an obvious failure compared with the South's idyllic slave society, pointing to the North's radical countercultures as evidence of its dysfunction: "Why have you Bloomer's and Women's Right's men, and strong-minded women, and Mormons, and anti-renters, and 'vote myself a farm' men, Millerites, and Spiritual Rappers, and Shakers, and Widow Wakemanites, and Agrarians, and Grahamites, and a thousand other superstitious and infidel isms at the North?" According to Fitzhugh, these fringe leftists unintentionally endorsed slavery when they critiqued capitalism and called for a harmonious, collaborative integration of work and private life. He claimed that southern plantations had already brought about the utopian society that the Fourierists imagined, except without the atheism and wild sex.[16]

With the western territories seized from Mexico in 1848, the southerners proposed an ambitious expansion of the peculiar institution, which, they argued, was favored by God and the Constitution. They also hoped to annex Cuba and parts of what remained of Mexico as territories for a great slaveholding empire. As a Mississippi senator explained in 1858, "I want these countries for the spread of slavery. I would spread the blessings of slavery, like the religion of our Divine Master, to the uttermost ends of the earth, and rebellious and wicked as the Yankees have been, I would even extend it to them." The free states had already been turned into hunting grounds for fugitives, and many northerners feared that the South would extend "the blessings of slavery" to them even more assertively by rejecting all territorial limits placed upon the institution.[17]

A major step toward this expansion came with the Kansas-Nebraska Act of 1854, which overrode a previous agreement between the sections, the Missouri Compromise, which had declared

36°30′ as slavery's northern boundary. When this compromise had been adjudicated three decades earlier, Thomas Jefferson had regarded it with prophetic alarm: "This momentous question, like a firebell in the night, awakened and filled me with terror. I considered it at once the knell of the union." Although the recognition that slavery would ultimately prove a life-or-death question for the American experiment might have waked up Jefferson in some way, the compromise had been designed to lull the population generally into a false repose. But the landgrab of the Mexican-American War had reopened the question. Overturning the geographical limits on the institution established by the Missouri Compromise, Congress decided that the matter of whether slavery could be extended into the territories of Kansas and Nebraska would be decided by "popular sovereignty"; that is, settlers there would take a vote.

Pierce signed the bill while Boston was under martial law that summer. Amos Lawrence, the millionaire being waked up just then by Anthony Burns's rendition, jumped into action and became a chief financial backer of the Massachusetts Emigrant Aid Company, which defrayed the expenses of antislavery settlers moving west. Around a thousand northerners headed to Kansas, motivated by the economic opportunities that settling new territory offered or by abolitionist principles or both. Antislavery ministers shifted at this time from preaching moral suasion to packing crates with guns and kegs of blasting powder to help them. Much to Garrison's dismay, the two most famous liberal ministers in the nation, Theodore Parker and Henry Ward Beecher (Harriet Beecher Stowe's brother), raised money in their churches to buy weapons. Because boxes of breech-loading Sharps rifles sent from these abolitionist Christians were often marked "books" or "tools" for transport to the territory, the guns came to be called Beecher's Bibles. Antislavery homesteaders were met by settlers on the opposing side of the issue as well as Missouri residents who flowed over the border to add their strength and numbers to the pro-slavery effort. This tinderbox came to be known as Bleeding Kansas, a period of sham elections and armed skirmishes between "Free-Staters" and "Border Ruffians."

A disastrous sequence of events in May 1856 brought this guerrilla violence to a head and closed the distance between the remote territories and the heart of the nation's government. On the nineteenth, the Massachusetts senator Charles Sumner took the floor to deliver a rancorous speech that stretched over two days, decrying the violence in Kansas and criticizing southern senators by name. On the twenty-second, Preston Brooks, a representative from South Carolina, entered the Senate chamber after the session adjourned and approached Sumner, who was writing at his desk. Insulted by Sumner's remarks against a senator from his state, Brooks had determined not to challenge him to a duel as a gentleman and a social equal but rather to reproach him as he would a slave. Informing Sumner of his offense, he raised a hardwood walking stick with a large metal head and began thrashing his face and head. Shocked and blinded with blood, Sumner tried to escape under his desk but became trapped. Eventually, he tore the bolted-down furniture out of the floor to get free and staggered up the aisle. Senators who might have intervened to stop the attack were held at bay by associates of Brooks brandishing guns and canes. Even after Sumner lost consciousness and lay on the floor covered in gore, Brooks held him by the lapel and continued to pummel him. Physical violence erupting on city streets and the prairie, and now even in the halls of Congress, signaled that the opportunity for civil debate on the "slavery question" and the long era of compromise in the name of union were speeding to a close.

Just as accounts of Brooks's shocking attack on Sumner inflamed the North, news came from Kansas that the day before the beating, the town of Lawrence—named for the antislavery millionaire whose funds had helped build it—had been raided and destroyed. After the pro-slavery territorial government passed drastic laws, including one mandating two years of hard labor for the felony of expressing antislavery views, the Free-Staters in Lawrence had set up their own government and were indicted for treason. Hundreds of Border Ruffians, some deputized to arrest the traitors, descended on Lawrence with cannons and other weapons. They were joined by a huge mob of southerners who had marched into the territory under a banner proclaiming "The Supremacy of the White Race."

Together, they destroyed the offices of two Free State newspapers, burned the town's hotel and the home of its governor, and ransacked houses and businesses. Some 150 civilians were killed.[18]

Continuing the chain of retribution, news of the attack on Sumner reached Kansas, catalyzing one man in particular to action. John Brown was an austere and intensely religious abolitionist, a New England–born pioneer who worked in the wool business, leather tanning, and other concerns. Like his father, who had been an early subscriber to *The Liberator,* he was an exacting old-school Calvinist obsessed with the wages of sin. He had publicly consecrated his life to the destruction of slavery after the murder of the abolitionist printer Elijah Lovejoy in 1837 and privately called his wife and children to kneel with him in their home and solemnly pledge to fight the institution of slavery even unto death. They lived very humbly, saving every penny for the patriarch's ultimate campaign, but the financial panic of that year wiped him out completely. A year later, cholera struck, and four of his young children died within days. Burying them together in one common grave, Brown also wanted to die. But he was determined to live for the antislavery cause and fulfill the role he was preordained to play in it as God's instrument to kill men and eradicate a great evil.

In 1849, Brown moved his family to upstate New York as part of an experiment called Timbuctoo conceived by Gerrit Smith, the wealthy political abolitionist and Liberty Party stalwart. Smith divvied up over a hundred thousand acres of land he owned in an area of the Adirondacks called North Elba, giving it to black families to farm, aiming to provide them with sustainable homes and the assets they would need to meet the property threshold to vote in New York. Brown approached Smith with an offer to buy one of the parcels and lend what help he could to the black settlers, teaching them the skills they would need to hack homesteads out of the region's inhospitable land. But in fact he was there to recruit an army.[19]

For at least three years at that point, Brown had been sharing with select black men his plan for a campaign of strategic incursions into slaveholding territory from a series of natural fortifications in the Allegheny Mountains. His goal was to rally slaves to run away

John Brown, ca. 1847.
National Portrait Gallery, Smithsonian
Institution; purchased with major
acquisition funds and with funds donated
by Betty Adler Schermer in honor of her
great-grandfather August M. Bondi

and join his ranks, battling to the death anyone who stood in their way. He planned to start with twenty-five armed men, grow their number to a hundred, and start drilling as a proper army that could liberate a widening area, sending some people on to Canada through a system he called the Subterranean Pass Way while others stayed to fight. He never lost sight of this large-scale plan that he believed would be the ultimate deathblow to the institution, but the battle against slavery was hot in Kansas, so he headed west.

In 1855, he arrived in the territory, walking next to a sick horse pulling a wagon loaded down with weapons and the corpse of one of his grandchildren, which he had disinterred en route. He joined his family members already homesteading there: six of his sons plus two of their wives, one of his daughters and her husband, and two brothers-in-law. He was named captain of a group called the Liberty Guards, a Free State militia. Brown allowed no swearing, no alcohol, and no indecent behavior among his men. They camped in open tents, suffering frostbitten toes in the winter, or on top of rough blankets on wet grass in warmer weather. They ate beans and a little milk when they could get it but usually managed only two meals a day of skillet bread washed down with creek water. In leaner times, they would smash corn between two rocks, roll it into a ball, and bake it in the ashes of the campfire, sometimes pairing it with a piece of jerky from the last time they allocated a bullet to wild game. Brown was turning fifty-six years old, but his sons noted that he had never looked better; after many years of preparation, his opportunity to assail the slave power directly had finally arrived.[20]

In retribution for the beating of Sumner and the sack of Lawrence, Brown and his men rode into a pro-slavery settlement near Pottawatomie around 11:00 p.m. on May 24, 1856, and started knocking on doors, informing the inhabitants that they represented "the Northern army." Over a period of four hours, they dragged five pro-slavery men out of three homes. At daybreak, the terrified wives and children of these settlers ventured out of their cabins to discover the gruesome handiwork of Brown and his posse. A bullet hole in a forehead indicated one execution-style shooting, but even more disturbing was the damage done with swords: the men's skulls had been hacked open, holes carved into their chests, throats cut. The bodies had also been mutilated—fingers, hands, and arms cut off. These killings, which came to be known as the Pottawatomie Massacre, touched off a period of heightened violence; two hundred men were killed in the coming months. Pro-slavery forces burned the Browns' homestead and shot one of his sons dead in the road. But the event also "startled alike the brave and timid in free-state ranks with a triumphant, yet serious, feeling, that on their side at least a Man had arrived."[21]

For this man, Kansas was an important battle, but he was planning a war. As Brown headed out of Kansas that fall on one of his many cross-country journeys, Higginson came in. He had recently returned from a long vacation in the Portuguese islands with his chronically ill wife. As their returning ship approached the New England coast, the harbor pilot came on board with newspaper reports of the beating of Charles Sumner and the intensifying violence in Kansas. From his first night back in Worcester, Higginson leaped into raising money and purchasing weapons to win Kansas for freedom, and he went to check it out for himself in September. In a dispatch from Lawrence, he wrote, "A single day in Kanzas makes the American Revolution" truly imaginable; indeed, "the same event is still in progress here."

Bleeding Kansas seemed to him like an ongoing battle in the Revolutionary War, but it also revealed the failure of that exalted conflict of the previous century. Reflecting on all the southerners he saw who had come to Kansas specifically to fight men from the North, Higginson reflected, "People speak of civil war as only a thing that may be, when there is scarcely a State in the Union which has not been already involved in civil war, through its representatives here. The simple fact is, that slaveholders and freemen are always two nations." He forecast "a struggle which will convulse a continent before it is ended, and separate forever those two nations of North and South, which neither Union nor Constitution has yet welded into one." Higginson anticipated, indeed hoped, that this war would soon be declared in Kansas. By the fall of 1856, five years before the shots fired at Fort Sumter, Americans understood that a civil war was not just inevitable; it had already begun.[22]

———

THE PRESIDENTIAL ELECTION of 1856 seemed to some the last possible hope that a solution could begin within the political system. "Bleeding Kansas" and "Bleeding Sumner" became key rallying cries for a major new player on the American political scene—the Republican Party. The Republican platform pledged to halt the spread of slavery to the territories and beyond but not to abolish it in states where it already existed, exactly the kind of half measure that made politics disgusting to Garrison. Although many antislavery men joined their ranks, Republicans on the whole were by no means fired by the dream of racial equality. Indeed, they generally supported colonization. Although many abolitionist activists regarded them as too conservative on slavery, the mainstream press portrayed them as radical representatives not only of African American rights but also of Grahamites, socialists, women suffragists, and Free Lovers.

The Republicans hated slave owners because they curtailed the freedoms of white men, maintaining an unpaid labor force that devalued free workers, enforcing gag rules against antislavery speech in defiance of the First Amendment, and the like. They resented that southern aristocrats, whom they described as "one percent" of the population, controlled the political system with a majority in Congress and the cudgel of the slavery-protecting Constitution. For the presidential ticket, they nominated John C. Frémont, a former soldier and one of the first two senators from the new state of California. Frémont had struck it rich in the gold rush and had effectively no political record or experience, which was considered an asset in this climate. Unfit for the job by most standards, he still managed to rally an enormous surge of support in the North. In the final count, Frémont lost to the Democrat James Buchanan. But the new Republican Party did remarkably well and came into position for a win of world-historical significance four years later.[23]

With this last-ditch political effort exhausted, Higginson was determined to abandon all further compromise approaches and

The new Republican Party portrayed in 1856 as a collection of Grahamites, women's rights women, socialist followers of Charles Fourier, Free Lovers, Catholics, and African Americans.

Library of Congress

move directly to disband the Union. Rather than stand for four more years of pro-slavery federal government under yet another northerner who sympathized with the slave power, he spearheaded an attempt to organize antislavery secessionists. Garrison had advocated dissolution since the early 1840s, and even some political abolitionists agreed with him, although many charged that his movement damaged the antislavery cause by associating it in the public mind with disloyalty to the Union. In the lead-up to the election, it had been commonplace in antislavery circles to say that Frémont's candidacy was "the last hope for freedom" and that if he were not elected, the North must start the process of formal separation. Now Higginson wanted to hold them to it. He called a convention to establish a disunion agenda in January 1857. The press in both the North and the South took notice of the announcement, calling the participants a band of mischievous fanatics who should be executed for treason.[24]

The convention speakers frankly confirmed their status as traitors; Higginson called the label a compliment. They declared their determination to sever the "bloody bond" between the free and the slave states, to "unmake" the Constitution that had proved "a failure and a curse." One of many speakers to affirm that abolitionism was no longer a reform movement but a revolution, Garrison asserted, "We are engaged in a revolution more far-reaching, more sublime, more glorious than our fathers ever dream of." With justification from the spirit of 1776, they were openly looking to overthrow the existing government, which they regarded as merely a cloak of respectability over the slave power. Speakers described an unprecedented American state that would exist on the other side of this revolution, where radical abolitionists would be recognized as heroic freedom fighters and founders of a truer nation. One man in the audience needed no convincing on this score. It was John Brown, and he had something beyond disunion in mind.[25]

Brown had come to meet his New England admirers and hit them up for money. After Sumner's beating and the sack of Lawrence, a new committee had been formed in Boston to redouble support for the Kansas Free-Staters. These backers were eager to meet Brown, whose name had become famous among them after the Pottawatomie Massacre the previous summer. The committee's chairman, George Luther Stearns, and its secretary, Frank Sanborn, set up a tour of speaking engagements and private dinners that would occupy Brown for much of the first four months of 1857. He stepped into the affluent parlors of New England with his stiff, old-fashioned clothes and his fierce, charismatic face, a bowie knife strapped to his leg and a loaded revolver close at hand. Appearing in public despite the price on his head, Brown was determined that he would not be taken alive. He brought a whiff of the frontier and of righteous bloodshed under the noses of these deep-pocketed backers, making them feel sheepish that they had not done more. He could not stomach the rich fare that filled their tables, declining even to butter his bread, keeping himself ready to rough it in the campaign ahead.[26]

Brown met Garrison during this time at Theodore Parker's house, where they had a heated debate about the question of violence, Garrison citing the nonresistant teachings of Christ and Brown firing back with the bellicose Old Testament. Garrison had been a key inspiration for Brown, who had read *The Liberator* at his father's house in the 1830s and later become a subscriber himself. Although Garrison was actually five years younger than Brown, it is tempting to see them as representatives of two phases of the movement—the sword that was swiftly replacing the pen. But ultimately, violent insurgency worked hand in hand with nonresistance to secure the approaching victory. Years later, Wendell Phillips would call them the two greatest Americans of their time and claim that "Brown stood on the platform that Garrison built." Garrison had indeed played a role in Brown's conversion to the cause, but he would soon be converted in turn as Brown pushed the slave power to a tipping point.[27]

Brown made fast friends among the Concord set. At the end of a brief stay with Emerson, the two headed out together for a dinner at Stearns's house, joining Thoreau, Alcott, Higginson, Parker, and others. Everyone present, including Stearns's very young children, remembered afterward—and for the rest of their lives—Brown's arresting declaration that "it is better that a whole generation of men, women, children should be swept away than that this crime of slavery should exist one day longer." He made precisely the impression needed to secure the money and weapons he wanted, despite his refusal to explain what he planned to do with them. Sanborn authorized a contribution of two hundred Sharps rifles and ammunition from the Kansas committee. Stearns paid out of pocket for two hundred revolvers.[28]

In addition to all these guns, Brown had a custom weapon in mind. From a Connecticut forge master, he ordered a thousand pikes—flat, eighteen-inch-long metal spearheads, sharp on both sides, mounted to six-foot-long wooden poles. John Greenleaf Whittier, an antislavery poet and a Non-Resistant, later said, "It is not a Christian weapon; it looks too much like murder." Brown wanted a weapon that could be wielded successfully by people who had not been taught to handle firearms, namely enslaved people, including women.[29]

He crossed the country again that fall and directed a raid in Missouri in which a slave owner was killed. He ferried the freed people safely all the way to Canada in January 1858 and then turned up at Frederick Douglass's house in Rochester, New York, in February. A decade before, he had invited Douglass to his house, sharing his plan for insurrection over an exceedingly modest meal. Brown had

John Brown pike.
Division of Political and Military History, National Museum of American History, Smithsonian Institution

explained that God created the Alleghenies at the beginning of time for use in the battle that would win black freedom. Douglass raised a number of objections but soon understood that Brown would not be dissuaded; the worst that could happen is that he would die in the fight, which he was most eager to do. Now, in 1858, he felt it was time to tap a small and discreet group of white financial backers and the black men who would fill the most important roles in the liberating army and the government it would instate. With the snow piled deep outside Douglass's windows, Brown started writing.

He drew a map of a series of forts connected by tunnels and penned a new U.S. constitution. This instrument would govern his army of insurgents, the society that he imagined as an intermediary version of the nation-state in transition, the "Provisional United States." Its articles encourage all men and women to carry arms openly and at all times. It specifies that the marriage relation would be upheld; there would be no profanity, indecency, drunkenness, or unlawful sex. All members would be required to labor for the common good, and all property would be held in common. Brown assumes there would be a president and a full cabinet, a supreme court, an army, a congress, and "civil officers of every description and grade, as well as teachers, chaplains, physicians, surgeons, mechanics, agents of every description, clerks, and messengers." He included procedures for the trial and removal of the executive officers if the need arose, guidelines for what constitutes a quorum in the house of representatives, and other policies far too detailed to be practically applied to a makeshift band of guerrilla fighters drawn directly from bondage. Perhaps he imagined, as the Brook Farmers and other communitarians had, that his would be the "first" community, a model and epicenter from which a new society would spread. This constitution was not limited to Brown's idea for an antislavery coup; it reveals his vision for a racially inclusive utopian community called the United States, which his revolution would bring into being.[30]

Brown also wrote letters during his stay with Douglass. He

reached out to some of the Massachusetts men he had connected with on his visit the previous year, asking if they were interested in backing a special mission that would turn their theories into action. One of them, Frank Sanborn, agreed to meet with Brown at Gerrit Smith's house in Peterboro, New York. Smith was a close colleague of Douglass's and, of course, had known Brown for many years, because his family and permanent residence were still on the property Smith had sold him in North Elba. Like many others, Smith had been converted by Bleeding Kansas to the belief that violence alone would end slavery. On Washington's Birthday, Brown presented his new constitution to these men and outlined his plan of attack. They took a long walk in the snow around the grand estate. Sanborn and Smith doubted Brown's plan would work but felt they had to support such a stalwart warrior in the cause. Sanborn went to his friends in Boston who had been vigorous backers, both financially and ideologically, of Free-Stater violence in Kansas. Brown followed him there, staying in a hotel under an assumed name and barely leaving his room. Over the course of a few days, some of the men he had dined with a year before came to see him and pledged their support. Together, these backers formed a clandestine committee known as the Secret Six: Thomas Wentworth Higginson, Theodore Parker, George Luther Stearns, Frank Sanborn, Samuel Gridley Howe, and Gerrit Smith.

Having secured the white patrons he needed, Brown set out to find the black fighters and leaders who had always been central to his plan. He was in touch with Lewis Hayden, who enthusiastically recruited for him in Boston. Henry Highland Garnet accompanied Brown to Philadelphia for a week of meetings with black leaders there. He then headed to the expatriate African American communities in Canada West, stopping in St. Catharines, Ontario, to see Harriet Tubman, who had been in touch with Hayden about Brown's plan. Tubman's direct-action assault on slavery had begun a decade earlier with her own self-emancipation, followed by at least a dozen return trips into slave territory that had liberated many others. Brown called her "the General" and "the most of a man (naturally) I

Harriet Tubman, ca. 1868.
Library of Congress

ever met with." She had dreamed of him before they met, repeatedly seeing a vision of his bearded face on a serpent in the wilderness, beseeching her with a message. And indeed, he shared his plan and she pledged her help. But he had crossed the border with someone else in mind.[31]

CHAPTER 11

The Provisional
United States

C atherine Delany opened her front door in Chatham, Ontario, in April 1858, her young children likely peering around her, to find an old white man with a long scraggly white beard. He looked like a sad-eyed Old Testament prophet, as she later recalled. He wanted to talk to her husband, who was on a professional call out of the city that day. The stranger would not come in, give his name, or leave any message, except for a promise to return in two weeks. He tried again at that time and again failed to find the man he sought at home. Four days later, they met at last in the street: John Brown and Martin Delany.[1]

Brown took Delany to the comfortable two-story brick house of Isaac Holden, where he was staying. Holden was a black surveyor and civil engineer, born in Louisiana, who had lived in Canada for twenty-five years. The house's large windows, high gables, and two chimneys bespoke the promise of success and security that brought black Americans across the border. Looking over Brown's materials there, Delany agreed to convene a constitutional convention and elections for the government of Brown's "Provisional United States."[2]

On May 8, Delany helped to assemble dozens of the area's black leaders at a church in town, where they met in secret with Brown's raggedy band of self-described desperadoes. Brown read aloud the constitution he had written at Frederick Douglass's house that winter. The convention adopted the first forty-five articles with no changes. But Article 46 proved to be controversial and remains a crucial but puzzling articulation of Brown's project. It reads, "The foregoing Articles shall not be construed so as in any way to encourage the overthrow of any State Government, or of the General Government of the United States, and look to no dissolution of the Union, but simply to Amendment and Repeal. And our flag shall be the same that our Fathers fought under in the Revolution."[3]

George J. Reynolds balked at this, moving to strike the article. Reynolds was a coppersmith based in Sandusky, Ohio, and had attended Delany's emigration convention four years earlier. A leader in the League of Liberty, a secret all-black armed organization that ran fugitives to Canada at border crossings along the Great Lakes from Syracuse to Detroit, Reynolds had no intention of fighting under the Stars and Stripes. It was the flag of a slave empire pretending to be a democracy, from which he had risked his life helping hundreds of people escape torture and enslavement. Those black men and women, he felt, carried the true "stripes" of the United States on their backs. He fully advocated the overthrow of the American government and thus could not support any statement to the contrary.[4]

Brown wouldn't hear of it. Article 46 was the core of his position; he saw himself not as an insurrectionist but as a defender of the true United States against pro-slavery usurpers. African Americans were the rightful inheritors and representatives of the flag of the founders. In the ensuing discussion, Delany was among those who spoke in favor of the article. His interpretation was that Brown proposed "an independent community," separate and in many ways oppositional to the official nation, that would nevertheless exist "*within* and *under* the government of the United States," much like the Mormons or the Cherokee at that time, or the black communes in Ontario. Reynolds's motion was put to a vote, but his was the only voice of support. The constitution as a whole was unanimously adopted, and Delany asked the attendees to sign the bottom of the document. Looking over their signatures, Brown called them the new John Hancocks, these black Canadian founding fathers of another United States, within and under the nation.[5]

In his account of this convention, Delany claims that the plan Brown presented was the Subterranean Pass Way, a variant underground railroad that would funnel fugitives to a site in the Kansas territory that would serve as the kernel of their separatist America. Other sources indicate that Brown and some of his followers had theorized a "Free State of Topeka" for admission to the Union, where all men and women would have the right to vote. Its official seal would bear the image of a black man standing on a cannon and holding a drawn sword.[6]

Delany's account of the Chatham Convention conflicts with most others, but in truth Brown had likely not explained his plans fully to the black delegates there or even to the men who followed him south to carry them out. Still, the group reconvened for elections to fill the government they understood would soon come into being. They chose congressmen, a secretary of state, a secretary of the treasury, a secretary of war, and the military commander in chief. Delany agreed to be president of the Subterranean Pass Way. But this African American president whom Brown had journeyed to Canada to find was not by his side the following year, when he put his plan into action. Delany was ten thousand miles away, establishing a provisional nation of his own.

AFTER YEARS OF planning and fundraising, and a lifetime of frustrated dreaming about a place where black people might live in both peace and power, Delany sailed in May 1859 for West Africa. Utopian ideas about the continent were wound into his earliest memories, as his grandparents on both sides had been born in Africa and remembered it well. According to Delany, his father's father had been a Gola chief who, after being sold into American bondage, was killed in a fight with a white slave owner who was trying to punish him. His mother's father was a Mandingo prince from the Niger Valley region named Shango Peace, a sacred name inherited only by chiefs and royal heirs. He was only briefly enslaved in the United States before gaining his liberty and returning to Africa. His grandmother Graci lived with Delany's family until she died. Her stories about the family's lost regal inheritance, with "all the gorgeous imagery of the tropics," he recalled, "shaped itself in the dreams of his childhood."[7]

While the ACS had poisoned the idea of an African settlement for many would-be migrants, Delany believed the continent was worth another look, as he explained in his 1852 proposal. In the intervening years, he and others, especially the militant minister Henry Highland Garnet, turned their attention to an area in the Niger Valley called Yorubaland, part of contemporary Nigeria. While Garnet had in mind "the civilization and Christianization of Africa" and Delany wanted secular black nationhood that would also be commercially lucrative, they worked together to put an African colony back on the table for black Americans. They proposed to fuel the economy with cotton, competing with the southern states on the international market, pitting free black labor against the slave economy. Frederick Douglass charged that in proposing a new "King Cotton" on another continent, Garnet and Delany were "singing the same tune" as the plantation owners.[8]

En route to Yorubaland, Delany sailed first for Liberia, as he had promised some of his backers, landing in Monrovia, where his former classmate at Harvard Medical School had settled. After partially recovering from a bout of malaria, he continued to Lagos, where he stayed for five weeks. He declared that this urban center was "destined to be the great black metropolis of the world." He traveled up the Ogun River for three weeks into the interior and was welcomed with a festival in Abeokuta, a beautiful walled city with homes of red clay. Along with a colleague, Delany soon negotiated a treaty with Egba leaders that would permit black Americans to move in. They would be allowed to settle any area of land not currently in use and would be subject to local laws, but they would retain the right to work out issues within their own community that did not involve the native Africans, suggesting that they intended to remain a separate people.[9]

It was there in Abeokuta that Delany saw an American newspaper, the headlines seeming to scream out directly to him from so far away: John Brown was dead. He discovered that Brown's ultimate mission took him not to Kansas but to Harpers Ferry, Virginia, less than ten miles from Delany's hometown. Together, they had imagined a revolutionary black-led American government and plotted secretly to bring it about, but now Delany had given up on the United States utterly, seeing a future only in his new nation within and under the Egba. How very strange for Delany to learn that Brown and his remaining raiders had been held in the very jail where his own father had once been locked up for resisting an assault.[10]

———

BROWN HAD HEADED for Virginia with a band of men and several crates of weapons. Among his army were three of his sons and two other young men related to them by marriage, some Free State fighters who had followed him out of Kansas, and a number of freeborn black men recruited in Canada and Cleveland. Osborne Perry Anderson had attended Oberlin College, then worked as a printer for Mary Ann Shadd Cary and contributed to the Chatham Convention; another free black Oberlin alumnus, John Anthony Copeland, joined as well. The band also included a formerly enslaved man, Dangerfield Newby, who hoped to liberate his wife and children who were still in bondage. Among the white soldiers were a hugely muscular, hotheaded Spiritualist named Albert Hazlett, and Francis Jackson Meriam, the one-eyed, syphilitic grandson of a Boston abolitionist who had been a primary financial backer of Garrison's entire career, recruited at the last minute by Lewis Hayden. Brown had entreated Frederick Douglass to join them right up to the final weeks before their departure. Douglass thought the Harpers Ferry plan was disastrous, even suicidal, and declined to take part. But at their final meeting, he brought along a fugitive from slavery named Shields Green, who joined Brown on the spot.

Harriet Tubman, who was unable to participate in the raid because she was ill, had suggested the Fourth of July as the best date for Brown to launch his attack. But due to delays, they did not arrive in the area until around that time, renting a farmhouse on the Maryland side of the Potomac. One of Brown's daughters and a daughter-in-law came for a time to help with domestic work and to make the situation look somewhat less suspicious to the neighbors. For three months, the men read Thomas Paine, held debates, ran reconnaissance missions, and played cards sitting on cases full of guns. They wrote a "Declaration of Liberty" on a long scroll, borrowing the form and much of the language from the Declaration of Independence and quoting Jefferson's other writings as well, except with bad spelling and eccentric punctuation. They nominated themselves representatives of the enslaved population and demanded equal rights, privileges, and justice to all, irrespective of race or sex.

Finally, the day was upon them. Brown gathered the men and read aloud the Constitution of the Provisional United States, swore them into its Provisional Army, and presented some with official written commissions from its War Department. He had shared with them by this time his final plan. Their first move would be to capture the federal armory across the river in Harpers Ferry, Virginia, where guns and ammunition were manufactured and stored. Some of the men balked, believing they would become trapped inside and be shot like fish in a barrel, unable to escape to the mountain hideouts that had been the crux of Brown's long-standing strategy. But their commander believed that their seizure of a sensitive government facility and millions of dollars in weapons, so close to the nation's capital, would send precisely the right message. Poised for attack on the United States as the Provisional United States, they would be the fulcrum of the turning wheel of patriotism and treason.

In the past century and a half, many fine histories have recounted in detail the choreography of the next thirty-six hours, to which a certain dark magic still clings. Brown and his men marched into town at night, cut telegraph wires, and took hostages at gunpoint, including the armory's guard. Having forced entrance into the armory, Brown sent a delegation to capture slave owners from their homes, free enslaved people to join the fight, and spread the word that the revolution had begun. They entered the mansion of Lewis Washington, great-grandnephew of George Washington, on his

Aaron Stevens's commission in the Provisional Army of
the United States, signed by John Brown.
Massachusetts Historical Society

plantation five miles from Harpers Ferry, breaking into his elegant
hallway with a flaming pine torch, and ordering him out of bed.
They stole some family heirlooms of symbolic importance, including a pair of pistols given to the first American president by his
friend the Marquis de Lafayette, loaded their hostage into his own
carriage alongside several of the men he enslaved, and headed back
to the armory, making stops at other plantations on the way.

When they arrived, they put the white prisoners in a small room
with a stove and gave each black man a pike. They took more armory employees prisoner and were holding around forty men there
by dawn. Brown's second-in-command urged him to lead the men
out that morning and head for the mountains before they became
trapped. But Brown did not budge. He expected enslaved people in
Maryland and Virginia to flock to them, swelling their numbers to
a force that could overpower any local resistance.

Townspeople began arming themselves, and by 10:00 a.m. a
volunteer militia of around a hundred men had gathered, eager to
kill the invaders. They picked some of them off on the armory
grounds, shooting and mutilating their corpses for hours in grisly
retaliation; in the town, Brown's men had killed an Irish grocer, the

town's mayor, and a black railroad employee. The town's defenders returned fire, killing and capturing some of the raiders. Brown sent out two men to negotiate, including one of his sons, along with a hostage waving a white handkerchief. Both of the raiders were shot.

Brown and his remaining soldiers were holed up in a small room with their hostages and the bloody bodies of dead and badly wounded raiders. Federal troops had been called, but the best that could be found nearby was a regiment of ninety inexperienced Marines. When Jeb Stuart, who had been brought in to lead them alongside Robert E. Lee, came to the armory door to deliver a message, he recognized Brown from his time in Kansas and asked for his surrender. Brown refused. The troops immediately attacked the door with sledgehammers and then, unable to breach it, used a heavy ladder as a battering ram. They broke through and stormed in; a few were shot, a few of Brown's men run through with bayonets. While reloading a gun, Brown was slashed and then stabbed and then beaten with the hilt of a dress sword. The engagement lasted only a few minutes. Washington, no longer a hostage, stepped out, pulling on a pair of kid gloves, and asked for breakfast.

There had been twenty-two soldiers in the Provisional Army of the United States, including their commander in chief, John Brown. Ten were mortally wounded in the course of the two-day battle. Seven were captured and later executed. Five got away, including Osborne Anderson, who made it all the way back to Chatham, Ontario, without being apprehended and later served in the Union army. The raid did not directly free any slaves, though a number escaped and self-emancipated in the uproar around the time of the event; two of the people Brown's men liberated from the Washington plantation ended up dead. But there is evidence to suggest that the insurrectionaries had been in touch with enslaved people in the surrounding areas and that many were armed and poised to join the fight. In the weeks after the raid, mysterious fires were set on nearby farms, suggesting to many that these collaborators intended to carry out the uprising Brown had started, despite his capture.[11]

If the Virginia authorities thought at first that they had put down an isolated terrorist act by a ragtag band of criminals, their perspective shifted when they searched the farmhouse and another location where Brown's men had stashed supplies. They found an impressive cache of weapons, easily enough to carry out a legitimate military campaign and support an army in the mountains—big crates of rifles, revolvers, ammunition, bayonets and swords, clothes and tools, a swivel gun. Thousands of copies of Brown's constitution were tied up for mass distribution, and there were maps of the southern states, with marked areas where the black population outnumbered whites. Brown had also left letters and documents incriminating himself and his high-profile northern supporters.

Considering that he had been planning for over a decade, Brown's disastrous decisions on the day of the raid raise the possibility that he actually intended to fail. He had written to Sanborn the previous year that he expected his success to "be like the last victory of Samson." That is, he would die while pulling down the enemy's great temple. In a sense, the raid's success began only after its failure, in the six weeks that remained of Brown's life.[12]

Virginia's governor, Henry Wise, arrived and took command of the scene. In their first conversation, Wise advised Brown to consider the condition of his immortal soul, especially because he was an old man. Brown countered that he doubted Wise was any younger and he was positive he had much greater sins to worry about. At every turn, he calmly avowed that his mission had been to free slaves as the Bible directed. Like many southerners who encountered him in jail, Wise admired the prisoner in spite of himself. He said anyone who thought Brown a madman was mistaken. He was a "fanatic," to be sure, he remarked, but also "a bundle of the best nerves I ever saw." Brown used his captors' interrogations as opportunities to remind them—and the reporters and, through them, the American people—that they, too, would die and face judgment. They were committing a great sin while he had done right. As W. E. B. DuBois later observed, "From the day John Brown was captured to the day he died, and after, it was the South and slavery that was on trial—not John Brown."[13]

In his previous northern tours, when Brown delivered lectures to raise money, people had sometimes remarked that he was an inferior public speaker, that his genius was action, not words. But his action had apparently failed, or else he had sacrificed whatever success would have been possible precisely to gain a national platform from which to communicate. From his cell in Virginia, Brown wrote to his family in the Adirondacks, "At this time to seal my testimony for God and humanity with my blood will do vastly more toward advancing the cause I have earnestly endeavored to promote than all I have done in my life before." He made the most of his time in captivity, with the whole country hanging on his every word. Many who had not initially supported him found his interviews, letters, and court testimony irresistible. Letters flowed into his cell from all corners of the country, from activists like Lydia Maria Child and Frances Harper, and also from Mahala Doyle, a woman whose husband and sons Brown had murdered in the Pottawatomie Massacre in Kansas. She let him know she was "gratified" that his "fiendish career" had been stopped and he would soon meet his "just reward." Of the men who had followed him into battle, the jailhouse writings of those who were captured alive indicate that they were just as firm in their resolve and as confident in the action they had taken as their commander. John Anthony Copeland urged his family not to sorrow for his imminent death on the scaffold. He said he had served under a general as brave as George Washington "and engaged in a cause no less honorable and glorious." In fighting for "the freedom of this country," he placed himself in the tradition of Crispus Attucks, the black man who fell as the first casualty of the American Revolution.[14]

When his trial began, Brown was still seriously wounded, having been stabbed multiple times by the Marines who had captured him. He lay on a cot through most of the proceedings. On the fifth day, the lawyers made their final statements, and the jury deliberated for forty-five minutes. When they returned, Brown stood, along with the rest of the men crowded into the courtroom, waiting expectantly but in absolute silence, to receive their verdict. He was found guilty of conspiring and advising slaves to rebel, first-degree murder, and treason. His face registering no response whatsoever to this news, Brown turned after a moment to adjust his covers and then stretched out again on the cot. Brought in again for sentencing the following day, he was offered the opportunity to speak. Brown stood and addressed the court, affirming once again, "I did no wrong, but right. Now, if it is deemed necessary that I should forfeit my life for the furtherance of the ends of justice, and mingle my blood further with the blood of my children and with the blood of millions in this slave country whose rights are disregarded by wicked, cruel, and unjust enactments, I say, let it be done." He stood, unsteadily but with complete composure, when the judge pronounced his fate: execution by public hanging.[15]

———

FROM THE FIRST ISSUE of *The Liberator* in 1831, Garrison had prophesied that slavery would eventually result in a bloody scourge on American soil, as had David Walker before him. An avowed Non-Resistant, Garrison preached peace without exception, but in the 1850s he was well aware that his colleagues were taking a new direction, actually hoping to hasten and contribute to the violent apocalypse he had long anticipated. In 1858, he noted that "a sad change has come over the spirit of anti-slavery men, generally speaking. We are growing more and more warlike, more and more disposed to repudiate the principles of peace." He insisted that the weapons of despotism—revolvers, swords, cannons, and bombshells—could not be repurposed as tools for liberty. Seeing their increasing impatience, he urged abolitionists, "Do not make yourselves familiar with the idea that blood must flow. Perhaps blood will flow—God knows, I do not; but it shall not flow through any council of mine." In his initial notice of the Harpers Ferry raid, Garrison called it "misguided, wild, and apparently insane," and yet his pacifism and anti-Americanism seemed already to waver: "Our views of war and bloodshed, even in the best of causes, are too well known to need repeating here; but let no one who glories in the Revolutionary struggle of 1776 deny the right of the slave to imitate the example of our fathers." So profound was the turning tide during the time of Brown's imprisonment that even Garrison's long-standing opposition to violence was shaken.[16]

Garrison's colleague Henry C. Wright, the marriage reformer and founding Non-Resistant, held a convention in the days before Brown's execution, issuing the "Natick Resolution," which made it clear that he had abandoned the controversial pacifist principles he helped to suffuse into the movement two decades earlier. Wright now believed that "it is the right and duty of the slaves to resist their masters, and the right and duty of the people of the North to incite them to resistance, and to aid them in it." Wright had long rejected the American founders and yet, like Garrison, was moved to resignify them by Brown's revolutionary death: "He was as innocent as were Washington, Lafayette, Franklin, Jefferson, Hancock, and Patrick Henry, and far more deserving the approval of mankind."[17]

It was the Transcendentalists, however, whose support was most crucial in securing Brown's place in national memory. A number of the Secret Six had ties to Transcendentalism, but even more important was the role Emerson and Thoreau played in constructing an appealing narrative around Brown at this time. Always suspicious of collective politics, they described Brown as a self-reliant individual who took matters into his own hands, an interpretation that, while reductive, still appeals to many. They had hosted Brown in their homes, sitting long after dinner in conversation, and, with Alcott, attended lectures at which money was raised for Brown's direct-action plot, which, although he kept the details sketchy, was understood to involve armed violence.[18]

As Brown awaited execution, both Emerson and Thoreau offered rousing encomiums to the man they considered a hero. At a meeting to raise money for Brown's family, Emerson described him as a saint whose martyrdom "will make the gallows as glorious as the cross." Thoreau lifted Brown up as "the most American of us all." He said that since Brown's arrest, he had been unable to sleep and criticized the lethargy of his fellow Americans: "The modern Christian is a man who has consented to say all the prayers in the liturgy, provided you will let him go straight to bed and sleep quietly afterward. All his prayers begin with 'Now I lay me down to sleep,' and he is forever looking forward to the time when he shall go to his 'long rest.'" But according to Thoreau, Harpers Ferry had succeeded in a goal far beyond merely waking people up: Brown's transformational contribution was that he had "taught us how to die."[19]

Despite Brown's powerful example, some of his supporters were not yet ready to die. Once the incriminating documents were discovered, most of his backers fled the country and denied their role in the plot in order to avoid execution. Higginson stood by him, irreversibly committed to treason and ready to face the consequences. Parker also remained loyal, but by that time he was dying of tuberculosis in Italy. Stearns, Sanborn, and Howe fled to Canada and burned all of their correspondence. Smith suffered a mental breakdown and was committed to an asylum in Utica. Even a decade after the end of the Civil War, he was still cast into periods of mental illness when reminded of anything connected to John Brown. Douglass also fled the country, first to Canada and then on to England. Higginson regarded his colleagues' ducking for cover with disdain and immersed himself instead in further treasonous conspiracy, defiantly signing his name at the bottom of a letter discussing plans to rescue Brown, followed by the note "There is no need of burning this."[20]

Higginson went to see Brown's wife in North Elba a month before the execution to escort her to the Virginia jail, perhaps still hoping she would persuade her husband to go along with an escape plan. He and others had hatched a plot to take Governor Wise hostage, exchange him for Brown's release, and speed away on a gunboat. Plan B was to hire a band of rescuers to approach on foot and ride out with Brown on stolen cavalry horses. Both plans proved too expensive and were abandoned. Brown then sent word that he did not wish to see Mary before he died; he was not sure he could maintain his stoic resolve in her presence. She traveled south anyway, staying at the Raritan Bay Union commune in New Jersey and with Lucretia Mott in Philadelphia. When her husband consented, she made her way to Virginia, obtaining permission from Governor Wise to take Brown's body out of the state after the hanging.[21]

Execution day arrived: December 2, 1859. Only military and prison personnel were allowed on the grounds to watch, but across the North, thousands turned out to bear witness. Black congregations held vigils for "Brother Brown." All over New England, church bells tolled, some continuously from ten to noon. In Albany, there was a hundred-gun salute. Massive assemblies crammed the largest venues in all major cities, and many more stood in the streets, singing dirges and reading poems that celebrated Brown as a "glorious traitor" who "made treason holy and sublime." In Cleveland alone, five thousand people mourned in a hall they had draped in black. A huge crowd turned out in Montreal as well. Samuel Gridley Howe joined one group primarily composed of people of color there, showing his support for Brown at a distance he hoped would make him safe from extradition as an accomplice.

The vigil at Boston's Tremont Temple overflowed into the street. When William Lloyd Garrison stood to address the crowd, it became clear that his brand of pacifist abolitionism was finished. "How many non-resistants are there here tonight?" he asked. Only one man said, "I." In the strange and momentous vacillation that followed, Garrison identified himself as an "ultra peace man" but then wished "success to every slave insurrection at the South," which was greeted with enthusiastic applause from the crowd of four thousand. He added, "I thank God when men who believe in the right and duty of wielding carnal weapons" do so against oppression, because God takes retribution on the tyrant through these agents of violence. "Rather than see men wearing their chains in a cowardly and servile spirit, I would, as an advocate of peace, much rather see them breaking the head of the tyrant with their chains. Give me, as a non-resistant, Bunker Hill, and Lexington, and Concord, rather than the cowardice and servility of a Southern slave-plantation." For Garrison to refer to nonviolent submission as cowardly and call for breaking the heads of tyrants was an astounding shift, and one that was accompanied as well by a clear, if begrudging, admiration for the American founders and the violence of the revolution, which he had long decried.

Placards around the auditorium displayed Brown's picture and a cross alongside quotations from founders including Washington, Jefferson, and Patrick Henry—all Virginians—as well as the Marquis de Lafayette, who was like Brown, Garrison observed, in that he fought for the freedom of another people, not in his own self-interest. The state seal of Virginia also featured prominently at this demonstration: Virtue, holding a spear not unlike one of John Brown's pikes, stands astride defeated Tyranny, under the phrase "Sic Semper Tyrannis." Garrison said that this "terrible motto" justified Brown's attack, affirming as it did "the right of the oppressed to trample their oppressors beneath their feet, and, if necessary, consign them to a bloody grave!" Brown's attempted coup d'état in Virginia had wrested from the South the Revolutionary heritage it claimed, recasting the roles of virtue and tyranny. In New York City, Henry Highland Garnet declared that "Virginia will be famed in history for having been the home of Washington and the theatre of John Brown's cowardly execution." He declared that December 2 should thenceforth be observed as "Martyr's Day."[22]

In Philadelphia, "an immense crowd of whites and blacks" took

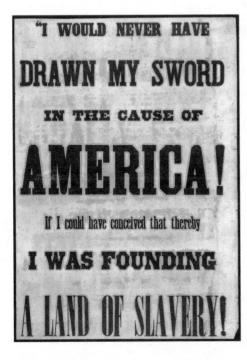

Placard with an antislavery quotation attributed to the Marquis de Lafayette, displayed by Boston abolitionists on the day of John Brown's execution. *Boston Public Library*

over National Hall, and after every remark hisses competed with applause from the crowd, half sympathetic to Brown and half glad to see the traitor executed. Theodore Tilton spoke as a representative of Henry Ward Beecher's church in Brooklyn, where crates of rifles labeled "Bibles" had famously been packed for shipment to Kansas, some of which might have ended up in Brown's stockpile. He was followed on the platform by Lucretia Mott. When Robert Purvis rose to speak, he was greeted with "a burst of applause, hisses and groans." It was several minutes before the crowd would let him begin. Over the "wild confusion" he declared, "This day marks the most eventful epoch in the history of our country. It is the beginning of the end, and I thank God for this unmistakable sign of the times." Thrilling the crowd to near hysteria, he swore that in time "John Brown shall be looked upon as the Jesus Christ of the nineteenth century." After this, the anti-Brown contingent took over the stage, offering loud cheers for Governor Wise, for Virginia, and for the United States. Clearly, public sentiment in the North was by no means unified. In Boston, a group announced "an anti-Brown meeting" in "support of the Union and the Constitution" and "to rebuke domestic treason" at Faneuil Hall.[23]

Martin Delany was in West Africa that day, oblivious to the historic actions and imminent deaths of his colleagues. But strangely enough, one of his childhood friends, John Avis, was the jailer and executioner charged with implementing Brown's sentence. Brown and his men grew to like Avis so much during their imprisonment that they wrote him farewell letters and willed him a rifle and a pistol. Perhaps they had even chatted about their mutual friend Delany, whose name had surfaced during the investigation as one of the many conspirators, the minutes of the Chatham Convention having been found among Brown's effects. When Avis and the guards came into Brown's cell that morning, he handed one of them a slip of paper with his last words: "I John Brown am now quite <u>certain</u> that the crimes of this <u>guilty land</u>: will never be purged away; but with Blood. I had <u>as I now think: vainly</u> flattered myself that without <u>very much</u> bloodshed; it might be done."

The guards restrained his arms with a cord, led him out to an undertaker's wagon, and sat him on top of the wooden crate that held his coffin. The scrawl on the scrap was his final statement on slavery, but he did not remain silent on the ride to the gallows, gazing at the farmland of the Shenandoah River valley and tracing the line of the Blue Ridge Mountains. "This is a beautiful country," he said. "I never had the pleasure of seeing it before."[24]

They had erected the gallows in an anonymous field, hoping not to create a pilgrimage site for those who regarded Brown as a martyr. He walked quickly up the scaffold steps and did not tremble or shrink back from the noose when Avis put it over his head. He shook hands with his executioners, the jailer and the sheriff, and they tied his ankles. They made him stand for ten or fifteen minutes on top of the trapdoor with the noose around his neck and the hood over his head—an inhumane delay. Thousands of uniformed Virginia militiamen stood guard in formation around the scaffold. A number of southerners who would soon show up on the wrong side of treason themselves were looking on that day. Robert E. Lee stood by silently. Stonewall Jackson prayed for Brown's soul and noted his "unflinching firmness," even "apparent cheerfulness." Also present was a young actor who was so eager to see the hanging that he cobbled together a military uniform and snuck into the

John Brown's execution.
Virginia Military Institute Archives

lineup. John Wilkes Booth would soon become a traitor and assassin even more infamous than the one he came to see killed.[25]

At last, the sound of the trapdoor's hinges shrieked across the hushed field, and the prisoner dropped through the platform. Ideally, when a man is hanged, his neck snaps, killing him instantly. This rope was too short for that; Brown struggled and convulsed for five minutes, his hands trying to reach for his throat, though his arms were tied. Brown had met his death at the hands of the state with composure that impressed everyone present. He seemed not a craven criminal or a madman but someone deeply sure that he had done the right thing and was prepared to meet divine judgment for it. They left him hanging there for half an hour, bringing up several different doctors to make sure he was really dead. Finally, they cut down the gaunt corpse and dropped it into the coffin along with the rope.

Mary Brown traveled north by train with her husband's body for burial on their farm in the Adirondacks. The mourners, including what remained of his family and their African American neighbors, sang "Blow Ye the Trumpet, Blow," a hymn Brown liked to sing to his children and grandchildren at bedtime, even though it's about waking up for all eternity. Wendell Phillips, the antislavery leader who had been indicted for treason himself after the Anthony Burns riot five years earlier, gave a eulogy. They lowered Brown into the grave next to his son Frederick, who had been killed in Kansas. For a marker, Brown had repurposed in advance the tombstone of his grandfather, also named John Brown, a soldier in the first American Revolution who had died in 1776. Years later, when the Civil War was long over, the bodies of eleven of the other raiders were collected and reinterred alongside their commander in chief. These white and black men, would-be founders of a revolutionary utopia called the Provisional United States, lie buried together in the frozen ground of Timbuctoo.

CHAPTER 12

Under the Flag

A new session of Congress opened days after Brown's execution. In both houses, nothing was discussed except Harpers
Ferry. Southern senators accused their northern colleagues of having personally known about the plot, of having attended Henry
Wright's militant Natick convention, of celebrating as a hero a
homicidal traitor who wanted to butcher southerners, of being dis-
unionists, and so on. On the day that Brown was buried, Senator
Jefferson Davis of Mississippi took the floor. He made it clear that
the South was inflamed not simply by the actions of John Brown
and his men but by a whole culture in the North that refused to "arrest the march of abolitionism." He argued that the North's support
of murderous fanatics represented a clear violation of the constitutional protection of the institution of slavery: "John Brown, and a
thousand John Browns, can invade us, and the Government will not
protect us." He warned that "to secure our rights and protect our
honor we will dissever the ties that bind us together, even if it rushes
us into a sea of blood."[1]

In nearby Virginia, Henry Wise similarly warned of influences
and forces "more potent far than the little band of desperadoes" at
Harpers Ferry: *"John Brown's invasion startled us; but we have been
tamely submitting to a greater danger, without confessing it."* That greater
danger, he declared, was that "an evil spirit of fanaticism has seized
upon negro slavery as the one subject of social reform, and the one
idea of its abolition has seemed to madden whole masses of one

entire section of the country." In other words, the problem wasn't Brown specifically but antislavery activism stretching back to the advent of radical immediatism, which had produced and supported not only Brown but an untold number of other antislavery vigilantes. Like Davis, he noted with outrage that money for the spears that would cut southerners' throats had been raised in the churches of the North. For Wise, the required response was clear: "We must take up arms."[2]

Conservatives in the North who sympathized with this position jumped to express their solidarity in an attempt to prevent the schism that was beginning to seem inevitable. An article in the *Boston Post* declared simply, "The North is in the wrong." Calling antislavery forces "the aggressors" in this internecine battle, they declared that there were plenty in New England who "intend to live under this Constitution, maintain this Union, and protect Southern rights and Southern men; and they will do it, if need be, with arms in their hands. Whenever the contest comes between the South and Republican fanaticism, the Democrats of the North will be with the South." Arguing that the ideological conflict was not truly sectional but limited to a few dangerous ultras, they swore that "Wendell Phillips and his Republican cohorts will never get out of New England to fight anybody—They will rather at the point of the bayonet be driven into the sea by the outraged men who love the Union and cherish the memories of the revolution."[3]

The presidential election year of 1860 dawned with two of the Harpers Ferry raiders still in prison awaiting execution. Southerners swore that if a candidate was elected who opposed the maintenance and spread of slavery, they would immediately secede and form a separate slaveholding republic. Some abolitionists, meanwhile, turned back to politics after years of conscientious objection. Although some of his friends, including Stephen S. Foster and Gerrit Smith, wanted a more radical party than the Republicans, Higginson liked Abraham Lincoln and supported him, as did Garrison. The South proclaimed in advance the lengths they were willing to go to, to resist a Lincoln presidency. "Whether the Potomac is crimsoned in human gore, and Pennsylvania Avenue is paved ten fathoms deep with mangled bodies," one Georgia newspaper declared, "the South will never submit to such humiliation and degradation as the inauguration of Abraham Lincoln." This kind of hyperbole turned out to be a fair forecast of what soon transpired. Triumphing where Frémont had failed, Lincoln was elected on the Republican ticket that November. His popularity in northern states handed him the Electoral College, but he took only 40 percent of the national popular vote. In most of the southern states, Republican ballots were not even available.[4]

Within days, the South Carolina General Assembly passed a resolution declaring Lincoln's election "a hostile act" and stating its intention to withdraw from the United States. In December, it voted unanimously to declare its separation, dissolving the Union instantiated by the Constitution because "non-slaveholding states" had not held up their end of the deal. Specifically, the North had allowed the existence of abolitionist organizations: "They have permitted the open establishment among them of societies, whose avowed object is to disturb the peace and to eloign the property of the citizens of other States. They have encouraged and assisted thousands of our slaves to leave their homes; and those who remain, have been incited by emissaries, books and pictures to servile insurrection. For twenty-five years this agitation has been steadily increasing."[5]

Other slave states soon joined South Carolina, many explicitly referencing John Brown and the antislavery societies in their declarations of secession as well. Georgia proclaimed, "For twenty years past the abolitionists and their allies in the Northern States have been engaged in constant efforts to subvert our institutions and to excite insurrection and servile war among us. . . . These efforts have in one instance led to the actual invasion of one of the slave-holding States." Mississippi denounced the radicalism that "advocates negro equality, socially and politically, and promotes insurrection and incendiarism in our midst." This faction of the North had "formed associations to carry out its schemes of emancipation in the States and wherever else slavery exists." In one case, "it has invaded a State, and invested with the honors of martyrdom the wretch whose purpose was to apply flames to our dwellings, and the weapons of destruction to our lives."

Thus, the Civil War began as a reaction against abolitionists, not against slavery. The North never dissolved its union with the slave-holding states or launched a military attack to demand the end of the institution. It was the South that regarded its political connection to northern reform culture as untenable, refusing any longer to be constitutionally tied to it. Indeed, southerners had seen this coming for a long time. From the rise of the radical antislavery movement back in the 1830s, South Carolina's senator John C. Calhoun had argued that Congress should not acknowledge abolitionist petitions because they would ultimately bring about a shift in the culture that would lead to national schism. He warned in 1837 that if the "incendiary spirit" of "this fanatical portion of society" managed to convince a large portion of the North that slavery is a sin, they would feel morally obliged to abolish it, and that would mean the end of the Union. He stated plainly, "Abolition and the Union cannot coexist." Since that time, mainstream newspapers, politicians, and public sentiment generally in both the North and the South had decried the explosive potential of social protest, accusing antislavery activists of endangering the Union, a charge many of them fully owned. They had enjoined their fellow northerners to sever their connection with values and practices they found intolerable, but the South beat them to it. They had declared a war against dissent that the North took up as a war to save the Union, turning it only later into a war to end slavery.[6]

In the first week of February, the states that had seceded met to approve a constitution and found a new nation, the Confederate States of America. They adopted a "Provisional Constitution" and elected Jefferson Davis president. The war officially began on April 12, 1861, when about six thousand Confederate troops gathered around Charleston harbor and began firing on the sixty men at Fort Sumter, who surrendered after thirty-six hours. That same week, Henry Wise, the former governor of Virginia who had overseen the execution of John Brown for treason, commanded a band of conspirators to seize the U.S. armory at Harpers Ferry for the Confederacy.[7]

———

THE CHAIN REACTION leading from Brown's raid to the Civil War unfolded as Martin Delany continued his venture abroad, sailing from West Africa to Europe to raise money for a new black nation. While he was in Glasgow securing deals to sell his colony's cotton, he learned that Abraham Lincoln had been elected president. He departed from Liverpool in December, setting foot on American soil after eighteen months abroad just as South Carolina formally seceded from the Union and declared itself an independent nation, the Palmetto Republic.

In the early days of the war, no one knew what it would mean for black Americans, whether enslaved or free; it would be more than a year before Lincoln made emancipation part of the Union's strategy. Until 1862, some African Americans were still actively attempting to organize a separate black state in the American West, while others were still emigrating from America to Haiti. So Garnet and Delany went on planning for their Niger Valley colony, recruiting 186 settlers. In his lectures, Delany presented glowing accounts of his African travels; sometimes he wore a dashiki and other times a more elaborate chief's wedding costume.[8]

But then Delany's prospects in Abeokuta fell apart. British missionaries there worked to destroy his agreement with the tribal leaders, convincing them that the "two races"—that is, black Americans and the Egba community—would not successfully mix. The prospective immigrants were essentially American, they argued, with American values, including racial prejudice: "The introduction of a large number of free blacks from America filled with certain notions of freedom, republicanism, and contempt for their uncivilized fellowmen, with whom at a distance they claim a relationship, but with whom they will not sit down and dwell as brethren of the same family, cannot but be attended with the greatest danger to the native governments and people." Moreover, as a separatist nation, they would remain a troublesome, alien people who would not assimilate with the majority population. The Alake, Oba Okukenu, ultimately denied signing any agreement that would have created a nation within and under his nation, declaring, "We will not have another people among us with another government."[9]

With the African option foreclosed and the Civil War in full swing, Delany shifted his attention back to the United States for the first time in a decade. Like many other black Canadian settlers who chose to move back across the U.S. border during the war years, the Delanys relocated to Ohio, forming part of a community springing up around the new Wilberforce, a college founded by the AME Church and a group of black leaders including Delany's Pittsburgh mentor, Lewis Woodson.

———

GARRISON GREETED THE NEWS of the South's secession with joy, declaring the "covenant with death" and "agreement with hell" annulled and throwing his support behind the federal government. While other hard-line abolitionists refused to start waving the flag and beating the war drums until slavery was formally abolished, Garrison was surprisingly confident that this ultimate victory would now be clinched in due time through political channels.

In Boston, on April 21, 1861, he and Wendell Phillips officially embraced the symbol of the Union they had for so long denigrated, and they appeared "under the flag" for the first time. Before this point, they often displayed the Stars and Stripes hung upside down and dressed with black mourning crape. Garrison had said that the banner of a country in which four million people were enslaved "is a flag to be abhorred, disowned and trodden under foot by every true friend of freedom, every advocate of the oppressed, and never with his consent to be unfurled to the breeze." He had published poems in *The Liberator* describing the American flag as "hate's polluted rag" and demanding that it be torn down and destroyed. But in their faith that the war would ultimately free the slaves, they dropped the long-standing anti-Americanism of their movement and proclaimed, "Today the abolitionist is merged in the citizen, in America."[10]

Garrison and his followers called on Lincoln to use his wartime powers to free the slaves, but the president resisted; he was doubtful that he had the constitutional authority to do so and knew that the Confederate states, no longer governed by that instrument or by his office, would be unlikely to care. He discouraged the efforts of military leaders on the ground to emancipate slaves in their regions of command and thought it wise to colonize those who ran to the Union forces. Declaring emancipation, he believed, "would be equivalent to a John Brown raid, on a gigantic scale."[11]

All through that summer, abolitionists increased the pressure, addressing letters, editorials, and petitions to the White House and visiting in person to plead their case. In September 1862, after Union forces drove the Confederates out of Maryland in the Battle of Antietam, the bloodiest day in American history, Lincoln issued an order that promised freedom to enslaved people in rebel territories on January 1. In the issue of *The Liberator* in which he printed this initial Emancipation Proclamation, Garrison ended his decades-long standoff with the United States and encouraged his followers to do the same. If the government is on the side of liberty, he declared, *"such a government can receive the sanction and support of every abolitionist, whether in a moral or military point of view."* Noting this total about-face among the former Non-Resistants, Gerrit Smith observed that it was not they who had switched sides, but everyone else: "The 'Garrisonian abolitionist' was formerly a Disunionist, and is now a Unionist; and hence he is charged with being inconsistent, or at least with being a convert. . . . There is a conversion. It is, however *to* him, and not *of* him. There is a change; but it is *around* him, and not *in* him." As Wendell Phillips crowed, explaining how the moderate Lincoln had evolved into the Great Emancipator, "Why did he grow? Because we watered him."[12]

HIGGINSON HAD STAYED HOME up to this point in the war, caring for his invalid wife. But once emancipation was declared, he decided that if he did not fight, "I shall forfeit my self-respect & be a broken man for the remainder of my days. I have sacrificed the public duty to this domestic one as long as I can bear." He anticipated a short conflict, which the North would win. The North would demand the abolition of slavery as a condition of the South's defeat, and then, he believed, the two nations would remain separate. Thus, this disunionist would be fighting not to preserve the Union but to end it formally and forever. He had been exercising, boxing, fencing, drilling the boys in Worcester for the Massachusetts 51st Regiment. Then Higginson got an invitation that he could not turn down.[13]

Very early in the war, the U.S. Navy had bombarded Confederate batteries on the Sea Islands of South Carolina and landed troops who seized the area and now occupied it. All the white residents had evacuated, except for one man who was too drunk to move. The landowners set fires on their way out but left huge mansions and other property, including ten thousand enslaved people. Abolitionists from Boston and New York poured in to work with them, starting schools and offering whatever help they could to a population transitioning to life after enslavement—it was known then as the Port Royal Experiment and was the first iteration of Reconstruction. The "queer farrago" of reformers at Port Royal were called Gideonites, or Gideon's Band. They were described even by a fellow abolitionist as "bearded and mustached and odd-looking men, with odder-looking women," resembling "the adjournment of a John Brown meeting or the fag end of a broken-down phalanstery!" The band comprised "clerks, doctors, divinity-students; professors and teachers, underground railway agents and socialists," and also included James Forten's granddaughter, Charlotte, and Harriet Tubman. Tubman worked in the hospital and wherever else she was needed but also took part in military maneuvers. Most famously, she played a crucial part in the raid on Combahee Ferry, which freed more than seven hundred people. The few activists who remained Non-Resistants at this time were turned away from Port Royal, because one of the most important "experiments" with these newly freed people was to turn them into a regiment of U.S. soldiers, the First South Carolina Volunteers.[14]

Rufus Saxton was the commanding officer on the Sea Islands.

His father was a Transcendentalist, and his brother had gone to the Brook Farm school, learning the printing trade working on *The Harbinger*. Saxton knew Higginson from Boston abolitionist and women's rights circles and offered him a commission to lead this first American military regiment of formerly enslaved men into the war against slavery. Higginson wrote, "I had been an abolitionist too long, and had known and loved John Brown too well, not to feel a thrill of joy at last on finding myself in the position where he only wished to be." He arrived and accepted his mission, directed at last by the government to carry out what he and his collaborators had been plotting sub rosa for a decade.

Higginson was with his black troops and the rest of the Port Royal crowd on New Year's Day 1863, when emancipation became official. The army commanders arranged a party for thousands of guests from around the region in a beautiful grove, gnarly live-oak trees trailing Spanish moss overhead, a glimpse of glittering blue water beyond. They spit-roasted ten lean cows and flavored barrels of water with molasses, ginger, and vinegar to drink. For dessert, there was hard bread with molasses and a ration of tobacco. A military band played patriotic tunes.

The event began as planned with a prayer, then a reading of the proclamation and a ceremonial presentation of the American flag. Higginson accepted the silk Stars and Stripes that the regiment's color-bearer would carry into battle, mounted on a staff and embellished with the regiment's title and "the year of Jubilee has come." He waved it for the assembled crowd to see. At that instant, the strong, clear voice of a black man near the platform arose: "My country, 'tis of thee." Two women immediately joined in harmony, and the song "America" spread through the assembled crowd of newly free people. Up to that point, the day's festivities had stuck strictly to an official program, in keeping with an air of military discipline, but they sang on, verse after verse.

"I never saw anything so electric; it made all other words cheap; it seemed the choked voice of a race at last unloosed," Higginson wrote. "Just think of it!—the first day they had ever had a country, the first flag they had ever seen which promised anything to their

Emancipation Day at Port Royal.
Frank Leslie's Illustrated Newspaper, *January 24, 1863*

people." This newly bestowed country and its flag—the one that had for so long upheld and perpetuated their enslavement, and then, at so very late a date, declared their nominal freedom and called immediately for their service, even their lives. Higginson was scheduled to deliver concluding remarks, later recalling that "spectators stood in silence, waiting for my stupid words," but "the life of the whole day was in those unknown people's song." White abolitionists were struck dumb, their words rendered "cheap" and "stupid," even in their own ears, by these black voices raised in radical hope, despite the solemn certainty that only more violence and sacrifice lay ahead. Charlotte Forten noted in her journal that Higginson had tears in his eyes and that the whole occasion had seemed "a brilliant dream," the "most glorious day this nation has yet seen."[15]

———

THE MEN WHO FOUGHT with Higginson numbered among the nearly 200,000 African Americans who served in the Civil War.

Many were eager to prove their courage and to contribute personally to the defeat of the slave power, hopeful that military service would lead to full citizenship rights when the war was over. In this long tradition of black soldiers, none were more famous than the first regiment of free men raised in Boston, under the command of Robert Gould Shaw.

As a child, Shaw attended school at Brook Farm and lived nearby. His parents were wealthy but committed activists, especially of abolition and Association. Shaw's mother's best friend was the abolitionist Lydia Maria Child, and his childhood was populated by Boston's progressive elite: Garrison, Stowe, Emerson, Hawthorne, Fuller. His father, Francis Shaw, a leading Fourierist and major financial backer of Brook Farm, had contributed articles and translations to *The Harbinger*. He often galloped over to visit his socialist Transcendentalist friends with his little son beside him on his own pony. Shaw had romped through the commune with his brothers and sisters and sledded through its snowy forests by the light of the full moon. Two of his sisters later married Brook Farmers, one of them the tutor who helped him get into Harvard.

Fifteen years after the phalanstery fire, Shaw had reason to visit again under very different auspices. On May 19, 1861, he wrote to his mother, "It is very odd to be at Brook Farm." Indeed it must have been. The property, rechristened "Camp Andrew," had undergone yet another conversion into a training site for Union troops headed into the Civil War. Military drills were carried out where no gunshot had been heard for the six years the commune lasted, where woodland animals would walk up to the farmhouse door to be fed. Perhaps this new generation of young men, wearing the uniform of the United States hung with sabers and revolvers instead of the socialists' bright peasant blouses, felt hope for the world that they would bring about, but their feelings on the precipice of war might have been closer to dread.[16]

Shaw fought at Antietam and elsewhere before his father persuaded him to take command of a regiment of black volunteers being recruited in Boston by abolitionists, members of the Secret Six, and black leaders including Delany, Frederick Douglass,

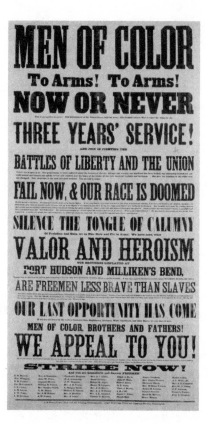

Recruiting broadside.
The Library Company of Philadelphia

Robert Purvis, Henry Highland Garnet, and Charles Lenox Remond. Indeed, so many men of color answered the call to arms that they also filled a fifty-fifth regiment. Garrison's oldest son was offered a commission as their second lieutenant. Still a committed pacifist, Garrison reminded his son of the many reasons that he should not go. But he did not stand in his way, urging him to do his duty as he saw it.

In May 1863, Garrison adjourned the opening session of the NEASS meeting in Boston so that the abolitionists could all turn out to watch the Massachusetts 54th Regiment march through the streets on its way south to war; soldiering had supplanted convention speeches for these activists. Twenty-five-year-old Shaw was at the lead. Garrison had known him all his life. He might also have recognized one of Frederick Douglass's sons among the troops, and one of Delany's was there as well. Garrison later recalled how his "heart was deeply stirred" as he thought about the dangers the regiment faced: the Confederacy had made it clear they would enslave black soldiers and put their white officers to death. Garrison would never have picked up a rifle, but he knew something about facing the threat of violence for principle.

The poet Henry Wadsworth Longfellow was there to watch the parade, too, recording in his journal that the black regiment was "an imposing sight, with something wild and strange about it, like a dream." The 54th marched down State Street, singing,

> John Brown's body lies a-mouldering in the grave,
> John Brown's body lies a-mouldering in the grave,
> John Brown's body lies a-mouldering in the grave,
> His soul is marching on!

For his armed attack on the pro-slavery nation, John Brown met a traitor's death. But within a few short years, his unquiet soul had become a guiding light for Union soldiers, agents of the very government that had executed him. The song, written by Union soldiers, was soon adapted by Julia Ward Howe, the wife of one of the Secret Six, into "The Battle Hymn of the Republic." She transposed John Brown and Jesus Christ, who "hath loosed the fateful lightning of His terrible swift sword." The song stirred northerners not to preserve the American Union but to take up the mantle of martyrdom in the slaves' cause: "As He died to make men holy, let us die to make men free." Freeing men through violence was God's work and America's work now, no longer the treasonous scheme of a lunatic fringe.

Garrison was fifty-seven years old. In a career spanning three decades up to that point, he had denounced the U.S. government as the ultimate enslaver. Now, it seemed, it would be the agent of freedom. In the name of union with the South, black men were armed for a mission of divine liberation. By chance, Garrison was standing on the corner of what was then called Wilson's Lane, where a mob had dragged him by a rope in 1835. "With emotion too deep for words," he watched the soldiers march past.[17]

———

RECRUITING FOR THE 54TH and other black regiments serving under white officers gave Delany an idea for something more: a whole black army, separate "colored troops" with, importantly, black commanders. He took this idea all the way to the top, meeting with Lincoln for forty-five minutes at the White House in February 1865. The president liked the idea and directed Delany to his secretary of war with a letter introducing "this most extraordinary and intelligent black man." The lead article in *The New York Times* blasted the news that Delany had been appointed the first black field officer in American history. *The Anglo-African Magazine* sold postcards featuring a portrait of the "Black Major" in full military dress. Delany, the black nationalist and treasonous conspirator, was suddenly an icon of patriotism. Just as Thomas Wentworth Higginson had done eighteen months before, Delany reported in April 1865 to Rufus Saxton, the brigadier general overseeing the Union occupation of the South Carolina Sea Islands. But the Black Major had missed almost all of the official fighting; Robert E. Lee surrendered to Ulysses S. Grant at Appomattox Courthouse on April 9.

Delany went to Charleston for the victory party on April 14, the anniversary of the Battle of Fort Sumter. Four years after the American flag was lowered there in defeat, the same Stars and Stripes would be raised by the same man, in triumph. Lincoln invited Garrison to attend as an honored guest. He traveled along with a bevy of his abolitionist colleagues to the city in which he had been burned in effigy. With profound relief, Garrison and Delany both reunited with their sons in Charleston; the war was over, and they had survived to march victoriously into the former heart of American slavery singing the John Brown song. Thousands of others, including their comrade Robert Gould Shaw, lay heaped in unmarked graves.

The celebration was a citywide spectacle: one hundred guns firing, ships decked out, flags billowing, thousands of African Americans celebrating in the street. Henry Ward Beecher gave an address after the flag was raised, extolling the Stars and Stripes as the em-

Martin Delany.
National Portrait Gallery,
Smithsonian Institution

blem of their fathers, made newly meaningful in this terrible test and cleansed of all its prior associations as the icon of a slave society. Garrison told the assembled free people, "Once I could not feel any gladness at the sight of the American flag, because it was stained with your blood, and under it four millions of slaves were daily driven to unrequited labor. Now it floats purged of its gory stains; it symbolizes freedom for all, without distinction of race or color." They carried Garrison on their shoulders, they tearfully introduced him to children whom they could finally claim as their own, they brought him any present they could think of—a basket of nuts, fancy pastries, lots of flowers. The celebration continued even at the wharf as Garrison and his retinue left the city, where the crowd thrilled to a speech from the Black Major.[18]

The morning after this grand jubilee, Garrison, along with Beecher and his protégé Theodore Tilton, visited the grave of John C. Calhoun, the South Carolina statesman who had spearheaded the militant turn in pro-slavery rhetoric by popularizing the idea that the institution was a "positive good." Garrison placed his hand on the marble slab and said, "Down into a deeper grave than this slavery has gone, and for it there is no resurrection." American slavery was dead forever, its defenders vanquished, and Garrison had lived to see his much-maligned principles triumph. But what he did not yet know was that, five hundred miles to the north, the Great Emancipator was dying even as he spoke.

Around 10:00 p.m. on the fourteenth, only five days after the Confederacy admitted defeat, John Wilkes Booth, an actor from Maryland, crept into the box at Ford's Theatre in Washington, D.C., where Abraham Lincoln was watching a comedy with his wife and friends. On a mission to strike a sensational final blow against the Union, Booth entered the balcony behind the president and fired a single bullet into the back of his head. As he jumped onto the stage, entangling his foot in a flag, some witnesses heard him shout the Virginia state motto: *Sic semper tyrannis!* Lincoln never regained consciousness and died the next morning. Andrew Johnson was sworn in as his successor to the White House and inheritor of the Reconstruction project. Johnson was from Tennessee and had only recently liberated the people he enslaved himself.

It was Easter weekend. The churches were all poised to celebrate Christ's resurrection, coinciding that year with the resurrection of the nation from war and the longer pall of slavery. The celebration turned into a funeral overnight, "from frantic joy to frantic grief," as one South Carolinian recalled. Local women quickly sewed black borders onto the celebratory flags, which were lowered to half-mast. Mount Zion Church was dressed in mourning for a year. On the Sea Islands, white teachers distributed scraps of black fabric for freewomen to pin on their children. Union military posts were draped, and soldiers' arms were banded. Grown men cried in public. Confederates celebrated. Free people feared they would be snatched back into slavery.[19]

Delany would soon learn that on the same strange night that the American president was murdered in the midst of their grand celebration, another not unrelated tragedy was also under way. In far-off Ohio, a vandal set fire to the main building at Wilberforce while the black students and faculty were in town at a victory party. This arson, clearly motivated by bitter and vindictive racism, destroyed classrooms, the dining hall, the chapel, and all of Delany's papers, correspondence, manuscripts, and keepsakes from Africa. For Delany, and for every American left alive at this time, the very ground seemed to yawn with the threat of destruction, even with the hideous war years ended and a new era of freedom dawning. Slavery was dead, along with some 600,000 young men and now the president. All old things had violently passed away. What unprecedented future would arise from this scorched earth?[20]

PART IV

The Radicals' Reconstruction, 1865–1877

CHAPTER 13

To Write Justice
in the American Heart

Less than a month after Lincoln's assassination, Garrison convened the American Anti-Slavery Society in New York City for what he assumed would be its final meeting. He was turning sixty that year; many of the society's original backers were dead or very old. It no longer had agents in the field, and after the Emancipation Proclamation, donations had dried up. And yet this meeting was packed to the balconies, drawing a huge crowd to oppose what Garrison saw as the triumphant and natural end of the organization's work: its dissolution. The church was hung with mourning drapery to honor the slain president, and speakers kept remarking somberly that the assembly felt like a funeral for their movement. Garrison was astounded. Surely they weren't nostalgic for the bad old days? He suspected that some of his colleagues had simply gotten used to being abolitionists—the drama, the annual round of conventions, the moral righteousness of their cause, which the nation had finally embraced in the war—and wouldn't admit that the prize was won. "Practically, absolutely, slavery is dead," he declared, chastising some society members for seeming so "gloomy over the triumph of universal justice."

Garrison reminded the crowd that when the society was organized in the 1830s, indeed even a mere four years earlier, "the religious societies, the government and the people were against us, and now they are for us. We held up our little torch when all was darkness, and we need not do it now when the whole heavens are ablaze." Now, he insisted, "we are no longer alone. The government is with us, the people are with us, the millions are with us, the armies are with us; abolitionism is no longer distinctive, but common." With slavery abolished, he believed, all racial prejudice would inevitably fall away.[1]

Yes, Congress had written the Thirteenth Amendment to the Constitution abolishing involuntary servitude, his opponents in this debate granted. But was slavery really limited to a legal status? Was mere emancipation the same thing as freedom? As the states of the former Confederacy convened that year to pass new constitutions, they were required to ratify the amendment as a condition of their return to the Union. But along with it, they created Black Codes, sets of laws that would govern only African American residents, in order to ensure that they remained subordinate to white citizens and that their labor could continue to be exploited. In some states, the newly free people would have to register themselves with county clerks, just as free people had been required to do in many states before the war; if they did not, they could be sold into forced labor. The same punishment could be enacted for "vagrancy," a vague crime of which any African American might be accused. Black men—but not white men—would be executed if convicted for the crime of rape, and people of color were not allowed to testify in cases involving whites, so any whiff of a charge of this kind meant certain death. In many places, they were not allowed to possess guns, and special taxes could be levied against them. For these reasons and others, many at the convention countered Garrison by insisting that as long as "any discrimination exists between white and black at the South," as Frederick Douglass declared, "slavery exists."

The demand to keep the organization running came both from young guns who were new to the scene but still wanted a piece of the action and from veterans like Stephen S. Foster, the Come-Outer and one of the original Non-Resistants. "Is our work done?" Foster asked the crowd. "What did we organize to do? Our object was first the abolition of slavery; and second, the elevation of the negro to an equality with the white. Now, Sir, is that work done?

Are the colored people equal with the whites?" He insisted that the AASS continue its work until the dawn of an era when "there will be no colored cars" on passenger trains and "no hooting" when white ladies walk "arm in arm, with the black men." Their goal as abolitionists, as Foster saw it, had been not simply legal manumission but rather sweeping transformation: "We wanted to write the idea of justice in the American heart."

This debate reveals something essential about the nature of social justice activism: it can never fully achieve its aim. In the fight for a perfectly equal and just society, every victory, no matter how great, leaves something else undone. Abolitionism was among the most successful protest movements in American history, and yet by the standards outlined by Foster and Douglass in 1865, the goals of the AASS remain unmet today. It also illuminates a defining turn in radical activist cultures after the Civil War. Given the anti-Americanism and distrust of electoral politics that had long defined the movement, the faith that both Garrison and his leading opponents placed in the federal government and the Republican Party is truly astounding. Douglass, Phillips, and others threw their energies into the fight for African American suffrage, in part for its symbolic import, but also because they believed it would allow black voters to protect their own interests at the polls. A hardcore Non-Resistant before the war, Garrison now felt confident handing his life's work over to the state, going so far as to declare that "the American army was now the American antislavery society."[2]

The AASS voted to remain in operation, but for the first time in its thirty-two-year history, Garrison would not be at its helm. He retired from the society and published the final issue of *The Liberator* at the end of the year, declaring its work complete. Wendell Phillips took over leadership of the AASS, vowing to champion a range of causes including the rights of women, Chinese immigrants, laborers, and Native Americans but first and foremost to win the vote for black men. They adopted a new motto, "No Reconstruction without Negro Suffrage."

MEANWHILE, REPORTS MADE their way north of the devastation the war had wrought on the former Confederacy. One northern journalist, traveling through South Carolina in late 1865, described "a city of ruins, of desolation, of vacant houses, of widowed women, of rotting wharves, of deserted warehouses, of weed-wild gardens, of miles of grass-grown streets, of acres of pitiful and voiceful barrenness." This, he wrote, was "the dead body of Charleston" after four years of the war that had begun there. The grand center of the Confederacy had nearly been destroyed by Parrott gun bombardment, three dozen or more exploding shells weighing 150 pounds each, fired from a 16,000-pound cannon four miles away. Charleston's residents were evacuated in the final months of the war, although many formerly enslaved people remained, and the city was occupied by the Union army, which would remain there for years. White officers chose from the luxurious homes that had fared well in the shelling. Black troops patrolled the streets, which were generally deserted. There was little commerce to speak of, and basic supplies were scarce. A few white Charlestonians remained, mainly women in mourning garb who sneered at the occupying force; otherwise, soldiers mostly encountered wayward goats and rangy mutts feeding on trash and creeping flora.[3]

Cities like Richmond and Atlanta were burned-out husks as well. All over the region, the farms that had not been torched lay fallow and choked with weeds. Soldiers on both sides had tactically destroyed homes and barns; bridges, fences, and rail lines; crops and livestock; even family heirlooms. Where there was cotton in the fields, no one knew who would bring in the harvest and how they would be paid; the currency was, of course, so much trash.

Meanwhile, four million formerly enslaved people had been "turned loose," as it was commonly said, with nowhere to go, having been deprived of all resources for generations. Emancipation had come to them unevenly. Some had run to Union lines as soon as fighting broke out and became "contraband of war"; others learned of abolition through hearsay or from halting announcements by their bewildered enslavers or from Yankee soldiers on horseback. They were free, but with no land of their own on which

Charleston in ruins, 1865.
Library of Congress

to grow or hunt food, no access to healthcare, and no education, including basic literacy, to fall back on. Now they faced the task of surviving a perilously unscaffolded freedom, a smallpox epidemic that swept through their communities after the war, and most of all the defeated white southerners who themselves had little more than water gruel to eat and who hated them and the United States with equal vehemence.[4]

The fate of these brand-new Americans was a defining question for the entire nation, not just for the remaining abolitionists arguing in far-off northern cities. Foreseeing something of this challenge back in 1863, Lincoln's War Department had established a task force to explore how best to address the needs of millions of people who were homeless and impoverished, many long separated from kinship networks. The members of the American Freedmen's Inquiry Commission might have seemed unlikely choices for official government business only a few years before. Samuel Gridley Howe was a former member of John Brown's Secret Six and the Boston Vigilance Committee who had previously founded pioneering institutions for the education of the blind and the mentally disabled. Robert Dale Owen was a socialist and labor organizer whose advocacy of birth control and Free Love had made him nearly as scandalous as his colleague Fanny Wright. James McKaye, a wealthy abolitionist from New York, rounded out the group. Men formerly involved with socialist communes and treasonous plots were now leaders of the federal project that would shape the American future—proof of their vindication but also their containment.

This task force visited black communities around the nation, as well as the settlements in Canada West. To counter the ubiquitous claim that the free people would not work unless they were physically compelled to do so, the commission gathered proof that black Americans were more than capable of establishing productive, healthy communities provided they also had the rights and opportunities that white Americans enjoyed. Its official recommendation was that the government "offer the freedmen temporary aid and counsel until they become a little accustomed to their new sphere of life; secure to them, by law, their just rights of person and property; relieve them, by a fair and equal administration of justice, from the depressing influence of disgraceful prejudice." The commission's most critically important but as it turned out tragically unrealized directive was that the government "guard them against the virtual restoration of slavery in any form, under any pretext, and then let them take care of themselves." With this charge, the Freedmen's Bureau was formed to manage the protection, employment, and education of freed people in the South. The bureau's agents would settle disputes, register marriages, negotiate labor contracts, and provide food and medical care. Their jurisdiction stretched from Washington, D.C., to Texas, where they would oversee millions of people and countless acres of abandoned or confiscated land.[5]

Some white southerners adapted themselves to the astonishing changes of the postwar years, including their own temporary disenfranchisement while black men went to the polls. Many others fought them tooth and nail, destroying the schoolhouses for black children that the bureau established, knocking down every person of color they encountered on the street. Looking back to evaluate the work of the bureau from his vantage point in the early twentieth century, W. E. B. DuBois said that the herculean task of Reconstruction "was in large part foredoomed to failure. The very name of the Bureau stood for a thing in the South which for two centuries and better men had refused even to argue,—that life amid free Negroes was simply unthinkable, the maddest of experiments."[6]

Into this maddest of experiments went the Black Major. Delany was mustered out of the army at the war's end and accepted a post with the Freedmen's Bureau on the South Carolina Sea Islands, where Reconstruction had effectively begun early in the war with the Port Royal project. Like the other military leaders there, as well as the black community itself, Delany saw property ownership and the economic power it represented as the key to Reconstruction, encouraging the population under his leadership to "get up a community and get all the lands you can." He believed that the most important measure the government could undertake for the entire economy would be to help four million penniless black southerners secure small farms of their own. Once they had a little money at their disposal, they would come to constitute a massive new consumer market, looking to purchase things like shoes in the short term and eventually fine furniture and luxury goods.[7]

Land redistribution had gotten an early start in 1864, when Lincoln set aside some acres on the Sea Islands to be sold to black families at preferential rates. Rufus Saxton and others at Port Royal had pushed for more, and the following year a far more sweeping opportunity arose. In January 1865, concluding his infamous scorched-earth march to the sea, the Union general William Tecumseh Sherman had met with twenty black leaders in Savannah, Georgia. The questions he, along with Secretary of War Edwin Stanton, posed were simple: What did they most want for their people? How could the government best help them? The group chose Garrison Frazier, a sixty-seven-year-old minister, as their spokesman. His answer was clear: "The way we can best take care of ourselves is to have land." By working their own farms, he believed, African Americans could "soon maintain ourselves and have something to spare." He asked that they be placed on land until they were able to purchase it "and make it our own." Asked if they would prefer to live among white people "or in colonies by yourselves," Frazier answered, "I would prefer to live by ourselves." Only one of his nineteen colleagues disagreed with him.[8]

Two days later, Sherman issued a field order claiming a tract of some 400,000 acres of land, a thirty-mile-wide strip of coastline running all the way from Charleston to the northeast corner of Florida, to be distributed in 40-acre plots to African American families. The black population of the occupied Sea Islands doubled as hundreds poured in behind Sherman's troops, many emaciated and dying of disease. Saxton was to administer Sherman's order, and bureau agents like Delany were charged with parceling out the land. By the middle of 1865, they had settled 40,000 free people in this area, sometimes assigning as many as 5,000 acres a day. From time to time, groups came together to choose a larger, combined area, with plans to lay out a village.

Geographically, it was a superb location for the kind of community so many black leaders had sought for decades. Some of the finest cotton in the South grew there, a staple cash crop in demand internationally, which could provide them with an economic base. In their own gardens, families raised tomatoes, okra, chickens, and pretty much anything else they wanted with ease. Waters teeming with fish and oysters, thickets full of berries, and other wild delicacies were abundant and free to all. The Carolinas would need a port city, and many assumed that Charleston would never recover. A new urban center would arise from the Sea Islands, they thought, bustling with trade up and down the Eastern Seaboard and to Europe. This community would have concentrated political power, a voting bloc, and their own representatives.

But with the war over, the previous landowners, Confederates driven out when the Union captured the area, started trickling back into town, many impoverished to the point of starvation, gazing on the shards of family china that glimmered from the weeds overtaking the blackened shells of their mansions, the people they had claimed as property now in possession of the fields. In the fall of 1865, President Johnson came to their rescue. Congress had passed a bill with a land provision that seemed to make Sherman's field order permanent, but Johnson vetoed it, revoking the freedmen's land grants and declaring that white southerners could reclaim all of their property, except for the formerly enslaved people themselves, that had not been sold outright, simply by paying the overdue taxes and taking an oath of allegiance to their once and future nation, the United States.

The black population was distraught and furious as these promised lands were torn from their grasp. A group on Edisto Island, where black residents had been assigned sixteen thousand acres of land, wrote an impassioned letter to the president, asking that the government break up the land monopoly that slave-owning whites had held in the area before the war, allowing the free people a chance to work for the purchase of their own small farms. "This is our home," they declared, "we have made these lands what they are." Of course, they received no answer. Except for the very few freed people who had managed to buy property outright, the only options that remained were to lease land from whites or else to work for the "new masters," northern cotton agents who had come into the region to make their fortunes. Working someone else's cotton field for someone else's profit did not feel like a new dawn of freedom, especially because African Americans suffered under restrictions that did not apply to white laborers, including legal limitations on their physical movement on public roads and between plantations. Threats of violence and imprisonment were ever present.[9]

As the free people's hope for landownership evaporated, Delany focused on building relationships between black workers and white planters. He published newspaper articles urging these groups to cooperate to rebuild the economy on which they both relied. Indeed, he had a shockingly forgiving attitude toward the defeated Confederates and supported a Reconstruction plan that would grant them total amnesty and reintegration into the political system. He believed that if the South was ever going to knit together into a functional, peaceful society in which black people would be safe and slowly accrue financial and political power, they would have to be paragons of forgiveness and patience. In his insistence that the free people of South Carolina compromise with their former enslavers, the increasingly conservative Reconstruction-era Delany seems far removed from his previous radicalism.

Having swept the 1866 elections, Radical Republicans held the majority in Congress; indeed, they wielded power enough to override the presidential veto. Led by Thaddeus Stevens and Charles Sumner, who had healed from his assault on the floor of the Senate and returned to his seat, this wing of the party advocated for strong federal Reconstruction policies that would punish the defeated Confederate traitors and bring African Americans into full citizenship. They sought to strike at the root of racial inequality and effect a broad transformation of American society, making them more racially progressive than Lincoln, much less his North Carolina–born successor. Whereas Johnson spoke of a "restoration" of the South, Stevens demanded a "revolution" instead, "a radical reorganization in Southern institutions, habits and manners." This would have to include, in his opinion, not only African American suffrage but a radical program of land redistribution: "We shall not approach the measure of justice until we have given every adult freedman a homestead on the land where he was born and toiled and suffered. Forty acres of land and a hut would be more valuable to him than the immediate right to vote. Unless we give them this, we shall receive the censure of mankind and the curse of Heaven."[10]

Overpowering, for a time, the president and his allies who declared that the United States would always be "a white man's country" with "a white man's government," the Radicals argued that the aim of the founders had been a thoroughly egalitarian society. While slavery remained, they were unable to realize this goal. Now, with the Civil War over, it was Congress's "duty to complete their work." Stevens saw Reconstruction as a "revolution to correct the palpable incongruities and despotic provisions of the Constitution" in order to make the nation what it never yet had been: "a true republic." Activists going back to Owen had called for a second revolution that would put the nation's most progressive political ideals into practice. For a brief moment in history, their dream was shared by a number of government leaders with both the political power and the will to go after it. Over President Johnson's veto, they passed the Reconstruction Acts of 1867, requiring southern states to recognize black male citizenship before being readmitted to the Union and sending twenty thousand federal troops to the "defunct states" of the South, as Stevens called them, as districts under military occupation.[11]

Delany feared that Radical Republicans would push the president and the South too far. He wrote to a delegation of black leaders who had visited the White House, including his longtime colleague and sometime adversary Frederick Douglass, urging them not to expect too much from Johnson, who had expressed to them his belief that black people should be colonized outside the United States. In your dealings with him, Delany advised, "be mild, as is the nature of your race." Of course, he supported black suffrage, and indeed wrote a letter to the president advocating for it, but Delany's focus remained on the gradual acquisition of the economic power that property ownership would bring. He did not think the time had come for social integration or black political leadership at the national level.

In 1867, for example, Wendell Phillips and other Radical Republicans wanted the party to nominate a black man for the vice presidency. Delany wrote a letter to Henry Highland Garnet dismissing their proposal as "nonsense." He suggested that African Americans should slowly fit themselves for small local offices instead, arguing that outsize political ambition would inevitably lead to blunders, which would be powerful ammunition for their enemies. When Delany himself was floated as a potential candidate for the House of Representatives the following year, he declined to run, declaring, "It is not necessary for our claims as American citizens, nor important for the accomplishment of that end, that a black man at this period be a representative in the national halls of legislation." He insisted that "the American people generally" were not ready for high-ranking black officials, and he seemed quite willing to accept the possibility that they may "never become ready." He urged African American southerners to resist the "ill-timed and extravagant advice" of Radical Republican troublemakers and to embrace moderation. Unaccountably, he even asked them to accept their inferiority. "We are not equal to our white friends in many ways," he wrote. "Not equal in general intelligence." As black Americans claimed their civil rights, Delany warned them not to "elbow the white people out of their own places."[12]

This, from the man who has been heralded as a father of black nationalism, who had once proclaimed, "We must declare ourselves to be the equals of white men, if not their superiors," who had spearheaded a multinational movement for a black-ruled republic, who had aided and abetted the insurrectionist John Brown. How do we explain Delany's advocacy of not just political compromise but black subordination in the late 1860s, a moment that seemed to vibrate with radical possibility? Clearly, he did not trust white reformers to end racism, so perhaps he was playing the long game, anticipating a time when southern blacks would have to live with the relationships now being forged with their neighbors—a dynamic that would indeed prove more lasting than the support of whites in the North. Plenty of other activists, including Stephen S. Foster and northern black community leaders, never invested their full hope for civil rights in the Republican Party. Higginson had insisted that the vote would be meaningless without land, that northern well-wishers needed to secure for the free people not just money and old clothes or even teachers and schoolbooks but reparative justice in the form of landownership so that "they can dispense even with our love."[13]

But Delany's growing opposition to the radical wing of the party was driven by a brand of racial accommodationism that is difficult to square with his earlier career as one of the most important black militant visionaries in American history. Conservative whites started to look favorably on him as a spokesman of black humility and prudence, in contrast to the "arch-agitator" Phillips. Just two years after the end of the war, *The New York Times* quoted him to support its view that black people should stay out of politics because intermarriage and other unnatural horrors would follow.[14]

―――――

DELANY WAS NOT the only activist whose uncompromising utopian radicalism incrementally gave way to political pragmatism and
expediency after the war. As he took on the mantle of the abolitionist movement, Wendell Phillips entered a period of political influence that he never could have foreseen. He was becoming a
radical standard-bearer against President Johnson, who, it was increasingly clear, posed a major obstacle to post-emancipation black
rights. To conservatives, Phillips was seen as the vanguard of outrageous social ideas that the Republican majority in Congress would
then adopt. Johnson said he should be hanged for treason, while
Phillips contributed to mounting calls for the president's impeachment. Most of all, Phillips aimed to wring as many victories for
African Americans as he could out of the Republicans while they
were still engaged and in power, even if it meant abandoning the
perfectionist mandates that had fired the antebellum movement to
"break *every* yoke" and to "come out" of the world's corruption. In
May 1867, he explained, "I only want that if we sell out, we sell in
the dearest market and get the best price. If I cannot get the whole
that I ask for, then I want to get as much as I can."[15]

This willingness to sell out for the right price, to accept less than
the whole he had always asked for, steered Phillips's approach to the
additional constitutional amendments under discussion at this time.
In 1865, when proposals for a Fourteenth Amendment to the Constitution that would grant citizenship status and equal protection
under the law to African Americans had started to circulate, Robert
Dale Owen brought the matter to the attention of Elizabeth Cady
Stanton and Susan B. Anthony. He hoped that legislators would
consider a draft using the term "persons" to describe American citizens, opening the possibility of suffrage for women as well. But the
text legislators eventually agreed on included "male" three times so
there could be no mistake, the first time women's exclusion from
constitutional rights was made explicit.

Stanton and Anthony assumed that the colleagues with whom

The Reconstruction Amendments excluded not only women
but Native Americans from suffrage.
Harper's Weekly, *April 22, 1871*

they had long worked on the overlapping causes of abolition and
women's rights would denounce this advance toward one goal positioned in antagonism to the other, but they were mistaken. Higginson, who had been very active in the movement before the war,
declined Stanton's request to join the fight for women's suffrage at
this time, writing to her that he felt "a little less strong than formerly" on this issue after his time in the South. He said that in his
experience even "the women otherwise most radical seem usually
indifferent" to suffrage although men encouraged them to pursue
that path. But in the South, the black demand for suffrage was "in-
destructible," he explained, "no oppression could even blunt it."[16]

When they approached Phillips about merging their movement
with the evolving American Anti-Slavery Society to work for equal
rights and suffrage for all, he was not interested. Although he had
vocally supported women's rights throughout his career, he began
blocking discussion of gender issues at the society's conventions.
Foster opposed him, urging their colleagues to support women's
suffrage as a matter of conscience, political expediency be damned.

But this was "the Negro's hour," Phillips insisted, and women would have to wait. In high dudgeon, Stanton asked him, "Do you believe the African race is composed entirely of males?"

Stanton and Phillips had tangled before. At the women's rights convention in 1860, Stanton had launched into an attack on marriage and expressed "the most profound respect and loving sympathy for those heroic women, who, in the face of law and public sentiment, have dared to sunder the unholy ties of a joyless, loveless union." Intense debate followed about whether marriage was "merely a contract," as Stanton said, and if it was even appropriate to discuss the subject at all, given that the public would accuse their movement of further dallying with Free Love. For Phillips, there was no question. He took the floor and declared that the laws of marriage and divorce rest equally on women and men and that this was not, after all, a marriage convention. Indeed, he moved to strike the foregoing discussion from the recorded proceedings, an attempt to suppress material that he deemed too risky. Anthony boomed in response, "Nearly all the wrongs of which we complain grow out of the inequality, the injustice of the marriage laws, that rob the wife of the right to herself and her children—that make her the slave of the man she marries." Phillips's motion was defeated, as was Stanton's about divorce, although the convention did affirm women's right to "the control and custody of our persons in marriage."[17]

Then the war came. Stanton and Anthony founded the Women's Loyal National League, agreeing to pause agitation specifically aimed at women's rights and throw their energy behind the Union cause, spearheading an enormous petition campaign that ultimately contributed to emancipation and the Thirteenth Amendment prohibiting slavery. Before long, Stanton would come to regard the suspension of women's rights agitation during the war years as a "blunder," yet another instance of women putting other people ahead of themselves and being silenced by male reform leaders rather than driving an independent movement forward.

Like Phillips, Stanton and Anthony knew that the war had provided a rare opening for transformational change. As Frederick Douglass observed in 1865, "We may not see, for centuries to come, the same disposition that exists at this moment." They felt an urgency to seize that momentum before it was too late. If the Constitution was going to be changed, now was the time to usher in as many of the reforms they sought as possible so that, as Stanton put it, American women might walk into citizenship rights on the arms of black soldiers.[18]

When the National Woman's Rights Convention met in 1866, the first time since the war, its members rebranded as the American Equal Rights Association, with a platform advocating for both women and African Americans. Speakers including Henry Ward Beecher, Theodore Tilton, Frederick Douglass, Sojourner Truth, Abby Kelley, and Stephen S. Foster affirmed the unity of these aims. Charles Lenox Remond, a stalwart of both movements, declared, "All I ask for myself I claim for my wife and sister." Indeed, his sister, Sarah Remond, was also in attendance.[19]

Frances Harper delivered the final and most compelling speech on the intersectional agenda that she hoped would define the new organization. A well-known author and a traveling lecturer for the AASS, Harper began her talk with a personal story about the financial problems she faced when her husband died suddenly and the obstacles that arose in her path because of her sex, her race, and her

Frances E. W. Harper.
Schomburg Center for Research in Black Culture, Manuscripts, Archives, and Rare Books Division, The New York Public Library. The New York Public Library Digital Collections, *1893*

economic position. She supported women's suffrage but implored the white women present to understand that the ballot would not cure the massive injustices that she as a woman of color endured. She spoke of the travails of black Union veterans, including Harriet Tubman, who often encountered violent racism in daily life in the postwar years. She described her own experiences on trains and streetcars in northern cities like Philadelphia, where she had been ejected from her seat multiple times. The last time a conductor had approached her, she explained, she had refused to budge: "I felt the fight in me; but I don't want to have to fight all the time." She said that white women, just as much as any group in the country, must overcome their ignorance of the harsh realities facing people of color. Her core message was, "We are all bound up together." This was the promise of the Equal Rights Association, a place where multi-issue activists could collaborate across social differences to grasp systems of social inequality at the root. But it didn't last long.[20]

IN 1867, REFORMER ATTENTION turned once again to Kansas. With the announcement of two ballot propositions there that would extend the right to vote, one to black men and the other to women, East Coast reformers flooded in with leaflets flying. Elizabeth Cady Stanton and Susan B. Anthony traveled fifteen hundred miles to "the sacred soil where John Brown and his sons had helped to fight the battles that made Kansas a free State." Anthony's two brothers had been among the Free State settlers who ultimately triumphed there in a guerrilla war against slavery's expansion. Positioning themselves as the inheritors of that fight, Stanton and Anthony chased what they described in utopian terms as "one green spot on earth where women could enjoy full liberty as citizens of the United States." They spoke in log cabins, barns, mills, and unfinished schoolhouses. They were eaten up by bugs at night, sleeping either outdoors in a carriage with wild animals snuffing at the door or in the dirty sheets of whatever farmhouse would invite them in for the night, once with a mouse nest in the bed. They often dined on nothing more than an apple and slippery elm bark to chew and became used to forgoing luxuries like milk and sugar, to which Stanton was particularly attached and certainly accustomed.[21]

When the two suffrage propositions had been announced, local politicians and the press began playing the two movements against each other, insisting that they were mutually exclusive and antagonistic, that if one succeeded it would be at the expense of the other, even though many of the activists on the ground supported both aims. The Kansas Republican Party decided to back only black male suffrage and formed a committee to actively oppose female suffrage. Local newspapers ridiculed women's rights activists and warned Kansans that women voters would usher in a social revolution against men and overturn Christianity.

Fearing that the ludicrous vision of women at the polls might discredit the movement for black suffrage, and determined not to let the two causes "mix," Phillips made a decision that sealed his relationship with his former colleagues Stanton and Anthony. He was in charge of two pots of money bequeathed to the use of reform causes and decided to cut off the women's movement as beneficiaries of these funds, hamstringing their ability to drum up support for the women's ballot initiative. With two weeks left until the day of the vote, they took an infusion of funds from an unexpected source.

George Francis Train was a showman, a shrewd entrepreneur, and a "great American humbug," as one contemporary called him. Onstage, he was an oddball combination of serious orator and stand-up comedian, nationally known for his rapid-fire monologues of impersonations, jokes, and political opinions. Because of his reputation as a highly influential crowd-pleaser, the Union Pacific Railroad paid him off the books as a promoter and lobbyist; he made a fortune on real estate speculation in Nebraska, because he knew in advance where new rail lines would be laid. A southern sympathizer during the war, he was vocally opposed to black suffrage. Despite his peculiar manic energy and rumored mental illness, Stanton and Anthony held their noses and teamed up with Train, who became a major backer of their movement.

Garrison, for one, was flabbergasted. He wrote to express his

Flyer for a suffrage meeting featuring George Francis Train, 1876.
American Antiquarian Society

dismay that Stanton and Anthony were aligning themselves and the movement with a "crack-brained harlequin and semi-lunatic" who tossed off racial slurs in his stage performances. "He may be of use in drawing an audience," Garrison observed, "but so would a kangaroo, a gorilla, or a hippopotamus." They responded pointedly that they were glad to have the support of a man like Train who intended to see women's suffrage accomplished: "Though many of the leading minds of this country have advocated woman's enfranchisement for the last twenty years, it has been more as an intellectual theory than a fact of life, hence none of our many friends were ready to help in the practical work of the last few months." Stanton also wrote a letter to Higginson asserting, "The position of such men as Garrison, Phillips, Sumner in their treatment of our question today proves that we must not trust any of you." She said that abolitionists had never used women's rights as a litmus test for their backers: "Do they ignore everyone who is false to woman? by no means. Why ask us to ignore everyone who is false to the negro?"[22]

Both of the Kansas suffrage propositions went down in flames, teaching Stanton "that it is impossible for the best of men to understand women's feelings and the humiliation of their position" and that women must awake "to their duty to themselves" ahead of all others—namely, black men. But these were the wrong lessons. This antagonistic perspective, eschewing collaboration across difference and spoiling for a fight with other groups seeking redress, soon led to a split in the movement and the narrowing of its capacious vision.

The question of black male suffrage would soon be settled at the federal level. As the Fifteenth Amendment, which made it illegal to deny a citizen the right to vote on the basis of race, color, or previous condition of servitude, wended its way toward ratification, those who had insistently deferred the question of votes for women until black suffrage was secure felt in 1868 that it was time to take it up. Many former abolitionists advocated a sixteenth amendment that would make women the next constitutional priority. But Stanton and Anthony would not let it go, attacking black suffrage in increasingly incendiary terms and opposing the amendment to the bitter end.

It's worth noting that a few African American activists, including Sojourner Truth, also opposed the Fifteenth Amendment for its exclusion of women. Robert and Harriet Forten Purvis faced off with their own sons over it. Charles Purvis, James Forten's grandson, regarded white women as "the bitterest enemies of the negro" in this moment. He was in no hurry to enfranchise the southern women in whose names black men were being tortured and burned alive. But his father countered firmly that he would not support his acquisition of rights denied to his daughter.[23]

Meanwhile, Stanton's racist rhetoric only heightened. In their new magazine, *The Revolution*—funded by Train and with editorial help from the Come-Outer Parker Pillsbury, a colleague from the antislavery days—she and Anthony fomented outrage that men of color would soon have rights that were denied to white women. Stanton's attacks were particularly virulent and calculated. "Think of Patrick and Sambo and Hans and Yung Tung," she fumed, making laws for educated, refined, native-born white women whose grandfathers were heroes of the American Revolution. Stanton had long indulged in this invidious comparison. Even the Seneca Falls declaration rails against "the most ignorant and degraded men—both natives and foreigners"—holding rights withheld from women. By February 1869, her editorials suggested that black men were sexual predators, a tactic then being deployed by white-supremacist terrorists to justify grisly lynchings. The Fifteenth Amendment, she pretended to worry, would "culminate in fearful outrages on womanhood especially in the southern states."[24]

After all of this, Stanton and Anthony still had the gall to walk into the 1869 meeting of the Equal Rights Association to face long-time colleagues like Frederick Douglass, who had stood to advocate women's suffrage at the Seneca Falls Convention over twenty years earlier, when white women themselves were afraid to go so far. Even before that, Stanton had seen Remond and Garrison stand with Lucretia Mott in London, refusing to take part in any antislavery debate that did not acknowledge the full equality of women. Black women had been essential to the annual conventions of the 1850s that cemented the movement. As Stanton and Anthony entered Steinway Hall, they might have locked eyes with Frances Harper, whose calls for a truly inclusive approach to women's oppression they had heard for years but had proved unwilling to heed.

Stephen S. Foster led the attack, demanding that Stanton resign her position as president. She called for a vote of confidence and won it. The abolitionist Charles Burleigh tried to speak multiple times but was drowned out by loud hissing from the crowd of women. Paulina Wright Davis shared her observation on a recent trip to the South that black men were the worst of tyrants and beat their wives once a week on principle. Douglass then took the floor, registering his dissent from this claim and from a number of Stanton's other offensive remarks about "ignorant bootblacks" and "degraded Chinese" that had cropped up in Stanton's remarks earlier. Anthony started down the aisle toward him, but Douglass raised his hand, saying, "No, no, Susan," and she returned to her seat. He insisted that they hear him out.

Douglass, who had no doubt been deeply offended by a long-time friend throwing around slurs like "Sambo," never resorted to personal disrespect or even to casting doubt on Stanton and Anthony's political aims. He was still all in for women's rights, he told them, but given the dire situation in the South, African Americans were in a state of emergency and needed every possible tool to protect themselves. He explained that "when women, because they are women, are hunted down . . . when they are dragged from their houses and hung upon lamp posts," then they will "have an urgency to obtain the ballot equal to our own." Someone in the crowd called out, "Is that not all true about black women?" Yes, of course it was, Douglass answered, "but not because she is a woman but because she is black." Harper backed him up, observing that those who agitated for the rights of "women" or even "working women" never seemed to mean black women, too. She supported anything that advanced the cause of black men, she affirmed, and when it was a question of race, she was willing to "let the lesser question of sex go."[25]

This meeting was so rancorous that it destroyed the organization. Condemning Stanton's racism, a Boston-based splinter group including Lucy Stone, Higginson, Garrison, Douglass, Harper, Foster, and Clara Barton pledged to pursue women's suffrage full bore, but only after the vote for black men was secure. While they were far more committed to racial justice than Stanton and Anthony's group, they were more moderate on all other issues. Theodore Tilton tried to arbitrate a reunion between the groups the following year. Lucretia Mott joined him, in her seventies at this point and nearing the end of her activist career. Always insistent on a unified battle for human rights, she was physically sickened by the vicious infighting between her friends and former colleagues. When the warring factions refused to reconcile, she wrote that she was "glad to be out of it all, & never mean to join another Organizat[io]n."[26]

By the time the Fifteenth Amendment was ratified in 1870, the activist alliances that had laid the groundwork for it had splintered. Mott could barely recognize Stanton; Douglass was increasingly alarmed by Delany; Phillips and Garrison avoided each other as well, having gone to court over the use of movement funds. The final text of the amendment made it illegal to deny an American citizen the right to vote on the basis of race, color, or previous condition of servitude. "Sex" did not appear there, as Stanton had hoped, and it was anemic in other ways as well. Previous drafts had offered more robust protections against the backdoor methods that southern states used to exclude eligible African American voters— poll taxes, literacy tests, and the like. Soon even those methods would seem quaint.

Even in this diminished state, Wendell Phillips stood by his trust in the franchise as synonymous with equality and empowerment, arguing that "a man with the ballot in his hand is the master of the situation." He learned of the amendment's ratification while on the road lecturing and wrote to a friend, "Our long work is sealed at last." The United States had finally declared independence for all:

Print celebrating the Fifteenth Amendment. Martin Delany
is given pride of place at top center alongside Frederick Douglass
and Hiram Revels, the first U.S. black senator. Abraham Lincoln
and John Brown are positioned symmetrically below.
Library of Congress

"Today is its real 'Birthday.'" The second revolution was complete, and a new republic founded, he confidently declared.[27]

Privately, he knew that wasn't quite true. Phillips called the American Anti-Slavery Society together one last time. Five years after he had replaced Garrison, he told the crowd that now, and finally, the victory was won, and it was time to disband. Stephen S. Foster disagreed, declaring that the Fifteenth Amendment was no guarantee of the protection and future well-being of the free people, that the vote alone meant next to nothing given the intimidation by white southerners that would accompany it. Their organization should hold out, he argued, until the government adopted a plan of land redistribution that would put black southerners on more equal footing in the long term. There was still considerable momentum behind these economic proposals even as political solutions won the day; thousands of abolitionists had signed a petition the previous year asking Congress to help freed people acquire tracts of southern land and receive loans for building materials, tools, and seed. But Phillips, the traitor, fanatic, and arch-agitator who had also championed land-based reparations, not to mention universal suffrage, insisted that "the Constitution of the United States had absorbed" the constitution of the AASS and that "the mighty arm of the nation" was raised to implement it. Still, he could not help but admit, "I am no longer proud, as I once was, of the flag or of the name of an American. . . . I am no longer proud of the Declaration of Independence." But it was time to shift focus to the "crusades of the future," he advised them. "We sheathe no sword. We only turn our front upon a new foe."[28]

CHAPTER 14

A Revolution Going Backward

The Civil War marked a key moment of economic modernization in the United States, and not only because it freed four million workers and abolished the slave labor system on which the country, indeed global capitalism, had been built. The mid-nineteenth century also saw rapid industrialization that transformed the entire working class. Artisans with hand tools in small shops gave way to enormous factories full of machines, and American life became increasingly urban as concentrations of workers lived in proximity to these manufacturing centers. Laborers had made Union victory possible, not only because they were disproportionately represented in the army (richer men could send a "substitute" for $300), but also because they powered the manufacturing boom the war required. They churned out factory-made boots and firearms and assembled sloops and frigates in navy shipyards. Railway workers laid thousands of miles of new track to carry troops and supplies south into battle.[1]

But the cost of living was on the rise—the prices of food, fuel, and rent climbing while real wages fell. The war was enriching factory owners but creating an unprecedented wealth gap, so that workers were increasingly aware of their exclusion from the prosperity they produced. Strikes and other forms of labor unrest were widespread during the war years. Trade unions and associations of workingmen resurged as the vast population of Americans who worked for a living aimed to harness their power to demand higher wages. Sailmakers, nail makers, horseshoers, grave diggers, coopers, locomotive engineers, typographers, cigar makers, piano makers, spinners, glass cutters, miners, ironworkers, wheelwrights—all sought to organize during this time. Their agitation shed light on the failings of the wage labor system into which formerly enslaved people were being initiated.

As the war between the North and the South came to a close, a new conflict seemed to be right on the horizon. Many Americans saw a reckoning with capitalism as inevitable and considered justice for working people a critical piece of the Reconstruction revolution that would also place African Americans and women on new footing. As Wendell Phillips declared, "We have now but one purpose; and that is, having driven all other political questions out of the arena, having abolished slavery, the only question left is labor,—the relations of capital and labor." He had been a delegate at the first meeting of the New England Workingmen's Association back in 1845, where Brisbane, Ripley, and the Brook Farmers sought to organize millworkers under Fourierist Association. In those days,

Women shoemakers on strike in Lynn, Massachusetts.
Frank Leslie's Illustrated Newspaper, *March 17, 1860*

he insisted that the issue of slavery take precedence over labor and rejected comparisons between the two systems. By the end of the Civil War, however, he was wielding the metaphor of "wage slavery" himself and became a major figure in the Boston-area movement. Indeed, he claimed that "the Anti-Slavery cause was only a portion of the great struggle between Capital and Labor. Capital undertook to own the laborer. We have broken that up." Phillips saw the labor cause, unlike women's suffrage, as compatible with his fight for black rights and worked to integrate these movements at the same time he was muzzling Stanton and Anthony.[2]

When Kansas considered its two suffrage propositions in the summer of 1867, the Radical Republican senator Ben Wade of Ohio spoke in favor of both in Lawrence, which had been rebuilt after its destruction by Border Ruffians. During the war years, Kansas had seen strikes by tailors, cabinetmakers, and others. Reflecting this climate, much of Wade's speech concerned a reform battle that was neither black male suffrage nor the movement for women's rights. Now that the nation had disposed of slavery, he declared, the question "of labor and capital must pass through the ordeal." Warning that the shadow of this approaching class struggle was already darkening the land, he called for a more equal distribution of property and wealth. The people and the government "which had done so much for the slave cannot quietly regard the terrible distinction which exists between the man that labors and him that does not." Wade's remarks were widely circulated, and the press accused him and his party of threatening a war on private property to follow the war on slavery. The speech even caught the attention of a German philosopher living in London, whose *Communist Manifesto* and new release, *Capital,* were still little known outside European radical circles.[3]

Karl Marx had watched the Civil War with great interest. He was familiar with the American political scene, having written almost weekly for the *New-York Tribune* over the course of a decade at the invitation of the editor Charles Dana, a former resident of Brook Farm. Marx was a stalwart supporter of the Union cause and a fan of Wendell Phillips and the antislavery movement. On behalf of the International Workingmen's Association (IWA or First International), a group of European labor activists, socialists, and anarchists that had recently been founded in London, he had written a letter to congratulate Lincoln on his reelection in 1864.

Marx interpreted the debate over the expansion of slavery that roiled the country in the 1850s as a contest over which of the nation's labor systems would become dominant. The existence of slavery, he believed, had made it impossible for white American workers to identify as a class, embracing African American laborers and others around the world, "but this barrier to progress has been swept off by the red sea of civil war." Marx believed that the emancipation of slaves at the hands of a president he called "the single-minded son of the working class" opened the door for a radical reorganization of the nation's economy.[4]

A group of German American socialists in New York City under the leadership of Friedrich Sorge converted their "Communist Club," which had been an antislavery organization for over a decade, into the first American section of the IWA in 1869. Like many Americans, they hoped that the abolition of slavery would soon lead to a reckoning with the widening socioeconomic divisions created by industrial capitalism, which seemed to be at odds with the principles of the nation's founding. In the aftermath of a war that had reshaped the landscape and toppled existing hierarchies, it seemed possible to address in relatively short order the inequalities on the basis of race, sex, and socioeconomic class that the first revolution had left unaddressed.

The leading goal of the labor movement that emerged at the end of the war was to limit the workday to eight hours. This agenda was articulated and pursued most aggressively by the Boston activists Ira Steward and George McNeill, whose Eight-Hour League supported radical Reconstruction and African American rights, demanding "freedom north and south" and equality in both "the cotton fields of South Carolina" and the "cotton mills of Massachusetts." Like Marx, Steward held that the Civil War made workers newly receptive to reform arguments because the American laborer "instinctively feels that something of slavery still remains, or that something of freedom is yet to come." Eight-Hour activists saw utopian potential in the extra time that laborers would be able to invest in their own advancement. They envisioned a future in which poverty would be "abolished and human life lengthened" and "the wages system" would "finally cease to exist." But just as many abolitionists understood emancipation to be a necessary but nowhere near sufficient victory, Steward saw the goal of a shorter workday as an initial step toward greater reforms.[5]

As local unions and workers' movements gained steam, labor leaders called for an organization that would bring them all together. In 1866, the National Labor Union was founded in Baltimore. It was the first organization of its kind, offering an inclusive platform that claimed to observe "no north, no south, no east, no west, neither color nor sex, on the question of the rights of labor." And yet this group was hostile to certain groups of immigrant workers, namely the Chinese men working on the railroads that were beginning to crisscross the nation. At their 1868 convention, the leaders agreed to seat Susan B. Anthony but not to support her "peculiar ideas." In 1869, an African American labor organizer named Isaac Myers, who had founded a trade union of black ship caulkers, was invited to the meeting, but only so that white labor leaders could encourage him in his separate efforts, not to suggest that the two groups join forces.

Myers organized his own convention that year in Washington, D.C. Positioning black workers' agitation as a necessary sequel to Reconstruction, the assembly declared, "The colored man's struggle until now has been for naked existence, for the right to life and liberty; with the fifteenth amendment, henceforth his struggle will be in pursuit of happiness." This group commended the women's suffrage movement and specifically applauded black women for charting new territory in their professional aspirations, encouraging them to learn trades and organize.[6]

The question of what role women workers would play in the movement was one that all the strands of labor organization had to address. Since the time of the Fourierist Sarah Bagley and her many activist colleagues among the Massachusetts "mill girls," women had played leading roles in American labor agitation. After the war, Edith Daniels, Jennie Collins, and Aurora Phelps had founded the Boston Working Women's League and worked alongside the Eight-Hour League and other organizations run by men. The First International had admitted one woman as a representative to its General Council, the British freethinker Harriet Law. Still, there was no question that the movement's core constituency was white men. In the postwar years, as Stanton and Anthony burned their bridges with antiracist activists, they stepped up their efforts to build connections with women labor leaders.

Indeed work and wages were the issues that had brought Anthony into the women's movement. A single woman supporting her family on a teacher's salary, she was outraged to learn that her male colleagues were paid twice as much. Economic concerns, wages, and employment had all been broached at Seneca Falls and were major topics of discussion at the Rochester and Worcester conventions that followed. In her lectures of this period, Anthony made a clear case for women's suffrage as an economic issue and a labor strategy, arguing, "With the right of suffrage to all comes an end to the dynasty of capital over labor." Moreover, a working woman had even more to complain of than workingmen: "She is doomed to work for half pay, always a subordinate." Anthony and Stanton endorsed the eight-hour campaign in the first issue of *The Revolution* and declared that "labor and women suffrage are the twin issues of the hour."[7]

Not everyone was convinced of this mutually beneficial path forward for feminism and labor. An important goal for some trade unionists was that male laborers be paid "a family wage" in order to support dependents, including a wife who stayed at home. And many labor reformers had long held that the women's movement would yield no meaningful results for those obliged to labor for a living. After Seneca Falls, one labor newspaper had called the women "theoretical reformers" who "belong to a class that is, for the most part, unaffected by the serious evils that weigh so crushingly" on working women. Their goal of women's political empowerment, this critic argued, was fanciful: "These schemes are Utopian, and will never be realized."[8]

After the war, when so much that had once seemed impossible had come to pass, perhaps it was harder to write off reform goals as utopian. After the astounding victory of emancipation, as civil rights activists in Congress, convention halls, and cotton fields debated black suffrage as a practical measure alongside the more visionary plan of a black colony on tens of thousands of seacoast acres, workers and women similarly questioned how best to seize the singular opportunity of Reconstruction, whether to pursue concrete reforms or full-blown liberation. While many in this period took a decidedly conservative turn, one Garrisonian turned labor activist and Free Lover brought the defiant utopianism of antebellum reform culture to the questions that dogged the second founding.

———

ON THE DAY that John Brown was executed, when Garrison asked the massive crowd at Tremont Temple if anyone present was still a Non-Resistant, the one man who said "I" was probably Ezra Heywood. Heywood was from an old New England family and had been prepping for the ministry at Brown in the 1850s when the antislavery movement took its revolutionary turn. He had regarded William Lloyd Garrison as a dangerous infidel until two women at his boardinghouse gave him a copy of *The Liberator*. Inspired by Phillips at an event in Providence, he became acquainted with Frederick Douglass and Charles Remond, who were working for the rights of black public-school students there, and turned infidel himself, coming out of the church and into full-time work as an abolitionist in 1858. He became a dedicated Non-Resistant, sworn to the perfectionist pacifism that Henry C. Wright and Garrison had developed with the help of the socialist Free Lover John Humphrey Noyes. Indeed, his dedication to that cause soon outstripped that of Garrison himself.[9]

Heywood found it impossible to follow his mentors in embracing the Civil War as divinely ordained to end slavery, when they had all believed so fervently that violence and nationalism were just other sinful faces of the same corruption. In an 1861 speech taking issue with Phillips and other colleagues who greeted the outbreak of war with enthusiasm, he declared, "It is a greater crime to kill a man than to enslave him." Before printing the speech, Garrison asked Heywood if he might consider deleting this line. Heywood was astounded that a fellow Non-Resistant wanted to censor him on this point and responded that he would rather delete every other line in the address and save that one. After the Emancipation Proclamation, when the abolitionist movement had almost unanimously abandoned pacifist and anti-American principles, Heywood stood firm. While others pitched in to help troop enlistment drives, he spoke out against the draft and praised the very few who resisted the demand to join the fight. When Garrison finally embraced the Union cause and joined Phillips "under the flag," Heywood maintained that all war is wrong and all "war government" must be repudiated.

In one powerful speech critiquing the abolitionists for sacrificing their principles, he quoted from the founding manifestos of the American Anti-Slavery Society and of the New England Non-

Ezra Heywood.
*Labadie Collection, University of
Michigan Library*

Resistance Society, which Garrison had composed decades earlier. Although he was being called out personally as an apostate, Garrison continued to print Heywood's contrarian speeches, but with editorial notes registering doubt about the "felicity" of trumpeting these views during wartime. In his most direct critique of Heywood, he writes, "We know of an exceptional non-resistant who is so unwise or so unfortunate in his treatment of the awful struggle through which the nation is passing, as to give aid and comfort to those traitorous dissemblers 'who cry peace, peace, when there is no peace.'"[10]

In June 1863, as his relationship with the Garrisonians frayed, Heywood met Josiah Warren, the socialist co-founder of Modern Times, who inspired him to take up the cause of labor reform. Over the next five years, he would develop an ideology that combined Warren's critique of capitalism, the Non-Resistance of Garrison and Noyes, and an individualist anarchism adapted from Emerson and the Transcendentalists. In 1869, in the very month that the Equal Rights Association imploded, Heywood called to order the first convention of the New England Labor Reform League. It brought together old antislavery colleagues like Wendell Phillips, who called for the equitable treatment of Chinese workers; Stephen S. Foster, who advocated the equal distribution of all property; the shoemakers' union; the Eight-Hour men; and others, including a number of women's suffragists, who covered it approvingly for *The Revolution*.[11]

In his opening remarks, Heywood declared, "We are all negroes . . . because wealth centralizes in a few, and the working classes are the poorer classes, and woman is reduced and held in wretched pecuniary servitude." The Associationist and former Brook Farmer John Orvis echoed Heywood's infelicitous analogy, proclaiming that the labor movement represented "Reconstruction come North" and declaring "the real question is, whether the laboring classes shall work as freemen or slaves." For labor activists who wanted immediate improvements in workplace conditions, Heywood and other veterans of more diffuse social movements often seemed off target, too insistent on tangential and possibly divisive issues like women's rights. Ira Steward's speech at the convention pulled attention back to the specific goal of the eight-hour day. Orvis, however, opposed eight-hour legislation, holding that it would merely provide a steam valve for workers' dissatisfaction, convincing them that the wage labor system was tolerable. He wanted them to push further in their demands for cooperatively owned factories and stores under their own control. For his part, Heywood found the eight-hour agitation too focused on legal reform; as an anarchist committed to "individual sovereignty," he scorned solutions that worked within the existing framework of the state instead of aiming for more abstract but revolutionary alternatives.[12]

Heywood continued to trumpet his anticapitalist message in the coming years, calling to his conventions a network of multi-issue thinkers and agitators including Albert Brisbane, Elizabeth Cady Stanton, and Stephen Pearl Andrews, with an honorary position for J. K. Ingalls, longtime land reformer and founding member of the first English-speaking section of the First International in the United States. Although many industrial workers found Heywood's philosophical approach inadequate, the overlap on his organization's roster of Marxists and Fourierists, Free Lovers and women's rights activists, indicates that anticapitalist critique in this moment provided a fruitful junction for radical thought. Stanton stood alongside Brisbane, who had opened her eyes to women's oppression in the isolated households of capitalism years before; perhaps she had originally met Orvis, who had carried Brook Farm's Associationism into the postwar labor movement, during her stay at the phalanx in the 1840s. Andrews, of course, had been the talk of the women's convention of 1858 by attempting to make the Free Love implications of the women's movement explicit. The lineup also included a new friend of his who would push this issue much further, propelling the reform scene into the spotlight of a national scandal.[13]

———

SHE WAS BORN Victoria Claflin, a dirt-poor nobody in Ohio, to a family who made a living as traveling snake-oil salesmen. As a toddler, she began seeing visions, and her gifts as a clairvoyant and magnetic healer were soon added to the family's offerings. At fifteen, she married Canning Woodhull, an alcoholic; they had two children together and later divorced. After the war, Victoria Woodhull married Colonel James Harvey Blood, a reformer and Spiritualist. In 1868, she was visited by the spirit of Demosthenes, who had been in touch with her a number of times before and who directed her to move to New York City, where she met Cornelius Vanderbilt, the railroad baron. Back to plying her metaphysical skills, she advised him in a few lucrative trades, and he set her and her sister up with a brokerage in early 1870. They were the first women on Wall Street. Susan B. Anthony stopped in to congratulate them; she had always regarded employment and earnings as the keys to women's independence. With her financial windfall, Woodhull secured a mansion on East Thirty-eighth Street in which she, her sister, her parents, her children, her first and second husbands, and friends like Stephen Pearl Andrews and his wife took up residence.

Strangely enough, while she was raking it in on Wall Street, Woodhull became a forceful critic of capitalism, delivering fiery speeches about corporate greed, the concentration of wealth in the hands of the few, and the exploitation of workers. If those in power did not do justice to laborers, she warned, "before our next centennial birthday, July 4, 1876, you will have precipitated the most terrible war that the earth has yet known." Having prophesied the Civil War with her "spiritual senses" three years before it began, she continued, "I already hear and see the approach of a more terrible contest." Moreover, the needed changes could not be accomplished under the present Constitution, and a new government would need to be formed: "What our fathers failed to do is left for this generation to perform; and it must not shirk the duty."[14]

In May 1870, the sisters began publishing a major reform newspaper, *Woodhull and Claflin's Weekly.* It became the organ of Section 12 of the First International, which they helped to organize. By the late 1860s, there were about fifty sections in the United States with a total membership of around five thousand. Reflecting the makeup of American reform culture, English-speaking IWA sections were

Victoria Woodhull, ca. 1870.
*Fogg Museum, Historical Photographs
and Special Visual Collections
Department, Fine Arts Library,
Harvard University*

generally full of Spiritualists, Free Lovers, former abolitionists, and Associationists. Section 12 was kookier than most. Nevertheless, from their headquarters in Woodhull's downtown newspaper office, this group played a vital role in disseminating socialist thought in the United States. Woodhull printed thousands of pamphlet copies of one of Marx's major addresses and published Stephen Pearl Andrews's translation of *The Communist Manifesto,* the first in the United States. These texts helped to convince many in the reform community, like Theodore Tilton, that "the same logic and sympathy—the same conviction and ardor—which made us an Abolitionist twenty years ago, make us a Communist now."[15]

Communism grabbed the attention of not only American radicals but the entire world in 1871, when an insurrection of French socialists called the Paris Commune ruled the city for two months before being put down in a bloodbath. For many Americans, the specter of violent revolution that workers' rights agitation had always vaguely threatened now seemed alarmingly real. *The New York Times* warned that "every great city has within it the communistic elements of a revolution." Just like Paris, the underbelly of New York held a "dark boiling, explosive mass of population" awaiting an opportunity "to burst out with terrific violence against property, Government, and the Church." On a gloomy day in December, Woodhull and multiple sections of the First International marched with thousands of others through the streets of lower Manhattan in sympathy with their slaughtered French colleagues. She and her sister were near the front of the parade, as were a group of Cuban activists with their national flag, and an Irish band, who demanded that a few white Internationals be positioned between themselves and a company of black soldiers known as the Skidmore Guards. Nearly everyone wore mourning crape and waved red flags. Six gray horses draped in black pulled a mahogany coffin on a platform under a banner proclaiming, "Honor to the Martyrs of the Universal Republic." The International was well represented, but some communists claimed it was a distraction from the movement's goals and that workers would only lose a day's pay and gain nothing by participating. It was a sign of an approaching schism between orthodox Marxists and the "reformers and phantastics" who, as Friedrich Sorge complained, "tried to force the workingmen to kill their time with idle talk about women's rights and suffrage, universal language, social freedom"—a euphemism for Free Love—"every possible kind of financial and civil reform and the like."[16]

The Free Love sentiments of Section 12 that galled the German American IWA were only becoming more pronounced. Although Marx had previously corresponded warmly with Woodhull, in 1872 he denounced Section 12 as "almost exclusively consisting of middle-class humbugs and worn-out Yankee swindlers in the reform business," which "never ceased to make the I.W.A. the vehicle of issues some of which are foreign to, while others are directly opposed to, the aims and purposes of the I.W.A." At the IWA's congress in The Hague, Marx expelled Woodhull's section because of the precedence it gave to "talk of personal liberty, social liberty, dress regulation, women's franchise, [and] universal language," instead of carrying out the work of the First International as a workingmen's organization. Although he was essentially correct in calling Woodhull "a banker's woman, free-lover, and general hum-bug," her excision marked a moment of divergence in American activist culture. Socialist ideas from Europe—namely those of Owen and Fourier—had been mainstays of the American tradition for fifty years. Both of these thinkers put women's rights and a cri-tique of marriage at the center of their theories of economy and exploitation. The shuttering of Section 12 foreclosed the evolution of that feminist socialist tradition by those who had been among the first American champions of Marx. While a new generation of labor agitators won important victories for workers in the coming decades, they generally considered American home life part of a separate agenda when they considered it at all.[17]

Of course, Marx's disapproval did not end Woodhull's political career. Up to this point, she had been advocating women's rights with no connection to the long-standing movement already dedi-cated to this cause and headquartered in the same city. Stanton had failed to pursue the diverse suffrage movement she had proposed with the short-lived Equal Rights Association, but a new alliance with Woodhull opened a radical new avenue for the women's move-ment.

———

IN JANUARY 1871, Woodhull became the first woman to address the House Judiciary Committee, laying out her argument that the Re-construction Amendments against which Stanton and Anthony had fought so viciously had actually enfranchised women as well as black men. Stanton, Anthony, and others in their circle embraced this "new departure," vowing to cast their ballots as fully empow-ered citizens in the election the following year. Hundreds of women, including black suffragists like Mary Ann Shadd Cary, were determined to march into polling places to cast their ballots in the coming election and, if they were arrested, to fight their disen-franchisement in the courts. Woodhull decided to take it a step fur-ther and run for president.[18]

The lead-up to the election of 1872 was already scattering the field of progressives and reformers. The Republican president,

Ulysses S. Grant, was running for reelection, but there was dissension within the party ranks. A faction calling itself the Liberal Republicans rose up to challenge Grant and the Radical Republicanism that had dominated Reconstruction policy, putting Horace Greeley at the top of the ticket. A number of antebellum reformers had taken conservative turns by this time, but Greeley had always annoyed more radical activists with his wishy-washiness. Having been a leading Fourierist in the socialist zeitgeist of the 1840s, crucial to Brook Farm's conversion and the general dissemination of Associationist doctrine, he had since come out strongly against the Free Love implications of the movement and remained a stalwart voice for traditional marriage as the women's movement and others called for reforming the institution. He was no great cheerleader for women's suffrage, and worst of all he championed a conciliatory approach to Reconstruction. He held that the North should stop meddling with the South and leave it to govern itself, arguing that white Americans should "clasp hands across the bloody chasm" of the war. He called for amnesty for even the highest-ranking Confederates; indeed he and Cornelius Vanderbilt had bailed Jefferson Davis out of prison. In his first term, Grant took active measures to enforce the Reconstruction Amendments and crack down on the KKK and other white-supremacist paramilitary organizations terrorizing black southerners. Reformers like Higginson and Phillips who refused to "clasp hands" with Klansmen considered Greeley a "turncoat" and a "traitor." But he did attract the support of a few in the reform community, including the women's rights leader Theodore Tilton and Frank Sanborn, who had once been a member of John Brown's Secret Six.

Woodhull's unprecedented presidential bid divided the field further. Woodhull was a lightning rod for suffragists just as she was for socialists. Some refused to sit next to her on the lecture platform. She carried an undeniable whiff of sexual scandal in her wake that some women reformers, especially the Boston contingent, would not come near. Her sex radicalism was not merely a rumor but a position she proudly and publicly embraced, declaring in one speech, "Yes, I am a Free Lover. I have an inalienable, constitutional and natural right to love whom I may, to love as long or as short a period as I can; to change that love every day if I please, and with that right neither you nor any law you can frame have any right to interfere." Her platform for the "Cosmo-Politan Party," written by Stephen Pearl Andrews and read aloud at the May 1871 women's convention, did nothing to suggest she had recanted these views.[19]

While women who cared about social respectability blanched, Stanton remained unfazed. Even though she was not swinging with the Free Love clique at the Club in Manhattan in the 1850s, she nonetheless voiced a position on marriage and divorce that aligned with theirs and seemed to borrow from their lexicon as well. In this sense, the two movements' shared origin in Fourierist socialism was always apparent. From her Declaration of Sentiments at Seneca Falls, Stanton had pointed to marriage as a stumbling block for women. She had advocated for open divorce laws before some well-known Free Lovers were even on the scene, arguing in 1850, "If, as at present, all can freely and *thoughtlessly* enter into the married state, they should be allowed to come as freely and *thoughtfully* out again." In 1860, she wrote to Anthony that this aspect of their movement was gaining prominence for her: "This marriage question grows on me. . . . It lies at the very foundation of all progress."[20]

In *The Revolution,* Stanton wrote so many impassioned articles condemning loveless indissoluble marriages that letters poured in asking if the magazine was officially opposed to the institution. In response, she presented her objections "to our *present system,* which I call the 'man marriage.'" She rejected the version of marriage upheld by religion and the state, claiming that hundreds of women are "dragging out miserable, dependent lives in those living sepulchers called home, where the light of love has all gone out." Until women and men are equals, "marriage will be, in most cases, a long, hard struggle to make the best out of a bad bargain." In another piece, she declares, "Marriage, as it now exists, is a curse to society and to the human race; it is a source, far more frequently, of misery than of happiness." This is all straight out of the Free Love playbook.[21]

By 1870, Stanton was explicitly advocating Free Love by name as the inevitable end point of the women's movement. In a speech titled "On Marriage and Divorce," she called for the end of legal marriage in favor of "true and harmonious relations" that arise spontaneously. She said that even happy couples working together for women's equality nevertheless make "abject slaves" of each other with their claims to ownership and possession in marriage. Articulating an expansive set of goals for the women's movement, she proclaimed, "What is wanted therefore is not merely suffrage and civic rights," or even the social equality of the sexes, "but Freedom, freedom from all unnecessary entanglements and concessions, freedom from binding obligations involving impossibilities, freedom to repair mistakes, to express the manifoldness of our own natures." She called for "nothing short of unlimited freedom of divorce, freedom to institute at the option of the parties new amatory relationships, love put above marriage, and in a word the obnoxious doctrine of Free Love." Reinforcing the accusation so long hurled by the anti-reform press, she confirmed that there was indeed a slippery slope from women's rights to Free Love, so those merely "dabbling" in the suffrage movement should get out of the boat now.[22]

Thus, while many communists and women's rights women watched warily when Woodhull announced a "Combination Convention" for May 1872, Stanton fully backed the rising star who she hoped would unite her movement with the Spiritualists and the First International. Woodhull's goal was to consolidate all social radicals across the country—"Labor, land, peace, and temperance reformers, and Internationals and Women Suffragists"—into one political party and nominate candidates for federal office. Stanton also issued a call for this event but described it simply as a women's suffrage convention "to be held in cooperation with the International in New York." Still, it was clear from her announcement that this would be a different sort of convention than many of her readers were used to: "instead of simply rehearsing the time-worn arguments on suffrage," she invited "those women who are prepared for a more revolutionary step."

The convention proved to be a rare source of discord between Stanton and Anthony, in part because it interfered with the regular meeting of the "respectable wing" of the women's movement, as the press called it. Incensed, Anthony tried to have the owner of the hall withdraw his permission for the meeting, and when that didn't work, she posted police outside and charged an entry fee of twenty-five cents. When Woodhull changed the venue, Anthony had the gaslights cut off, leaving women clinging to one another in the pitch dark. But the event came off successfully despite these machinations: a diverse group of several hundred delegates met to champion women's rights and racial egalitarianism, all under an explicitly socialist program that would include the abolition of private corporations. The New York papers described a multiracial crowd of gender benders and their communist slogans: "Government Protection and Provision from the Cradle to the Grave"; "Nationalization of Land, Labor, Education, and Insurance"; "The Products of the Past Should Be the Equal Inheritance of the Living Generation." The following month, the People's Party, which was renamed the Equal Rights Party, held another meeting to officially nominate Victoria Woodhull as their candidate for the U.S. presidency, with Frederick Douglass as her running mate (which came as a total surprise to Douglass). A promising coalitional effort "to secure and maintain human rights" was brewing here—but it wouldn't last long.[23]

———

As STANTON EMBRACED her Free Love views more explicitly, contributing to Heywood's radical periodical *The Word* and seeking connections with communists, perhaps she was relieved that Woodhull had so dramatically entered the scene. Given Stanton's own privileged, conventional private life and the tight-laced colleagues who had been trying to muzzle the anti-marriage implications of the movement for twenty years, the younger woman must have seemed like a breath of fresh air. So Stanton befriended Woodhull when others were distancing themselves. And because Stanton could not keep a secret (and perhaps because she was accustomed to gossiping only with women who would rather have died than plunge themselves into the middle of a public sex scandal), she whispered to Woodhull a juicy tidbit that riveted the American public for three years, redirected social movements, and sent multiple people to jail.

This piece of gossip involved two men who were already well known to the reading public. Henry Ward Beecher had been a mainstay on reform platforms for years, his very name bound up with the revolutionary turn in antislavery sentiment he had helped foment by sending crates of Sharps rifles to Free-Staters in Kansas. As the minister of Plymouth Church in Brooklyn, he was regarded as the most accomplished orator of his time and a moral leader of the nation. Theodore Tilton was his protégé, parishioner, and colleague, and the two had an unusually intense friendship. When they were apart, they exchanged passionate letters, and they often traveled together in their reform work, including a visit to Charleston alongside Garrison for the victory party and flag raising at Fort Sumter. After the war and their antislavery work was complete, Beecher became a relatively moderate supporter of women's suffrage and an opponent of the goals of organized labor. Tilton, however, wandered toward the wilder side of reform culture and away from the church. In 1870, he learned that something had happened between his wife, Elizabeth Tilton, and Beecher. It was never altogether clear what that something was. She confessed that she had sinned in the way she had "known" Beecher but was never able to offer much clarity on the nature of this knowing. She admitted to adultery and then recanted it, possibly under duress, confessed again, and so on. The three of them met privately to hash it out and, after exchanging kisses all around, promised to keep whatever had happened under their hats to spare the minister's reputation and the Tiltons' marriage.[24]

Sometime that year, at dinner after work with Stanton and another suffragist colleague, Tilton told them the story of his cuckolding by America's leading churchman, presenting it as an anecdote related to their work on the marriage institution. Anthony was having dinner with his wife that very night. When he returned home,

Henry Ward Beecher.
Historical Picture Collection,
Yale University Manuscripts
and Archives

the couple got into a heated fight, and both admitted to breaking their marriage vows. Anthony excused herself to an upstairs bedroom. Soon Elizabeth came running up with Theodore chasing her, and the women bolted the door while he hammered with his fists on the other side. Afraid he would strike Elizabeth or worse, Anthony called to him, "If you enter this room it will be over my dead body." The women climbed into bed together for the night, and Elizabeth sobbed out the whole story while her husband fumed down the hall.

Stanton and Anthony compared notes the next day, but they handled the information in characteristically divergent ways. In the media circus that eventually ensued, Anthony refused to breathe a word to the reporters who hung around her lectures, but Stanton gave interviews to anyone who asked. Even though she and Tilton were close friends and collaborators, the story was too good for Stanton to keep to herself. She soon spilled it to Woodhull, who first tried to use the information to blackmail Beecher privately and then made it national news. Woodhull wanted to expose the hypocrisy of middle-class marriage, but she was hoping to settle a few personal scores as well. She and Tilton were close friends—lovers, she claimed. He had written a glowing biography of her and often slept over at her Murray Hill mansion—on the sofa, he claimed.

But she was furious that he supported Greeley's presidential campaign instead of hers. Moreover, Beecher's sisters had been attacking her in the press. Catharine Beecher found Woodhull odious on the same grounds that she and her father, the Reverend Lyman Beecher, had criticized Fanny Wright nearly fifty years before. Her sister Harriet Beecher Stowe, author of the antislavery juggernaut *Uncle Tom's Cabin,* had published an anti–Free Love novel, *My Wife and I,* that satirized both Woodhull and Stanton.

So, first at a Spiritualist convention in September and then in her newspaper in November, Woodhull exposed Henry Ward Beecher's affair with Elizabeth Tilton, even suggesting that he was the father of some of her children. Branding Beecher "the king of Free Love," she did not condemn the extramarital sex, just the hypocrisy, and invited him to own up publicly to his radical beliefs and join her in "the grand social revolution." This kicked off a media firestorm that made Woodhull more notorious than ever, dragging along a number of previously respectable members of the reform community in her wake.

When Election Day dawned later that month, Woodhull did not cast a vote for herself. First of all, she was a woman and therefore was prohibited from voting, and second, she was locked up in federal prison on obscenity charges. In her crusade against Beecher, she had run afoul of Anthony Comstock, a self-appointed warrior against obscenity who proved to be a formidable opponent of social activists in this period.

Like Graham before him, Comstock lived in terror that lewd thoughts and masturbation were degrading the Republic. As a young Union soldier, he had been shocked by the widespread use of profanity in the ranks, and in postwar New York City he confronted much worse. A one-man morality crusade with bushy muttonchops, he persuaded legislators to pass a law, which he then personally enforced, making it illegal to circulate through the U.S. mail any lewd or indecent text. The law targeted pornography and information on the prevention of sexually transmitted infections, birth control, or the termination of pregnancy—or any device intended or adapted for an immoral use. He confiscated tens of thousands of dildos and other "articles for self-pollution" in his roundups of prohibited material. For each offense, the Comstock law allowed for a fine of up to $5,000, imprisonment at hard labor for up to ten years, or both.[25]

Comstock nabbed Woodhull and her sister for the issue of their newspaper that had broken the Beecher scandal. They served four weeks before the case was dismissed. Upstate, Susan B. Anthony marched into the polling place and cast an illegal vote for Ulysses S. Grant. She was later arrested at her home in Rochester.

IN MOST STATES, Woodhull's name did not actually appear on ballots on Election Day 1872, but in South Carolina, Martin Delany's did. He ran for lieutenant governor on a ticket with a white ex-Confederate, although he and his son had both risked their lives in the Union army not a decade before. Like Greeley's Liberal Republicanism, the moderate platform of Delany's fusion ticket aimed to break down Radicalism with a conciliatory approach to Reconstruction.

Delany's stump speeches claimed that Republicans had cultivated ongoing racial hostility in the South and that people of color stood to lose the most from this antagonism. He even went so far as to claim that Democrats had done more to abolish slavery than Republicans, a truly head-spinning revisionist claim: "Before and during the war I was a conductor on the Underground Railroad. You all know what that was—a society to carry off slaves and give them freedom. This required money, and I tell you we got ten dollars from a Democrat where we got one dollar from a Republican, and, what is more, we didn't refuse the money because it came from Democrats. Don't let us now refuse assistance because it comes from Democrats." He sought to convince African Americans that Democrats were their friends while reassuring whites that economic partnerships did not mean social integration.[26]

By this time, Delany's criticism of the Republican Party and its Reconstruction strategy was well established, and his startling racial conservatism was only intensifying. In 1871, he published an article

claiming that South Carolina was crawling with conniving northern carpetbaggers who called themselves Republicans to gain the
trust of the black population, who, he complained, used to be polite and agreeable but had become quarrelsome and sullen. Douglass
published an outraged response to Delany, declaring that if he did
not know the author personally, "I should say that the man who
wrote thus of the manners of the colored people of South Carolina
had taken his place with the old planters." He said the "good manners" of southern blacks in the past that Delany apparently admired
were inspired by the lash. "I know too well your own proud and
independent spirit, to believe that the manners of an enslaved and
oppressed people are more to your taste than those which are born
of freedom and independence." Black leaders were shocked by
Delany's perspective, but white southerners loved it. His local
newspaper used Delany to support its view that northerners were
the problem facing black southerners, not the ongoing grip of slavery and not the Ku Klux Klan.[27]

Frederick Douglass and most defenders of black rights regarded
the forces attempting to weaken Radical Republicanism that year as
"mischievous and dangerous." Even though the party was flawed,
he said that he would rather "put a pistol to my head and blow my
brains out, than to lend myself in any wise to the destruction or
defeat of the Republican Party." Delany lost at the polls, as did
Greeley at the national level. But the die was cast for a decisive turn
in the coming years toward the conservative Reconstruction policies they championed.[28]

Delany's bizarre nostalgia for black southerners who knew their
place was far from unique. Many of the white reformers who had
come to the Sea Islands to work with the freed people were bitter
and disillusioned as well. Like Delany, some complained of their
"social failings," bad habits, and "ingratitude." One of the Gideonites said she was glad the recently emancipated population had shed
their servility but sorry they were no longer obedient. This burn-
out with the hard work of Reconstruction increasingly infected
northerners as well, who were falling in love in these years with
the new idea of the "Old South." Pop culture was flooded with

The Penn School, founded by Laura Towne and Ellen Murray,
was one of the most successful aspects of the Port Royal Experiment.
Library of Congress

sentimental images of reconciliation between the sections, like marriage plots between Union soldiers and southern belles peppered
with moonlight and magnolias, picturesque plantations and loyal
slaves who spoke in thick dialect for comic relief. White northerners weary of the complex problems left in the wake of the war welcomed these celebratory visions of the antebellum South, the very
society that their sons and brothers had died to destroy.[29]

Meanwhile, those who continued to advocate for the rights of
black Americans often struggled to get a hearing. Wendell Phillips
was booed in Faneuil Hall in 1870 by someone who yelled that his
message was "played out." As the leader of the antislavery movement, he had gone from hated fanatic to national hero and now to
annoying relic. *The New York Times* affirmed that "the majority of
the Republican party have out-grown" the ideas of Garrison and
Phillips. *The Atlantic* agreed that the "national mind" was rather fatigued "by the thought of a race with which it was really occupied
a long time." Even some with no love for the former Confederacy
were moving on to other things a decade after the war. Higginson

had actively advocated black rights in the immediate postwar years, but by 1870 he was resigned to the idea that it would take "centuries of time" for white southerners to treat their black neighbors fairly.[30]

Fighting this culture eager to forget the Civil War, activists beseeched Americans not to abandon the Reconstruction project of black empowerment that would give meaning to its terrible sacrifices. Douglass was among those who tirelessly "waved the bloody shirt," attempting to preserve the fading public understanding of the war as the dear price the nation had paid to rout slavery. He delivered a powerful speech to this effect on Decoration Day, the precursor of Memorial Day, at Arlington, which had recently become the first national cemetery. The grounds had previously belonged to the Confederate general Robert E. Lee and his wife, who had inherited the vast plantation from her slaveholding ancestors George and Martha Washington. Having been seized and occupied by Union forces during the war, the land became home to a village of fifteen hundred free people, bustling with churches, schools, neat frame homes, and a "Garrison Street" in honor of the antislavery leader. But the region was overwhelmed with the war's carnage, and the government ultimately dedicated the site as the permanent resting place for many thousands of Union soldiers.

Addressing President Grant and others near the monument to the "Unknown Loyal Dead," Douglass took the opportunity to note the alarming drift toward minimizing the political content of the war, a desire to remember it as a shared experience of suffering for the North and South, and a demand to grieve all that the Confederacy had lost as well as the Union deaths. He remarked, "We are sometimes asked, in the name of patriotism, to forget the merits of this fearful struggle, and to remember with equal admiration those who struck at the nation's life, and those who struck to save it—those who fought for slavery, and those who fought for liberty and justice." Countering this trend, he recalled the horror of mass death and mutilated young bodies, "the war that filled our land with widows and orphans" and "made stumps out of men" and "sent them off on the journey of life armless, legless, maimed, and mutilated."

Imploring his audience to remember that one side fought to destroy the United States and enslave men, while the other saved the Union and destroyed the "hell-black system of human bondage," he asked, "If this war is to be forgotten, I ask, in the name of all things sacred, what shall men remember?"[31]

CHAPTER 15

This Electric Uprising

At twenty minutes to midnight on July 3, 1876, a crowd began pouring into Union Square from Fourth Avenue in New York City. Lines of marching militiamen were illuminated by rows of torchbearers, followed by bands playing and people dancing. Lanterns hung in the windows of nearly every home they passed. Outdoor gas jets were wide open, too, spelling out patriotic mottoes in flames licking the summer night. The commercial buildings were covered with Stars and Stripes from roof to basement, red, white, and blue shields, and portraits of presidents obscuring even the doors and windows. The city was festooned, wrapped, overtaken by American flags: large floating flags, double rows of small flags on a line, banners, bunting, long slender ribbon flags. Entering the square, the parade met a throng already assembled there, teeming around the statue of George Washington on horseback, which had been hung with streamers and flowers. Rockets and Roman candles whizzed overhead. Fireworks burst into serpents and bouquets. Women on the rooftops cried shrilly at each boom, waving handkerchiefs, "and some wept from the excitement and from a passionate sense of patriotic love."[1]

As midnight struck, "the hubbub became indescribable, for all the bands appeared to be playing different airs, and the shouting and cheering was excessive, for the crowds had now increased in the square to an amazing extent, and were in many places a mere mass of swaying humanity so jammed together that individual motion was lost, and they could only move together like a tide." Drums thumped, steam whistles screamed, the crowd cheered wildly. "Every one's nostrils are filled with sulphur," a witness reported, their eyes smarting and ears ringing. Full-throated singing of "Hail, Columbia" and "Yankee Doodle" was occasionally audible in the din.

At the same moment in Philadelphia, 300,000 people watched a similar parade of Union veterans marching by torchlight, bearing tattered flags unfolded for the first time in ten years, their route punctuated by fireworks and gunfire, gaslight and rockets. The new Liberty Bell was rolled out in front of Independence Hall to a street "crowded with people, wild and transfigured with patriotism." The square was still packed at dawn; even the trees were full of men and boys who had climbed up for a better view.

The official plans for July 4, 1876, the nation's hundredth birthday, had been in the works for four years. They centered on the Centennial Exposition in Philadelphia, a massive campus covering hundreds of acres that had taken two years to build. In the six months it was open, ten million people would visit. The temporary structure erected as the main exhibition hall was the largest building in the world at that time. Along with two hundred other buildings on the grounds, it housed a glittering showcase of industrial modernity: new weapons and farming equipment, the latest steam-powered technologies, mass-produced sewing machines and typewriters, the first monorail. You could sample foods made in factories and branded, like Heinz ketchup, as well as a tropical fruit with an exotic name: "banana." Alexander Graham Bell's first telephone was set up for a demonstration; you could hear someone whisper into your ear all the way across Machinery Hall. The right forearm of the Statue of Liberty was there, too. For fifty cents, you could climb a ladder up to the torch in its hand.[2]

At least thirty-five countries contributed to the Centennial Exposition, and foreign dignitaries were given pride of place at the major events. Indeed, at the national centennial headquarters in Philadelphia as well as urban celebrations like the one in Union

"Colossal Hand and
Torch" at the Philadelphia
Centennial Exposition
in 1876.
Library of Congress

Square, Manhattan, the flags of many other nations flew alongside
the Stars and Stripes, representing the diverse origins of America's
population, united in the new nation founded one hundred years
before. The message was that the United States was a rising titan
that combined the strength of many old-world nations. All thirty-
seven states in the reunited Union sent representatives to confirm
that on its hundredth birthday, the nation had "No North, No
South, No East, No West." The blotting out of the recent war's
political meaning was evident. There were portraits of Lincoln,
Sumner, and Grant, but also Confederate figures like Stonewall
Jackson and Robert E. Lee, somehow transubstantiated already
from militant traitors to American heroes.

But one group of Americans was conspicuously underrepre-
sented. The new citizens that the war had made received no trib-
utes, no embrace of reconciliation, no flags to represent their
origins. As one journalist noted, "The great show of the American
people's industry and independence will close with one link in the
chain of its complete history left out." Calling out this exclusion
in the lead-up to the festivities, he observed, "The negro stands before the law a freeman, covered with the habiliments of citizenship,
yet the prejudice against him, the results of his previous condition,
have prevented him from taking any part or having a prominent

part of this marvelous undertaking in celebration of one hundred years of American independence, save that of a menial, the water-drawers and hat-takers."[3]

African Americans had high hopes for the centennial. Many looked forward to joining in the celebration with everyone else, abandoning the long-standing tradition of protest meetings on July 5 and alternative liberation holidays like August 1 to claim their place as Americans on Independence Day. But black Philadelphians were pointedly excluded from the preparations for the Centennial Exposition; none were even hired as guards for the fair. Out of thirty thousand exhibits, there was only one statue, *The Freed Slave,* by a white artist, of a nearly naked black man holding a broken chain and a copy of the Emancipation Proclamation. Disappointed at the lack of attention to the role of African Americans in the nation's history and life, African Americans wanted to add their heroes to the iconography of the day. One group raised enough money to commission the black sculptor Edmonia Lewis to create an elaborate pedestal twenty-two feet high, which would hold a marble bust of Richard Allen. The centennial organizers agreed to provide space for the statue but insisted that it be removed within sixty days of the exposition's end. Many other statues, including other religious memorials from Catholics and Jews, were to remain on the grounds permanently. After a string of delays, the Allen statue was finally dedicated on November 2, a week before the exposition closed. From there, it was sent to Wilberforce University and largely forgotten until 2010, when it was returned to Philadelphia and put on view at Mother Bethel, the church and cultural institution Allen founded, where free African Americans in 1817 had voiced a "tremendous no" in protest against forced deportation.[4]

Frederick Douglass was at the Centennial Exposition that Fourth of July. A supporter had floated the idea that the organizing committee should ask him to read the Emancipation Proclamation after the Declaration of Independence, a nod to the second founding effected by the recent war. The committee refused this request but invited Douglass to sit on the stage with President Grant and other bigwigs. When the day arrived, however, the police guarding the platform denied Douglass entrance, even though he presented the appropriate ticket. As he was being turned away, a white senator on the stage recognized him and brought him up, reassuring the police that he belonged there.

Also on the platform sat Susan B. Anthony, waiting for her cue. She and her colleagues had written to the committee to request enough seats on the stage for at least one female representative from each state and a place on the official program to read a women's declaration of rights. The organizers responded that this would be impossible but sent six invitations as a peace offering. Stanton and Mott refused this consolation prize and held their own separate convention. Anthony and a group of other women's rights activists, insisting that women were taxed to pay for the event and had a right to be there, accepted the tickets and decided to present their declaration anyway, immediately after the reading of the original document penned by the founders, "as an impeachment of them and their male descendants for their injustice and oppression."

The Declaration of Independence was read by a descendant of one of its original signers, Richard Henry Lee of Virginia, a cousin of the late Confederate general Lee. Taking his final word as her signal, Anthony rose and presented the protest pamphlet to the presiding officer, whose face drained of color. As they walked across the platform, the women scattered other copies to eager hands outstretched on either side of them, some attendees standing on their chairs to snag one. "While the Nation is buoyant with patriotism," its preamble declares, "we cannot forget, in this glad hour, that while men of every race, and clime, and condition have been invested with the full rights of citizenship, under our hospitable flag, all women still suffer the degradation of disenfranchisement." Men on the stage shouted, "Order!" as the women left the hall and climbed up on a bandstand outside, under Washington's statue and the Liberty Bell. Anthony read the "Declaration and Protest of the Women of the United States" with a colleague holding an umbrella over her head to block the scorching sun.[5]

The centennial celebration was in some sense a good representation of America one hundred years in. Purporting to encompass a riotous collection of everything representing everyone, it was in fact a strategically orchestrated and exclusionary space. Yet by fighting to be included, some of those omitted managed to form part of the tableau in spite of efforts to bar them. Unfortunately, these unrelenting agitators sometimes carried out the same kind of exclusion themselves. Soon after the centennial protest, Mary Ann Shadd Cary, suffrage activist and former black emigrationist leader, wrote to Stanton and Anthony on behalf of ninety-four African American women who wished to add their names to the list of signers of the women's declaration, but they were not included.[6]

The vast, showy, months-long parade of events for the national centennial, which a cynical few recognized at the time as "an overgrown and spread-eagle Fourth of July," papered over a low point in the life of the nation, a time of alarming violence and instability that threatened the republic so recently emerged from war. Indeed, a significant portion of the white population had begun to protest the holiday, an inversion of the long-standing abolitionist tradition before the war. Black activists had once fasted and mourned on July 4 and avoided going out on the street for fear of being attacked by white revelers. But in the years immediately following the Civil War, African Americans in the South reclaimed the date for themselves. In Charleston, black residents poured into the city square each year to rally around the Stars and Stripes, while resentful ex-Confederates stayed indoors and shut the curtains. Thanks to the battles fought and won there under the flag, the Fourth of July became, for a time, a black holiday.[7]

Indeed, on that centennial Fourth, while the official program in Philadelphia was under way, two white men in a carriage approached the main road of the small, predominantly black town of Hamburg, South Carolina, where a black National Guard company was parading for the holiday. The visitors demanded that the company part to let them through, and after a tense exchange they did just that. But two days later, the white men took the issue to court, charging that the militia had obstructed a public throughway. Their lawyer, a Confederate veteran named Matthew Calbraith Butler, demanded that the militia disband and hand over all of their weapons. The trial judge was Prince Rivers, who had served in the Union army under the command of Thomas Wentworth Higginson and was also a leader of the militia in question. When he refused to enforce the white counsel's demand, Butler declared that he would "have the arms in a half hour or lay the damned town in ashes."[8]

Meanwhile, a crowd of at least two hundred armed white men had assembled in the street. Word spread that they had retrieved a cannon from a neighboring town. Pointing its mouth into the courtroom, they fired three times, but the black crowd had escaped through the back door into some surrounding buildings. Shots were exchanged, and a white man fell dead. Two militia members were killed and many were captured. Around 2:00 a.m., the white mob took the captives, as well as some other black men they had rounded up from private homes, to the bank of the Savannah River near a train bridge and shot four of them execution-style. Then they returned to loot the town, destroying black homes and businesses. Ninety-four white men were indicted for their participation in these murders, but none of them were ever prosecuted. Indeed, one went on to serve as a U.S. senator, and another became the state's governor.

While it could have been purely bad timing or personal mischief that led those white men to drive a carriage through a black military demonstration on the nation's centennial, the Hamburg Massacre is better understood as one incident in a series of calculated efforts to kill and intimidate black South Carolinians and their allies in the lead-up to that year's election. The entire region had been consumed by white-supremacist violence since the end of the war, with major outbreaks in Memphis and New Orleans in 1866 in which eighty African Americans were killed and countless others raped and wounded. In 1870, the first Reconstruction governor of occupied South Carolina wrote to the president to report that "colored men and women have been dragged from their homes at the dead hour of night and most cruelly and brutally scourged." He described one group being lashed on their bare backs until "the flayed flesh hung dripping in shreds," and then hinted that "they were subjected to nameless indignities too gross and disgusting to be even remotely alluded to."

Grant often received reports of this kind. In 1875, a school-teacher in Mississippi wrote in alarm that "these Southern people are simply carrying out a kind of guerrilla war and I know they are planning to continue in this course until they have succeeded in killing thousands of colored men and reducing the remnant to a condition of slavery." She said that the president had no doubt heard a great deal about the atrocities plaguing black southerners, "but you do not hear the worst. It cannot be told." The violence spiked around elections, and with Radical Republicanism waning by 1872, Democrats across the South devised an aggressive "Redemption" agenda to suppress the black vote and take back control of local governments to reinstall white rule in 1876. They formed "Rifle Clubs" to intimidate black citizens and carry out nighttime raids on their homes, running many out of town and killing more than a hundred by Election Day.[9]

In addition to the threat of murder and the unnameable outrages ominously alluded to by these witnesses, vigilantes sought to prevent African Americans from voting by sabotaging polling places in black neighborhoods and carrying out untold varieties of voter fraud. A white justice of the peace wrote to Grant to report "stupendous frauds committed at the polls" in 1876: "On the day of Election, a crowd of white men Stood at the Polls & knocked, kicked, pushed, pulled hair & stuck pins & small bladed knives in the col. voters, and would not let a col. man vote unless he casted a Democratic ticket. The managers of the Polls would throw down the Republican tickets openly, or tear them up, & put in Democratic ones." This kind of violent subterfuge was in many cases not even necessary, because the U.S. Supreme Court had recently sanctioned a range of bureaucratic ways of disenfranchising black voters. That centennial year, after an official in Kentucky refused to register a black voter, the Court had ruled in *United States v. Reese* that "the Fifteenth Amendment does not confer the right of suffrage upon any one." Thus the amendment in which activists and

Radical Republican congressmen alike had placed so much faith, had made the centerpiece of their postwar efforts, had fought and fallen out over, had dreamed of and celebrated, was swiftly rendered unenforceable by the Supreme Court. The ruling held that it was illegal to bar a person from voting because of his race, but it was not illegal to do so with a biased literacy test, a selective poll tax, or a "grandfather clause" limiting suffrage to only those whose ancestors could legally vote—even if the end result was functionally the same. All southern state constitutions soon enshrined these practices and disenfranchised black citizens well into the twentieth century.[10]

As the consequential 1876 election approached, and the intimidation of black voters intensified, especially in South Carolina, Martin Delany made his endorsement for governor. He would be supporting the Democrat Confederate war hero Wade Hampton. In the midst of the deadly racial warfare of Redemption, Delany urged black South Carolinians to embrace "their native white people, whose interests were identical with theirs," aligning himself with the unreconstructed rebels bent on reversing the gains African Americans had made since the war.[11]

Delany's slide into conservatism was exacerbated by personal problems. He was sued for breach of trust and grand larceny in 1875, accused of stealing $212 from a black church five years earlier. During the trial, the lawyer verbally abused him, mocking as bogus his learning and respectability, and then pointed in his face, a finger nearly jabbing his nose, shouting, "You are a DAMNED INFERNAL LIAR!!!!" The jury came back in ten minutes with a guilty verdict. He was sentenced to twelve months in the penitentiary. Although Delany was eventually pardoned, he had no money, no prospects, and no good name. He assembled a pamphlet about his trial and conviction, arguing that it had been a Republican conspiracy to disgrace him and take away his influence, describing the party as the "worst class of white political adventurers from the North." He ended by saying that if black people continued to antagonize whites in the

South, "the whole country will rise up and rush to arms. Our race, shall only be remembered among the things of the past."[12]

Delany's unaccountable alliance with avowed racists was not lost on the black population with whom he had lived and worked for a decade. In October 1876, when he took the stage at a political rally, the black crowd started shouting and beating drums and pointing angrily at him until he was "howled down" and abandoned his speech. At another rally days later, when a schoolteacher took the stage, some black audience members mistook him for Delany, broke out concealed weapons, and opened fire. Seven people were killed that day. In his embrace of the southern Democrats, which he insisted was in the best interest of black South Carolinians, Delany's about-face was more dramatic than the turn to compromise and expediency of many antebellum ultras who shed their fanaticism in the postwar period. But his supposed pragmatism proved just as unsuccessful as his radical utopianism, indeed much more so. Before the war, plenty of black people disagreed with his ideas, but none were trying to kill him.

On the national stage, southerners threatened a second civil war if the Democrat Samuel Tilden did not defeat the Republican Rutherford B. Hayes. In response, President Grant stationed troops around the nation's capital and a warship in the Potomac to defend it. General William Tecumseh Sherman marched soldiers through the streets in a show of force. But after the Election Day that saw the biggest turnout in American history, it was unclear who the next American president would be. Tilden had won the popular vote and seemed to have triumphed in the Electoral College as well, but a number of his electoral votes were disputed or discredited. The election remained undecided into February, when it was solved with secret negotiations between the parties that came to be called the Corrupt Bargain, just as the disputed election of 1824 that Fanny Wright witnessed had been half a century before. Ultimately, the Democrats ceded the victory to Hayes in exchange for his vow to end Reconstruction and leave white southerners to govern the region as they would. Hayes took the oath of office on March 4, 1877, in a private ceremony in the White House—the election outcome was so controversial that the ongoing threat of insurrection made a public inauguration seem unwise. Charles Dana, prominent editor and former Brook Farmer, kept this controversy fresh in the public mind throughout Hayes's presidency. He ran the president's picture with the word "FRAUD" stamped across his forehead on the front page of the *New York Sun,* summing up the disgust of many Americans with the corruption of their much-vaunted hundred-year-old democracy.

The sequence of race riots, armed intimidation, and lynchings of African Americans in that national centennial year had succeeded. Hayes soon put his "pacification" plan into action, ordering federal Reconstruction troops to stand down on April 10, 1877. African Americans in the South were effectively enslaved again by the very same people as before, except those people now had more reason to resent them and less reason to spare their lives. The second revolution had been met with a violent counterrevolution, and the nation's singular, hard-won opportunity for a new founding in liberty and justice was foreclosed.

AS FEDERAL FORCES withdrew from the South, people of color there weighed their options for leaving the region. Disabused of

President "Rutherfraud"
B. Hayes.
New York Sun, *March 3, 1881*

whatever hope emancipation had offered for a livable future in America, many looked again to Liberia. The ACS, now over fifty years old and so long the enemy of black leaders and white anti-racists, came into surprising favor at the close of Reconstruction. The society reached out to black community leaders and elected black board members, including a bishop of the AME Church who forecast in a July 1876 speech that colonized African Americans were divinely predestined to develop a "United States of Africa." The following year, three men of color in Charleston formed the Liberian Exodus Association, aiming to relocate African Americans to Liberia under the community's own direction, as opposed to the ACS. Hundreds of emigrants came to Charleston in January 1878, ready to embark even before there was a ship to take them. The *Azor,* a converted slave ship that had already crossed the Atlantic almost a hundred times, was finally christened on March 21. The company called it the black *Mayflower,* resuscitating language the ACS had used on its first voyage in 1820. Delany, a supporter of the venture, spoke at the ceremony, and a ladies' group presented him with the Liberian flag.[13]

The ship sailed a month later, past the ruins of Fort Sumter, with 206 emigrants singing that they were bound for the promised land. Twenty-three of them died en route from drinking polluted water. Twenty-seven more died in Liberia within two years, and 19 ultimately returned to the United States. This first voyage was also the company's last; unplanned costs and delays had bankrupted it. But this was far from the end of the dream of black emigration. For the rest of his life, Delany tried every way he could think of to return to Africa, including two unsuccessful bids to become minister to Liberia (Henry Highland Garnet was appointed instead), but he never set foot on the continent again. Thousands of African Americans in the mid-South sent petitions and pleading letters to President Hayes, asking that he either protect them on their native soil or aid their relocation to another country where they could be safe. But these calls went unanswered. Instead, the troops that had formerly enforced Reconstruction marched out of the South and into the streets of northern cities, where they trained their rifles not on resurgent traitors but on American workers.

———

IN ITS CENTENNIAL YEAR, the country was in the grips of the worst economic depression in its history. Initially triggered by a financial panic in 1873, the economic downturn dragged on for years, far longer than the Great Depression of the 1930s later would. The New York Stock Exchange closed for ten days; unemployment climbed and wages fell. Villages of homeless people, living in small shelters made of junk and scraps, sprang up in major cities. It was common to see people eating out of trash cans. As workers faced these hard times, they often had difficulty sustaining the labor organizations that had sprung up hopefully in the postwar years; the National Labor Union disbanded in 1873. In Pennsylvania, workers in the anthracite mines had been unionized since 1869, but when their agreement with company owners expired in 1874, the employers would not renew it. Indeed, the owners broke up the union by stockpiling coal and then closing the mines for six months. Driven to starvation, the workers accepted a 20 percent pay cut and returned to work. Soon after, the corporation targeted the most militant of the workers with accusations of murder, theft, and destruction of property, presenting them to the public as an Irish terrorist organization called the Molly Maguires. Twenty workers were publicly executed for these crimes in 1877, declaring their innocence until the end. Although the whole thing was likely fabricated by the owners to destroy workers' agitation, this episode added to growing public sentiment that labor organizers were dangerous foreign criminals.[14]

Meanwhile, the Centennial Exposition displayed the country's admiration of industrial capitalism, even as the dire economic climate revealed how poorly it served the people whose labor powered it. Middle-class Americans who had not been cast out into the streets by the depression hated and feared the roving bands of impoverished men, or "tramps," that suddenly dotted the country.

The mainstream press vilified the unemployed masses as lazy and degenerate. Still addressing his huge congregation in Brooklyn weekly as the most famous and highly paid minister in the country (although many Americans regarded him as a liar, a libertine, and a "dung hill covered with flowers"), Henry Ward Beecher declared, "No man in this land suffers from poverty unless it be more than his fault—unless it be his *sin*." He admitted that a workingman's wage of $1 a day might not be enough for a workingman to support a family of five children if he insisted on smoking and drinking beer but declared that any man who couldn't survive on bread and water "is not fit to live." This remark from a wealthy celebrity notorious for his own excessive appetites stuck in the craw of workingmen for years. At one of the "Bread and Water Beecher Banquets" held at union lodges around the country, a laborer derided "the pot-bellied millionaires who eat Porterhouse steaks, drink champagne, smoke 15 cent cigars, who will ride out with their wives, or more likely other people's wives."[15]

In the depression years, labor unrest escalated, and the response from corporations, the police, and eventually the federal government became increasingly violent. In 1874, workers in Manhattan had agitated for public programs to provide job opportunities. There were sensational rumors that the protesters were armed with weapons funded by the Paris Communards; all labor activists at this time were accused of being connected to this group and of aiming to take over American cities in comparably bloody proletariat revolutions. The workers had gotten a permit to demonstrate in Tompkins Square Park, but the city had revoked it the night before, and the protesters did not get the message. Seven thousand workers gathered, the largest demonstration in city history at that point. Mounted police cracked heads with billy clubs to disperse the crowd.

Three years later, in the summer of 1877, this tension exploded into a massive uprising, a defining moment in the relationship between the government, the American people, and corporate capitalism. The railroads were the largest industry in the nation, as well as a source of patriotic pride. They served as the circulatory system of the entire economy, moving grain, mail, people, and goods from coast to coast over thousands of miles of track. They were also the nation's largest employer. For the Pennsylvania Railroad alone, 200,000 men laid track, slung ties, and drove spikes, working as brakemen, switchers, firemen, mechanics, shop workers, engineers, firemen, conductors, and so on.[16]

Railroad work was dangerous. Men were frequently killed and maimed on the job, thrown from cars onto the tracks, their limbs pinched off in the massive couplings between cars, crushed in derailments or while unloading freight, run over when signals failed. It was also a source of huge wealth for owners, who received generous financial incentives from the government during the war years. This led to overspeculation, and the bursting of the railroad bubble was responsible in part for the economic crash under which American workers were suffering. When the railroads moved to slash wages an additional 10 percent after cuts of more than 30 percent over the previous three years, workers in West Virginia went on strike on July 18, 1877, grinding all train service to a halt.[17]

Over the next ten days, the strike scorched across the country, through Maryland, across New York and Pennsylvania, west to Chicago, and south to Texas, paralyzing the economy. Militias were dispatched to scatter the angry workers who packed the nation's streets. Some of the militia men deserted, shouldering their rifles and refusing to kill their neighbors and fellow workers, especially when so many of those workers had recently worn the Union uniform themselves. But others did as they were instructed, answering the strikers' shouts and hurled stones with bullets and bayonets. In Baltimore, they fired into a crowd, killing eleven and wounding others. When a similar scene was repeated in Pittsburgh, the strikers drove the militia into a freight yard roundhouse and set a fire that spread for three miles, destroying railroad buildings and well over a thousand train cars. The militia shot their way out, killing twenty strikers. More were killed in Chicago as women and men battled police in the streets. The press was particularly nasty in

Seth Voss Albee, "Rear of Union Depot, with ruins of Gen'l. Sup't. Gardiner's Palace Car in the foreground," 1877.
Carnegie Museum of Art, Pittsburgh: Second Century Acquisition Fund, 95.17.35

its descriptions of the women and people of color who took part in the Great Strike, describing on the Chicago scene, for example, a foulmouthed, "brawny," "unsexed mob of female incendiaries."[18]

Under headlines shrieking of bloodshed and gore, newspapers painted workers as feral anarchists, their explosive discontent inspired by devious foreigners rather than years of domestic privation and exploitation. This was six years after the Paris Commune, which the press had trotted out with every whisper of workers' protest to associate it firmly in the public mind with insurrection and mass death, stoking the country's first Red Scare. In truth, the strike had no overarching leadership and was certainly not backed by a centralized socialist cabal. It had arisen spontaneously from aggrieved workers pushed to the breaking point by corporate greed to demand fair wages, an eight-hour workday, and the end of child labor. But the Workingmen's Party of the United States did jump in with its full support once the action was under way.[19]

Socialist leadership became particularly instrumental in St. Louis, where the strike triggered the closest thing the country has ever seen to a revolutionary workers' government. All business effectively stopped as workers walked off the job—not just railroad employees, but also bartenders, bakers, washerwomen, newsboys, and steamboat roustabouts—in a general strike. A multinational, multiracial crowd of workers marched through the streets with torches and banners, tools of their trades, flags, and a loaf of bread on a pike, ending in massive rallies where they heartily pledged to stand with one another, "regardless of color." Controlling commerce, transportation, and public spaces, the workers had seized the city, which was home to over 300,000 people.[20]

Both its champions and its enemies declared that the Great Strike was no simple labor dispute but "a social revolution." Newspapers called it an "insurrection" and the "Railroad War." In many locations, strikers were indeed calling for armed engagement, declaring this the Lexington and Concord of a war between capital and labor that so many had forecast. Ezra Heywood penned an exhilarated defense of the Great Strike, describing it as "the Bunker Hill of a new Revolution." Comparing the actions of the workers in "this electric uprising" to "the sublime heroism of John Brown at Harper's Ferry," he declared, "Between capital and labor there can be no truce and no compromise; the conflict is as inevitable and irrepressible as between Northern liberty and Southern slavery." He criticized the press for fooling Americans into thinking that

Scene from the Great Strike of 1877.
Frank Leslie's Illustrated Newspaper, *August 4, 1877*

communism is the foe of law and order when in fact what they call "the bloody International," he claimed, "is the coming peace party of the world." Rejecting the idea that socialism was an alarming new foreign invasion, he declared that these ideas had been part of the American intellectual and political tradition for a very long time: they were proclaimed by Robert Owen "from New Harmony, Indiana, in 1830" and, even before that, immortalized in "the Declaration of 1776" by Thomas Jefferson.[21]

Calls came from all corners, even from reformers, to rout out communists and hang them for treason. In the suffrage paper she edited with Garrison and Higginson, Lucy Stone called for the "insurrection" to be violently suppressed. But labor papers prophesied that the Great Strike would in the future be recalled as "the beginning of the second American Revolution, which inaugurated the independence of Labor from Capital." Indeed, claiming that workers were waging war on the United States, President Hayes called in the army to put down the "unlawful and insurrectionary" action with violence. Perhaps the railroad corporations felt that they had earned the right to flex some military muscle: Hayes owed his position in large part to Thomas A. Scott, the president of the Pennsylvania Railroad, who in the decisive moment of the "corrupt bargain" had won the votes of southern congressmen on the electoral commission in return for the promise of a new Texas-Pacific Railroad. Hayes had ridden to Washington in Scott's own private train car.[22]

The president sent twelve hundred federal troops to occupy Pittsburgh and Reading on July 26. They broke the strike in city after city until normal railroad operations resumed nationwide by August 1. More than a hundred workers were buried. Some participants received hefty jail sentences for inciting riots, possessing stolen property, setting fires, and the like, but the vast majority were not charged with any crimes and went back to their jobs, some receiving cash payouts from the railroads for their "loyalty." Workingmen's parties enjoyed a spike in interest, and their candidates prevailed in a number of state elections the following year.

Confronted with the menace of working-class political engage-

Militia firing on a crowd in Philadelphia during the "Railroad Riot."
Frank Leslie's Illustrated Newspaper, *August 4, 1877*

ment, rich industrialists and government officials looked to the measures white southerners had developed to suppress the black vote. A judge in Indiana who would later serve as the secretary of state believed that "our revolutionary fathers" had taken the idea of popular government too far. "Democracy is now the enemy of law & order & society itself & as such should be denounced." In the aftermath of the Great Strike, businessmen contributed funds to expand police forces around the country and to stock armories with weapons to be used in the protection of private property. The standing army was enlarged as well, breaking from American tradition; most of the relatively small federal force at this time was tied up fighting the Sioux and Nez Percé in the Northwest, and many felt that troops should be more readily available to put down other domestic insurgents. Militias were reorganized into National Guard units composed of middle- and upper-class men. In the coming years, they would be trained in riot suppression and urban warfare, readying to combat future American revolutions.[23]

CONCLUSION

On Radical Failure

We may be personally defeated, but our principles never.

—Lucretia Mott (1833)

A month after his stirring defense of the Great Strike, Ezra Heywood went to jail. In 1876 he had published *Cupid's Yokes,* a twenty-three-page pamphlet offering a bold critique of marriage in the tradition of works by Marx Lazarus and the Nicholses. It frankly addresses a number of issues that even Free Lovers sometimes left oblique, including advocacy of multiple partners: "Love is not burnt out in one honeymoon, or satisfied in one lover; the secret history of the human heart proves that it is capable of loving any number of times and persons, and that the more it loves the more it can love." Heywood also offered information on the menstrual cycle, advising readers to avoid conception by refraining from intercourse during fertile periods rather than resorting to abortion. He printed fifty thousand copies for distribution by hand and through the mail. One of these was sent to Anthony Comstock, who had requested a copy using a fake name.[1]

Comstock believed that literature of this kind would bring "sure ruin and death" to young Americans seduced into unclean habits by "indecent creatures calling themselves reformers—men and women foul of speech, shameless in their lives, and corrupting in their influences." He set out to arrest Heywood at an event he must have regarded as the rotting core of American degeneracy, a convention of the New England Free Love League at Boston's Faneuil Hall. Comstock arrived around 8:30 that November night in 1877 and bought a ticket. Heywood's wife and collaborator then took the stage and delivered what Comstock called "the foulest address I ever heard."

Angela Heywood's writings feature frank and admiring descriptions of the penis, so we can only imagine the ways in which her address offended Comstock's sense of decency, which was likely already outraged by the very fact of a woman standing on a stage for any reason. Comstock fled outdoors for fresh air, unsure that he could continue with his plan. He drove himself back inside with the thought "It is infamous that such a thing as this is possible in any part of our land, much more in Boston. It must be stopped. But how? I resolved that one man in America at least should enter a protest." He found Ezra Heywood backstage and dragged him by the neck down a flight of stairs and into a waiting carriage as the audience of around 250 began to riot.[2]

Though *Cupid's Yokes* contained no explicit sexual descriptions, Heywood was found guilty of circulating obscenity and thrown in the same Dedham jail that would hold the anarchists Sacco and Vanzetti during their infamous trial fifty years later. While incarcerated, he decided to stop using the Christian calendar. Issues of his magazine, *The Word,* were subsequently dated Y.L. for Year of Love and dated in relation to the founding of the New England Free Love League. Heywood intended this new system as a blow against the despotism of a "mythical god" and Christianity's "crass penis tyranny," represented by the phallic symbol of the cross. From inside, he critiqued the prison-industrial complex that exploited inmate labor and denied fair pay to free workingmen in the community. Still a proud Non-Resistant long after that group had disappeared in the smoke of the war, he wrote that he "looked forward to a new world—churches without a hell, states without a sword, and society without a jail."

Thousands of people organized to demand Heywood's release. He received a presidential pardon in 1878 from Hayes, who acknowledged that "it is no crime by the laws of the United States to advocate the abolition of marriage." In his diary, the president noted that he did not find *Cupid's Yokes* obscene or lewd. Heywood continued to publish *The Word,* following in the tradition of Robert Dale Owen, boldly advertising birth control devices like the cervical cap and vaginal syringe in his paper, opining that Comstock's mother ought to have used them. Heywood was arrested four more times and served another two years at hard labor. He caught tuberculosis in jail and died soon after his release.[3]

Free Love suffered many similar defeats at the hands of Comstock and the moral crusaders of the late nineteenth century, who succeeded in elevating "family values" over civic ideals in American political culture. His government-backed war on free speech was waged in the name of defending the nation, just as previous attacks on the First Amendment rights of protesters had been. But Free Love was also deteriorating from the inside. In 1875, the Tilton-Beecher scandal had culminated in a sensational, six-month-long trial, during which both men were accused of being Free Lovers—Beecher by Tilton, and Tilton by his estranged wife. The defense dug up all kinds of dirt on the women's rights community to support this idea: that Tilton sometimes played chess with Stanton until three in the morning, that Anthony had once sat on his lap, that a witness had spotted him in Woodhull's mansion in tousled nightclothes.

Free Lovers hoped the spectacle would expose middle-class sexual respectability as a sham, that the institution, more than Beecher, would be found guilty and ruined. But though it likely confirmed most Americans' suspicion that all progressives had kinky private lives, the trial achieved nothing toward sexual liberation. One reformer had tried to bring government action against another, embracing the restrictive legal sanctions on intimacy that the movement was meant to challenge. In the end, the trial reduced "Free Love" to banal marital infidelity and resulted in a hung jury. Beecher was off the hook for possibly having sex with another man's wife, but Victoria Woodhull had gone to jail for writing about it.

Woodhull left the country in 1877, likely paid off by one of the late Cornelius Vanderbilt's sons in the hubbub over his disputed will. She married an English aristocrat and soon charmed the landed gentry just as she had so many Americans before. She continued to write on sex reform, contributing to a decisive turn in Free Love toward eugenics, a racist misreading of Darwinian evolution that pronounced some people more biologically fit to reproduce than others. Free Lovers had long hinted at the implications of their movement for the hereditary optimization of the population, claiming that children conceived in abusive and loveless marriages were "deformed." John Humphrey Noyes, the man who likely coined the term "Free Love," had carried out a selective breeding project called "stirpiculture" at his Oneida commune for a decade. At the turn of the twentieth century, birth control advocates hitched their wagon to a conservative, scientifically respectable ideology to advance their goal of reproductive freedom for white women. This led to the involuntary sterilization of disabled people and women of color, among other horrors. And Free Lovers were not the only reformers to embrace scientific ideas with troubling consequences. The widespread influence of Social Darwinism was also a factor in the abandonment of civil rights work, because some whites regarded the subordination and even extermination of African Americans in the South as the regrettable but natural course of racial competition and the survival of the fittest.

By the end of Reconstruction, the mainstream public was fatigued by reform, and Gilded Age greed supplanted the era of activist zeal this book recounts. Many of the reformers themselves were also disillusioned by the grisly realities of war and the high price paid for what, in the end, felt like qualified victories. Although some of the activists in these pages lived to good old age in the struggle, dancing and skinny-dipping at communes until the end, and some made change as government insiders, plenty of others turned traitor to their own values. The genteel interventions of Progressive Era reformers bore few traces of the radical utopianism that had defined social protest for most of the century. Northern intellectuals became interested in social science instead of social justice, addressing inequality with detached interest rather than empathetic fervor. American philosophy turned away from the mysticism and nonconformity of Transcendentalism to embrace pragmatism. One former radical turned archconservative, Orestes Brownson, opined that the Civil War had forever discredited the kind of activist worldview that had defined antebellum movements. He granted that the ideals of the abolitionists and other social radicals were indeed those of the Declaration of Independence, as they had always insisted, but he argued that the war had thankfully crushed these Enlightenment holdovers once and for all. Patriotism had inspired men to fight and die, and slavery was abolished to create a more stable government; the survival of the Union was a triumph of state power, not the humanitarian ideas of "theorists, radicals, and revolutionists, no-government men, non-resistants." The war had forced the nation to grow up and abandon "the wild theories and fancies of its childhood."[4]

This grown-up resignation found its way into activists' agendas as well. Having abandoned their nascent alliances with African Americans, workers, Free Lovers, and communists, then forded the sewer of the Beecher-Tilton scandal, Stanton and her colleagues turned away from their most radical ideas, damming a potentially capacious women's movement into the narrow stream of suffrage reform. Beginning work on a mammoth six-volume *History of Woman Suffrage,* published from 1881 to 1922, they re-narrated the movement as a long battle for the vote, a diminishment of its previously far-reaching vision. Their pragmatic approach eventually won its finite victory, of course, but it took nearly another half a century. Although they reduced Mary Gove Nichols to a single sentence, they featured Fanny Wright on the frontispiece of the first volume and included her in the list of women to whom the book is dedicated, one defiant nod to the origins of their movement in a wilder tangle of radical thought, when women's rights had burst onto the scene alongside socialism, sexual freedom, religious freethinking, race mixing, and marriage abolition.

This tribute to Wright's legacy from her heirs in the activist tradition differed sharply from her daughter Silva's perspective, which was that Wright's work was "infidel trash." In 1874, she testified against women's suffrage before a congressional committee, describing her mother as the woman "the Female Suffragists are pleased to consider as having *opened* the door to their pretensions." She declared that women's political empowerment could only bring "misery and degradation upon the whole sex" and "wreck human happiness in America." Publicly, Wright is remembered today on a historical marker in a highway median in Memphis, between a Taco Bell and a Dollar General store. It describes her as a "Scottish spinster heiress" and Nashoba as a plantation where "cooperative living and other advanced sociological experiments" were enforced. In addition to this inaccurate biography, it indicates the wrong location and the wrong dates. But what would be a fitting memorial to Wright and to the other nineteenth-century American radicals? As statues commemorating the Confederacy are taken down all over the country, family names removed from university buildings as their ties to slavery are acknowledged, would we lift up these activists as the period's heroes instead?[5]

By the dawn of the twentieth century, the Supreme Court upheld Jim Crow segregation as the law of the land, ruling in *Plessy v. Ferguson* (1896) that a drop of "black blood" was enough to disqualify African Americans from privileges reserved for white citizens. Anti-immigrant sentiment heightened, with harsh legal restrictions that singled out the Chinese but also an increasingly explicit strain in American political culture discriminating against all foreign-born residents. The project of imperialist expansion that had pushed the United States to the Pacific Ocean extended overseas in 1898 as the country went to war with Spain for Cuba, the Philippines, and other territories. After fifty years of peak activist foment, Americans were not living in phalansteries among roving anti-lions, nor are we now. Capitalism has expanded beyond reckoning, and ongoing inequalities across race, gender, and socioeconomic class are still measurably immiserating American lives. Perhaps this is why so much of the work of nineteenth-century radical activists is forgotten, their contributions relatively obscure and marginalized in our narrative of the nation's past. They are history's losers.

At least that's how they look from one perspective. On the other hand, it is impossible to deny the victories of specific reform goals like the legal abolition of slavery, suffrage for black men and later women, readily available divorce, and the eight-hour workday. The devastating period of both white supremacy and white neglect that followed Reconstruction was met by a new generation of antiracist leaders, some with ties to the abolitionist movement, who founded the NAACP and other civil rights organizations that still endure. Some of the educational ventures of the Reconstruction government remain, notably Howard University, named for the head of the Freedmen's Bureau. Despite harsh anticommunist crackdowns after the Great Strike of 1877, the following decades saw a spike of American interest in socialism. Young workers like Samuel Gompers and Eugene Debs had been profoundly influenced by the uprising and went on to play pivotal roles in the next generation of the labor movement that made unions a major player in twentieth-century politics.

Indeed, the activist playbook developed in this sixty-year period has been internationally influential, just as Garrison promised. After the founding of the Non-Resistance Society, he wrote that it "will make a tremendous stir, not only in this country, but, in time, throughout the world." The radical pacifism of the early antislavery movement shaped the peace theories of Leo Tolstoy and, through him, Mahatma Gandhi, through whom its core ideas came back to the United States to influence the twentieth-century civil rights movement and antiwar activism. Non-Resistance also offers a key precedent for those fighting to abolish prisons and capital punishment, if only it were better known in the history of antislavery activism and American thought.[6]

But while we have forgotten the names of many of the radicals who figure in this story, American life today bears subtle but unmistakable evidence of their legacy, if you know where to look. Free Love ultimately triumphed, at least as surely as abolitionism and women's suffrage. Robert Dale Owen went on to serve in Congress and liberalized divorce statutes in Indiana, the state where his father had initiated a socialist society denouncing religion and marriage. His work created a legal precedent that made no-fault divorce accessible nationwide. Today, state and religious control over Americans' sex lives has been dramatically curtailed, and marital rape has been criminalized. Although marriage has not been abolished, as the Free Lovers had hoped, it has been redefined in extraordinary ways, perhaps most sweepingly by the widespread acceptance of their core idea that couples who fall out of romantic love should part ways.[7]

Our food culture, in both its mainstream and its elite iterations, bears the mark of Sylvester Graham's abstemious backlash against commercial plenitude, the diet of choice for nineteenth-century countercultures. Graham died at age fifty-seven at his home in Northampton, Massachusetts, after issuing a public apology for his relatively early decline, admitting that he had resorted to some of the very substances he condemned, like meat and alcohol, in an attempt to regain his strength. On the site of his house, there is now a restaurant called Sylvester's, serving eggs with verified provenance from organically fed chickens in a neighboring town. A palimpsest of twenty-first- and nineteenth-century dietary preoccupations, Sylvester's current proprietors seem to be as anxious about bread as its namesake. "Almost everything on our menu has a GLUTEN FREE ALTERNATIVE," the website shouts reassuringly. While Graham would no doubt appreciate this earnest pursuit of nutritional purity, he would be appalled at his namesake, "Sylvester's Special," a burger with bacon and cheese, and also by the teddy-bear-shaped cookies bearing his name in grocery stores across the country. Through one of his many followers, John Harvey Kellogg, Graham's preference for a bland breakfast resulted in granola, corn flakes, and the $37 billion cereal industry. Traces of his legacy linger as well at the low-rise walk-up apartment building in the East Village where Marx Lazarus and Mary Gove Nichols lived. A health-food café now occupies the ground level, selling raw vegan foods and cold-pressed organic juices, trumpeting the health benefits of dietary cleanses and the dangers of "high pressure processing" and other practices of the commercial food industry, a distinct echo of Grahamite dietary utopianism.[8]

In this sense, history validates the fears of critics who argued that the apparent failure of certain radical projects actually effected a greater and more insidious success. Robert Owen's ideas were better disseminated when his community at New Harmony folded, one critic noted: "Its failure tended more to the spread of his doctrines, than a moderate success would have done; for his disciples were scattered over the country, and have not been idle. They have insinuated their principles in a thousand quarters which the knowledge of their Community never could have reached, and have planted the seeds of infidelity and socialism in various sections of the Union." Noyes forecast that although the Owenite and Fourierist phases of American socialism were short-lived, they had embedded in the society forever a radical impulse: "These socialistic paroxysms have changed the heart of the nation; and that a yearning toward social reconstruction has become a part of the continuous permanent, inner experience of the American people."[9]

In the course of this slow-release radicalism, some failures have turned into successes with time. John Brown is the ultimate case in point. His raid on the arsenal at Harpers Ferry was a disaster, nothing like what he had planned; instead of installing a new black-led U.S. government in a mountain fort, it trapped him and his men to be captured and killed. But within a couple of years, Brown's contemporaries universally acknowledged that his raid pushed the South to secession, inflamed the moral courage of the North, and sped the onset of the war that ended slavery. As one supporter wrote, "We admit that in the particular object he had in view, John Brown *failed,* [but] in the hour of his disaster began his triumph— a triumph greater than his own wildest dreams had hoped."[10]

The mainstream nineteenth-century press loathed social radicalism as a rule and particularly reveled in the collapse of communitarian ventures. Historians have generally echoed their judgments, declaring flatly that projects like Brook Farm "failed." The term "failure" in this period often narrowly meant bankruptcy, and by this standard the socialist communes were indeed absolute failures— except for the ones that evolved into corporations turning out Oneida silverware and Amana refrigerators. The urban progressives who founded these pastoral utopias always seemed to choose the worst land for farming, right before the worst winter on record. But of course, their aim was not to strike it rich but to abandon the capitalist profit motive altogether.[11]

When the Brook Farm phalanstery stood in blackened ruins and the commune was nearly deserted, one labor paper defiantly declared Brook Farm a success: it had proved that people across social classes and genders could live together equally and harmoniously with no one working as a servant to anyone else. Labors like scrubbing pots were indeed rendered pleasurable there, just as Fourier said they would be. In truth, some working-class residents of this and other communes believed that something of the outside world's snobbery remained, but there were nevertheless moments, flashes of a kind of radical sociality that this context enabled, laying possible groundwork for future developments.[12]

The Brook Farmers went on to astonishing prominence in American culture and letters in the postbellum period. The names of those shaped by the Fourierist zeitgeist, as well as their children who never forgot the intoxicating intensity and promise of that period, form the core of our literary canon: Nathaniel Hawthorne, Emerson, Thoreau, Henry James, and Louisa May Alcott, to name a few. George William Curtis, who had delighted the community with his drag performance at one of their masquerade picnics, became editor of *Harper's Weekly* starting in 1863, a huge platform from which he advocated abolition, women's rights, and industrial reform. John Sullivan Dwight, who had come in sweating from garden work to teach piano lessons to the commune's students, became the first significant American music critic. In his time at the *Tribune,* George Ripley pioneered the modern book review, becoming a national arbiter of literary and cultural taste. It took him over a decade to pay off his debts from Brook Farm, but he died a millionaire, slumped over his desk on July 4, 1880.[13]

Pronouncements of the commune's failure seem to hinge on the fact that it didn't last forever. Countering this perspective in perhaps the most striking defense of Brook Farm, Noyes declared, "If a man's first-born, in whom his heart is bound up, dies at six years old, that does not turn the whole affair into a joke." He noted that it was easy for detractors "to ridicule the fervor and assurance of the actors in this enthusiastic drama, by comparing their hopes and predictions with the results. But for our part we hold that the hopes and predictions were true, and the results were liars."[14] As Thoreau observed, sometimes ending a project is necessary so that critique can continue: no single intervention can remain revolutionary and also endure forever. He said he closed his experiment at Walden because he had worn a literal rut into the ground, the kind of rut he wanted to escape. After coming out of society, he was amazed to find how quickly one man can make a lasting impression in a trackless forest: "I had not lived there a week before my feet wore a path from my door to the pond-side." Years later, he noted, the rut remained, and other visitors automatically walked in its path and made it even deeper. "How worn and dusty, then, must be the highways of the world, how deep the ruts of tradition and conformity!"

Thoreau lived at Walden for two years with nothing more complex than his own meals and safety to worry about. That site is now a state-funded shrine to the philosopher, where swarms of locals and tourists splash all summer in the glow of history. Brook Farm lasted three times as long, ran businesses, educated children, and coordinated hundreds of people. The site stands in weeds, marked by little more than a yellowed bulletin board with a typed paragraph about Transcendentalism and a vague silhouette of George Ripley cut from construction paper. Thoreau is revered, the Brook Farmers forgotten; iconoclastic individuals remain far more palatable to Americans than collective movements.

Although a scant handful of the many thousands engaged in social protest in this period have been elevated to a pantheon of "reformers" in national memory, this process requires a degree of simplification and defanging, the weirder elements of the counterculture that nourished them edited out. Looking now at their portraits in waistcoats and lace collars, preserved in brass frames and tooled leather cases, one easily forgets that they were hated, mocked, and feared by most of their countrymen as aggravating oddballs looking to overthrow American life as they knew it. These activists knew their aims were utopian and had every reason to expect defeat, but they tried for them anyway. All that they accomplished was fired by this mix of radical hope and unrelenting antagonism, their willingness to hazard failure rather than accept the world as they found it.

On the day Abba Alcott arrived at Fruitlands, trudging through a steady rain with her husband, their four small daughters, a cranky socialist colleague, and all of their belongings in a wagon, she wrote in her journal, "Tho we may fail it will be some consolation that we have ventured what none others have dared." Although the travelers claimed that day marked the beginning of the world's regeneration, Alcott likely already suspected that their venture would not last. It was June 1, which is far too late to begin cultivating enough food to survive the winter in Massachusetts. In six months, she and her little girls would be subsisting on apples and bathing in water so cold that it froze at the edges, because they had run out of firewood. Fruitlands failed, but as Alcott's journal reveals, exposing oneself to failure and rejecting mainstream measures of success were, in part, the point. They ventured to live as normal people would not dare rather than to betray values that they knew might be too lofty ever to realize.[15]

Thus, a history of radical thought must be a history of a certain kind of failure. We have so completely metabolized the wild ideas of nineteenth-century America that succeeded—women in pants, the telephone, regular bathing—that their original implausibility is lost. Success carries with it a feeling of inevitability, as though it represents merely the inexorable march of history, not a stray Hail Mary pass miraculously, just barely caught. Only the ideas that were dropped look impossible or silly to us now. But the stories of these activists summon a variety of potential Americas that have not come to be. At least not fully. At least not yet.

So with what success can we credit the radicals of the glorious social revolution? Not spotless personal virtue, certainly. The achievement of some crucial goals, to be sure, but nowhere near the realization of their full ambitions. Following their lead, we might look not to the perpetuity of their outcomes but to the rightness of their principles, their success in prefiguring, at least for a time, a different and better world, and most of all their motivation to act on those principles in the face of failure, to try something when it is easier and safer by far to do nothing. Devoting their lives to a struggle with no end, they dared to begin.

Acknowledgments

It has been a great privilege to immerse myself in the shocking, occasionally funny, and profoundly consequential history of the high-impact activism of the American nineteenth century. As galvanizing as this material is on its own, my work has been inspired and urged forward by the radical foment of our own moment, the waves of mobilization in recent years that continue the long battle against inequalities of race, class, gender, and sexuality in American life and politics, struggles in which the past powerfully echoes. Writing this book at this time and thus dwelling in both eras at once has convinced me that protest is meaningful and effective in ways I have sometimes doubted, even though its work is never done. Before I thank those who personally contributed in some way to the research, writing, and publication of this book, I want to sincerely acknowledge my debt more generally to the scholars who have treated various strands of this history in greater depth, shaping my understanding of the material and making it possible for me to offer this interpretation in response.

Thanks to John Kaag, whose collegial generosity I will never forget, and to Markus Hoffman, who helped me shape this project at its inception and made its realization possible. Emma Berry has been more than a careful editor but a brilliant collaborator on every page. My thanks as well to everyone else at Crown who shepherded this book along. For early advice on crossover publishing, I thank Matthew Pearl, Kevin Birmingham, Kent Greenfield, and Susan

Shulman. Aaron Lecklider, Lara Cohen, Jill McDonough, Jennifer Delton, Allyson Hobbs, Betsy Duquette, and Priscilla Wald offered valuable feedback on various iterations of this work. A number of other friends and colleagues provided crucial suggestions and encouragement along the way: Jen Manion, Elaine Showalter, Megan Marshall, Ramie Targoff, Tony Horwitz, Brian Halley, Paul Lewis, Shirley Samuels, Christopher Hanlon, Jennifer Schuessler, Jamie Ryerson, Dennis Rasmussen, Emily Wiemers, and Chuck and Louise Weed. I have benefited as well from the generosity of my colleagues and students at UMass Boston, especially Samantha Regan, Cheryl Nixon, and Tori McCandless. Thanks to Sarah Blackwood, Sarah Mesle, and my colleagues in their C19 seminar for commenting on a portion of the project and championing scholarly writing for the general public; and to Nadia Nurhussein and the participants in the Early Black Utopias Symposium for responding positively to ideas elaborated here. I am grateful for assistance from the staff of the Houghton Library, the Schlesinger Library, and the Andover-Harvard Theological Library of Harvard University; the David M. Rubenstein Rare Book & Manuscript Library at Duke University; the South Carolina Historical Society; the American Antiquarian Society; the Boston Athenaeum; and the Boston Public Library Rare Books and Manuscripts department, especially Kim Reynolds. Diane Duggan, I can't thank you enough for your work, which has allowed the time and space for mine. Thanks to my parents, Percy and Karen Jackson, and all of my in-laws for cheering me on; Sari Edelstein, for everything, forever. Jane and Adam Jackson-Edelstein, writing this book while caring for your cherished baby selves has been the most rigorous, vital time of my life. Remember that you have it in your power to begin the world over again; you've already done it for me.

Notes

Introduction: A Second and More Glorious Revolution

1. To minimize the number of citations in the body of the text, sources for multiple paragraphs often appear in one note. On the nation's fiftieth anniversary celebrations, see Adam Criblez, *Parading Patriotism: Independence Day Celebrations in the Urban Midwest, 1826–1876* (DeKalb: Northern Illinois University Press, 2013); Andrew Burstein, *America's Jubilee: A Generation Remembers the Revolution After Fifty Years of Independence* (New York: Vintage, 2001); and the collected pamphlets in *Fourth of July Orations*, vol. 1 (1826). For Owen's "Declaration of Mental Independence," see *New Harmony Gazette*, July 12, 1826. For a description of the natural environment around New Harmony, see Prince Maximilian of Wied, *The North American Journals*, vol. 1, *May 1832–April 1833* (Norman: University of Oklahoma Press, 2008).

2. *National Anti-Slavery Standard*, May 25, 1867.

3. Seth Cotlar, *Tom Paine's America: The Rise and Fall of Transatlantic Radicalism in the Early Republic* (Charlottesville: University of Virginia Press, 2011); Paul Collins, *The Trouble with Tom: The Strange Afterlife and Times of Thomas Paine* (New York: Bloomsbury, 2010).

4. *Liberator*, July 2, 1852.

Chapter 1: A Tremendous NO

1. For accounts of Lafayette's visit, see Auguste Levasseur, *Lafayette in America in 1824 and 1825; or, Journal of a Voyage to the United States*, trans. John D. Godman (Philadelphia: Carey and Lea, 1829), and Samuel Lorenzo Knapp, *Memoirs of General Lafayette* (Boston: E. G. House, 1825).

2. On anxiety about the passing of the founding generation, see Jay Fliegelman, *Pilgrims and Prodigals: The American Revolution Against Patriarchal Authority, 1750–1800* (Cambridge, U.K.: Cambridge University Press, 1982), and Russ Castronovo, *Fathering the Nation: American Genealogies of Slavery and Freedom*

(Berkeley: University of California Press, 1995). On Lafayette, see Lloyd S. Kramer, *Lafayette in Two Worlds: Public Cultures and Personal Identities in an Age of Revolution* (Chapel Hill: University of North Carolina Press, 1996), and Laura Auricchio, *The Marquis: Lafayette Reconsidered* (New York: Vintage, 2014). On the problem of the revolution's end in constitutional government and a permanent state, see Hannah Arendt, *On Revolution* (New York: Penguin Books, 1963).

3. *Liberator,* Jan. 31, 1840, reprinted from *Pittsburg Saturday Evening Visitor.*

4. Frances Wright, preface to *Course of Popular Lectures* (New York: Free Enquirer, 1829), 7. My account of Wright throughout this study relies heavily on Celia Morris Eckhardt's indispensable biography, *Fanny Wright: Rebel in America* (Cambridge, Mass.: Harvard University Press, 1984).

5. Frances Wright, *Views of Society and Manners in America* (London: Longman, 1821), 517, 522.

6. Quoted in Eckhardt, *Fanny Wright,* 53.

7. Quoted in Kramer, *Lafayette in Two Worlds,* 166.

8. Wright, preface to *Course of Popular Lectures,* 8; Wright to Julia Garnett, Oct. 30, 1824, Houghton Library, Harvard University.

9. Jane Blair Cary Smith, "The Carys of Virginia" (ca. 1864), 72–74, MSS 1378, University of Virginia Library.

10. Levasseur, *Lafayette in America in 1824 and 1825,* 203, 219.

11. Thomas Jefferson, *Notes on the State of Virginia,* 8th ed. (1801), 241–42, 213–14. See Peter S. Onuf, *Jefferson's Empire: The Language of American Nationhood* (Charlottesville: University Press of Virginia, 2000), 149–51, which quotes from Jefferson's 1821 autobiography.

12. Wright to Garnett, Nov. 12, 1824, Houghton Library.

13. Robert Finley, "Thoughts on the Colonization of Free Blacks," *African Repository and Colonial Journal* 9 (1834): 332–35; Henry Clay, "Speech at Organization of American Colonization Society," *Washington National Intelligencer,* Dec. 24, 1816. On the ACS, see James Ciment, *Another America: The Story of Liberia and the Former Slaves Who Ruled It* (New York: Hill and Wang, 2013); Eric Burin, *Slavery and the Peculiar Solution: A History of the American Colonization Society* (Gainesville: University Press of Florida, 2008); Beverly C. Tomek, *Colonization and Its Discontents: Emancipation, Emigration, and Antislavery in Antebellum Pennsylvania* (New York: New York University Press, 2011).

14. See Forten's description of the event in *Liberator,* Aug. 1, 1835, and in his letter to Paul Cuffee on Jan. 25, 1817.

15. Julie Winch, *A Gentleman of Color: The Life of James Forten* (New York: Oxford University Press, 2003), 351–52; my account of Forten relies on this excellent biography throughout. On Richard Allen, see Richard S. Newman, *Freedom's Prophet: Bishop Richard Allen, the AME Church, and the Black Founding Fathers* (New York: New York University Press, 2009), 259. For a recent treatment of early birthright citizenship discourse and discussion of colonization/emigration in free black communities, see Martha S. Jones, *Birthright Citizens: A History of Race and Rights in Antebellum America* (New York: Cambridge University Press, 2018).

16. Quoted in Winch, *Gentleman of Color,* 82.

17. Robert Purvis, *Remarks on the Life and Character of James Forten, Delivered at Bethel Church, March 30, 1842* (Philadelphia: Merrihew and Thompson, 1842), 6.

18. Pennsylvania Assembly, "An Act for the Gradual Abolition of Slavery" (1780).

19. Quoted in Winch, *Gentleman of Color,* 283.

20. Gary B. Nash, *Forging Freedom: The Formation of Philadelphia's Black Community, 1720–1840* (Cambridge, Mass.: Harvard University Press, 1991), 213.

21. James Forten, *Letters from a Man of Colour, on a Later Bill Before the Senate of Pennsylvania* (1813).

22. Ciment, *Another America,* 4–18.

23. Newman, *Freedom's Prophet,* 20.

24. Quoted in Eckhardt, *Fanny Wright,* 86.

25. Robert Owen, *Discourses on a New System of Society as Delivered in the Hall of Representatives of the United States* (Louisville, Ky.: Tanner, 1825), 11, 20, 14, 21.

26. Wright to Lafayette, Feb. 11, 1822, quoted in Kramer, *Lafayette in Two Worlds,* 158.

27. "Persons of all ages and descriptions, exclusive of persons of color, may become members of the Preliminary Society," *New Harmony Gazette* 1, no. 1 (Oct. 1, 1825).

28. *Genius of Universal Emancipation,* Feb. 24, 1827.

29. Jefferson to Wright, Aug. 7, 1825, Library of Congress.

30. Carol A. Kolmerten, *Women in Utopia: The Ideology of Gender in the American Owenite Communities* (Syracuse, N.Y.: Syracuse University Press, 1998), 35.

31. On the Jacksonian period, see Daniel Walker Howe, *What Hath God Wrought: The Transformation of America, 1815–1848* (New York: Oxford University Press, 2007), and Sean Wilentz, *The Rise of American Democracy: Jefferson to Lincoln* (New York: Norton, 2005).

32. Stuart Banner, *How the Indians Lost Their Land: Law and Power on the Frontier* (Cambridge, Mass.: Harvard University Press, 2007); Anthony Wallace, *The Long Bitter Trail: Andrew Jackson and the Indians* (New York: Hill and Wang, 1993); Alisse Portnoy, *Their Right to Speak: Women's Activism in the Indian and Slave Debates* (Cambridge, Mass.: Harvard University Press, 2005).

Chapter 2: One Bold Lady-Man

1. Fanny Trollope, *Domestic Manners of the Americans,* ed. Elsie B. Michie (1832; Oxford: Oxford University Press, 2014), 25–26.

2. *Genius of Universal Emancipation,* Sept. 30, July 15, June 10, 1826.

3. The historian Gail Bederman puts it plainly: "Wright's relationship with her slaves was no different from that of any other benevolent slave mistress, and her slaves bore the brunt of her visionary schemes" (439). Gail Bederman, "Revisiting Nashoba: Slavery, Utopia, and Frances Wright in America, 1818–1826," *American Literary History* 17, no. 3 (2005): 438–59.

4. Eckhardt, *Fanny Wright,* 148.

5. *Genius of Universal Emancipation,* July 28 and Aug. 18, 1827.

6. Quoted in Eckhardt, *Fanny Wright,* 144.

7. See ibid., 155. Frances Wright, "Explanatory Notes, Respecting the Nature and Object of the Institution of Nashoba, and of the Principles upon Which It Is Founded, Addressed to the Friends of Human Improvement, in All Countries and of All Nations"; *Genius of Universal Emancipation,* April 26, 1828.

8. Robert Dale Owen, "My Experience of Community Life," *Atlantic Monthly,* Sept. 1873, 343.

9. George Browning Lockwood, *The New Harmony Communities* (Marion, Ind.: Chronicle, 1902), 194–95. On the New Harmony costume, see Gayle V. Fischer, *Pantaloons and Power: A Nineteenth-Century Dress Reform in the United States* (Kent, Ohio: Kent State University Press, 2001), 35–41.

10. Paul Brown, *Twelve Months in New-Harmony* (Cincinnati: Woodward, 1827); Robert Sutton, *Communal Utopias and the American Experience* (Westport, Conn.: Greenwood, 2004); Donald Pitzer, "The New Moral World of Robert Owen and New Harmony," in *America's Communal Utopias* (Chapel Hill: University of North Carolina Press, 1997); Arthur Bestor, *Backwoods Utopias: The Sectarian Origins and the Owenite Phase of Communitarian Socialism in America, 1663–1829* (Philadelphia: University of Pennsylvania Press, 1950).

11. *New Harmony Gazette,* July 9, 1828.

12. *New York Commercial Advertiser,* Jan. 12, 1829; *Christian Reflector,* Dec. 25, 1839.

13. Quoted in Eckhardt, *Fanny Wright,* 258, 249–50.

14. *New-York Spectator,* June 18, 1830; Nov. 17, 1829.

15. Frances Wright, "Existing Evils and Their Remedy" (1829), 167; Robert Dale Owen's minority report, May 19, 1830. Also see Frank T. Carlton, "The Workingmen's Party of New York City, 1829–1831," *Political Science Quarterly* 22, no. 3 (Sept. 1907): 401–15.

16. Orestes Brownson, *The Convert; or, Leaves from My Experience* (New York: Sadlier, 1889), 129–30.

17. Wilentz, *Rise of American Democracy,* 282–86, 283. Also see Edward Pessen, *Most Uncommon Jacksonians: The Radical Leaders of the Early Labor Movement* (Albany: State University of New York Press, 1967), and Mark Lause, *Young America: Land, Labor, and the Republican Community* (Urbana: University of Illinois Press, 2005).

18. Thomas Skidmore, *The Rights of Man to Property!* (1829); the party's resolution of May 19, 1830, quoted in Carlton, "Workingmen's Party of New York City."

19. Sean Wilentz, *Chants Democratic: New York City and the Rise of the American Working Class, 1788–1850* (New York: Oxford University Press, 1984), 211.

20. On these disappointments, see Sara Fanning, *Caribbean Crossing: African Americans and the Haitian Emigration Movement* (New York: New York University Press, 2015), 99–123.

21. Robert Dale Owen, "An Earnest Sowing of Wild Oats," *Atlantic Monthly,* July 1874, 67–78.

22. Robert Dale Owen, *Moral Physiology* (London: Watson, 1841), 28.

23. *Free Enquirer,* June 19, 1830.

24. Eckhardt, *Fanny Wright,* 233–34.

Chapter 3: O America, Your Destruction Is at Hand!

1. Wright, preface to *Course of Popular Lectures*, 8.
2. *Freedom's Journal*, June 6, 1828.
3. *Freedom's Journal*, Dec. 12, 1828; Jan. 16, 1829.
4. *Freedom's Journal*, March 16, 1827; Dec. 19, 1828.
5. *Freedom's Journal*, Sept. 7, 1827, and March 7, 1829; Floyd Miller, *The Search for a Black Nationality: Black Emigration and Colonization, 1787–1863* (Urbana: University of Illinois Press, 1975), 84. Also see Jacqueline Bacon, *Freedom's Journal: The First African-American Newspaper* (Lanham, Md.: Lexington Books, 2007); and especially Sandra Sandiford Young, "John Brown Russwurm's Dilemma: Citizenship or Emigration," and Timothy Patrick McCarthy, " 'To Plead Our Own Cause': Black Print Culture and the Origins of American Abolitionism," both in *Prophets of Protest: Reconsidering the History of American Abolitionism*, ed. Timothy Patrick McCarthy and John Stauffer (New York: New Press, 2006).
6. *Walker's Appeal, in Four Articles; Together with a Preamble, to the Coloured Citizens of the World, but in Particular, and Very Expressly, to Those of the United States of America, Written in Boston, State of Massachusetts, September 28, 1829*. See Peter Hinks, *To Awaken My Afflicted Brethren* (University Park: Pennsylvania State University Press, 1997).
7. *Free Enquirer*, Aug. 12, 1829.
8. Lincoln wrote to Daniel Chamberlain in April 1865, "I have only been an instrument. The logic and moral power of Garrison, and the anti-slavery people of the country and the army have done all." Quoted in Michael Burlingame, *Abraham Lincoln: A Life*, vol. 2 (Baltimore: Johns Hopkins University Press, 2008). *Camden Journal* of South Carolina as quoted in *Liberator*, Jan. 15, 1831.
9. Garrison to Jacob Horton, June 27, 1829. Wendell Phillips Garrison and Francis Jackson Garrison, *William Lloyd Garrison, 1805–1879: The Story of His Life Told by His Children* (New York: Century, 1885), 1:25.
10. See Robert Levine, "Fifth of July: Nathaniel Paul and the Construction of Black Nationalism," in *Genius in Bondage: Literature of the Early Black Atlantic*, ed. Vincent Carretta and Philip Gould (Lexington: University Press of Kentucky, 2001).
11. *Garrison's First Anti-slavery Address in Boston: Address at Park Street Church, Boston, July 4, 1829* (1907).
12. Garrison and Garrison, *William Lloyd Garrison*, 1:178.
13. Archibald Henry Grimké, *William Lloyd Garrison, the Abolitionist* (New York: Funk & Wagnalls, 1891), 90. The Massachusetts General Colored Association had been active since 1826. On free black activism in the city before Garrison, see Christopher Cameron, *To Plead Our Own Cause: African Americans in Massachusetts and the Making of the Antislavery Movement* (Kent, Ohio: Kent State University Press, 2014).
14. Henry Mayer, *All on Fire: William Lloyd Garrison and the Abolition of Slavery* (New York: St. Martin's Press, 2000), 109.

15. Manisha Sinha, *The Slave's Cause: A History of Abolition* (New Haven, Conn.: Yale University Press, 2016), 217; Benjamin Quarles, *Black Abolitionists* (New York: Da Capo Press, 1991), 20.

16. *Liberator,* May 7 and 21, 1831.

17. *Liberator,* April 2, 1831.

18. Daina Ramey Berry, *The Price for Their Pound of Flesh: The Value of the Enslaved, from Womb to Grace, in the Building of a Nation* (Boston: Beacon, 2017); Thomas Gray, *The Confessions of Nat Turner* (Richmond: T. R. Gray, 1832); Patrick Breen, *The Land Shall Be Deluged in Blood: A New History of the Nat Turner Revolt* (New York: Oxford University Press, 2015).

19. Sinha, *Slave's Cause,* 211; Mayer, *All on Fire,* 122–23; *Liberator,* Sept. 3, 1831.

20. Quoted in *Liberator,* Oct. 24, 1835.

21. *Liberator,* June 16, 1832; Sinha, *Slave's Cause,* 223.

22. Newman, *Freedom's Prophet,* 269.

23. On Wilberforce and the other Canadian settlements, see William Pease and Jane Pease, *Black Utopia: Negro Communal Experiments in America* (Madison: State Historical Society of Wisconsin, 1963).

24. *Minutes and Proceedings of the Second Annual Convention for the Improvement of the Free People of Color* (Philadelphia, 1832), 18. I'm grateful to the Colored Conventions Project for making this and many other primary texts I cite here available online, http://coloredconventions.org.

25. William Lloyd Garrison, *Thoughts on African Colonization; or, An Impartial Exhibition of the Doctrines, Principles, and Purposes of the American Colonization Society. Together with the Resolutions, Addresses, and Remonstrances of the Free People of Color* (Boston: Garrison and Knapp, 1832), 5.

26. *Minutes and Proceedings of the Third Annual Convention for the Improvement of the Free People of Color* (Philadelphia, 1833), 23.

27. Sinha, *Slave's Cause,* 225; Mayer, *All on Fire,* 177.

Chapter 4: To Break Every Yoke

1. Carol Faulkner, *Lucretia Mott's Heresy: Abolition and Women's Rights in Nineteenth-Century America* (Philadelphia: University of Pennsylvania Press, 2011), 2, 57; Julie Roy Jeffrey, *The Great Silent Army of Abolitionism: Ordinary Women in the Antislavery Movement* (Chapel Hill: University of North Carolina Press, 2000), 1.

2. Julie L. Holcomb, *Moral Commerce: Quakers and the Transatlantic Boycott of the Slave Labor Economy* (Ithaca, N.Y.: Cornell University Press, 2016), 113–32.

3. Quoted in Faulkner, *Lucretia Mott's Heresy,* 54, 69.

4. Quoted in Jeffrey, *Great Silent Army of Abolitionism,* 57. See Jeffrey on racial prejudice in the movement; also see Shirley Yee, *Black Women Abolitionists: A Study in Activism, 1828–1860* (Knoxville: University of Tennessee Press, 1992). For the pamphlet written by Abby Kelley, Angelina Grimké, Lucretia Mott, Lydia Maria Child, and Grace Douglass at the Anti-Slavery Convention of American Women in May 1837, see Dorothy Sterling, *Ahead of Her Time: Abby Kelley and the Politics of Antislavery* (New York: Norton, 1994), 48.

5. Sinha, *Slave's Cause*, 234; Mayer, *All on Fire*, 206.

6. Amos Gilbert, *Memoir of Frances Wright: The Pioneer Woman in the Cause of Human Rights* (Cincinnati, 1855), 49; Eckhardt, *Fanny Wright*, 246.

7. Faulkner, *Lucretia Mott's Heresy*, 78; Sterling, *Ahead of Her Time*.

8. *Philadelphia Spirit of the Times*, reprinted in *Liberator*, July 20, 1838; *New York Commercial Advertiser*, reprinted as "Riots in Philadelphia," *Niles' National Register*, May 26, 1838; *Philadelphia Gazette*, May 18, 1838.

9. Noyes to Garrison, March 22, 1837, printed in *Liberator*, Oct. 13, 1837.

10. Garrison and Garrison, *William Lloyd Garrison*, 2:289. In his genealogy of the Free Love movement, Austin Kent puts Noyes's letter in the *Battle-Axe* at the very beginning, quoting Noyes's declaration that in a state of holiness "every dish is free to every guest." Austin Kent, *Free Love* (Hopkinton, N.Y., 1857), iv.

11. Quoted in Sterling, *Ahead of Her Time*, 58.

12. For an example of their opposition to capital punishment, see Charles C. Burleigh, *Thoughts on the Death Penalty* (Philadelphia: Merrihew and Thompson, 1847); Garrison and Garrison, *William Lloyd Garrison*, 2:228.

13. *Liberator*, Sept. 28, 1838.

14. Maria Weston Chapman, *Right and Wrong in Massachusetts* (1839), 51.

15. Garrison and Garrison, *William Lloyd Garrison*, 2:260, 267.

16. Stanton to William Goodell, Feb. 18, 1839, quoted in William Birney, *James G. Birney and His Times: The Genesis of the Republican Party* (New York: Appleton, 1890), 3:302.

17. C. Peter Ripley, ed., *The Black Abolitionist Papers* (Chapel Hill: University of North Carolina Press, 1991), 3:298–99.

18. Garrison and Garrison, *William Lloyd Garrison*, 2:383; Elizabeth Cady Stanton, *Eighty Years and More* (New York: European Publishing, 1898), 83.

Chapter 5: Coming Out from the World

1. *Liberator*, Oct. 16, 1840.

2. *Eighth Annual Report of the Board of Managers of the Massachusetts Anti-Slavery Society* (Boston, 1840), 30.

3. Reprinted in *Liberator*, Nov. 6, 1840.

4. David S. Reynolds, *Waking Giant: America in the Age of Jackson* (New York: HarperCollins, 2009), 124–30; Wright, preface to *Course of Popular Lectures*, 9.

5. See Lydia Maria Child, *Memoir of Benjamin Lay* (New York: AASS, 1842); Marcus Rediker, *The Fearless Benjamin Lay: The Quaker Dwarf Who Became the First Revolutionary Abolitionist* (Boston: Beacon, 2017).

6. Histories of middle-class reform that posit the roots of social activism in religious revivalism include Ronald G. Walters, *American Reformers, 1815–1860* (New York: Hill and Wang, 1978), and Steven Mintz, *Moralists and Modernizers: America's Pre–Civil War Reformers* (Baltimore: Johns Hopkins University Press, 1995).

7. Elizabeth Oakes Smith, "Fanny Wright," *Revolution*, April 29, 1869.

8. James Porter, *Modern Infidelity, Alias Come-Out-Ism: As Taught by Ultra Non-*

resistants, Transcendentalists, Garrisonians, and Other Revolutionists (Boston: Waite, Peirce, 1845), 11. Quoted in John McKivigan, *The War Against Proslavery Religion: Abolitionism and the Northern Churches, 1830–1865* (Ithaca, N.Y.: Cornell University Press, 2009), 67.

9. 2 Corinthians 6:17; Revelation 18:4.

10. Lewis Perry, *Civil Disobedience: An American Tradition* (New Haven, Conn.: Yale University Press, 2013), 106.

11. Robert Carter, "The Newness," *Century Illustrated Monthly Magazine,* Nov. 1889.

12. Newman, *Freedom's Prophet,* 63–65.

13. Forten to Cuffee, Jan. 25, 1817. Forten's letter to Cuffee is held in the Cuffee Collection, New Bedford Free Public Library. A digitized copy is available on the town website of Westport, MA. Also, black Bostonians protested segregation at the Park Street Church; see Marc Arkin, " 'A Convenient Seat in God's Temple': The Massachusetts General Colored Association and the Park Street Church Pew Controversy of 1830," *New England Quarterly* 89, no. 1 (2016): 6–53.

14. Quoted in Garrison and Garrison, *William Lloyd Garrison,* 2:426; quoted in *Liberator,* Dec. 4, 1840.

15. Kneeland's paper heartily praised the Chardon Street Convention, finding it "*most encouraging* to the friends of human rights." Quoted in Porter, *Modern Infidelity,* 9. Also see Philip Gura, *American Transcendentalism: A History* (New York: Hill and Wang, 2007), 110.

16. Ralph Waldo Emerson, "Fourierism and the Socialists," *Dial* 3, no. 1 (July 1842).

17. Robert Owen's first major work presenting his theories about the formation of character was *New Views of Society.* In its own time, Transcendentalism was often called the "new views."

18. See Robert D. Richardson Jr., *Emerson: The Mind on Fire* (Berkeley: University of California Press, 1995), 302. On Very's encounter with Elizabeth Palmer Peabody, see Megan Marshall, *The Peabody Sisters: Three Women Who Ignited American Romanticism* (Boston: Houghton Mifflin, 2005), 327–48. For his biography, see Edwin Gittleman, *Jones Very: The Effective Years: 1833–1840* (New York: Columbia University Press, 1967).

19. See Theodore Maynard, *Orestes Brownson: Yankee, Radical Catholic* (New York: Macmillan, 1943).

20. Orestes Brownson, *The Convert; or, Leaves from My Experience* (New York: Dunigan, 1857), 238; Orestes Brownson, "Church of the Future," *Boston Quarterly Review,* Jan. 1842.

21. Barbara Packer, *The Transcendentalists* (Cambridge, U.K.: Cambridge University Press, 1995), 53.

22. *Journals and Miscellaneous Notebooks of Ralph Waldo Emerson,* vol. 5, *1835–1838* (Cambridge, Mass.: Harvard University Press, 1965), 332–34.

23. Brownson, *Convert,* 228, 188; "The Rich Against the Poor," *Methodist Quarterly Review,* 3rd ser., 1 (Jan. 1841): 92–122; "Orestes A. Brownson," in *The Transcendentalists: An Anthology,* ed. Perry Miller (Cambridge, Mass.: Harvard University Press, 1950), 446. Also see Packer, *Transcendentalists,* 110–111.

24. Emerson, *Journals,* 5:298. On the impact of Brook Farm and socialism on Emerson's philosophy, see Sacvan Bercovitch, "The Problem of Ideology in American Literary History," *Critical Inquiry* 12, no. 4 (Summer 1986): 631–53.
25. Ralph Waldo Emerson, "Man the Reformer" (1841).
26. On Fruitlands, see John Matteson, *Eden's Outcast: The Story of Louisa May Alcott and Her Father* (New York: Norton, 2007), and Richard Francis, *Fruitlands: The Alcott Family and Their Search for Utopia* (New Haven, Conn.: Yale University Press, 2010).
27. Quoted in Peter Brock, *Radical Pacifists in Antebellum America* (Princeton, N.J.: Princeton University Press, 1968), 131.
28. On Thoreau's experiment at Walden in relation to Brook Farm and other communal living experiments, see Packer, *Transcendentalists,* 164, and Richard Francis, *Transcendental Utopias* (Ithaca, N.Y.: Cornell University Press, 1997). On Thoreau and antislavery activism, see Sandra Harbert Petrolionus, *To Set This World Right: The Antislavery Movement in Thoreau's Concord* (Ithaca, N.Y.: Cornell University Press, 2006).
29. Some accounts note Thoreau's attendance at the Chardon Street Convention, while others do not. See, for example, Henry Steele Commager, *Theodore Parker: Yankee Crusader* (Boston: Little, Brown, 1936).
30. Henry David Thoreau, "Resistance to Civil Government" (1849).

Chapter 6: Brook Farm on Fire

1. George Ripley, *A Letter Addressed to the Congregational Church in Purchase Street by Its Pastor* (Boston, 1840), 14. On Ripley, see Charles Crowe, *George Ripley: Transcendentalist and Utopian Socialist* (Athens: University of Georgia Press, 1967); Philip Gura, *Man's Better Angels: Romantic Reformers and the Coming of the Civil War* (Cambridge, Mass.: Harvard University Press, 2017); Octavius Brooks Frothingham, *George Ripley* (Boston: Houghton Mifflin, 1883).
2. Ripley, *Letter,* 14.
3. "A Glimpse of Christ's Idea of Society," *Dial* 2, no. 2 (1841). Italics mine. Megan Marshall notes that "of all the Transcendentalists not actually living on the commune, Elizabeth [Palmer Peabody] worked the hardest to ensure the success of the project." *The Peabody Sisters,* 415. Alcott is quoted in the *Liberator* coverage of the Chardon Street Convention and also in Amos Augustus Phelps, *The Sabbath* (New York: M. W. Dodd, 1844), 23.
4. Emerson to Ripley, Dec. 15, 1840. This letter is collected in *The Letters of Ralph Waldo Emerson* (New York: Columbia University Press, 1941), 368–71. On Brook Farm, see Lindsay Swift, *Brook Farm: Its Members, Scholars, and Visitors* (New York: Macmillan, 1900), and Sterling Delano, *Brook Farm: The Dark Side of Utopia* (Cambridge, Mass.: Harvard University Press, 2004).
5. Packer, *Transcendentalists,* 135.
6. Nathaniel Hawthorne, *American Notebooks,* entry for April 16, 1841. Hawthorne joined Brook Farm not to protest capitalism but because he thought it would allow him time to write and possibly make a home for himself and his

fiancée, Sophia Peabody. He later published a fictional account of life on a similar commune, *The Blithedale Romance.*

7. See Scott Gac, *Singing for Freedom: The Hutchinson Family Singers and the Nineteenth-Century Culture of Reform* (New Haven, Conn.: Yale University Press, 2008), 15.

8. Albert Brisbane, *Social Destiny of Man; or, Association and Reorganization of Industry* (Philadelphia: Stollmeyer, 1840), 132. See Adam Max Tuchinsky, *Horace Greeley's "New-York Tribune": Civil War–Era Socialism and the Crisis of Free Labor* (Ithaca, N.Y.: Cornell University Press, 2009).

9. On Fourier and his philosophy, see Jonathan Beecher, *Charles Fourier: The Visionary and His World* (Berkeley: University of California Press, 1986). On Association and Fourierist thought in America, see Carl Guarneri, *The Utopian Alternative: Fourierism in Nineteenth-Century America* (Ithaca, N.Y.: Cornell University Press, 1991).

10. Brisbane, *Social Destiny of Man,* 132. Emerson was ambivalent about marriage, noting in his journal that it should be "a temporary relation," just as Fourierist Free Lovers would argue in the following decade. Margaret Fuller wrote that nothing made her feel "so anti-marriage" as talking to Emerson's second wife, Lidian. See Megan Marshall, *Margaret Fuller: A New American Life* (New York: Houghton Mifflin, 2013) 192.

11. Guarneri, *Utopian Alternative,* 3, 60.

12. Christopher Clark reminds us that "many institutions and systems that would ultimately become established parts of American life were themselves new, experimental, and of questionable practicality at this point: penal systems, school reforms, science and technology, railroads, suburbs, large publishing firms, paper money, and a host of other institutions, schemes, and proposals were as 'utopian' in their inception as these communities." In this malleable and rapidly changing context, these socialist communities were certainly perceived as "a radical challenge, but not to a fixed social and cultural hegemony." Christopher Clark, *The Communitarian Moment: The Radical Challenge of the Northampton Association* (Amherst: University of Massachusetts Press, 1995), 10. Carl Guarneri also notes the utopianism of the mainstream American outlook at this time. See Guarneri, *Utopian Alternative,* 147, and John O'Sullivan, "The Great Nation of Futurity," *United States Democratic Review* 6, no. 23 (1839): 426–30. Brisbane also published articles on Association in this magazine in the same period.

13. "Women of the Boston Anti-slavery Fair," *Harbinger,* Oct. 1845; Crowe, *George Ripley,* 201. For an abolitionist critique of Association, see "The Associationists and the Abolitionists," *National Anti-Slavery Standard,* reprinted in *Harbinger,* Oct. 30, 1847.

14. John Van Der Zee Sears, *My Friends at Brook Farm* (New York: Desmond Fitzgerald, 1912), 159.

15. See Philip Dray, *There Is Power in a Union: The Epic Story of Labor in America* (New York: Anchor, 2010).

16. See "Workingmen's Convention," *Phalanx,* Dec. 9, 1844. On the role of Association in the labor movement, see Guarneri, *Utopian Alternative;* David Zon-

derman, *Uneasy Allies: Working for Labor Reform in Nineteenth-Century Boston* (Amherst: University of Massachusetts Press, 2011); Lause, *Young America*.

17. "New England Convention at Lowell, Mass.," *Phalanx*, May 3, 1845. Also see *Awl*, March 29 and April 5, 1845, and Zonderman, *Uneasy Allies*, 44–57.

18. On Association as sanitized Fourierism mixed with American exceptionalism, see Guarneri, *Utopian Alternative*, 93; *Industrial Association* pamphlet from the American Union of Associationists, 23; Crowe, *George Ripley*, 194; and "The Fourth of July," *Harbinger*, June 21 1845. See examples in *Present*, Sept. 1843; *Harbinger*, April 1, 1848; and *Phalanx* 1, no. 6 (1844).

19. *Phalanx*, May 3, 1845, 337.

20. Amelia Eloise Russell, *Home Life of the Brook Farm Association* (Boston: Little, Brown, 1900), 81, 105.

21. "Fire at Brook Farm," *Harbinger*, March 14, 1846.

22. Russell, *Home Life of the Brook Farm Association*, 127; Dwight to Anna Parsons, March 4, 1846, *Autobiography of Brook Farm*, ed. Henry W. Sams (Englewood Cliffs, N.J.: Prentice-Hall, 1958); John Thomas Codman, *Brook Farm: Historic and Personal Memoirs* (Boston: Arena, 1894), 191.

Chapter 7: Wheat Bread and Seminal Losses

1. For critiques of the persistence of marriage at Brook Farm, see Charles Lane, "Brook Farm," *Dial*, Jan. 1844, 351–57; and John Humphrey Noyes, *History of American Socialisms* (Philadelphia: J. B. Lippincott, 1870), 139–43.

2. Victor Hennequin, *Love in the Phalanstery*, trans. Henry James Sr. (New York: De Witt and Davenport, 1849). Discussions of this work were already appearing in *The Harbinger* in late 1848; see "Love in the Phalanstery," Nov. 11, 1848, for example. Albert Brisbane, *Theory of the Functions of the Human Passions* (New York: Miller, Orton, and Mulligan, 1856); Albert Brisbane and Henry Clapp Jr., *The Social Destiny of Man; or, Theory of the Four Movements* (New York: De-witt, 1857).

3. Beecher, *Charles Fourier*, 303–16.

4. Kent, *Free Love*, 92; *Nichols' Monthly*, Jan. 1855, quoted in J. W. Daniels, *Spiritualism Versus Christianity; or, Spiritualism Thoroughly Exposed* (New York: Miller, Orton, and Mulligan, 1856), 254; Francis Barry, "What Is Marriage?," *Social Revolutionist* 3 (Feb. 1857): 42–43. Also see Taylor Stoehr, *Free Love in America: A Documentary History* (New York: AMS Press, 1979), 6; Joanne Passet, *Sex Radicals and the Quest for Women's Equality* (Urbana: University of Illinois Press, 2003), 2. Also on the Free Lovers, see John Spurlock, *Free Love: Marriage and Middle-Class Radicalism in America, 1825–1860* (New York: New York University Press, 1988). Not all utopian socialist projects advocated "Free Love," but as John Humphrey Noyes asserted, they were united by a desire for *"the enlargement of home—the extension of family union beyond the little man-and-wife circle."* John Humphrey Noyes, *American Socialist*, March 30, 1876.

5. See Sylvester Graham, *Treatise on Bread and Bread-Making* (Boston: Light and Stearns, 1837). Stephen Nissenbaum notes that for Graham "commercially

baked bread was only a metaphor of the Jacksonian marketplace itself—a place of fevered chaos, laden with products manufactured by invisible men and corrupted with invisible poisons." Stephen Nissenbaum, *Sex, Diet, and Debility in Jacksonian America: Sylvester Graham and Health Reform* (Westport, Conn.: Greenwood, 1980), 19. Also see James Whorton, *Crusaders for Fitness: The History of American Health Reformers* (Princeton, N.J.: Princeton University Press, 1982), 126.

6. Sylvester Graham, *A Lecture to Young Men on Chastity* (Boston: Light and Stearns, 1837).

7. Nissenbaum, *Sex, Diet, and Debility in Jacksonian America,* 167.

8. Herman Melville, *Pierre; or, The Ambiguities* (1852).

9. M. Edgeworth Lazarus, *Love vs. Marriage* (New York: Fowler and Wells, 1852), 142, 109, 44, 288, 297, 298. In defending his preference for "variety in love," a bone of contention among marriage abolitionists, he says, "I have only to say with Emerson, if I am the devil's child, I will do the devil's work" (313). Lazarus was also a fan of Melville's novels and was likely acquainted with him personally. The will was signed on March 30, 1847. See David Faflik, *Boarding Out: Inhabiting the American Urban Literary Imagination, 1840–1860* (Evanston, Ill.: Northwestern University Press, 2012), 312n33. The best source on Lazarus's biography is Emily Bingham, *Mordecai: An Early American Family* (New York: Hill and Wang, 2003).

10. In backpedaling follow-up articles at that time, James indicated his hope that compulsory monogamy would be replaced with a freer system in which individuals would not need to call on external authorities to sanction sex, whether in "exclusive" or "varied" alliance. *Harbinger,* Dec. 2, 1848. Also see Guarneri, *Utopian Alternative,* 355, and Tuchinsky, *Horace Greeley's "New-York Tribune,"* 112–20.

11. Madeleine Stern, *The Pantarch: A Biography of Stephen Pearl Andrews* (Austin: University of Texas Press, 1968), 76–83; Moncure Conway, *Autobiography, Memories, and Experiences of Moncure Daniel Conway* (Boston: Houghton Mifflin, 1904), 1:234–37.

12. Stephen Pearl Andrews, *Love, Marriage, and Divorce and the Sovereignty of the Individual* (New York: Stringer and Townsend, 1853), 22, 70–73; April Haynes, *Riotous Flesh: Women, Physiology, and the Solitary Vice in Nineteenth-Century America* (Chicago: University of Chicago Press, 2015), 107.

13. See Jean L. Silver-Isenstadt, *Shameless: The Visionary Life of Mary Gove Nichols* (Baltimore: Johns Hopkins University Press, 2002). A number of Free Lovers championed varieties of nonreproductive sex for similar reasons in this time of high mortality for mothers and infants and no birth control. Noyes developed his theory of male continence after his wife had five births in six years, in which only one of the babies was born alive. He swore that he would "never again expose her to such fruitless suffering." He declared that a man should no more have sexual intercourse with his wife just to have an orgasm than he should fire a gun at his best friend in order to unload it. John Humphrey Noyes, *Male Continence* (Oneida, N.Y., 1872), 11.

14. Silver-Isenstadt, *Shameless,* 80–86.

15. T. L. Nichols and Mary Gove Nichols, *Marriage: Its History, Character, and Results* (New York: Nichols, 1854), 114. Also see Patricia Cline Cohen, "The 'Anti-marriage Theory' of Thomas and Mary Gove Nichols: A Radical Critique of Monogamy in the 1850s," *Journal of the Early Republic* 34 (Spring 2014).

16. "A Bad Book Gibbeted," *New-York Daily Times,* Aug. 17, 1855.

17. "The Free Love System: Origin, Progress, and Position of the Anti-marriage Movement," *New-York Daily Times,* Sept. 8, 1855.

18. "The Free Lovers," *New-York Daily Times,* Oct. 10, 1855; "A Rich Development," *New-York Daily Times,* Oct. 19, 1855; "The Free Lovers," *New-York Daily Times,* Oct. 23, 1855.

19. Remarriage was itself a controversial issue; see Nancy Cott, *Public Vows: A History of Marriage and the Nation* (Cambridge, Mass.: Harvard University Press, 2000), 109.

20. "Wife Holding," *Word,* April 1877, 3. Also see Passet, *Sex Radicals and the Quest for Women's Equality,* 81, 97.

21. "Mr. Heywood's Reply to Mr. Barry," *Word,* April 1877, 3.

22. Stoehr, *Free Love in America,* 5; Passet, *Sex Radicals and the Quest for Women's Equality,* 135–51; Charles J. Reid Jr., "The Devil Comes to Kansas: A Story of Free Love, Sexual Privacy, and the Law," *Michigan Journal of Gender and Law* 19, no. 1 (2012).

23. Lockwood, *New Harmony Communities,* 176.

24. *Mariposa Gazette,* Aug. 11, 1877.

25. T. W. Higginson, "Marriage of Lucy Stone Under Protest," *Liberator,* May 4, 1855.

26. On Free Love and eugenics, see Wendy Hayden, *Evolutionary Rhetoric: Sex, Science, and Free Love in Nineteenth-Century Feminism* (Carbondale: Southern Illinois University Press, 2013).

Chapter 8: Marriage Slavery and All Other Queer Things

1. Brisbane, *Social Destiny of Man,* 431.

2. Stanton, *Eighty Years and More,* 145–48.

3. On the cultivation of this story later in the movement, see Lisa Tetrault, *The Myth of Seneca Falls: Memory and the Women's Suffrage Movement* (Chapel Hill: University of North Carolina Press, 2014).

4. Scrapbooks, On the Woman's Rights Convention, prepared by Elizabeth Cady Stanton, 1848, Miscellany, 1840–1946, Elizabeth Cady Stanton Papers, Library of Congress.

5. Elizabeth Cady Stanton, *History of Woman Suffrage* (Rochester, N.Y.: Anthony and Mann, 1881), 1:73–75. Also see Sally McMillen, *Seneca Falls and the Origins of the Women's Rights Movement* (New York: Oxford University Press, 2009).

6. Cohen, "'Anti-marriage Theory' of Thomas and Mary Gove Nichols," 16.

7. *Proceedings of the Woman's Rights Convention, Held at Worcester, October 23d and 24th, 1850* (Boston: Prentiss and Sawyer, 1851), 17; Martha S. Jones, *All Bound*

Up Together: The Woman Question in African American Political Culture, 1830–1900 (Chapel Hill: University of North Carolina Press, 2007), 91–93.

8. *Proceedings of the Woman's Rights Convention, Held at Worcester,* 34. On the slavery analogy in the women's movement, see Karen Sánchez-Eppler, "Bodily Bonds: The Intersecting Rhetorics of Feminism and Abolition," in "America Reconstructed, 1840–1940," special issue, *Representations,* no. 24 (Autumn 1988): 28–59.

9. John B. Ellis, *Free Love and Its Votaries; or, American Socialism Unmasked* (New York: A. L. Bancroft, 1870), 430, xvl, 394; Henry C. Wright, *Marriage and Parentage; or, The Reproductive Element in Man* (Boston: Bela Marsh, 1854), 194, 200.

10. "Free Love Fairly Stated," *Social Revolutionist,* Feb. 1857, 52–56; Nichols and Nichols, *Marriage,* 92–93.

11. Lazarus, *Love vs. Marriage,* 170; Guarneri, *Utopian Alternative,* 264–66.

12. Lori Ginzberg, *Elizabeth Cady Stanton: An American Life* (New York: Hill and Wang, 2009), 20; Stanton, *History of Woman Suffrage,* 1:680.

13. Mark Lause, *The Antebellum Crisis and America's First Bohemians* (Kent, Ohio: Kent State University Press, 2013); Dolores Hayden, *The Grand Domestic Revolution* (Cambridge, Mass.: MIT Press, 1981), 95.

14. *New York Times,* May 15, 1858, quoted in Faye Dudden, *Fighting Chance: The Struggle over Woman Suffrage and Black Suffrage in Reconstruction America* (New York: Oxford University Press, 2011), 35.

15. *Proceedings of the Free Convention, Held at Rutland, Vt., [June] 25th, 26th, and 27th, 1858* (Boston: Yerrinton, 1858), 52, 5.

16. Quotations from Stoehr, *Free Love in America,* 136, and Lewis Perry, *Childhood, Marriage, and Reform: Henry Clarke Wright, 1797–1870* (Chicago: University of Chicago Press, 1980), 181–201.

17. *Proceedings of the Free Convention, Held at Rutland,* 23, 57, 98–99. For the *New York Times* coverage, see "Radicals in Council" and "The Free Convention," June 29, 1858; "The Reform Convention at Rutland, Vt," June 28, 1858; and "The Rutland Reformers," June 30, 1858.

Chapter 9: The Aliened American

1. Madeline Stern, "Stephen Pearl Andrews, Abolitionist, and the Annexation of Texas," *Southwestern Historical Quarterly* 67, no. 4 (April 1964): 491–523; William W. Freehling, *Road to Disunion* (New York: Oxford University Press, 1990), 1:372–95.

2. Calhoun quoted in Stern, "Stephen Pearl Andrews, Abolitionist, and the Annexation of Texas," 517; Joshua Giddings, *Speeches in Congress* (Boston: Jewett, 1853), 17.

3. James McPherson, *Battle Cry of Freedom: The Civil War Era* (New York: Oxford University Press, 1998), 58–68, 73.

4. "Great Meeting at Faneuil Hall," *Liberator,* June 8, 1849, and "Horrors of the Mexican War," *Liberator,* Aug. 23, 1850.

5. Quoted in Irving H. Bartlett, *Wendell Phillips: Brahmin Radical* (Boston: Beacon, 1961), 117–18.

6. Smith was nominated as the Liberty Party's presidential candidate in 1848 on a platform that included universal suffrage. On the Liberty Party, see Richard Sewell, *Ballots for Freedom: Antislavery Politics in the United States, 1837–1860* (New York: Norton, 1980); Reinhard Johnson, *The Liberty Party, 1840–1848: Antislavery Third-Party Politics in the United States* (Baton Rouge: Louisiana State University Press, 2009); Bruce Laurie, *Beyond Garrison: Antislavery and Social Reform* (Cambridge, U.K.: Cambridge University Press, 2005).

7. Frank Rollin, *Life and Public Services of Martin R. Delany* (Boston: Lee and Shepard, 1883), 27. My biographical sketch of Delany relies most heavily on Dorothy Sterling, *The Making of an Afro-American: Martin Robison Delany, 1812–1885* (New York: Doubleday, 1971).

8. Floyd Miller, "The Father of Black Nationalism: Another Contender," *Civil War History* 17, no. 4 (Dec. 1971): 310–19; Gayle Tate, "Prophesy and Transformation: The Contours of Lewis Woodson's Nationalism," *Journal of Black Studies* 29, no. 2 (Nov. 1998): 209–33.

9. Sterling, *Making of an Afro-American*, 60–67.

10. David Blight, *Frederick Douglass: Prophet of Freedom* (New York: Simon & Schuster, 2018), 205–12.

11. Quoted in Robert Levine, *Martin Delany, Frederick Douglass, and the Politics of Representative Identity* (Chapel Hill: University of North Carolina Press, 1997), 41.

12. Henry Highland Garnet, "An Address to the Slaves of the United States of America" (1843). It was later printed alongside David Walker's *Appeal* in 1848. See the Colored Conventions Project's online exhibit on Garnet's speech and its reception at the convention, curated by Harrison Graves, Jake Alspaugh, and Derrick Spires, edited by P. Gabrielle Foreman and Sarah Patterson, http://coloredconventions.org.

13. Jones, *All Bound Up Together*, 59–60; *Report of the Proceedings of the Colored National Convention, Held at Cleveland, Ohio, on Wednesday, September 6, 1848* (Rochester, N.Y.: North Star, 1848), 12.

14. See Sterling, *Making of an Afro-American*, 140.

15. *North Star*, Sept. 5, 1850; *National Anti-Slavery Standard*, Sept. 5, 1850. Manisha Sinha's recent history of antislavery, *The Slave's Cause*, provides an excellent account of the movement's turn to violence in the 1850s.

16. Martin Robison Delany, *The Condition, Elevation, Emigration, and Destiny of the Colored People of the United States* (Philadelphia, 1852), 212–14. Bizarrely, Delany had just been elected mayor of Greytown, Nicaragua—represented there by a friend while he worked in New York. See Levine, *Martin Delany, Frederick Douglass, and the Politics of Representative Identity*, 63. Levine sees Delany's earlier speech "Political Destiny" as wielding the rhetoric of manifest destiny.

17. *Frederick Douglass' Paper*, July 23, 1852. Delany's involvement with *The North Star* ended in June 1849. On their debates of *Uncle Tom's Cabin* and other aspects of Delany's relationship with Douglass, see Levine, *Martin Delany, Frederick Douglass, and the Politics of Representative Identity*, on which I have relied here. Also see Miller, *Search for a Black Nationality*, 132. Delany also responded to

Stowe with a novel of his own, the militant *Blake; or, the Huts of America,* which was serialized in *The Anglo-African Magazine* in 1859–1860 and in the *Weekly Anglo-African* in 1861–1862.

18. Quoted in Eckhardt, *Fanny Wright,* 294.

19. Harriet Beecher Stowe, *Uncle Tom's Cabin; or, Life Among the Lowly* (Boston: Jewett, 1852).

20. *Frederick Douglass' Paper,* April 1, 1853.

21. *Pennsylvania Freeman,* April 29, 1852; *Liberator,* March 26, 1852. Quoted in Levine, *Martin Delany, Frederick Douglass, and the Politics of Representative Identity,* 90.

22. See *Proceedings of the Colored National Convention* (Rochester, N.Y.: Frederick Douglass' Paper, 1853.)

23. "Speech of H. Ford Douglass, in Reply to Mr. J. M. Langston Before the Emigration Convention, at Cleveland, Ohio: Delivered on the Evening of the 27th of August, 1854"; *Proceedings of the Emigration Convention of Colored People, Held at Cleveland, Ohio* (Pittsburgh: A. A. Anderson, 1854).

24. *Frederick Douglass' Paper,* Nov. 18, 1853.

25. William Pease and Jane Pease, *Black Utopia;* W. E. B. DuBois, *John Brown* (Philadelphia: G. W. Jacobs, 1909), 99–100.

26. Richard Disney, *AME Church Review* 2 (1895): 5.

27. Jane Rhodes, *Mary Ann Shadd Cary: The Black Press and Protest in the Nineteenth Century* (Bloomington: Indiana University Press, 1998); Frances Harper, "The Air of Freedom," in *The Freedmen's Book,* ed. Lydia Maria Child (Boston: Ticknor and Fields, 1866), 243; Frederick Douglass, *The Heroic Slave: A Cultural and Critical Edition,* ed. Robert S. Levine, John Stauffer, and John R. McKivigan (New Haven, Conn.: Yale University Press, 2015), 26.

Chapter 10: Treason Will Not Be Treason Much Longer

1. Charles Emery Stevens, *Anthony Burns: A History* (Boston: John P. Jewett, 1856), 20.

2. Daniel Webster, "To the New York Committee for the Celebration of the Birthday of Washington," Feb. 20, 1851, quoted in William Spencer, *The Boston Slave Riot and Trial of Anthony Burns* (Boston: Fetridge, 1854), 31, 38.

3. Thomas Wentworth Higginson, *Cheerful Yesterdays* (Boston: Houghton Mifflin, 1900), 140–45.

4. Stevens, *Anthony Burns,* 291–95.

5. See Joel Strangis, *Lewis Hayden and the War Against Slavery* (North Haven, Conn.: Linnet, 1999), 5; Stanley J. Robboy and Anita W. Robboy, "Lewis Hayden: From Fugitive Slave to Statesman," *New England Quarterly* 46, no. 4 (Dec. 1973): 591–613; and the 1850 broadside "Declaration of Sentiments of the Colored Citizens of Boston, on the Fugitive Slave Bill," Bro. 10.67, Boston Athenaeum.

6. Thomas Wentworth Higginson, *Massachusetts in Mourning: A Sermon, Preached in Worcester, on Sunday, June 4, 1854* (Boston: J. Munroe, 1854), 5; and Higginson, *Cheerful Yesterdays,* 153.

7. The precise cause of Batchelder's death has long been a mystery, and accounts from that night note that a number of people nearby had guns. The version of the story related here is based on a document in Higginson's papers by an unspecified author reporting that Hayden had confided this series of events to him before leaving Boston while the investigation ensued. "Letters on the Anthony Burns Affair," typescript, Seq 354–358, Thomas Wentworth Higginson manuscript collection, Houghton Library. John T. Cumbler notes that other evidence points to Martin Stowell. See *From Abolition to Rights for All: The Making of a Reform Community in the Nineteenth Century* (Philadelphia: University of Pennsylvania Press, 2008), 198n82. For a full treatment of the Burns crisis, see Albert J. Von Frank, *The Trials of Anthony Burns: Freedom and Slavery in Emerson's Boston* (Cambridge, Mass.: Harvard University Press, 1998).

8. *Liberator,* June 9, 1854.

9. Spencer, *Boston Slave Riot and Trial of Anthony Burns,* 38.

10. Stevens, *Anthony Burns,* 135–43.

11. *Liberator,* Feb. 9, 1833; "From a Boston Correspondent: State of the Colored People," *Independent,* June 15, 1854.

12. See Higginson's journal entries for May 14 and 31 and July 20, 1842.

13. Higginson to Garrison, June 28, 1854, Boston Public Library.

14. "The Meeting at Framingham," *Liberator,* July 7, 1854.

15. Thoreau, "Slavery in Massachusetts" (1854).

16. George Fitzhugh, *Sociology for the South; or, The Failure of Free Society* (Richmond, Va.: Morris, 1854), 177. George Fitzhugh, *Cannibals All!; or, Slaves Without Masters* (Richmond, Va.: Morris, 1857), 155. These fringe leftists, he argued, all admitted that free society did not work, and thus "the works of the socialists contain the true defense of slavery" (368).

17. Albert Gallatin Brown, *Speeches, Messages, and Other Writings* (Philadelphia: J. B. Smith, 1859), 595.

18. McPherson, *Battle Cry of Freedom,* 149.

19. On Peterboro and Timbuctoo, see John Stauffer, *The Black Hearts of Men: Radical Abolitionists and the Transformation of Race* (Cambridge, Mass.: Harvard University Press, 2009).

20. DuBois, *John Brown,* 67–69.

21. Richard J. Hinton, *John Brown and His Men* (New York: Funk & Wagnalls, 1894), 61–75.

22. Higginson, *Cheerful Yesterdays; Letters and Journals of Thomas Wentworth Higginson, 1846–1906,* ed. Mary Thatcher Higginson (New York: Da Capo Press, 1969), 142.

23. Eric Foner, *Free Soil, Free Labor, Free Men: The Ideology of the Republican Party Before the Civil War* (New York: Oxford University Press, 1995); William E. Gienapp, *The Origins of the Republican Party, 1852–1856* (New York: Oxford University Press, 1988).

24. Foner, *Free Soil, Free Labor, Free Men,* 165–68; Tilden G. Edelstein, *Strange Enthusiasm: A Life of Thomas Wentworth Higginson* (New Haven, Conn.: Yale University Press, 1968), 187–202; *Liberator,* Feb. 6, 1857.

25. *Proceedings of the State Disunion Convention, Held at Worcester, Massachusetts, January 15, 1857* (Boston, 1857); Garrison and Garrison, *William Lloyd Garrison*, 3:454; Higginson, "The New Revolution: What Commitment Requires" (1857).

26. DuBois, *John Brown*, 210.

27. Stephen B. Oates, *To Purge This Land with Blood: A Biography of John Brown* (New York: Harper & Row, 1970), 30. *Eulogy of Garrison: Remarks of Wendell Phillips at the Funeral of William Lloyd Garrison* (Boston: Lee and Shepard, 1884), 10.

28. DuBois, *John Brown*, 104.

29. Ibid., 88; David S. Reynolds, *John Brown, Abolitionist* (New York: Vintage, 2005), 213; William James Linton, *Life of John Greenleaf Whittier* (London: W. Scott, 1893), 132.

30. John Brown, "Provisional Constitution and Ordinances for the People of the United States" (1858).

31. DuBois, *John Brown*, 250. Kellie Carter Jackson's new book on political violence in black antislavery activism offers a chapter on Brown's African American network of backers, including the crucial and little-known Mary Ellen Pleasant. I join the author in the attempt to decenter Brown himself from the Harpers Ferry event in order to reveal its extensive roots in collectivism rather than as the act of one exceptional individual. See Kellie Carter Jackson, *Force and Freedom: Black Abolitionists and the Politics of Violence* (Philadelphia: University of Pennsylvania Press, 2019), 113. On Lewis Hayden's role in Brown's network, see Strangis, *Lewis Hayden*, 105–7.

Chapter 11: The Provisional United States

1. Rollin, *Life and Public Services of Martin R. Delany*, 85.

2. Hinton, *John Brown and His Men*, 175.

3. Accounts of the Chatham Convention vary widely. Some say there were thirty-three or thirty-four black men; Delany says there were sixty or seventy. Brown is said to have stayed in various homes in different accounts. Also Delany says he agreed to be president of the permanent organization to be established by the Subterranean Pass Way plan, but other accounts say that they were not able to fill the position of the president. I have relied primarily on Hinton, DuBois, and the minutes of the Chatham Convention as recorded by Osborne Perry Anderson.

4. Sterling, *Making of an Afro-American*, 172.

5. DuBois, *John Brown*, 108–9; Rollin, *Life and Public Services of Martin R. Delany*, 89; Tony Horwitz, *Midnight Rising: John Brown and the Raid That Sparked the Civil War* (New York: Henry Holt, 2011), 124, 265.

6. Reynolds, *John Brown, Abolitionist*, 247; Sinha, *Slave's Cause*, 551.

7. Rollin, *Life and Public Services of Martin R. Delany*, 16–18.

8. "African Colonization Society," *Douglass' Monthly*, Feb. 1859.

9. Quoted in Miller, *Search for a Black Nationality*, 205. Also see Cyril E. Griffith, *The African Dream: Martin R. Delany and the Emergence of Pan-African Thought* (University Park: Pennsylvania State University Press, 1975), 48–49.

10. Sterling, *Making of an Afro-American,* 202.
11. Hannah Geffert (with Jean Libby), "Regional Black Involvement in John Brown's Raid on Harper's Ferry," in *Prophets of Protest,* ed. Timothy Patrick McCarthy and John Stauffer (New York: New Press, 2006), 165–79.
12. Brown to Sanborn, quoted in DuBois, *John Brown,* 234; John Brown, "Words of Advice" (1851).
13. DuBois, *John Brown,* 152; Henry Wise, "Comments in Richmond, Virginia," Oct. 21, 1859.
14. John Brown, "Prison Letters," Oct.–Dec. 1859; Mahala Doyle, "To John Brown," Nov. 20, 1859. For a collection of primary materials related to Brown, see John Stauffer and Zoe Trodd, eds., *The Tribunal: Responses to John Brown and the Harpers Ferry Raid* (Cambridge, Mass.: Harvard University Press, 2012). On Copeland, see Steven Lubet, *The "Colored Hero" of Harpers Ferry: John Anthony Copeland and the War Against Slavery* (New York: Cambridge University Press, 2015).
15. *The Life, Trial, and Execution of Captain John Brown* (New York: DeWitt, 1859).
16. Garrison and Garrison, *William Lloyd Garrison,* 3:473; *Liberator,* Oct. 21, 1859.
17. Henry Clarke Wright, *The Natick Resolution* (Boston, 1859).
18. David S. Reynolds has made the strongest argument for the Transcendentalists' role in John Brown's raid and reputation, arguing that "Transcendentalism bred social radicalism" and that "it was the Transcendentalists alone who rescued him from infamy and possible oblivion." Reynolds, *John Brown, Abolitionist,* 217, 355.
19. Henry David Thoreau, "Plea for Captain John Brown" (1859).
20. Higginson [to Lysander Spooner], Nov. 28, 1859, Boston Public Library, Rare Books and Manuscripts.
21. Edelstein, *Strange Enthusiasm,* 228–36.
22. *Liberator,* Dec. 9, 1859; Stauffer and Trodd, *Tribunal,* 155.
23. *Gettysburg Compiler,* Dec. 12, 1859.
24. Quoted in Oates, *To Purge This Land with Blood,* 351.
25. Zoe Trodd and John Stauffer, eds., *Meteor of War: The John Brown Story* (Maplecrest, N.Y.: Brandywine, 2004), 251.

Chapter 12: Under the Flag

1. *Congressional Globe,* 36th Cong., 1st Sess., Dec. 1859. Also see Horwitz, *Midnight Rising,* 262–63.
2. Henry A. Wise, "Message I," *Journal of the House of Delegates of the Commonwealth of Virginia,* for the Session of 1859–60 (Richmond: Ritchie, 1859), 3–24.
3. *Boston Post,* Dec. 3, 1859.
4. Quoted in McPherson, *Battle Cry of Freedom,* 230. Also see Wilentz, *Rise of American Democracy,* 775.
5. *Declaration of the Immediate Causes Which Induce and Justify the Secession of South Carolina from the Federal Union; and the Ordinance of Secession* (Charleston, S.C.: Evans and Cogswell, 1860). The Georgia and Mississippi Declarations of Causes were approved in 1861.

6. *Speeches of John C. Calhoun* (New York: Harper & Brothers, 1843), 223–25.

7. Horwitz, *Midnight Rising,* 275.

8. Sterling, *Making of an Afro-American,* 219.

9. Griffith, *African Dream,* 73–76.

10. *Liberator,* July 9, 1858; *Liberator,* July 14, 1854, reprinted from the *New-York Tribune* poem "Hail to the Stars and Stripes."

11. Quoted in Horwitz, *Midnight Rising,* 278.

12. McPherson. *Battle Cry of Freedom,* 557, quoted in Garrison and Garrison, *William Lloyd Garrison,* 4:61; *Liberator,* May 9, 1862, quoted in Peter Wirzbicki, "Wendell Phillips and the Transatlantic Radicalism: Democracy, Capitalism, and the American Labor Movement," *Wendell Phillips, Social Justice, and the Power of the Past,* ed. A. J. Aiséirithe and Donald Yacovone (Baton Rouge: Louisiana State University Press, 2016), 169.

13. Quoted in Edelstein, *Strange Enthusiasm,* 252.

14. Willie Lee Rose, *Rehearsal for Reconstruction: The Port Royal Experiment* (New York: Oxford University Press, 1964), 45–46, and the Introduction by C. Vann Woodward, ibid., xii.

15. Thomas Wentworth Higginson, *Army Life in a Black Regiment* (Boston: Fields, Osgood, 1870), 4, 38–41. For an extract from Charlotte Forten's journal with her account of the celebration of emancipation, see "A Social Experiment: The Port Royal *Journal* of Charlotte L. Forten, 1862–1863," *Journal of Negro History* 35:3 (July 1950): 233–64.

16. Russell Duncan, ed., *Blue-Eyed Child of Fortune: The Civil War Letters of Colonel Robert Gould Shaw* (Athens: University of Georgia Press, 1992), 101; Crowe, *George Ripley,* 161; Delano, *Brook Farm,* 312.

17. Garrison and Garrison, *William Lloyd Garrison,* 4:81.

18. Edward Cary, *The Trip of the Steamer* Oceanus *to Fort Sumter and Charleston, S.C.* (Brooklyn, 1865); Garrison and Garrison, *William Lloyd Garrison,* 4:148.

19. Martha Hodes, *Mourning Lincoln* (New Haven, Conn.: Yale University Press, 2015), 47.

20. Sources conflict about when Delany's papers were destroyed, ranging from 1864 to 1866. But *The Xenia Sentinel* of Ohio, April 21, 1865, reports that an arsonist burned the institution to the ground while the black students and teachers were all in town taking part in the town's celebration of the Union victory on April 14, 1865.

Chapter 13: To Write Justice in the American Heart

1. Garrison and Garrison, *William Lloyd Garrison,* 4:159; "The Anti Slavery Society," *New York Times,* May 11, 1865.

2. Parker Pillsbury, *Acts of the Anti-slavery Apostles* (Concord, N.H., 1883), 498.

3. Sidney Andrews, *The South Since the War: As Shown by Fourteen Weeks of Travel and Observation in Georgia and the Carolinas* (Boston: Ticknor and Fields, 1866), 1–2.

4. On epidemics and death among the freedmen, see Jim Downs, *Sick from Free-*

dom: African-American Illness and Suffering During the Civil War and Reconstruction (New York: Oxford University Press, 2012).

5. *Final Report of the American Freedmen's Inquiry Commission to the Secretary of War,* May 15, 1864.

6. W. E. B. DuBois, "The Freedmen's Bureau," *Atlantic Monthly,* March 1901.

7. Quoted in Tunde Adeleke, *Without Regard to Race: The Other Martin Robison Delany* (Jackson: University Press of Mississippi, 2009), 81. For a collection of Delany's speeches and writings in South Carolina that also attends to this shift, see Robert Levine, ed., *Martin R. Delany: A Documentary Reader* (Chapel Hill: University of North Carolina Press, 2003).

8. *New-York Daily Tribune,* Feb. 13, 1865, 5.

9. Rose, *Rehearsal for Reconstruction,* 330–31, 351–74; Edisto Island Freemen to Johnson, Oct. 28, 1865, in *Reconstruction: Voices from America's First Great Struggle for Racial Equality,* ed. Brooks D. Simpson (New York: Library of America, 2018), 125.

10. Eric Foner, *Reconstruction: America's Unfinished Revolution, 1863–1877* (New York: Harper & Row, 1988), 230–31; Thaddeus Stevens speech at Lancaster, Pa., Sept. 1865, in Simpson, *Reconstruction,* 103–4; Thaddeus Stevens speech in Congress, May 1866, in Simpson, *Reconstruction,* 239–40.

11. Thaddeus Stevens, Dec. 18, 1865, *Congressional Globe;* Thaddeus Stevens speech in Congress on Reconstruction, Jan. 1867, in Simpson, *Reconstruction,* 302.

12. Quoted in Adeleke, *Without Regard to Race,* 87, 103–4.

13. Thomas Wentworth Higginson, "Fair Play the Best Policy," *Atlantic Monthly,* May 1865.

14. "Colored Officials," *New York Times,* Aug. 21, 1867.

15. James Brewer Stewart, *Wendell Phillips: Liberty's Hero* (Baton Rouge: Louisiana State University Press, 1998), 284.

16. Higginson to Stanton, Dec. 22, 1866, in *The Selected Papers of Elizabeth Cady Stanton and Susan B. Anthony,* ed. Ann Gordon (New Brunswick, N.J.: Rutgers University Press, 1997), 2:10.

17. *Proceedings of the Tenth National Woman's Rights Convention, Held at the Cooper Institute, New York City, May 10th and 11th, 1860* (Boston: Yerrinton and Garrison, 1860).

18. Frederick Douglass, "What the Black Man Wants" (1865).

19. On Sarah Remond, see Sirpa Salenius, *An Abolitionist Abroad: Sarah Parker Remond in Cosmopolitan Europe* (Amherst: University of Massachusetts Press, 2016).

20. *Proceedings of the Eleventh National Woman's Rights Convention, Held at the Church of the Puritans, New York, May 10, 1866* (New York, 1866), 45–48.

21. Stanton, *Eighty Years and More,* 245.

22. Dennis B. Downey, "George Francis Train: The Great American Humbug," *Journal of Popular Culture* 14, no. 2 (Fall 1980): 251–61; Patricia G. Holland, "George Francis Train and the Woman Suffrage Movement, 1867–70," *Books at Iowa,* no. 46 (1987): 8–29.

23. Quoted in Dudden, *Fighting Chance,* 171.

24. *Revolution,* Feb. 4, 1869.

25. *New York World,* May 13, 1869; *New York Times,* May 13 and 14, 1869; *Revolution,* May 27, 1869.

26. Quoted in Faulkner, *Lucretia Mott's Heresy,* 204–5.

27. Quoted in Stewart, *Wendell Phillips,* 293.

28. James M. McPherson, *The Struggle for Equality: Abolitionists and the Negro in the Civil War and Reconstruction* (Princeton, N.J.: Princeton University Press, 1964), 412.

Chapter 14: A Revolution Going Backward

1. On the global economic impact of emancipation, see Sven Beckert, *Empire of Cotton: A Global History* (New York: Vintage, 2015).

2. Quoted in Aiséirithe and Yacovone, *Wendell Phillips, Social Justice, and the Power of the Past,* 17.

3. "Senator Wade on Capital and Labor," *New York Times,* July 1, 1867. Also see Foner, *Reconstruction,* 309.

4. *Bee-Hive,* Nov. 7, 1865. Also see Robin Blackburn, *An Unfinished Revolution: Karl Marx and Abraham Lincoln* (London: Verso, 2011); and Andrew Zimmerman, "From the Second American Revolution to the First International and Back Again: Marxism, the Popular Front, and the American Civil War," *The World the Civil War Made,* ed. Gregory P. Downs and Kate Masur (Chapel Hill: University of North Carolina Press, 2015): 304–36.

5. David Roediger, "Ira Steward and the Anti-slavery Origins of American Eight-Hour Theory," *Labor History* 27, no. 3 (1986): 420–24; Ira Steward, *Poverty* (1873), 4; *Boston Eight Hour League, Its Object and Work: Annual Report of the President, Containing the Plan and Estimates of a Free Hall for Workingmen and Workingwomen* (Boston: Boston Eight Hour League, 1872), 2.

6. *Proceedings of the Colored National Labor Convention, Held in Washington, D.C., on December 6th, 7th, 8th, 9th, and 10th, 1869* (Washington, D.C., 1870), 4.

7. Ellen DuBois, ed., "On Labor and Free Love: Two Unpublished Speeches of Elizabeth Cady Stanton," *Signs* 1, no. 1 (Autumn 1975): 258.

8. *Mechanics Advocate* article in Elizabeth Cady Stanton scrapbook, Library of Congress. These feminists were also well aware of the politics of women's unpaid labor in the home. They supported efforts toward cooperative housekeeping and communal kitchens that would mitigate these burdens, often inspired by the Fourierist critique of the isolated household. See Guarneri, *Utopian Alternative,* 398, and Dolores Hayden, *The Grand Domestic Revolution: A History of Feminist Designs for American Homes, Neighborhoods, and Cities* (Cambridge, Mass.: MIT Press), 1981.

9. For Heywood's biography, I have relied on Martin Blatt, *Free Love and Anarchism: The Biography of Ezra Heywood* (Urbana: University of Illinois Press, 1989).

10. In 1865, Heywood joined with hundreds of others who dissented against the Civil War to establish the Universal Peace Society. They advocated not just individual objection but national disarmament and the abolition of war. See ibid., 35.

11. *New York Times,* Jan. 28, 1869.

12. Zonderman, *Uneasy Allies,* 120, 125–26.

13. Blatt, *Free Love and Anarchism,* 50.

14. Victoria C. Woodhull, *A Speech on the Impending Revolution, Delivered in Music Hall, Boston, Thursday, Feb. 1, 1872, and the Academy of Music, New York, Feb. 20, 1872* (New York: Woodhull, Claflin, 1872).

15. Quoted in Zonderman, *Uneasy Allies,* 106.

16. *New York Times,* June 7, 1871, 4. See coverage of "The Communist Parade" in *New-York Tribune* and *New York Times,* Dec. 18, 1871. Quoted in Zonderman, *Uneasy Allies,* 132.

17. Zonderman, *Uneasy Allies,* 205. See Timothy Messer-Kruse, *The Yankee International: Marxism and the American Reform Tradition, 1848–1876* (Chapel Hill: University of North Carolina Press, 1998), 200.

18. Rosalyn Terborg-Penn, *African American Women in the Struggle for the Vote, 1850–1920* (Bloomington: Indiana University Press, 1998), 34. Also see Hugh Davis, *We Will Be Satisfied with Nothing Less: The African American Struggle for Equal Rights in the North During Reconstruction* (Ithaca, N.Y.: Cornell University Press, 2011). Mary Ann Shadd married Thomas Cary in 1856; I use her married name after this point. On the extended use of "new departure" tactics by black women in the South, see Liette Gidlow, "The Sequel: The Fifteenth Amendment, the Nineteenth Amendment, and Southern Black Women's Struggle to Vote," *Journal of the Gilded Age and Progressive Era,* 17 (July 2018): 433–49.

19. Victoria Woodhull, *"And the Truth Shall Set You Free": A Speech on the Principles of Social Freedom, Delivered Nov. 20, 1871, and Music Hall, Boston, Wednesday, Jan. 3, '72* (New York: Woodhull & Claflin, 1874). See *Woodhull and Claflin's Weekly,* May 27, 1871, 3. Note as well the side-by-side coverage of the conventions of the two suffrage organizations, with the Boston group lampooned for its "self-assumed purity and arrogance" in refusing to associate with people regarded as unsavory, presumably Woodhull herself.

20. *Lily,* April 1, 1850.

21. *Revolution,* April 8, 1869; "What Justifies Marriage?," *Revolution,* Aug. 18, 1870.

22. Stanton, "On Marriage and Divorce" (1870).

23. Zonderman, *Uneasy Allies,* 123–25.

24. On Beecher, see Debby Applegate, *The Most Famous Man in America: The Biography of Henry Ward Beecher* (New York: Doubleday, 2006). On the Beecher-Tilton scandal, see Richard Wightman Fox, *Trials of Intimacy: Love and Loss in the Beecher-Tilton Scandal* (Chicago: University of Chicago Press, 1999). For an exhaustive account of the trial with relevant documents, see *The Great Brooklyn Romance* (New York: Paxon, 1874). Anthony's account of her night at the Tiltons' is quoted on 1848.

25. On Comstock, see Amy Werbel, *Lust on Trial: Censorship and the Rise of American Obscenity in the Age of Anthony Comstock* (New York: Columbia University Press, 2018). Also see Helen Lefkowitz Horowitz, *Rereading Sex: Battles over Sexual Knowledge and Suppression in Nineteenth-Century America* (New York: Knopf, 2002).

26. *News and Courier,* Oct. 7, 1874, 1. Also see Levine, *Martin R. Delany: A Documentary Reader,* and Adeleke, *Without Regard to Race,* 129.

27. Rose, *Rehearsal for Reconstruction,* 365–69; *Daily Republican,* June 22, 1871, quoted in Adeleke, *Without Regard to Race,* 119, 116; "Minority Representation," *New York Times,* Feb. 21, 1874.

28. Quoted in Blight, *Frederick Douglass,* 556.

29. David Blight, *Race and Reunion: The Civil War in American Memory* (Cambridge, Mass.: Harvard University Press, 2009); Nina Silber, *The Romance of Reunion: Northerners and the South, 1865–1900* (Chapel Hill: University of North Carolina Press, 1993).

30. Quoted in Edelstein, *Strange Enthusiasm,* 323–24; Robert V. Bruce, *1877: Year of Violence* (Indianapolis: Bobbs-Merrill, 1959), 25.

31. Frederick Douglass, "The Unknown Loyal Dead" (1871).

Chapter 15: This Electric Uprising

1. *New York Times,* July 4, 1876, 1–2.

2. J. S. Ingram, *Centennial Exposition Described and Illustrated* (Philadelphia: Hubbard, 1876), 563–65; Linda P. Gross and Theresa R. Snyder, *Philadelphia's 1876 Centennial Exhibition* (Charleston, S.C.: Arcadia, 2005); Russell Weigley, ed., *Philadelphia: A 300-Year History* (New York: Norton, 1982); Edward Strahan, ed., *A Century After, Picturesque Glimpses of Philadelphia and Pennsylvania* (Philadelphia: Allen, Lane & Scott and J. W. Lauderbach, 1875).

3. Quoted in Philip Foner, "Black Participation in the Centennial of 1876," *Phylon* 39, no. 4 (1978): 289.

4. Mitch Kachun, "Before the Eyes of All Nations: African-American Identity and Historical Memory at the Centennial Exposition of 1876," in "African Americans in Pennsylvania," special issue, *Pennsylvania History: A Journal of Mid-Atlantic Studies* 65, no. 3 (Summer 1998): 300–323; Susanna W. Gold, *The Unfinished Exhibition: Visualizing Myth, Memory, and the Shadow of the Civil War in Centennial America* (New York: Routledge, 2016); Foner, "Black Participation," 283–96.

5. Stanton, "The Spirit of '76," in *Eighty Years and More.*

6. Terborg-Penn, *African American Women in the Struggle for the Vote,* 41.

7. Kathleen A. Clark, *Defining Moments: African American Commemoration and Political Culture in the South, 1863–1913* (Chapel Hill: University of North Carolina Press, 2005), 41–48; Bruce, *1877,* 12.

8. "An Address to the People of the United States, Adopted at a Convention of Colored Citizens, Held at Columbia, S.C., July 20 and 21, 1876," 7–8. See the Colored Conventions Project, http://coloredconventions.org.

9. Robert K. Scott to Grant, Oct. 22, 1870, in Simpson, *Reconstruction,* 391; Sarah A. Dickey to Grant, in Simpson, *Reconstruction,* 596.

10. David Brundage to Grant, in Simpson, *Reconstruction,* 632; *United States v. Reese,* 92 U.S. 214 (1876).

11. Quoted in Adeleke, *Without Regard to Race,* 154.

12. Martin Delany, "Trial and Conviction," courtesy of the South Carolina Historical Society.

13. Quoted in Griffith, *African Dream*, 115, 107–8; Rev. Henry M. Turner is quoted in "Nationality the Hope of Race," *African Repository* 52 (July 1876): 83–86. Also see George B. Tindall, "The Liberian Exodus of 1878," *South Carolina Historical Magazine* 53, no. 3 (July 1952), and Sterling, *Making of an Afro-American*, 319–21. On post-Emancipation black emigration movements in the South, see Steven Hahn, *A Nation Under Our Feet: Black Political Struggles in the Rural South from Slavery to the Great Migration* (Cambridge, Mass.: Harvard University Press, 2003).

14. Joseph Rayback, *A History of American Labor* (New York: Free Press, 1966), 144; Philip Foner, *The Great Labor Uprising of 1877* (New York: Monad Press, 1977), 27. For a fuller account of the Molly Maguires, see Dray, *There Is Power in a Union*.

15. Henry Ward Beecher, "Economy in Small Things," in *Plymouth Pulpit* (New York: J. B. Ford, 1875), 263; Robert Shaplen, "The Beecher-Tilton Affair," *New Yorker*, June 12, 1954; Henry Ward Beecher, "Bread and Water Sermon," July 1877; Bruce Laurie, *Artisans into Workers: Labor in Nineteenth-Century America* (Urbana: University of Illinois Press, 1997), 154–55.

16. Foner, *Great Labor Uprising of 1877*, 14.

17. David T. Burbank, *Reign of the Rabble: The St. Louis General Strike of 1877* (New York: Kelley, 1966), 9.

18. Foner, *Great Labor Uprising of 1877*, 154.

19. These were the demands articulated by the executive committee of the Workingmen's Party of the United States in St. Louis. See ibid., 174.

20. Ibid., 173, 182. The WPUS denounced the cross-racial collaboration in St. Louis. Also see David Roediger, "'Not Only the Ruling Classes to Overcome, but Also the So-Called Mob': Class, Skill, and Community in the St. Louis General Strike of 1877," *Journal of Social History* 19, no. 2 (Winter 1985): 225–26.

21. Ezra Heywood, "The Great Strike," *Radical Review*, Nov. 1877.

22. "The Strikers and the Mob," *Woman's Journal*, July 28, 1877; *Labor Standard*, Aug. 4, 1877; Foner, *Great Labor Uprising of 1877*, 15.

23. Bruce, *1877*, 316–17. Also see chapter 1 of Nell Irvin Painter, *Standing at Armageddon: A Grassroots History of the Progressive Era* (New York: Norton, 2011).

Conclusion: On Radical Failure

1. Ezra Heywood, *Cupid's Yokes* (Princeton, Mass.: Co-operative, 1876), 14.

2. Anthony Comstock, *Traps for the Young* (New York: Funk & Wagnalls, 1883), 63–64. On Angela Heywood, see Wendy McElroy, *Individualist Feminism of the Nineteenth Century: Collected Writings and Biographical Profiles* (Jefferson, NC: McFarland, 2001).

3. Quoted in Blatt, *Free Love and Anarchism*, 120–21, 79.

4. Orestes Augustus Brownson, *The American Republic: Its Constitution, Tendencies, and Destiny* (New York: P. O'Shea, 1866), 3, 11. On this Brownson essay and the conservative turn in postwar thought generally, see George M. Fredrickson, *The Inner Civil War: Northern Intellectuals and the Crisis of the Union* (1965; repr., Urbana: University of Illinois Press, 1993), 183–88. On pragmatism and the Civil War, see Louis Menand, *The Metaphysical Club* (New York: Farrar, Straus and Giroux, 2001). On the cultural shift after Reconstruction, see Richard White, *The Republic for Which It Stands: The United States During Reconstruction and the Gilded Age* (New York: Oxford University Press, 2017), 345–55. On the reform culture of the Progressive Era, see Michael McGerr, *A Fierce Discontent: The Rise and Fall of the Progressive Movement in America, 1870–1920* (New York: Free Press, 2003), and Ian Tyrrell, *Reforming the World: The Creation of America's Moral Empire* (Princeton, N.J.: Princeton University Press, 2010).

5. Quoted in Eckhardt, *Fanny Wright,* 290.

6. Peter Brock, *Radical Pacifists in Antebellum America* (Princeton, N.J.: Princeton University Press, 1968), 97–99, 169; Garrison and Garrison, *William Lloyd Garrison,* 2:229.

7. "Under other names, the sexual revolution contemplated by the free-lovers has been largely accomplished by succeeding generations . . . free love may be said to have won out, under a series of other banners." Stoehr, *Free Love in America,* 7. Gilbert Seldes observes that the radical goals of the abolition of slavery, the prohibition of alcohol, and universal adult suffrage all eventually made their way into the U.S. Constitution and that these outcomes cannot be separated from their origins in experimental subcultures that dabbled in vegetarianism, non-monogamy, dress reform, and communication with the spirit world. Gilbert Seldes, *The Stammering Century* (New York: John Day, 1928), 249. On Free Love as a precursor to critiques of marriage in queer theory and activism, see Holly Jackson, "The Marriage Trap in the Free-Love Novel and Queer Critique," *American Literature* 87, no. 4 (Dec. 2015): 681–708.

8. Silver-Isenstadt in *Shameless* gives the address of the water-cure boardinghouse-commune as 261. The juice shop is at 201, the address provided by Bingham in *Mordecai.*

9. *New York Times,* Sept. 8, 1855; Noyes, *History of American Socialisms,* 24.

10. "John Brown's Failure and His Triumph," *Independent,* Dec. 8, 1859.

11. On the evolving definition of failure, see Scott Sandage, *Born Losers: A History of Failure in America* (Cambridge, Mass.: Harvard University Press, 2005).

12. *Liberator,* Nov. 12, 1847, reprinted from *Voice of Industry.*

13. Crowe, *George Ripley,* 239–41.

14. Noyes, *History of American Socialisms,* 108, 228; Henry David Thoreau, *Walden* (1854).

15. See Abba Alcott's journal for this period, MS Am 1130.14, Houghton Library, and Louisa May Alcott, "Transcendental Wild Oats" (1873).

Index

AASS. *See* American Anti-Slavery
   Society
Abeokuta, 212–13, 231–32
abolitionism (abolitionists), xiii, xv,
   18–19. *See also specific figures*
   violence and attacks against, 71–76,
      169–70, 171–72
   women's central role in, 70–71,
      72–76
Adams, John, ix–x
Adams, John Quincy, 22–23, 24
Adams, Samuel, 182
African emigration movement, 13–14,
   20–22, 231–32, 308–9
Africania, 166–67
African Methodist Episcopal (AME)
   Church, 13, 14–16, 64–65, 93
Age of Reason (Paine), 49
Alcott, Abigail May "Abba," 328
Alcott, Amos Bronson, 96–97, 103–4,
   142
   Fruitlands, 103–4, 134, 142, 328
   Non-Resistance Society and, 79,
      104
   Transcendentalism and, 96–97,
      108–9
Alcott, Louisa May, 326
Allen, Richard, 13, 89, 93, 300
   ACS and, 13, 16, 50, 64, 66
   Canada emigration and, 64–65

Haitian emigration and Granville,
   21–22
American and Foreign Anti-Slavery
   Society, 82–83
American Anti-Slavery Society
   (AASS), 148, 270, 278
   Declaration of Sentiments, 66–67,
      68, 71, 278–79
   disbanding of, 270
   Garrison and, 66–67, 76, 82–83,
      247–48, 249
   Phillips and, 249, 260, 270
   schism of 1840, 82–83, 164
American Civil War. *See* Civil War
American Colonization Society (ACS),
   12–16, 20–21, 25, 50, 57, 66, 186,
   212, 308
American Equal Rights Association,
   262–63, 267–69, 279
American Freedmen's Inquiry
   Commission, 251–53
American Revolution, 3–4, 7, 10–11,
   17
American Society of Free Persons of
   Colour, 64
Anderson, Osborne Perry, 213, 216
Andrews, Stephen Pearl, 280
   Modern Times and, 131–33, 135,
      136, 137
   in Texas, 161–64, 167

Andrews, Stephen Pearl (*cont'd*):
    at Woman's Rights Convention
        (1858), 151–52
    Woodhull and, 281, 286
Anglo-African Magazine, 240
Anthony, Susan B., 259–68, 281
    anti-slavery activism, 260–61,
        263–66
    at Centennial Exposition (1876), 301
    at Combination Convention (1872),
        287–88
    Equal Rights Association and,
        267–68
    Kansas suffrage referendum, 263–66
    labor alliance, 275, 276–77
    at National Women's Rights
        Conventions, 148, 261, 262–63
    Stanton and, 287–92
anti-abolitionists, 62–63
Anti-Slavery Convention of American
    Women (1837), 70
Anti-Slavery Society. *See* American
    Anti-Slavery Society
Appeal to the Colored Citizens of the World
    (Walker), 52–53, 60, 62, 166
Arizona, 163
Arkansas, 162, 167
Association (Fourierist doctrine),
    111–24, 272–73, 326
Attucks, Crispus, 54, 218
Avis, John, 224, 225
Azor (ship), 308

Bagley, Sarah, xiii, 117, 275–76
Ballou, Adin, 104
Barbadoes, James, 67
Barry, Francis, 138
Barton, Clara, 268
Batchelder, James, 187–88, 348–49*n*
Battle of Antietam, 233, 237
Battle of Appomattox Court House,
    240–41
Battle of Fort Sumter, 201, 230–31,
    240, 289
Battle of Yorktown, 3–4, 17

Beecher, Catharine, 39, 291
Beecher, Henry Ward, 196, 224, 262,
    290, 310
    Civil War and, 240–41
    Tilton-Beecher scandal, 289–91, 319
Beecher, Lyman, 39, 291
Bell, Alexander Graham, 298
Benschoter, Cordelia, 138
Bentham, Jeremy, 8
Berlin Heights, 138, 149, 150
Bethel African Methodist Episcopal
    Church. *See* Mother Bethel AME
    Church
Birney, James, 76
birth control, 45, 141, 252, 291, 319, 320
Black Codes, 248
Black Heritage Trail (Boston), 194
Black Lives Matter, 190
black nationalism, 93, 166, 177, 258
Blackwell, Henry, 140
Bleeding Kansas, 196–201
Blood, James Harvey, 281
Booth, John Wilkes, 225–26, 242
Border Ruffians, 196–201, 273
Boston Athenaeum, 58
Boston Common, 54
Boston Female Anti-Slavery
    Society, 72
Boston Latin School, 41
Boston Post, 228
Boston riot of 1835, 74
Boston Vigilance Committee, 183,
    184–85, 191, 251
Boston Working Women's League, 276
Bowdoin College, 49
Boyer, Jean-Pierre, 12, 21–22, 27,
    44–45
Branch, Julia, 152–53, 155–56
Brattle Street Church (Boston), 182
Brisbane, Albert, 111–15, 138–39, 280
    arrest of, 136–37
    Association doctrine, 111–15,
        117–18, 119, 123
    Social Destiny of Man, 112, 113–14,
        142

Brook Farm, 109–12, 115–22, 123,
126, 134, 191, 237, 280, 325–27
Brook Farm (Wolcott), *122*
Brooks, Preston, 197–98, 200
Brown, Frederick, 226
Brown, John, xiii, *199*, 325
actions in Kansas, 198–201, 203–4
at Chatham Convention (1858),
209–11, 213, 224, 350*n*
Douglass and, 205–7, 209–10, 213,
221
execution of, 212–13, 219–26, *225*
imprisonment and trial of, 218–19
"John Brown's Body" (song), 239,
240
liberation theology of, 89
in Massachusetts, 203–5
planning for raid, 206–9, 213
raid in Missouri, 205–6
raid on Harpers Ferry, 213–19,
227–28, 325
Brown, Mary, 221–22, 226
Brownson, Orestes, 99–102, 107, 142,
321
Buchanan, James, 202–3
Burleigh, Charles, 72, 267
Burns, Anthony, 182–91, 194
Butler, Matthew Calbraith, 302–3

Calhoun, John C., 63, 162, 163, 230,
241–42
California, 162, 163, 202
Canada emigration, 64–66, 179–81,
207–8
Canada West, 64–66, 207–8, 252
Cary, Jane, 9–10
Cary, Mary Ann Shadd. *See* Shadd,
Mary Ann
Castle Garden (New York), 5
Cazenovia Convention. *See* Fugitive
Slave Law Convention (1850)
Centennial Exposition (1876), 298–302,
299, 309–10
Centennial of 1876, 297–302
Channing, William Henry, 191

Chapman, Maria Weston, 72, 79
Chardon Street Convention (1840),
87–88, 90, 93–95
Charleston, South Carolina, 250, *251,*
302
Chatham Convention (1858), 209–11,
213, 224, 350*n*
Chatham settlement, 179–80, 181, 211
Chickasaw Indians, 28
Child, Lydia Maria, 72, 218, 237
Chinese Exclusion Act, 322
Chinese immigrants, 249, 267, 275,
279, 322
Cincinnati riots of 1829, 64–65
civil disobedience, xiv–xv, 105, 139,
189
Civil War. *See also specific figures*
African Americans serving in,
236–37
Battle of Antietam, 233, 237
Battle of Appomattox Court House,
240–41
Battle of Fort Sumter, 201, 230–31,
240, 289
Brown's raid leading to, 227–31
as reaction against abolitionists, 230
Clapp, Henry, Jr., 124
Clay, Henry, 22, 186
Codman, John, 121
Collins, Jennie, 276
Collins, John, 104
colonization, 11–22, 44–45, 50–51,
64–66, 167
Colorado, 163
Colored American, The, 166
Combination Convention (1872),
287–88
Come-Outerism, 91–93, 103, 104, 146,
167
Common Sense (Paine), xvi
Communist Manifesto (Marx), 101, 273,
282
Compromise of 1850, 163, 171–72,
183
Compromise of 1877, 307

Comstock, Anthony, 291–92, 317–18
Concord Lyceum, 105
Condition, Elevation, Emigration, and Destiny of the Colored People of the United States (Delany), 172–75
Confederate States of America, 230–33
Constitution, U.S., and three-fifths clause, 163–64, 194–95
Copeland, John Anthony, 213, 218
Cornish, Samuel, 48–50, 67, 166
Cornwallis, Charles, Lord, 17
Craft, Ellen, 185
Creek War, 27
Cuba, 195, 322
Cuffee, Paul, 13–14, 20, 93
Curtis, George William, 326

Dana, Charles, 273, 307
Daniels, Edith, 276
Davis, Jefferson, 227, 230–31, 285
Davis, Paulina Wright, 267
Dawn Settlement, 179, 186
Debs, Eugene, 323
Declaration of Independence, ix–x, xvi, 194–95, 214, 301
    Forten and, 16–17
    Garrison and, 67, 192–93
    Walker and, 53
    Wright and, 45–46
"Declaration of Mental Independence" (Owen), x–xi, xv–xvii
Declaration of Sentiments of the American Anti-Slavery Society, 66–67, 68, 71
Delany, Catherine A., 181, 209
Delany, Martin Robison, 89, 165–76
    Africa and emigration, 211–13, 224, 231–32, 308–9
    background of, 165–66
    Brown and, 209–11, 212–13, 224
    in Chatham, 179–80, 181, 209–10
    at Chatham Convention (1858), 209–11, 213, 224, 350*n*
    Civil War and, 231, 237–38, 240–41, *241*

Condition, Elevation, Emigration, and Destiny of the Colored People, 172–75
    conservative turn of, 292–94, 305–6
    Douglass and, 167–68, 169–70, 174–75, 176, 178–79, 212, 257, 293
    election of 1876 and, 305–6
    embrace of use of violence, 169–70, 171–72
    Lincoln and, 240, 242–43
    Marseilles, Ohio, riot, 168–69
    at National Emigration Convention (1854), 177–79, 181, 210
    Reconstruction and, 253–58
Delany, Samuel, 165–66
Demosthenes, 281
Dial, The, 108, 112
Dickens, Charles, 141
dietary reform, 89, 94, 125–126, 324
disenfranchment, 304–5
divorce, 124, 131–133, 137, 146, 261, 286–87, 324
Douglass, Frederick
    AASS and, 164, 248
    Brown and, 205–7, 209–10, 213, 221
    at Centennial Exposition (1876), 300–301
    at Chatham Convention (1858), 209–11, 213, 224, 350*n*
    Civil War and, 237–39, 261–62, 295–96
    Collins and, 116
    Delany and, 167–68, 169–70, 174–75, 176, 178–79, 212, 257, 293
    election of 1872 and, 288, 293
    Equal Rights Association and, 267–69, 288
    at Fugitive Slave Law Convention (1850), 172, *173*
    The Heroic Slave, 180–81
    Heywood and, 277
    Liberty Party and, 165
    Mexican-American War and, 164

at National Convention of Colored
Citizens (1843), 169
National Council of the Colored
People and, 177–78
at National Women's Rights
Convention (1866), 262
Reconstruction and, 257
at Seneca Falls Convention (1848),
146, 147–48, 170
Stowe and, 175–76
Douglass, Robert, Jr., *55*
Doyle, Mahala, 218
Dred Scott v. Sandford, 179
DuBois, W. E. B., 217, 253
Dwight, John Sullivan, 326
Dwight, Marianne, 121, 122

Edisto Island Freemen, 255
Egba, 212–13, 231–32
Eight-Hour League, 274–75, 276
eight-hour workday, 274–75, 280, 312,
323
elections
of 1824, 4, 22
of 1828, 28
of 1840, 102
of 1856, 201–3
of 1860, 228–29
of 1872, 284–86, 291–92
of 1876, 304, 305–7
Elgin settlement, 179, *180*
Elizabeth (ship), 20–21
Emancipation Proclamation, 233, 235,
247, 248, 300
Emerson, Ralph Waldo, 4, 95–103,
109, 110–11, 191
Brown and, 204–5, 220–21
"Nature," 95, 99, 100
Engels, Friedrich, 115
Enlightenment, 4, 9, 21, 88
eugenics, 320
evangelical Protestantism, xi, 88–89, 115
Evils of the Revolutionary War (Whipple),
80–81
evolution, 320

"failure," use of term, 325–26
Fall River Mechanics' and Laborers'
Association, 117
"family values," 319
Faneuil Hall, 117, 164, 184–85, 317–18
Fifteenth Amendment, 266–67,
268–69, *269,* 304–5
Finley, Robert, 14
First Amendment, 62, 202, 319
First International (International
Workingmen's Association), 274,
276, 280–84, 287
First Seminole War, 27
Fitzhugh, George, 195
Flower, George, 27
Forten, Charlotte, 69, 234, 236
Forten, James, xiii, 13–18, *16,* 48–49,
93, 176
background of, 16–17
Free Produce and, 69
Fugitive Slave Act and, 20
Garrison and, 58, 64, 66
Haitian emigration and, 21–22, 44
Forten, Sarah, 69, 70
Foster, Stephen S., *92,* 279
anti-slavery activism, 91–93, 193,
248–49
election of 1860 and, 228–29, 258
at Free Convention (1858), 155–57
women's suffrage activism, 148,
260–61, 262, 267
Fourier, Charles, 112–22, 141, 143–44
Fourteenth Amendment, 259–60
Fowler, Bathsheba, 58
Franklin, Benjamin, 18
Frazier, Garrison, 253–54
Free African Society, 93
Free Convention (1858), 152–57
Freedmen's Bureau, 252, 253, 255,
323
Freedom's Journal, 48–50, *51,* 51–52,
166
Freedom Trail (Boston), 194
Freed Slave, The (statue), 300
Free Enquirer, The, 40–41, 48, 100

Free Love, 135–41, 150–52, 285–87, 323–24
  Brisbane and, 138–39, 161
  Fourierism and, 124–25, 128, 141
  Graham and, 127, 128
  Greeley and, 131, 285
  Heywood and, 138–39, 277, 288, 317–19
  Lazarus and, 128–30, 138, 151, 344n
  Nicholses and, 135–37, 150
  Noyes and, 78–79, 277, 339n
  Owen and, 139–40, 252, 323–24
  Paine and, 89
  Stanton and, 147, 150–51, 261, 286–87
  Stowe's *My Wife and I,* 291
  Woodhull and, 285–86, 319–20
"free marriages," 139, 141
Free Produce, 68–69, *70,* 102
Free Thought, 40, 49, 88
Frémont, John C., 202–3, 229
French Revolution, 4
Fruitlands, 103–4, 134, 142, 328
Fugitive Slave Act of 1793, 19–20
Fugitive Slave Act of 1850, 177, 182–83, 185, 186, 193
Fugitive Slave Law Convention (1850), 172, *173*
Fuller, Margaret, 96, 110–11, 136, 143

Gandhi, Mahatma, 323
Garnet, Henry Highland, 169, 207, 223, 238, 257
Garrison, William Lloyd, xvii, *55*
  AASS and, 66–67, 71, 76, 82–83, 247–48, 249, 270, 278–79
  abolition doctrine and activism, 54–68, 66–67, 71–72, 76–77, 80–84, 87–88, 104–5, 116, 163, 203, 268–69. *See also Liberator, The*
  background of, 54
  Brown and, 196, 204, 219–20, 222, 277
  at Chardon Street Convention (1840), 87–88, 90, 93–95
  Civil War and, 232–33, 238–39, 241–42, 289
  Delany and, 167–68, 171, 174–75
  Graham and, 126
  Harmony Grove speech (1854), 192–94
  Heywood and, 277–79
  jailing of, 56–57
  at National Women's Rights Convention, 148
  Park Street Church address (1829), 54–56, 57–58
  Stowe's *Uncle Tom's Cabin* and, 176
gender equality, 69–70, 109
Genius of Universal Emancipation, 21, 26, 31–33, 57
Gilded Age, 320
Gompers, Samuel, 323
Gove, Hiram, 133, 135
Graham, Sylvester, 125–28, 133–34, 324
Grant, Ulysses S., 240, 285, 292, 295, 300–301, 304, 306
Granville, Jonathan, 12–13, 21–22, 26
Great Railroad Strike of 1877, 310–15, *312, 313, 315,* 323
Greeley, Horace, 111, 115, 131–33, 142, 285, 291, 292, 293
Green, Shields, 213
Greener, Jacob, 57
Grimké, Angelina, 73–74, 143

Haitian emigration movement, 12–13, 21–22, 26, 27, 44–45, 231
Haitian Revolution, 11, 21
Hall of Science (New York), *40,* 40–41, 98
Hamburg massacre of 1876, 302–4
Hampton, Wade, 305
Hancock, John, 182
Harbinger, The, 116, 123, 128, 151, 235, 237
Harman, Lillian, 139
Harman, Moses, 139
Harmony Grove, 192–94

Harper, Frances E. W., 180, 218, *262,*
      262–63
Harpers Ferry, 22
      Brown's raid on, 213–19, 227–28,
      325
Harper's Weekly, 326
Harvard Divinity School, 97, 99
Harvard Medical School, 170–71, 212
Harvard University, 191
Hawthorne, Nathaniel, 109, 189, 237,
      326, 341*n*
Hayden, Harriet, 186, 194
Hayden, Lewis, 186–88, *187,* 207
Hayes, Rutherford B., 306–9, *307,* 314,
      318–19
Hazlett, Albert, 213
Hegel, Georg Wilhelm Friedrich, 112
Henry, Patrick, 223
Heroic Slave, The (Douglass), 180–81
Heywood, Angela, 138, 318
Heywood, Ezra, 89, 277–79, 277–80,
      278
      background of, 277
      Cupid's Yokes, 317–19
      Free Love and, 138–39, 277, 288,
      317–19
      Great Strike and, 313
Higginson, Thomas Wentworth, 140,
      184, 193, 258, 260
      Bleeding Kansas and, 203–4
      Boston slave riot of 1854, 184–90,
      191–92, 194
      Brown and, 203–4, 207, 221, 235
      Civil War and, 233–34, 235–36,
      240, 303
      election of 1856 and, 201–3
      election of 1860 and, 228
      politics and anti-slavery activism,
      183–88, 200–204
      Reconstruction and, 265, 294–95
      Saxton and, 235–36
History of Woman Suffrage (Stanton), 321
Holmes, Oliver Wendell, 170
Hopedale Community, 104
Howard University, 323

Howe, Julia Ward, 239
Howe, Samuel Gridley, 207, 221, 222,
      251
Hutchinson, Ann, 38
Hutchinson Family Singers, 111

Ignatius of Loyola, Saint, 141
Indian Removal Act of 1830, 28
industrialization, xi–xii, 125–26, 271
inequality, 11, 23–24, 41–42, 100, 101,
      274
"infidel," 57, 90–91, 98–99
Ingalls, J. K., 280
International Workingmen's
      Association (First International),
      274, 276, 280–84, 287
interracial marriage, 49, 59–60
interracial sex, 11–12, 19, 25, 32–35, 39

Jackson, Andrew, 22–23, 27–28, 73
Jackson, Thomas Jonathan
      "Stonewall," 225, 299
James, Henry, xiv, 326
James, Henry, Sr., 123, 130
Jefferson, Thomas, ix–x, 4, 22, 214, 314
      Missouri Compromise and, 196
      Notes on the State of Virginia, 10–11
      views on slavery, 10–12
      Wright and, 9–11, 26–27, 62
Jim Crow laws, 322
John Brown Pike, 205, *205,* 223
"John Brown's Body" (song), 239, 240
John Brown's Provisional Constitution,
      214
John Brown's Provisional United
      States, 206, 209–11, 226
Johnson, Andrew, 242, 254–57, 259
Jones, Absalom, 93
Jubilee of Independence, ix–x

Kansas, 163, 195–201
      sacking of Lawrence, 197–98, 203
      suffrage referendum, 263–66, 273
Kansas Free-Staters, 196–201, 203–4
Kansas-Nebraska Act of 1854, 195–96

Kelley, Abby, 78–79, 82, 104, 126, 146, 156, 262
Kellogg, John Harvey, 324
Kneeland, Abner, 57, 96
Ku Klux Klan (KKK), 285, 293

"Laboring Classes, The" (Brownson), 101–2, 112
labor movement, xiii, xiv, 42–43, 117–18, 271–77, 323
    Great Railroad Strike of 1877, 310–15
Lafayette, Gilbert du Motier, Marquis de, 3–6, 22, 223, 223
    Hayden and, 186
    Jefferson and, 9–10
    Wright and, 5–6, 8–9, 10, 22–23, 24
land redistribution, 253–54
Lane, Charles, 142
Langston, Charles, 168–69
Lawrence, Amos Adams, 191, 196
Lay, Benjamin, 89
Lazarus, Marx Edgeworth, xiii, 128, 128–31, 134–35, 138, 141, 324
    Free Love and, 128–30, 138, 151, 344n
    Love vs. Marriage, 128–31, 151
League of Liberty, 210
Lee, Ann "Mother Ann Lee," 38
Lee, Jarena, 38
Lee, Richard Henry, 301
Lee, Robert E., 216, 240, 295, 299
Levasseur, Auguste, 10
Lewis, Edmonia, 300
Liberator, The, 58–60, 61–62, 77–80, 82, 87, 89, 154, 166, 174, 192, 198, 204, 219, 232, 233, 249, 277
Liberia (Liberian emigration), 20–21, 50, 64–65, 176, 212–13, 308–9
Liberty Guards, 199–200
Liberty Party, 164–65, 167
Lincoln, Abraham, 54, 253, 256, 269
    assassination of, 242
    Civil War and, 231, 233, 240
    Delany and, 240, 242–43

election of 1860, 228–29, 231
election of 1864, 274
Emancipation Proclamation, 233, 235, 247, 248
Long Depression, 309–10
Longfellow, Henry Wadsworth, 239
Louisiana, 162, 167
Love in the Phalanstery (James), 123
Lovejoy, Elijah, 76, 198
Love vs. Marriage (Lazarus), 128–31, 151
Lowell Female Labor Reform Association, 117
Lucifer, the Light-Bearer, 139
Lundy, Benjamin, 21, 26, 31–33, 35, 57
lynching, 169, 267, 307

McCrummell, James, 67
Mack, David, 104
McKaye, James, 252
McNeill, George, 274–75
"manifest destiny," 115, 163, 173–74
Mann, Horace, 41
marriage, 32–37, 42, 49, 59–60, 77–78, 114, 123–41, 146, 149–56, 177, 206, 261, 284–90, 317–24
Marriage: Its History, Character, and Results (Gove and Nichols), 135
Marriage and Parentage (Wright), 154–55
Marseilles, Ohio, riot, 168–69
Marx, Karl, 101, 115, 273–74, 282, 283–84
Mary Lyndon; or, Revelations of a Life (Nichols), 135–36, 137
Massachusetts Emigrant Aid Company, 196
Massachusetts General Colored Association, 51–52, 64
Massachusetts 54th Regiment, 238–39, 240
masturbation, 126–27, 130, 133, 291
Mechanics' Union of Trade Associations, 42
Melville, Herman, 127–28, 134
Memnonia Community, 141

Meriam, Francis Jackson, 213
Mexican-American War, 162–64, 195, 196
millenarianism, 77, 89, 98–99
"mill girls," 275–76
Minkins, Shadrach, 182, 185, 186, 191, 194
Mississippi, 229
Missouri, 205
Missouri Compromise, 163, 195–96
Modern Times, 131–33, 135, 151, 279
Molly Maguires, 309
monogamy, 43, 113, 123–24
Monroe, James, 21
Monticello, 10–11, 12
Mother Bethel AME Church (Philadelphia), 13, 14–16, *15,* 64–65, 93, 167
Mott, James, 69
Mott, Lucretia, 68–69, *74,* 133, 191, 221, 317
 anti-slavery activism, 68, 69, 84
 Equal Rights Association and, 268–69
 Free Produce movement, 68–69
 at Seneca Falls Convention (1848), 144–46
 Stanton and, 84, 144–45, 146–47, 301
Murray, Ellen, *294*
Museum of African American History (Boston), 194
Myers, Isaac, 275
Mylne, James, 7
Mystery, The, 167–68
My Wife and I, Or, Harry Henderson's History (Stowe), 291

NAACP (National Association for the Advancement of Colored People), 323
Nantucket Island riot of 1842, 92
Nashoba Commune, 24–28, 29–35, *30,* 44
Natick Resolution, 220, 227

National Convention of Colored Citizens (1843), 169
National Convention of Free People of Colour
 1830, 56, 93
 1832, 64, 66–67
National Council of the Colored People, 177–78
National Emigration Convention (1854), 177–79, 181, 210
National Labor Union (NLU), 275, 309
National Women's Rights Conventions, 149
 1850, 148–50
 1858, 151
 1860, 261
 1866, 262–63
Native Americans, 27, 28, 155, 249
"Nature" (Emerson), 95, 99, 100
Nebraska, 195–96, 264
Nell, William C., 168–69
Nevada, 163
Newby, Dangerfield, 213
New England Anti-Slavery Society (NEASS), 63–64
New England Free Love League, 317–18
New England Labor Reform League, 279
New England Non-Resistance Society, 79–82, 91, 104–5, 146, 183, 278–79, 323
New England Workingmen's Association, 117, 272–73
New Harmony, xvii, 24–25, 27, 35–39, 325
New Mexico, 162, 163
New Orleans massacre of 1866, 303
New View of Society, A (Owen), 23
New Views of Christianity, Society, and the Church (Brownson), 100
New York Stock Exchange, 309
New York Sun, 307
New York Times, 135–36, 152, 153, 155, 240, 258, 282–83, 294

New-York Tribune, 111–12, 130, 273
Nichols, Mary Gove, 133–37, *134,* 141,
    147, 321, 324
Nichols, Thomas, 135, 141
Nichols' Monthly, 135
Nigeria, 212
Non-Resistance, 79–82, 91, 104–5,
    146, 183, 278–79, 323
Northampton Association of
    Education and Industry, 104
North Elba, New York, 198, 207,
    221
North Star, The, 168–69
Norton, Andrews, 96
Notes on the State of Virginia (Jefferson),
    10–11
Noyes, John Humphrey, 77–79, 105,
    277, 320, 325, 326–27

Oberlin College, 126, 213
Oneida Community, 77–79, 320
"Oration Containing a Declaration of
    Mental Independence" (Owen),
    x–xi, xv–xvii
Orvis, John, 279–80
Owen, Robert, x–xii, 23–26
    Emerson and, 96–97
    later years of, 256–57
    New Harmony, 24–25, 27, 35–39,
        314, 325
    "Oration Containing a Declaration
        of Mental Independence," x–xi,
        xv–xvii
    utopian philosophy of, 23–26
Owen, Robert Dale, *43,* 319, 323–24
    marriage to Robinson, 139–40
    New Harmony, 35–36
    Reconstruction and, 251–52, 259
    Wright and, 40–45, 100

Paine, Thomas, xvi, xvii, 18, 40, 49,
    89–90, 214
Panic of 1837, 101–2, 107
Panic of 1873, 309
Paris Commune, 282, 310

Parker, Theodore, 96, 142, 185–86,
    188, 192, 196, 204, 207, 221
Park Street Church (Boston), 54–56
Paul, Nathaniel, 50, 58
Peabody, Elizabeth, 99
Peace, Pati, 165–66
Penn, William, 16
Penn School, *294*
Pennsylvania
    An Act for the Gradual Abolition of
        Slavery, 18–19
    slavery in, 12–22
Pennsylvania Anti-Slavery Society, *74*
Pennsylvania Constitution, 167
Pennsylvania General Assembly, 18
Pennsylvania Hall fire of 1838, 73–76,
    75, 78
Pennsylvania Railroad, 311, 314
Pennsylvania State House, 16, 74
Perfectionists, 77–79
Phelps, Aurora, 276
Philadelphia Convention of Free
    People of Colour (1832), 64,
    66–67
Philadelphia Female Anti-Slavery
    Society, 69–70
Philadelphia Gazette, 75
Phillips, Wendell, xiii, *148*
    anti-slavery activism, 164, 185, 188,
        204, 228, 249, 264, 278, 279,
        294
    Boston slave riot of 1854, 185, 188
    Brown and, 204, 226
    Civil War and, 232, 233, 278
    Heywood and, 277, 278, 279
    labor rights activism, 272–74, 285
    Reconstruction and, 257, 258,
        259–61
    women's rights activism, 148–49,
        268–70
Phiquepal d'Arusmont, William S.,
    44–47
Pierce, Franklin, 189, 196
Pierre (Melville), 127–28
Pillsbury, Parker, 266–67

Plessy v. Ferguson, 322
Plymouth Church (Brooklyn), 289
Poe, Edgar Allan, 134
Polk, James K., 162–63
poll taxes, 105, 269, 305
Port Royal Experiment, 234–36, *236,*
    253–54
Pottawatomie Massacre, 200, 203–4,
    218
Powell, William, 82
presidential elections
    of 1824, 4, 22
    of 1828, 28
    of 1840, 102
    of 1856, 201–3
    of 1860, 228–29
    of 1872, 284–86, 291–92
    of 1876, 304, 305–7
Progressive Era, 320–21
Provisional Army of the United States,
    215, 216–17
Purchase Street Church (Boston),
    107–8
Purvis, Charles, 266
Purvis, Harriet Forten, 64, 69, 75, 148,
    266
Purvis, Robert, 64, *74,* 75, 176, 224,
    238, 266
Putney Bible School, 77

Quakers (Quakerism), 18, 69, 89–90

Radical Republicans (Republicanism),
    256–58, 273, 285, 293, 304
Rapp, George (Rappites), 24–25,
    26, 37
Raritan Bay Union, 221
Reconstruction, xv, 242, 251–58, 295,
    323
Reconstruction Acts of 1867, 257, *260,*
    284
Remond, Charles Lenox, *83*
    AASS and, 83–84, 87
    Civil War and, 238
    Heywood and, 277

    at National Women's Rights
        Conventions, 148, 262
Remond, Sarah, 148, 262
Republican Party, 201–3, 249, 292–93.
    See also Radical Republicans
Republic of Texas, 161–63
Revels, Hiram, *269*
Revere, Paul, 54
Revolution, The, 276, 279, 286
Revolutionary War, 3–4, 7, 10–11, 17
Reynolds, George J., 210
Rifle Clubs, 304
Rights of All, The, 50, 166
Riley, Elizabeth, 58
Ripley, George, 96, *97,* 107–12,
    115–19, 123, 130–31, 326
Ripley, Sophia, 108–9, 120
Rivers, Prince, 303
Robinson, Mary, 140
Rush, Benjamin, 18
Russell, Amelia, 119–21
Russwurm, John, 49, 50
Rutland Free Convention (1858). *See*
    Free Convention
Ryckman, Lewis, 117–18

Sacco and Vanzetti, 318
sacking of Lawrence, 197–98, 203
Sanborn, Frank, 204–5, 207, 217, 221,
    285
Saxton, Rufus, 234–35, 240, 253, 254
Scott, Thomas A., 314
Scottish Enlightenment, 7
Second Coming of Christ, 99, 191
Second Great Awakening, 88–89
Secret Six, 207, 220, 237–38, 239, 251,
    285
"Self-Reliance" (Emerson), 103
Seneca Falls Convention (1848),
    144–47, 151–52, 170
Seward, William, 164
sexual abstinence, 126–27
sexual freedom, 32–35, 39, 40, 45,
    77–79, 123–25, 131–41. *See also*
    Free Love

Shadd, Abraham, 67
Shadd, Mary Ann, 180–81, 213, 284, 302
Shango Peace, 211–12
Shaw, Francis, 237
Shaw, Robert Gould, 237–40
Sherman, William Tecumseh, 253, 254, 255, 306
Siege of Boston, 182
Sims, Thomas, 183–84, 194
Skidmore, Thomas, 43
Skidmore Guards, 283
Smith, Adam, 7
Smith, Gerrit, 165, 172, *173,* 198, 207, 228–29
Social Darwinism, 320
Social Destiny of Man (Brisbane), 112, 113–14, 123–24, 142
Socialism, 23–25, 34–40, 96, 103, 114–17, 131–36, 151, 170, 201, *202,* 234–37, 252, 274–88, 312–14, 323–25
Solitary Vice (Gove), 133–34
Sorge, Friedrich, 274, 283
South Carolina, 229, 230, 231, 234–35, 250
South Carolina Sea Islands, 234–35, 242, 253–54
Spanish-American War, 322
Spiritualism, 150, 152–55, 195, 213, 281, 287, 291
Stanton, Edwin, 253
Stanton, Elizabeth Cady, 142–47, *144,* 191, 280, 286–91, 319
  Beecher-Tilton scandal, 289–91
  Free Love and, 147, 150–51, 286–87
  Gove and, 133
  ideological divergence with abolitionists and women's suffrage, 259–69
  labor activism, 276–77
  Mott and, 84, 144–45, 146–47, 301
  Paine and, 89–90
  at Seneca Falls Convention (1848), 144–47, 151–52, 286

women's suffrage and, 142–47, 151–52, 259–69, 302, 321
Stanton, Henry, 81–83, 84, 164–65
Statue of Liberty, 298, *299*
Stearns, George Luther, 204–5, 207, 221
Stendhal, 8
Stevens, Aaron, 215
Stevens, Thaddeus, 256–57
Steward, Ira, 274–75, 280
Stewart, Maria, 58
Stone, Huldah, 117
Stone, Lucy, 140, 152, 191, 193, 268, 314
Stowe, Harriet Beecher, 135, 175–76, 291
strikes, 42, 117, 271, *272,* 273, 311-14, 323
Stuart, J.E.B. "Jeb," 216
Subterranean Pass Way, 199, 211, 350*n*
suffrage, 146, 149–50, 242, 249, 256–70, 273–77, 286–87, 304–5, 321–23
Sumner, Charles, 197–98, 200, 256
Supreme Court, U.S.
  Dred Scott v. Sandford, 179
  Plessy v. Ferguson, 322
  United States v. Reese, 304–5

temperance movement, 191
Texas, 161–64, 167
Texas Constitution, 161
Texas-Pacific Railroad, 314
Texas Revolution, 161
"There's a Good Time Coming" (song), 111
Thirteenth Amendment, 248, 261
Thoreau, Henry David, 104–6, 126
  Brown and, 204, 220–21
  Brownson and, 100
  Harmony Grove speech, 193–94
  at Walden Pond, 104, 327
Thoughts on African Colonization (Garrison), 66
Tilden, Samuel, 306

Tilton, Elizabeth, 289–91, 319

Tilton, Theodore, 282, 285
  Beecher-Tilton scandal, 289–91
  Brown and, 224
  Civil War and, 241–42
  women's suffrage activism, 262,
    268

Timbuctoo. *See* North Elba, New
  York

Tompkins Square Park riot of 1874,
  310

Towne, Laura, *294*

Townsend, Hannah, *70*

Trail of Tears, 28

Train, George Francis, 264–65

Transcendental Club, 96, 108

Transcendentalism, 95–101, 220, 237,
  321

Treat, Joseph, 150

Truth, Sojourner, 148, 193, 262, 266

Tubman, Harriet, 207–8, *208,* 213–14,
  234, 263

Turner, Nat, 60–61, 65, 71

Una, The, 191

Uncle Tom's Cabin (Stowe), 135, 175–76,
  291

Underhill, Ned, 151

Union Pacific Railroad, 264

Unitarianism, 95, 96, 98–99

United States v. Reese, 304–5

University of Glasgow, 7

Utah, 163

Utopianism, 8, 14–15, 23–24, 99–105,
  112–16, 122, 140–41, 195, 206,
  211, 226, 275–77, 306, 320,
  324–27

"vagrancy," 248

Van Buren, Martin, 73, 102

Vanderbilt, Cornelius, 285, 319–20

Vashon, John, 50, 58, 166, 167

Very, Jones, 99, 191

Views of Society and Manners in America
  (Wright), 7–8

"Vigilance Committees," 183–85

Voice of Industry, 117

Wade, Ben, 273

Walden Pond, 104, 327

Walker, David, 50, 51–53, 58–62, 182,
  219
  *Appeal to the Colored Citizens of the
    World,* 52–53, 60, 62, 166

Walker, Edwin, 139

Walker, Jonathan, 71

War of 1812, 27

Warren, Josiah, 36, 131, 151, 161,
  279

Washington, George, xvii, 17, 214

Washington, Lewis, 214–15

Washington, Martha, 12

Water-Cure Journal, 138

Watkins, William, 57

Webster, Daniel, 183

Whipper, William, 69

Whipple, Charles, 80–81

White, Lydia, 69

Whiting, N. H., 94

Whitman, Walt, 124

Whittier, John Greenleaf, 205

Wilberforce colony, 65, 179, 232

Wilberforce University, 232, 242–43,
  300

Wilmot, David, 163

Wise, Henry, 217, 221–22, 224,
  227–28, 230–31

Wolcott, Josiah, *122*

Wollstonecraft, Mary, 68

Women's Loyal National League, 261

women's suffrage, 71, 90, 124, 142–53,
  259–66, 321–22. *See also* National
  Women's Rights Conventions;
  and specific figures
  Seneca Falls Convention (1848),
    144–47, 151–52

Woodhull, Canning, 281

Woodhull, Victoria Claflin, 126,
  280–89, *282,* 291–92, 319–20

Woodhull and Claflin's Weekly, 281–82

Woodson, Lewis, 166–67, 232
Word, The, 288, 318, 319
Workingmen's Party, 42–43, 45, 312
World Anti-Slavery Convention
    (1840), 83–84, 87, 142
Wright, Camilla, 6–7, 9, 22, 31, 32, 33,
    46
Wright, Frances "Fanny," *6,* 6–12,
    43–47, 56, 88, 90
    early life of, 6–7
    Emerson and, 98
    Granville and, 12–13, 26
    Hall of Science address, 40–41, 98
    Jefferson and, 9–11, 26–27, 62
    Lafayette and, 5–6, 8–9, 10, 22–23,
        24
    lecture tour, 38–43, 45–46, 48,
        53–54, 99–100
    legacy of, 321–22
    at Nashoba Commune, 24–28,
        29–35, 44
    New Harmony, 35–37, 38
    Owen and, 23, 24, 25–26
    Stowe's *Uncle Tom's Cabin* and, 175
    *Views of Society and Manners in
        America,* 7–8
    views on education, 40–43
    views on sex and marriage, 11–12,
        25, 33–35, 39, 40, 45–46
    views on slavery and slaves, 7, 9,
        10–12, 25–26, 30–31, 44–45, 73
Wright, Henry, 76–77, 91, 154–55,
    220, 227, 277
Wyoming, 163

Yorubaland, 212

ABOUT THE AUTHOR

HOLLY JACKSON is an associate professor of English at the University of Massachusetts, Boston. Her writing has appeared in *The New York Times, The Washington Post,* and *The Boston Globe,* as well as in a number of scholarly venues, including one previous book. She lives in Cambridge, Massachusetts.

ABOUT THE TYPE

This book was set in Bembo, a typeface based on an old-style Roman face that was used for Cardinal Pietro Bembo's tract *De Aetna* in 1495. Bembo was cut by Francesco Griffo (1450–1518) in the early sixteenth century for Italian Renaissance printer and publisher Aldus Manutius (1449–1515). The Lanston Monotype Company of Philadelphia brought the well-proportioned letterforms of Bembo to the United States in the 1930s.